The Old Steam Navy

VOLUME ONE

FRIGATES, SLOOPS, AND GUNBOATS, 1815–1885

The Niagara, *Late in the Civil War. A 4,500-ton sloop, she was designed by Henry Steers, architect of the schooner-yacht* America. *(Courtesy Peabody Museum)*

The Old Steam Navy

VOLUME ONE

Frigates, Sloops, and Gunboats, 1815–1885

DONALD L. CANNEY

Distributed by:
Airlife Publishing Ltd.
101 Longden Road, Shrewsbury SY3 9EB, England

Library of Congress Cataloging-in-Publication Data

Canney, Donald L., 1947–
The old steam navy / Donald L. Canney.
p. cm.
Contents: v. 1. Frigates, sloops, and gunboats, 1815–1885.
Includes bibliographical references.
ISBN 0-87021-004-1
1. United States. Navy—History. 2. Warships—United States—History. I. Title.
VA55.C28 1990 89-13675
359′.00973—dc20 CIP

Printed in the United States of America

9 8 7 6 5 4 3 2

First printing

To My Grandmother,
Alicia Humphreys Canney

Contents

Illustrations

Foreword

With volume one of *The Old Steam Navy* Donald L. Canney has done U.S. naval historians a great service. In the past, there has been a tendency to begin the story of U.S. warship design with the creation of the "New Navy," in 1883. Canney revives the memory of the older steam navy out of which that new navy grew. It was a very different organization, much less centralized than the modern U.S. Navy, with much of the design work carried out by the staffs of the individual navy yards. It also lacked any semblance of a centralized modern tactical organization like the office of the chief of naval operations (or, for that matter, the British Admiralty).

The old navy also existed in what seems to us a very alien strategic environment. Both before and after the Civil War, the only recognized probable enemy was Great Britain, and the Royal Navy was so powerful that the United States could not really hope to match it. In the event of war, U.S. strategy (as in 1812) would have been commerce raiding, to which end individually powerful ships, like the big steam frigate *Merrimack,* were built before the Civil War. As Canney recounts, they were not altogether successful. After the Civil War, the tacit assumption seems to have been that not even war with England was likely. The navy's main mission was what might now be called Third World presence.

The extent to which this organization, which had built only a relatively few (and relatively slow) steam warships before 1861, was able to mobilize for the Civil War was remarkable. So was the extent to which the navy itself, led by an aggressive secretary, was able to formulate a new strategy, not only for dealing with the Confederacy but also for deterring any potential foreign intervention. By the end of the war, the U.S. Navy was building ships whose performance exceeded those of any others in the world, and the United States had the potential, in its cruisers and in its armored ships (which Canney will describe in a later volume), to become a leading world naval power. Certainly by 1865 the United States had the necessary raw industrial power.

That potential was not realized, and from a naval point of view the national decision to retreat from world power must have been painful. From a national point of view, however, it was reasonably logical, for the time. No European power directly threatened the United States, no European power other than England had territory abutting that of the United States, and contemporary steam warships could not easily cross even the Atlantic in fighting order. A U.S. government determined to reduce expenditures could not be bothered to support a modern navy. Canney shows the consequences of this decision, for example, in the retreat from modern steam machinery.

One strategic problem for the United States was conveniently ignored at the time: Cuba. Although Spain was only a second- or third-rate European power, she did have a reasonably modern navy, and in Cuba she had a base within easy range of the United States. This potential problem was dramatized in 1873 when the United States almost came to blows with Spain over the seizure of an American ship, the *Virginius,* which was running guns to Cuba.

The administration of the navy at the time was forced to acknowledge that the remaining Civil War ironclads were obsolescent at best and not nearly as serviceable as had been imagined. The crisis ended before very much could be done, and the policy of reducing the navy to what was needed to deal with such minor Third World states as Korea continued. Remarkably, the *Virginius* crisis was not cited later—in the early 1880s—as a rationale for reviving and modernizing the navy. On the other hand, even in 1898, Cuba represented a unique situation: the Spanish fleet could not have crossed the Atlantic, fought in U.S. waters, and retreated. Based in Cuba, however, it directly threatened the U.S. East Coast.

Such observations do not negate the achievements or the rationale of the old steam navy. It was certainly true that the extraordinary steaming performances of the ships designed during the Civil War were thrown aside. On the other hand, after 1865 the navy's main role was to maintain a worthwhile presence in the Third World, at a minimum cost. Sailing performance had to be emphasized, since only sail could provide the sort of long endurance the navy's role demanded. Ships providing Third World presence did not then have to be able to fight modern warships. That came only somewhat later, when the remaining Third World states began buying ships in Europe.

At home, much of the available money was inevitably siphoned away in maintaining public and private yards. Some of that siphoning was corruption. Some of it, however, was also maintenance of the base from which a later navy could be built. Roach may have been the villain of the end of the old navy, but his was also the only modern yard available to build the first of the steel cruisers of the new navy.

History is written by the winners, and in the U.S. Navy the winners were those who persuaded a reluctant U.S. government, Congress and administration together, to build up a modern fleet after 1883. Part of their argument was that the happy circumstances of both the Civil War and the postwar period had passed. The navy of the Civil War had been built up remarkably quickly, for example, by the construction of the "ninety-day gunboats." That achievement in turn had been possible partly because wooden hulls could be built so easily and so quickly, and also because steam machinery was relatively simple. By 1883 high-performance warships were no longer so easy to build, and it seemed reasonable to argue that a wartime navy had to be created many years before any emergency.

The other new development was that steam machinery was now economical enough that a foreign fleet *could* reach the New World in fighting order. A favorite argument of the naval revivalists was that a European fleet could appear off the U.S. East Coast and reduce much of the country's wealth to ashes by naval bombardment. This argument eventually prompted the construction of a U.S. battle fleet; it also led to a revival of the army's coast defense artillery.

Between 1850 and 1885, the U.S. Navy found its fortunes changing more radically than ever before or since in its history: from a small but reasonably modern force to an extremely powerful and modern fleet, then down very quickly to obsolescence and neglect, and then back up toward its present preeminent position. For a modern reader, perhaps the most important lesson is that preeminent naval power, built up at enormous cost, can decay surprisingly fast, in the face of requirements for economy and government ignorance of the value of sea power. The revival of 1885 occurred not because the government moved itself but only because a few naval officers were able to convince it that a new combination of technical and strategic circumstances made a modern navy essential.

That lesson, that even the most powerful navy must make sure the government and public paying for it understand its rationale, may be the most valuable one in this extremely interesting book.

Norman Friedman

Preface

Many of the official unpublished types of sources (General Board minutes, design files, and others) available for the development of twentieth-century warships do not exist for the era of the old steam navy. This reflects the rather informal and unstructured procedures used in designing nineteenth-century warships. In rare instances, official design committees were formed for a particular class of vessels, but on the whole, only the chief naval constructor and the constructors at various navy yards were involved in the process. Most of the unpublished design information is scattered among the general correspondence files of the constructors and the secretary of the navy. Fortunately, the original plans for the majority of the vessels of the era are on file at the National Archives. Thus the plans are the most comprehensive and useful record of these ships.

Plans found in the National Archives may be filed, in one of three ways. "NARS Plan" plus a code number is the main filing designation. "NARS Alpha. File" indicates the plan is filed under the ship's name rather than a code number. "NARS BSE" plans are located in the plans from the Bureau of Steam Engineering, filed alphabetically by ship's name. All the above are from Record Group 19, located at the Cartographic and Architectural Branch of the archives in Alexandria, Virginia.

Other National Archives record groups used are RG 45 (Navy Department Records) and RG 74 (Bureau of Ordnance). Plans from the latter are listed by code number and are also found at the Alexandria branch.

Documents in all three record groups are identified by the record group number and entry number: for example, RG 45/209. The bibliography lists all entry numbers and the title or subject of the entry. Entry numbers prefaced by "M" are on microfilm. RG 45/OSF indicates a subfile referred to as the "Old Subject File" and will be followed by code letters and a file box number (RG 45/OSF AQ Box 88).

Reports of the North Atlantic Blockading Squadron (RG 45/OSF AD Box 52) are preprinted forms and have a generic date of November 1864; many have no identified reporting officer. Other types of reports also may not have listed reporting officers or recipients.

The dimensions and tonnage measurements of vessels are sometimes difficult to determine because contemporary sources varied in their standards and accuracy. "Length overall," for instance, is nearly meaningless in the primary sources. Tonnage was a particularly complicated subject that in its exact application was of more interest to insurers than seamen.

In this book, all length dimensions are "between perpendiculars," as indicated or calculated from the plans of the ships. This dimension was usually from the forward end of the main, or gun, deck to the aft side of the stern post; on screw steamers this was to the aft side of the forward stern post. Breadth dimensions are "molded" (or "moulded")—to the outside of the frames—rather than "extreme"—to the outside of the planking. Tonnage is given in displacement tons only. Deviations from these standards will be so noted.

Every attempt has been made to avoid one of the major problems of nautical books: the overuse of sailing jargon (although technical descriptions of ships require a certain number of specialized terms). Wherever possible, terms (particularly steam engineering) have been defined when introduced. A limited glossary emphasizing steam engineering vocabulary that is not likely to be found in other nautical books has been appended. Some general shipbuilding terms are also included. No attempt has been made to cover general sailing terminology (such as rig types and so on), since these terms are defined in other readily available sources.

As far as possible, reproductions of original plans have been used. These are primary documents and as such much to be preferred over copied drafts. Many factors, however, prevent extensive use of the originals. Their size (usually one-fourth inch to one foot) combined with the fineness of their lines results in infinitesimal detail when reduced to book format. Second, aging and wear have made many plans exceedingly difficult to reproduce photographically. Where photographic negatives were found unsuitable or photocopies could not be used, I have traced or drawn reproductions, usually simplifying them somewhat without eliminating essentials. Where highly detailed and attractive originals were available, I have attempted to include them in as large size as possible. These tracings and drawings from the original ship plans are designed to delineate salient features of the ships and may not be adequate for the ship modeler to work from directly. Wherever possible, National Archives code numbers are included, to enable the modeler or other interested individuals to have access to the originals.

Acknowledgments

Many individuals and institutions were necessary for the research and writing of this volume. The single largest repository used was the National Archives. In the main archives, I wish to thank Richard Von Doernhof and Terry Hammett.

The majority of the remaining plans of nineteenth century American warships are maintained by the Cartographic and Architectural Branch of the National Archives in Alexandria, Virginia. Paul Connor, Jeffrey Carter, and Brendan Kelly provided valuable assistance. Brendan was particularly conscientious in searching out obscure plans.

Other institutions to be acknowledged are the Mystic Seaport Museum and library (Mystic, Connecticut), the Mariners Museum of Newport News, the Society for the Preservation of New England Antiquities in Boston, the Wilson Library at the University of North Carolina (Chapel Hill), and the Franklin Institute of Philadelphia. Also, Kathy Flynn of the photographs section of the Peabody Museum of Salem, Massachusetts, was particularly helpful. The Ohio State University Library has one of the most extensive collections of early steam-engineering books extant, and I used their services extensively. The State Library of Ohio was also the source of many useful government documents.

The assistance and advice of the following individuals were invaluable: Jim Dolph at Portsmouth Navy Yard; Michael Winey at the U.S. Army Military History Institute (Carlyle Barracks, Pennsylvania); Dr. Charles Peery, who allowed the use of photographs from his collection, Mike Curtin at the Hampton Roads Naval Museum in Norfolk, and John Arrison of the Hart Nautical Collection at the Massachusetts Institute of Technology, (Cambridge). Thanks also to Frank Braynard of the American Merchant Marine Academy Museum in Kings Point, New York, for information on the engines of the *Ranger;* and Herbert Reynolds Spencer, Jr., for permission to use material from his father's booklet on the *Michigan.* Also, the late K. Jack Bauer provided much information on early steam technology.

Particular thanks go to Stephen S. Roberts for permission to use a great deal of previously gathered material on American cruising ships. This included compilations of ships' ordnance gathered from their logs, a summary of the building programs of Civil War cruisers, and a compilation of information on naval vessels of the era ("Recognition Data: U.S. Screw Corvettes, Sloops, and Gunboats, 1859–c. 1890"), based on information from deck logs and ships' plans.

Thanks to my father, Ladd L. Canney, for information on early steam engines.

Finally, Chuck Haberlein of the Naval Historical Center (Washington, D.C.), who is one of the few experts on nineteenth-century naval steamships, provided invaluable information, advice and introductions to other sources. I appreciate his assistance in obtaining photographs from the naval collection as well as his critique of the first draft.

My wife, Janice, assisted in preparing the manuscript and provided support in more ways than can be listed here.

Introduction

Like huge toy boats tossed aside by bored schoolboys, the battered hulks of once formidable warships were strewn on the beach, with holed bottoms on unseemly display; other equally substantial vessels seemed to have submitted to an immense hand that forced them to the shallow harbor bottom, leaving decks awash and tangled rigging where polished brass and neatly furled sails had been a few hours before.

The three wrecked U.S. Navy steamers in the harbor of Apia, Samoa, in March 1889, with their anomalous masts and spars towering over squat funnels, were the "Old Navy"—the relics—even in 1889 a quarter of a century out-of-date. They had been dispatched to face down British and German cruisers in a colonial dispute over the territory. The storm preempted the threatened showdown and left three American and three German vessels sunk or beached. Only a British warship escaped during the hurricane, and the question of the outcome of the unfought battle remained to be debated by later naval historians.

The loss of the *Trenton, Vandalia,* and *Nipsic,* three of the most advanced vessels of the American wooden navy, was indeed tragic, but the event is an appropriate symbol for the historical fate of the entire old steam-and-sail navy.

By the date of the Samoan storm, the modern steel ("new") navy was coming into its own and had captured the attention of the nation. The quaint old live-oak fleet was quickly eclipsed in the public mind and, with the exception of a few celebrated vessels of the Civil War, soon forgotten. This process of historical amnesia was no doubt expedited by the perception that the old fleet was in any case obsolete, consisting for the most part of vessels and armament dating from the 1850s.

The consequent lack of interest in the vessels of the post–Civil War era, when the navy was indeed in decline, became a phenomenon that encompassed the entire early steam navy, from 1815 onward. The only exceptions were a few famous ships of the Civil War. The most telling evidence of this inattention is seen in the paucity of literature on the subject of early naval steam vessels compared to the numerous books on both the sailing ships of the navy and the modern steel warships. The nearest approximation to a study of the ships of the steam navy is *The Steam Navy of the United States,* written in 1896 by Frank M. Bennett, a volume with serious shortcomings. Not only is the book rarely found, it is by no means a comprehensive study of the warships of the era. Bennett emphasized only their steam powerplants and the development of the corps of steam engineers, to the exclusion of the vessels' sailing qualities, hull designs, or construction. The small format and primitive photograph reproduction methods further limit the book's value as a tool for serious study of the warships of the era.

The present study has been written to fill an obvious need—to document the ships of the early steam navy, a neglected subject in naval literature. This volume covers the unarmored vessels built by or for the navy, beginning with Robert Fulton's steam harbor defense battery in 1815 and concluding with the last wooden sail-and-steam sloops of the 1880s. Excluded, therefore, are the monitors and riverclads, the purchased vessels, and various types of auxiliary and torpedo ships. Ironclads and torpedo vessels will be the subject of a later volume.

The purpose of the book is to detail these vessels, as well as the technological developments they represented. In the process the relevant naval policies will be explored, along with the individuals who contributed to the development of the navy in the nineteenth century.

The method used is both graphic and narrative, as well as historical. The plans and photographs in many cases will speak for themselves. The author is not by training a naval architect or sailor but a historian and researcher presenting a long overdue study of the warships of a neglected era.

The Old Steam Navy

VOLUME ONE

FRIGATES, SLOOPS, AND GUNBOATS, 1815–1885

A model of Fulton's Demologos *in the Smithsonian Institution. Note the four funnels located on the starboard side and rudders on each end. (Courtesy Smithsonian Institution)*

CHAPTER 1

From Harbor Batteries to Paddle-Wheel Frigates, 1815–1840

On 3 January 1815, the river side-wheel steamer *Enterprise,* commandeered by General Andrew Jackson, ran past British guns to supply the garrison at Fort Saint Philip, near New Orleans. According to Samuel Carter III in *Blaze of Glory: the Fight for New Orleans,* Jackson "saw in the *Enterprise,* free from dependence on wind and current, a valuable tool," and he used her several times during the campaign.[1] The use of a steam vessel in military operations at this early date was unprecedented: the successful commercial employment of steam vessels was less than a decade old.

This isolated incident cannot in any way be interpreted as a factor in the founding of the steam navy; however, it serves to emphasize the practicality of steam-powered vessels in wartime, even at that early date. Second, the incident serves as a fitting introduction for the U.S. Navy's pioneer steam warship, which was completed in the same year, 1815.

Fulton's Steam Battery

Robert Fulton's *Clermont,* or "North River Steamboat," the first commercially successful steam vessel, was six years old by 1813, when this quintessential Yankee inventor proposed a steam-powered floating battery for the defense of New York. Fulton obtained influential support from Stephen Decatur, Jacob Jones, James Biddle, and Oliver Hazard Perry, among others, and the project was approved by Congress on 9 March 1814.[2] The need for this unprecedented warship was clear: the British had blockaded U.S. harbors and invasion was imminent.

The *Demologos* ("Voice of the People," Fulton's own name for the vessel, but also called the Fulton Steam Battery or *Fulton I*) was laid down on 20 June 1814 at the civilian shipyard of Adam and Noah Brown. Her proportions were more rectangular than longitudinal, measuring 153 feet, 2 inches in length, by 56 feet breadth. The latter figure was "molded beam," that is, measured to the outsides of the frames rather than to the outside of the planking (extreme). With foot-thick planking, she was 58 feet in extreme breadth. This boxy hull structure has been described as a catamaran, implying that there were two complete hulls. More accurately, the vessel was composed of two identical half hulls, separated by the paddle-wheel race. The double hull was not unusual in this era and was used for ferryboats where extra breadth was necessary. (In fact, the double-hulled design with a centrally mounted paddle wheel was common to horse-powered ferryboats of the time.) Fulton himself had, beginning in 1812, built three steam ferryboats—the *Jersey, York,* and *Nassau*—on the catamaran principle.[3]

The interior sides of the battery's hulls were planked up flat and the ends of the vessel were identical. A rudder was placed at the end of each respective half hull, and each pair was linked by a yoke to permit their use in parallel, via tillers and wheels on the spar deck.[4]

The vessel had two decks, each complete except for a midship opening for the paddle wheel. The wheel's paddle buckets extended about two feet above the level of the spar deck, and this aperture was given a planking hatch over the wheel. There were no bulwarks on this deck, only iron stanchions set four feet inboard of the plank sheer to support a barricade of wet cotton bales for protection in action. The lower ends of the stanchions were mounted on the ceiling of the lower deck bulwarks. Beams for both decks were 1-foot square and continuous across the vessel, solidly connecting both hulls.[5]

Unlike standard hulls, where the frames were spaced at intervals along the keel, those of the *Demologos* were set hard against each other, forming a bottom of solid timber (probably oak). Above the turn of the bilge, the frames narrowed somewhat, allowing more conventional spacing on her sides. The external planking was one 12-inch layer of timber. Inside her frames, from the turn of the bilge upward, were a foot of ceiling and a second vertical set of frames covered by a second layer of ceiling. In total, her gundeck between gunports was protected by more than five feet of timber. This side protection extended down to protect the upper parts of engine and boilers, to a point below the ship's waterline.[6]

Yet another unusual feature of the hull was the use of timbers connecting each half hull along the keels, and thus across the paddle-wheel race. Twelve 12-inch-square timbers were used for this purpose, with obvious disregard for the considerable drag they would create some thirteen feet below the waterline.[7]

The machinery of the ship is the subject of some disagreement. The most commonly seen plan shows an inclined cylinder, with the piston rod acting directly on the paddle-wheel crankshaft. A draft recently located in the Danish Royal Archives, however, indicates the cylinder was vertical. The piston had a diameter of 4 feet, a stroke of 5 feet, and developed 120 horsepower. The piston rod worked a crosshead, which in turn operated side-levers that were approximately on the same level as the cylinder. The side-levers operated connecting rods to gears on the paddle-wheel shaft.[8]

The two boilers were copper and each had two flues. The Danish plans indicated there were two funnels per boiler, though another early source gave the vessel one per boiler. The Smithsonian Institution's model of the ship, built from the Danish plans, shows her with all four funnels, though speculation has it that later in her career the two on each boiler were trunked together.[9] In this vessel, boilers were located in one hull, and machinery was in the other. The external result was four funnels set on one side of the vessel, certainly unusual, but no more so than the vessel's entire concept.

The framework of the vessel's paddle wheel was iron and the wheel's diameter was 16 feet with eight wooden blades (or "buckets") measuring 14 feet 6 inches by three feet each. It could be driven with equal facility in either direction and the dip of the buckets was approximately three feet, at a draft of thirteen feet.[10]

Set behind the 5-foot bulwarks were twenty-six 32-pounders, most of which had been captured on the British vessel *John of Lancaster* earlier in the war. The effectiveness of the British blockade was such that they were transported overland from Philadelphia to New York.[11]

Fulton's early plans were to equip the ship with his "submarine gun." This was apparently nothing more than a standard Columbiad, suspended below a vessel's waterline for firing into the hull of an enemy vessel. A block-and-tackle arrangement raised the gun for loading. The effective use of the weapon required exceedingly close quarters with the enemy. Fulton envisioned a sailing battery using these guns, but Stephen Decatur convinced him of the danger of entangling the rigging with that of the enemy ship. This induced Fulton to consider steam power for the battery, leading eventually to the vessel actually constructed. There is no evidence that the submarine gun was ever tested, however, and none was on the steam battery. (Another unused idea for the vessel was a pump to defend the vessel with streams of water at 60 to 80 gallons per minute.)[12]

A two-masted lateen rig was added to the *Demologos* on the orders of her first naval commander, Captain David Porter, and she made her first trial trip on 10 June 1815. She had two subsequent trials and attained 5½ knots on the last run, in September 1815.[13]

A committee recommended the vessel be used for training, but the suggestion was disregarded and she was never commissioned in the navy. In 1817 she made one further trip under her own power—a "day-trip" to Staten Island with President Monroe aboard. In 1821 her machinery and guns were removed and she became a receiving ship. The vessel accidentally blew up in June 1829, the result of careless handling of gunpowder on board.[14]

Steam Batteries, 1815–1831

It is a matter of record that no steam vessels were built for the navy in the era between the *Demologos* and the *Fulton II* of 1837. The only steam-powered ship in the inventory during this interim period was the diminutive *Sea Gull,* purchased in 1822 to suppress pirates in the West Indies. This 100-ton side-wheel vessel had been built in Hartford in 1818 as the *Enterprise* and was powered by a rotary engine, the only such engine known in any U.S. naval vessel. Masts and sails were added to her by the navy and she was used until 1825. In 1840 she was sold at Philadelphia for $4,750, about one-quarter of her purchase price.[15]

Fulton's steam battery did, however, set a limited kind of precedent for steam-related activities in this

*Reconstructed Plans of Fulton's Steam Battery (*Demologos, *or* Fulton I*). The plans show the identical ends, location of engines and boilers in either "half-hull" of the vessel, and deck layout. Note the layers of timbering and the resultant thickness of side protection. Plans found in the Danish National Archives were reconstructed for the model in the Smithsonian Institution. See p. 2. (Courtesy Smithsonian Institution)*

5 HARBOR BATTERIES TO FRIGATES, 1815–1840

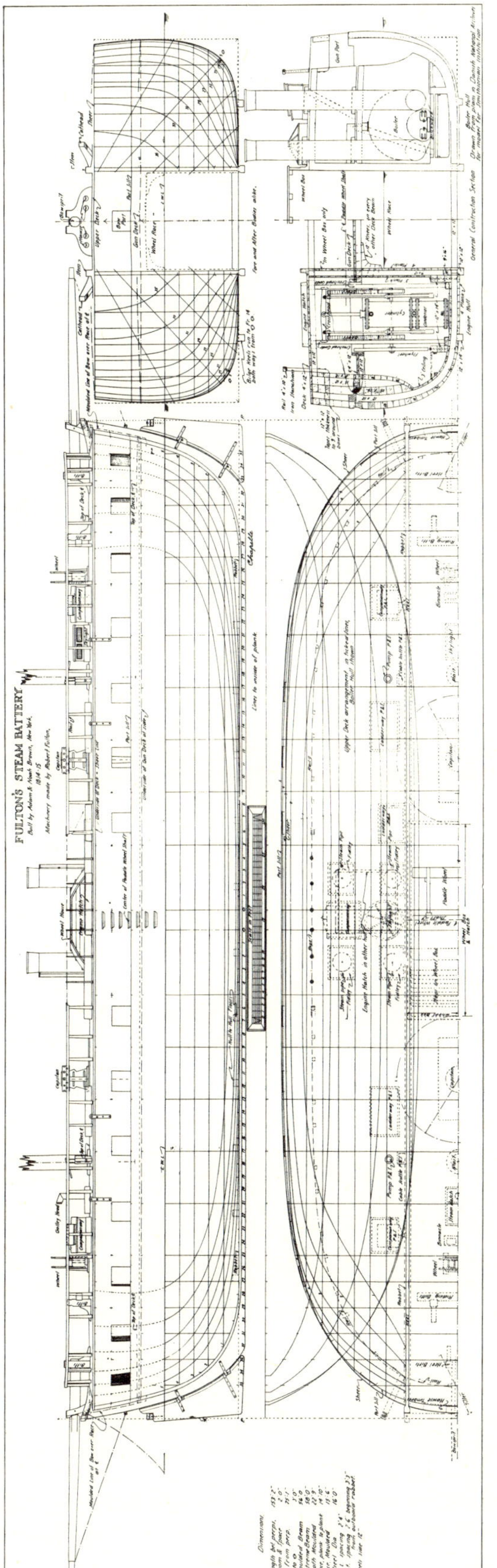

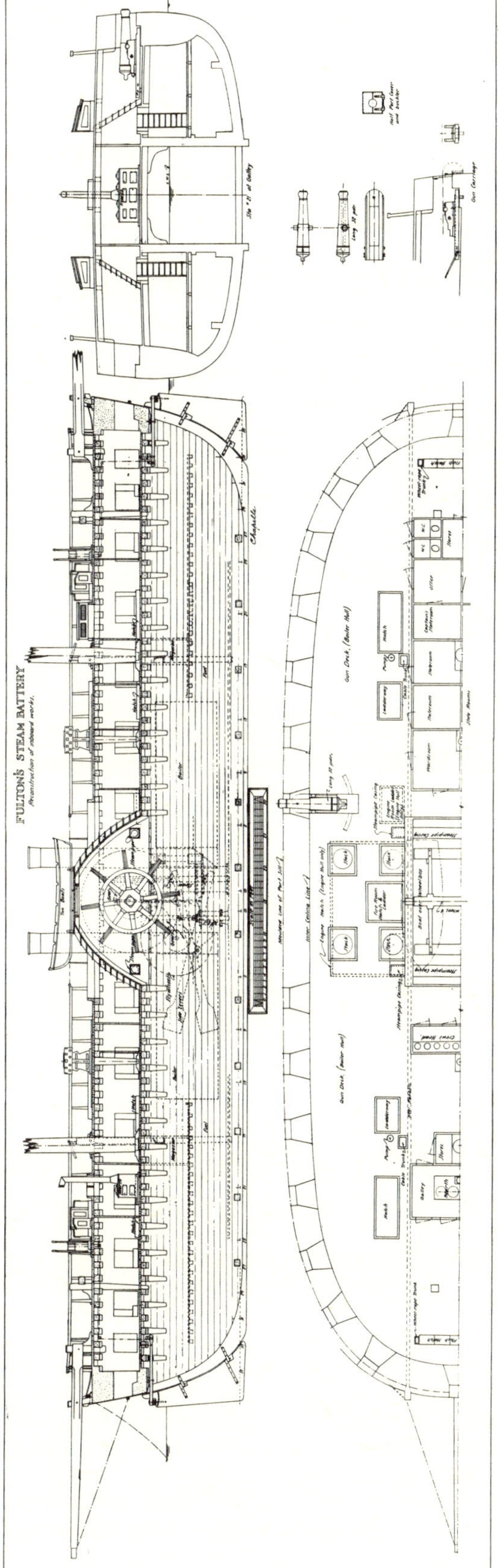

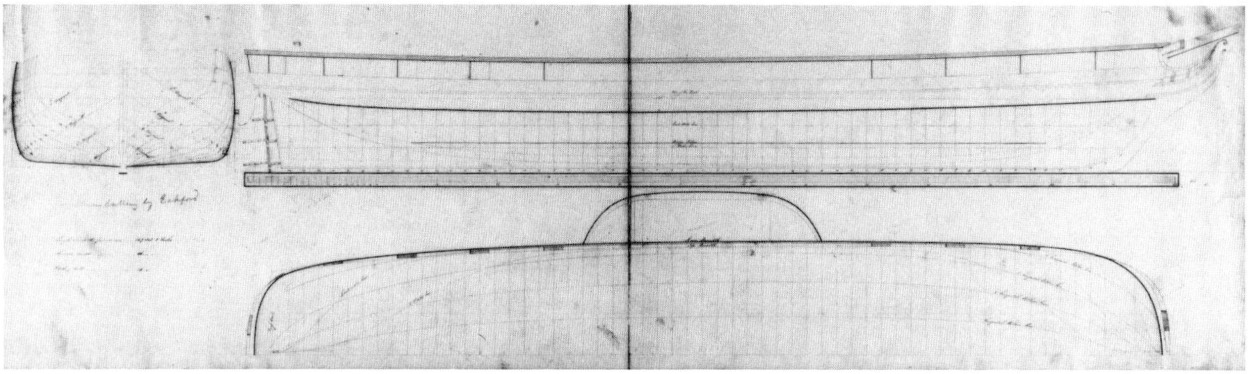

A Design for a "Steam Battery," by Henry Eckford, c. 1818. There is some evidence this "battery" was intended for ocean-going service, and she would have been a conventional paddle-wheel warship, based on Eckford's merchant vessel Fulton. *(NARS 107-9-14, National Archives)*

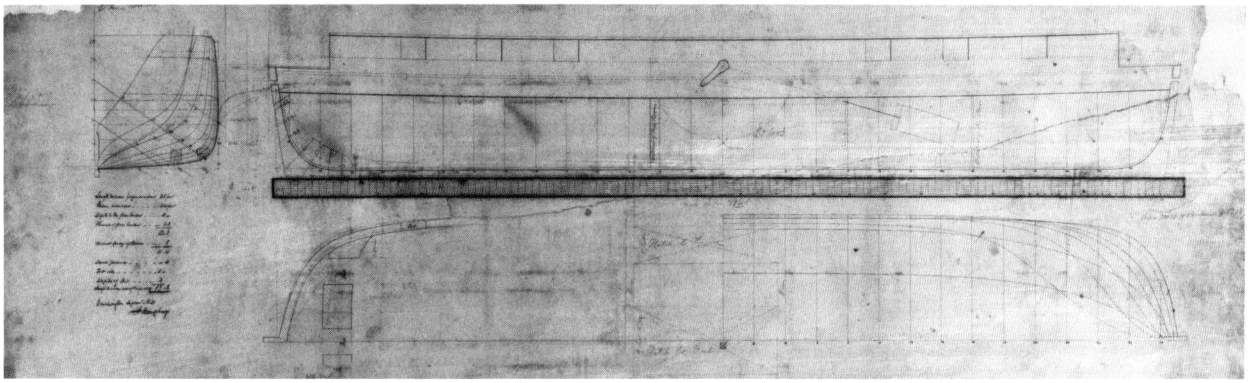

Humphreys's Proposal for a Double-Ended Steam Battery with Athwarthships Bulwarks, 1831. (NARS 40-6-2F, National Archives)

period. While the *Demologos* was yet uncompleted, a second battery was begun in Baltimore and another planned for Philadelphia. These projects were shelved with the cessation of hostilities in 1814.[16]

In 1816, Congress perpetuated the idea of a steam battery in a law for the "Gradual Increase of the Navy," which authorized accumulating the materials needed to build three such vessels. The Board of Naval Commissioners subsequently advertised for plans for these ships and began "procurement of the steam engines and all the imperishable materials" required. By 1822, the materials were available for two batteries at New York and a third at Washington Navy Yard, including engines and copper boilers as well as timber for frames.[17]

The navy's proposed plan for the ships was described in an official response to the inventor John Stevens in 1821. The plan was to be "entirely different from the first steam battery. . . . It was prepared by the naval constructor who built the steamship now plying between New York and New Orleans, and is believed to possess all her qualities of fleetness and ability to keep the sea."[18]

A draft in the National Archives (107-9-14) labeled "Eckford Steam Battery" is probably the plan referred to in the navy's response to Stevens. Henry Eckford, employed by the department from 1817 to 1820, had designed the merchant steamer *Robert Fulton* before 1820, a vessel described as the "first ocean-going steamship, both in conception and execution to appear in American waters." She was the largest steamer to date, 159 feet by 33 feet 5 inches, and was the only vessel of that era to regularly ply the New York to New Orleans run.[19]

Eckford's steam battery design was 147 feet 8 inches by 36 feet, broader and shorter than the *Robert Fulton,* and she was considerably flatter on the bottom. She was pierced for ten guns on a side and unlike the *Demologos* looked strictly conventional. The commissioners had rather higher expectations of these ships than the title "battery" implies, hence the patterning of the vessel on the lines of an ocean-going steamer.

The materials and plans were all that was accomplished on the project during the 1820s, indeed, all that Congress had required. By 1831, the board had decided to update the plans for the batteries and evaluate the materials gathered. The engines were found to be obsolete and the suggestion was made that they be exchanged on the open market for newer engines and boilers.[20] At this point Samuel Humphreys, now chief naval constructor, came into the picture and began the process of developing a new design for a steam battery.

Fulton II

On 7 October 1831, Humphreys was directed by the Board of Naval Commissioners to visit a "steam factory" in Baltimore and investigate costs and details of engines and boilers for a steam battery of 500 tons. Humphreys reported that $29,500 would procure a 120-horsepower engine with a 56-inch cylinder. It would require thirty-five feet of hold space fore and aft and drive paddle wheels 20 feet in diameter. All the machinery and boilers would be under the deck, with the exception of the paddle-wheel shafts.[21]

The chief constructor had apparently prepared a draft of such a vessel before his information-gathering trip to Baltimore, a plan now in the National Archives, dated September 1831 and signed by Humphreys. The ship was to be 125 feet by 34 feet; in pencil on the draft is the notation "430 tons." The below-deck machinery space is 35 feet long, and the paddle wheels are 20 feet in diameter. Other characteristics of the plan are noteworthy and unusual: her hull form is identical fore and aft; and bulwarks cross the bows of the vessel, set back somewhat from each stem. In addition to broadside ports, there are three ports on each endwork.

Because of the navy hierarchy's lack of interest or lack of funds, the design was shelved. Steam-related activities, however, arise sporadically in the records before 1835. A model of a steam battery is mentioned in a letter in 1833, and that same year "Wm. Humphreys" at Washington Navy Yard was ordered to "this day commence laying down the moulds for a steam battery." No substantive progress in the area was made.[22]

Only pressure from above persuaded the navy commissioners (the controlling body before the bureau system) to reallocate funds from sailing vessels to a steam-propelled ship. President Jackson provided the impetus in an order to Secretary of the Navy Mahlon Dickerson early in 1835, and by June the board was directed to build a steam battery "of a form and size best calculated for the defense of our ports and harbors."[23]

The secretary's instructions indicated no limitations were placed on the amount of money to be spent, and in fact, implied that the cost was secondary to accomplishing the ends set forth. The board retransmitted and somewhat reinterpreted those instructions, however, to a committee comprising the constructors Humphreys, Samuel Hartt, and John Lenthall. They were to design a vessel "of the least dimensions and at the least expense." She was to carry two long guns "to be worked in circles, one forward and one abaft the wheel house" and four 32-pounders in broadside. She was to have a crew of sixty, to stow provisions for twenty days, to have all machinery and boilers under the deck, and to average 10 knots. Finally she was to be capable of passing "with facility and safety from one harbour to another, as from New York to New Port or Philadelphia and from the latter place to Norfolk and with an ability to move with considerable speed with sail."[24]

The committee was obliged to consult various civilian experts in the field to accomplish their ends. Given the primitive state of the technology, problems and contradictions were inevitable. Furthermore, the scent of a government contract in the offing may well have skewed otherwise sound advice.

The counsel received on the hull design was sound only in principle, exaggerated and probably based on the practice of river steamers. A ten-to-one length to breadth ratio was recommended and experiments were cited wherein "artificial bows" had been added to existing steamers to test such proportions.

On the matter of machinery, an engine builder in New York recommended a high-pressure, vibrating cylinder engine because of the simplicity, safety, and power of that variety. The gentleman was, incidentally, prepared to supply the navy with just such a powerplant. The advantages of the vibrating (oscillating) cylinder engines were indeed considerable. They had few moving parts and were therefore relatively simple and maintenance free. High-pressure engines exhausted directly into the atmosphere and required no condensing apparatus, and their boilers were significantly smaller than low-pressure units.

For reasons now unknown, only one person was consulted on engines, and the committee's report recommended the high-pressure, vibrating cylinder engine. The board raised no objections or questions concerning the recommendations and the design procedure continued. The absence of further inquiries, however, would later redound to the detriment of the project.[25]

The board directed Humphreys to design two hulls, of 180-foot and 200-foot lengths.[26] Given the tenor of their earlier instructions to the committee, it was inevitable that the hull of the "least size" was selected. It is immediately obvious that the plan for the *Fulton II* was Humphreys's design of 1831, with 55 feet inserted amidships. The 34-foot beam was retained, as well as the identical fore and after bodies, and the athwartships bulwarks. The hull

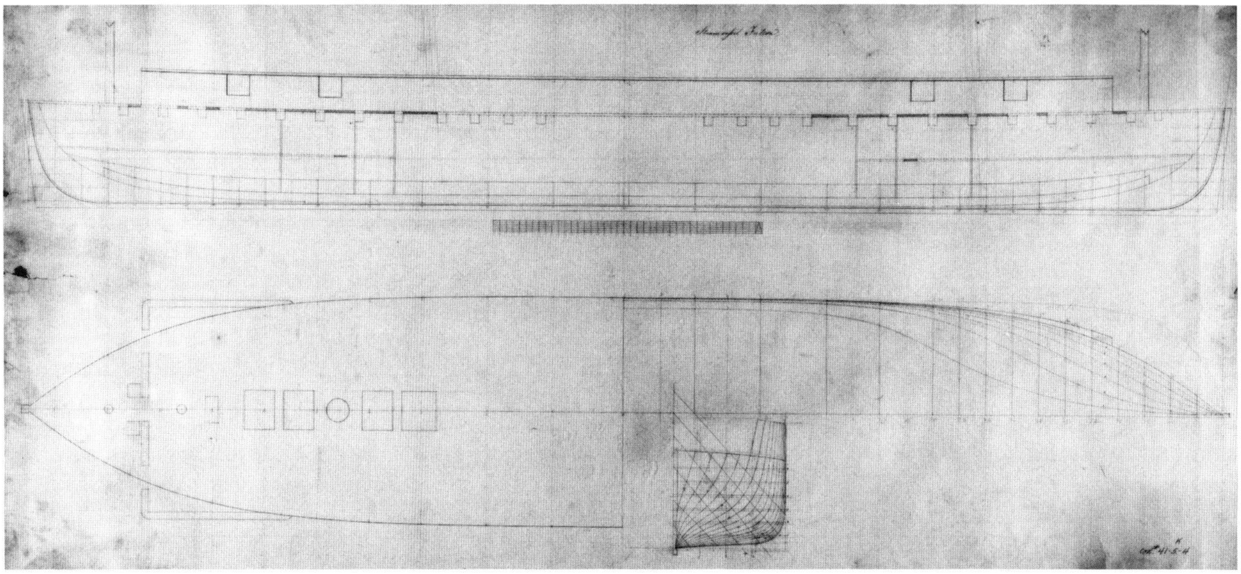

General Plan of the Fulton II. *Note the obvious development from Humphreys's design of 1831. On this plan both the original locations of masts on ends are seen, as well as the positions of masts when completed. (NARS Plan 41-5-4K, National Archives)*

was begun late in 1835 at the New York Navy Yard, supervised by constructor Hartt and Captain Matthew Calbraith Perry, the latter already known for his progressive views on the navy.

Even as the hull was being laid down, other events were casting doubts upon aspects of the design. A committee of the board ordered a test firing of a 32-pound cannon arranged to discharge "over a ship's deck, and the determine whether it could safely be attempted in the proposed steam vessel." The committee observed and reported in part: "The first discharge . . . tore up the platform which represented the deck."[27] The committee apparently shook their collective heads and went home. No further tests are on record, nor are specific recommendations for changes.

As early as November 1835, the board expressed doubts about the appropriateness of high-pressure engines, doubts that had not been officially raised when the engine committee had submitted its report. The board delayed its "final decision" until more information was available. It was not until three months later that members acknowledged their ignorance in the matter by advertising for and hiring a civilian steam engineer. Charles H. Haswell was given a two-month tenure and instructed to recommend suitable engines for the ship.[28]

Subsequently, on 12 July 1836, Haswell was appointed first chief engineer in the navy, and assigned to the *Fulton II.* Thus, the board's ignorance brought about the eventual (1842) institution of the Steam Engineer Corps, with Haswell its first member.[29]

Haswell dislodged the board from its shaky preference for high-pressure engines and recommended low-pressure, condensing machinery. Condensers, though more complicated, freed the vessel for operation at sea, allowing water to be condensed for reuse, thus reducing saltwater corrosion and the formation of deposits on boilers and pipes.

This critical alteration in the vessel occurred in July 1836, three months after the hull of the ship was essentially complete. Work had been suspended until the machinery could be installed; then decking and fitting out would be possible.[30] And yet further delays were necessary. The type of low-pressure engines was yet to be determined; the design and construction of the machinery was not yet accomplished; and, of course, the contract for the new machinery would have to be let out for bids.

Three types of engines were considered, designated according to the position of the cylinder: the vertical or "steeple" engine; inclined; and horizontal. The height of the steeple engine eliminated it immediately. The inclined engine, on the other hand, provided the most protection because the only portion exposed above deck was the paddle shaft. Horizontal cylinders would necessarily be entirely above deck.

The exposure of the horizontal engines was surprisingly inconsequential to Captain Perry. He was more concerned with the extra stowage space below decks that this type of engine would allow. In his letter to the board on the subject, however, he strongly advocated adding "30 or even 40 feet" to the vessel's length to accommodate the larger condensing engines. Others, including Commandant Ridgely of the navy yard, echoed this recommendation.[31]

Humphreys and the board disagreed. They voiced concern over the length-to-breadth ratio of the ship: should she be lengthened? Their chief concern, however, was the "forward state" of the hull and the expense involved in bisecting the hull and adding to it.[32] Practically, the addition would have been relatively uncomplicated, given the ship's long, straight midsection.

Consequently, the hull was launched in its original configuration in May 1837. The West Point Foundry Association supplied the engines and boilers as designed by Charles Haswell, and the ship was commissioned on 13 December 1837. More than two years had been consumed in construction time.

The product of this convoluted and hesitant process was certainly unique. The *Fulton II* measured 181 feet 6 inches between perpendiculars by 34 feet 10 inches, and displaced 1,011 tons at a mean draft of 10 feet 6 inches. (Though these dimensions are unimpressive by twentieth-century standards, it should be remembered that the average frigate of the era did not exceed 180 feet between perpendiculars.) She was strongly built of live oak and her hull lines, identical fore and aft, were sharp and somewhat hollow below the waterline. Her entrance lines shortly filled to a squared midship section, which occupied nearly a third of her length. Her lines owed much more to river vessels than ocean steamers, with nearly flat floors, straight sides, and hard bilges.

The engines of the vessel were by almost any standard astoundingly simple. Two 50-inch cylinders were mounted horizontally on deck, with each piston rod connected to the crank of one paddle wheel, measuring 22 feet 10 inches in diameter. The stroke of the piston was nine feet and the two cylinders and paddles were not connected in any way.

Four copper boilers measuring 10 feet by 16 feet each were below deck. Flues carried the gases through the boiler water and to the funnels. Copper was used in spite of the expense because of its resistance to corrosion. Each boiler was equipped with an exceedingly tall smokestack, reminiscent of those on the typical midcentury riverboat.

Adding to this formidable top-hamper was a topsail schooner rig. She was originally to have had two masts, but Perry added a third. Her complement numbered 137 and she was to stow thirty days' provisions. These two figures were inexplicably larger than the board's original requirements of a crew of sixty and provisions for twenty days.[33]

On deck, bulwarks extended forward and aft from substantially built wheelhouses (9 inches of planking), terminating abruptly some twenty feet from each stem. The athwartships bulwarks ("ramparts") were pierced for three guns each, and all bulwarks were three feet higher than the ports, with their sides sloped "to glance off an enemy's shot," according to an early source.[34]

Connecting the wheelhouses and extending aft over the engines was a light deck, referred to incongruously as a "promenade" deck. Though an engine house may have been added later in her career, at the outset her machinery was essentially

Drawing of the Fulton II *by Samuel Ward Stanton. The broadside profile does not reveal the second pair of funnels or the cross-bulwarks fore and aft. Note that her stern bulwarks have been built up, probably to protect her steering apparatus. (Naval Historical Center)*

exposed—protected only by the bulwarks and paddle housings on the perimeter of the deck.[35] Exposed engines were not unusual in riverboats of the era, but on a warship the practice was patently undesirable.

Descriptions of her armament are not consistent, and her later role as a gunnery-practice ship no doubt involved various battery changes. Perry at first used weapons available at the yard: four 32s and four to six light 18-pounders. As a test vessel, she had one large ordnance piece, an 8- or 10-inch Paixhans-type shell gun, mounted on pivot rails forward.[36]

The design of the *Fulton II* was highly unorthodox, but it is apparent that there was an overriding method at work: a rationale that emphasized both fore and aft fire as well as movement. The original committee report, no doubt written by Humphreys, explained: "The extreme breadth [is] to be placed in the center (longitudinally), both ends or bodies to be alike, with a rudder at each end, to be capable of advancing or retreating without turning around, or exposing her broadsides and wheels to the shot of the enemy."[37] The cross-bulwarks were logical extensions of this rationale, providing both protection and deck space for a substantial battery firing fore and aft. In confined harbors, the ship's reversing would have been useful. A second rudder was planned and discarded, no doubt because of the difficulties in protecting the steering apparatus from hostile shot and from the *Fulton II*'s own projectiles.

Early press reaction to the *Fulton II* was positive and emphasized her powerful engines and proposed battery. The latter was touted as "invaluable for harbor defense" because of the range of the large shell guns.[38] A Boston journal quoted her officers as saying she was a "rapid, easy boat in smooth water, 14 knots being frequently got out of her," and Captain Perry commented on her "astonishing rapidity." Later, even her critics claimed she could attain 16 knots.[39]

She demonstrated both strength and speed in public early in 1838, when she towed the new frigate *Macedonian* "with the ease of a canoe . . . turning a circle in her own length."[40] A theory then current on the use of steam vessels was their use in towing "real" sailing vessels of war into harm's way despite calms or contrary winds. Such notions may have sweetened the sailing leadership's distaste for smoke-belching steamers.

Later in 1838 she was ordered to New York, specifically to race with the British Atlantic steamer *Great Western*. According to F. M. Bennett, the battery easily overhauled her competitor. The inequality of the contest was obvious, however, because the commercial steamer was fully loaded as she sailed for Liverpool.[41]

It soon became apparent that speed may have been the vessel's only asset—and that a questionable one. The shortcomings of the ship became more emphatic as the department veered from the ship's intended role as a harbor defense battery. On her trial trip, she demonstrated that she was not adaptable to the open sea. Perry reported her very wet "even in a light sea way" and that eight men were required to steer her, four at the tiller ropes and four at the wheel. Undaunted, the board ordered her from the harbor onto the coast.

Perry replied with a protest, citing her huge appetite for fuel, which limited her to 70 hours under steam, as well as her poor model for sea service.[42] A Boston paper described her limitations: "The model of her bottom is nearly the same, stem and stern, being very sharp . . . what the sailors call very lean in the bows, so much so, that . . . in a heavy sea, she would be nearly buried." Furthermore, her paddle housings were as close as twenty inches from the water, and easily "choked," impairing her progress markedly.[43]

Such facts and suggestions for their remedy were dutifully forwarded to Washington. No response was given except for an order to take her to Washington in May 1838. The result was predictable, and public.

Subsequently, a letter appeared in the *Army and Navy Chronicle,* gleefully exposing the failure of the *Fulton II.* The correspondent related that the first notice of the vessel after departing from New York was that she had "taken shelter from a blow under the Delaware breakwater," a storm "which a passenger steamer would have scorned to run from." Her next appearance was off Norfolk, under equally embarrassing circumstances: she was out of coal.[44]

In an avalanche of criticism that had been building since her construction, little of the vessel was left unscathed. And the barbs came from both within and without the navy. Her engines, admittedly powerful and reliable, were called unsuitable for the ship. Her ease at attaining high speeds sufficed to prove their "unnecessary size, power and weight." The critics compared them to those of the *Great Western,* which displaced 500 tons more than the *Fulton II* but whose engines developed 400 horsepower, compared to 720 horsepower for the naval vessel. Attackers then noted the physical size of these engines and the consequent lack of stowage and bunker spaces.[45]

The exposure of the engines and the bulwark arrangement received much attention, some couched in typical nineteenth-century florid sarcasm: "At the same time that a raking shot is solicited, her maximum broadside of three guns has an opportunity of tearing up the deck and disjointing the timbers before and beyond it . . . thereby in a spirit of philosophic impartiality dealing alike to friend and foe. . . . Constructed . . . with the express design to engage head or stern on, every hostile shot which tells must be a raking one." Thus endangered were the ends of the cylinders, the paddle buckets and the smoke pipes, and only a "dextrous" shot could miss the latter.[46]

Other objects of ridicule were her wheelhouses, described as "immense fungi," and her draft. The latter was criticized—"when light, too bouyant; when full, too deep." The ungainly appearance of the ship drew hoots from all quarters. She was described as "ludicrous and unseemly" with her cut-down ends giving the appearance of a "canal boat."[47] Illustrations of the ship, not to be confused with those of the rebuilt *Fulton II* of 1852, support these impressions. The abrupt termination of her overhanging bulwarks, combined with a bowsprit detached from any suitable supporting cutwater and knee rendered her truly homely. The gaggle of 40-foot smokepipes, however, was sufficient to disgust any sailor of the era, who expected grace, if not beauty, from 100-gun ships-of-the-line.

Many of the practical criticisms, unfortunately, were justified, particularly in view of the department's mixed signals on the mission of the vessel. If her model was only suitable for harbor work, the addition of a sailing rig and larger crew and stowage requirements were inappropriate.

Regardless of her purpose, her large fuel consumption was objectionable, as were her lack of protection for her engines and her low-hanging wheel housings. Perry suggested iron-armored sloping bulwarks be erected around the engines, but his advanced idea was duly ignored by the department. In the next few years modifications were made, including removing two of her boilers and the lower three feet of her paddle housings. Continued efforts were made to improve her until she was laid up in 1842.[48]

The criticism was sufficient to warrant congressional interest to the extent that all of the pertinent documents in her case were published. No actual investigation ensued, but the onus of her failure should fall particularly on the Board of Naval Commissioners. Their salient error was ignoring the need to lengthen the hull when larger engines became necessary, and this decision was essentially economic, made to minimize the cost of the ship. The sail-versus-steam controversy arose in this budgetary decision. In January 1836, the department reported the amount in their treasury and stated that "part . . . must necessarily be devoted to the completion of the frigate *Columbia.*"[49] Thus, a sailing vessel, on the stocks since 1825, was given higher priority than the steam battery.

The board's attempt to make a cruiser out of the *Fulton II* was in any case doomed to fail. It would be some forty years before the state of the technology would permit engines efficient enough to approach the cruising capabilities of sailing vessels.

The *Fulton II* was not an admirable beginning for the steam navy. She was not a complete loss, however. After ten years of disuse, her hull was found solid enough to warrant rebuilding the vessel, and she became a useful adjunct to the service, as will be seen in a later chapter. Despite her shortcomings, she did indeed bring steam power into the navy.

Mississippi and *Missouri*

With the notoriety of the *Fulton II* still fresh, on 3 March 1839 Congress directed the construction of two steam frigates. These were designated "sea steamers" from the outset, possibly to avoid the ambiguity that had plagued the *Fulton II*'s genesis.

By this time, the navy's reluctance to embrace steam had placed it far behind other fleets. The British possessed at least fifteen paddle sloops and one frigate, and France at least sixteen steamers.[50] All this construction occurred despite the clear disadvantages of paddle-wheel vessels as warships. The practical underwater screw had yet to be introduced.

The commissioners appointed two committees to formulate the design of the new steamers: a board of five line officers to determine the "powers and properties" required from the vessels; and a group of three constructors, two engineers, and Captain Perry to set forth the specifications of vessels to fulfill the officers' requirements. (Perry was also a member of the officer board.)

Their consensus called for ocean-going vessels, two 8-inch and eight broadside guns, two months' provisions for crews of two hundred, and fuel for twenty days' steaming. Under steam the ships would cruise at 9 knots and be capable of performing all the duties of a cruising vessel with sails alone.[51]

On the question of propulsion, there was disagreement over whether to use the English type of side-lever engine or inclined cylinders. As a compromise, one of each was to be built, with the stipulation that each develop the same nominal horsepower, estimated by calculating the cubic capacity of the cylinders.[52]

Humphreys, Hartt, and Lenthall completed the design, and construction was begun at New York and Philadelphia. The latter vessel was named the *Mississippi,* the former, *Missouri.* In direct contrast to the building of the *Fulton II,* neither vessel's construction was marred by significant delays or mid-construction crises. One journalist commented after the launch of the *Missouri,* "There has not been any trammeling by instructions from Washington."[53] The board, which was under considerable

The Mississippi *As She Appeared Departing for the Japan Expedition. Note the port stripe and white-topped paddle housings. (From Charles Beebe Stuart's* Naval and Mail Steamers of the United States, *1853.)*

fire both for the *Fulton II* as well as unsuccessful sailing vessels, was keeping a low profile in this instance, though this posture did not long delay the dissolution of this body in 1842 and its replacement by the bureau system.

Both vessels were launched in 1841 and commissioned early the next year. Descriptions of the vessels confirm that the hulls were identical, having been built from the same molds.[54] They were 220 feet between perpendiculars, with a 39-foot beam and a deep draft of 20 feet. Their hull lines were unremarkable except in their traditionalism. They had moderately rising floors, and the area of greatest immersion was forward of the longitudinal center of the hull. The placement of the midsection before the vessel's center of length was standard sailing ship hull design. Their low bilges and straight sides, however, were considered requisites for the effective action of the side wheels on the water.

Both vessels were the longest naval vessels built to that time. By comparison, the 120-gun ship-of-the-line *Pennsylvania* measured 209 feet in length, but this large battleship's greater beam (56 feet) made her less prone to hogging ("drooping" at the ends because of insufficient longitudinal strength) than the new frigates. Consequently, "iron trusses" were incorporated in the new steamers: a series of parallel diagonal iron straps running from the turn of the bilge to the main deck. The ships were the first American naval vessels built with this feature and among the earliest ships in the country to have such strengthening.[55]

The hulls' live-oak frames were filled solid between the members. Thus their bottoms were solid from their keels to their bilges.[56] Another innovation was that of watertight bulkheads, which had not been used in earlier naval vessels and were rarely seen elsewhere in the early nineteenth century. Both plans and correspondence indicate that four such iron divisions were used on the *Mississippi.* Two delimited the machinery spaces, one was thirty-five feet from the stem, and the fourth, forty-six feet from the stern post.[57]

Both vessels were bark-rigged and carried 19,000 square feet of canvas, including topgallant sails. Because of the placement of the funnels, no mainsails were used.[58]

Below decks, the *Missouri* was described as "much superior" to her sister ship in arrangement and finish.[59] The *Mississippi* did boast a "handsome mahogany sideboard" and a "Turkey carpet" in the captain's cabin. As was normal for the day, midshipmen and other officers' quarters were aft in each vessel, and the crew was forward of the engine spaces. The complement for each was 226 and they carried provisions for four months and 15,000 gallons of water.[60]

Ten Paixhan-type shell guns made up the vessels' batteries. In broadside were 8-inch 68-pounders and on the bows were two 10-inch, 120-pounder guns.[61] The latter fulfilled the requirement that they "fire forward 2 degrees within the line of the keel and the shot of each would cross the other at a distance of 112 yards from the pivot, and aft 145 degrees . . . making a range of 146 degrees." To obtain this field of fire, pivot ports over 20 feet long were used, consisting of eight hinged segments each. To further clear the decks for the pivot guns, the anchors were catted in the fore chains rather than on the bows.[62]

The boilers of each vessel were identical. Four copper boilers were placed in pairs in each hull, back to back, with common smoke chimneys. The weight of the boilers and funnel was just under 300 tons in each vessel.[63]

Less is known of the *Missouri*'s engine because of her short career. Inclined engines, however, became the most frequently used type in American naval paddle steamers. Naval steam engineer Charles W. Copeland designed the *Missouri*'s engines and used inclined cylinders, air pumps, and valves.[64] The cylinders were 62 inches by 10-foot stroke and were rated at 517 horsepower. The framework for the cylinders and appurtenances was of massive wooden beams. The paddle wheels were 28 feet in diameter and weighed 30 tons each. Their framework was wrought iron and the paddle buckets were oak.[65]

The *Mississippi*'s side-lever engines were unique to the navy, and were the first such engines used in the United States. The type was virtually standard in trans-Atlantic steamers of the day. The British steamer *Comet* had first used side-lever machinery in 1820 and the type retained its popularity until the 1850s.[66]

The side-lever was essentially an inversion of the walking beam configuration popular on river

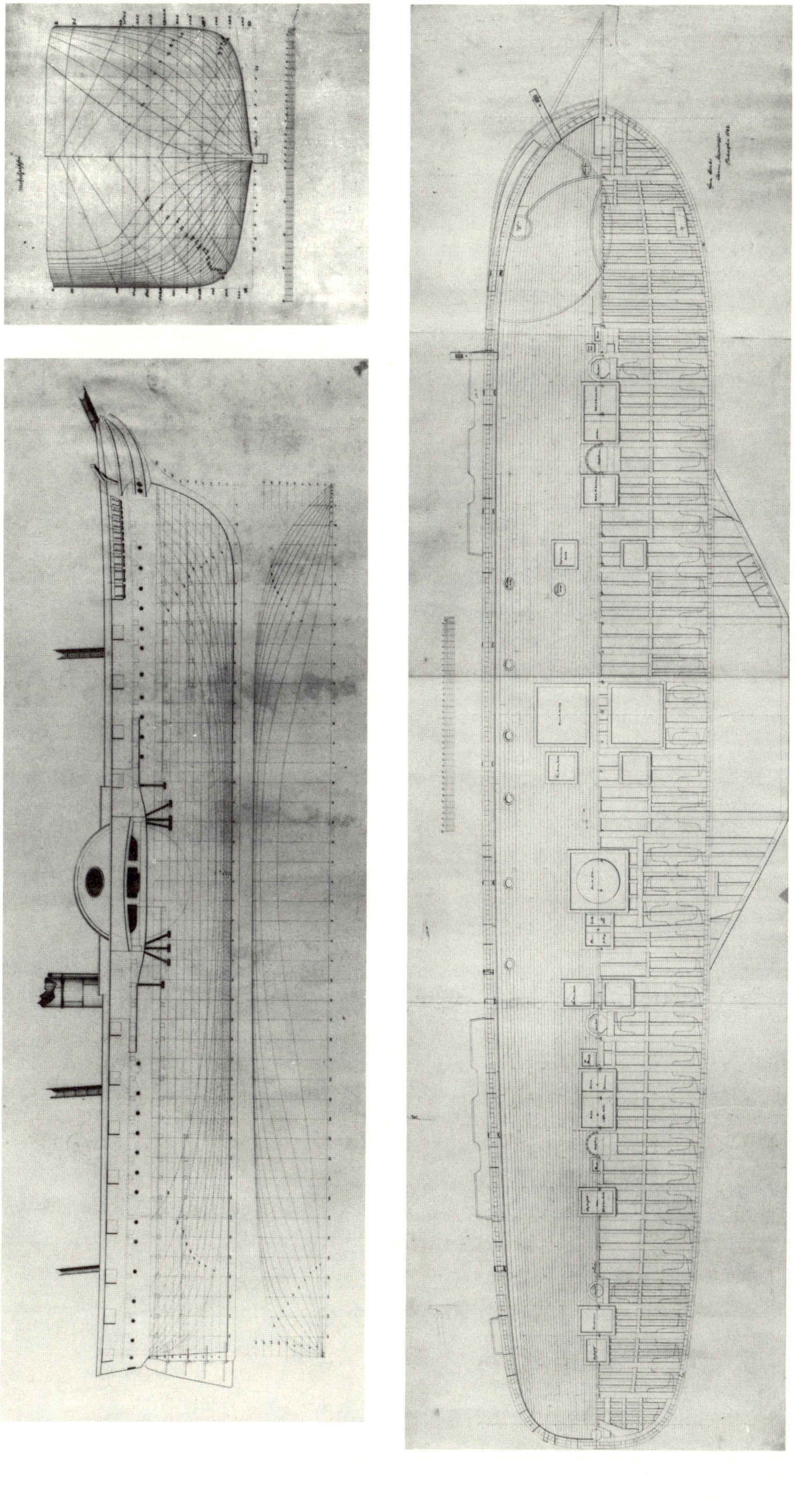

Sheer, Half-breadth, Body, and Deck Plans of the Mississippi, *1842. (NARS 79-1-6, 108-7-14G, 108-7-14S, National Archives)*

Side-Lever Engines of the Mississippi. *The Bureau of Steam Engineering collection at the National Archives has the original plans for a majority of the parts of this engine. The major components of the engine have been assembled in the drawing for a general view. The structure behind the center of the side lever is the condenser and to its right is the air pump. Details of the valve mechanism have been omitted, and lengths of linkages are estimates. Gothic architectural details are reproduced as per original plans. The engine was mounted with the cylinder forward. (Drawing by the author from the Bureau of Steam Engineering Plans, National Archives)*

steamers. In these engines, the vertical piston rod rocked one end of a see-sawing beam, and the other end drove a rod downward to crank the paddle-wheel shaft. The height of such engines precluded their use on warships. In the side-lever engine, the rods from the cylinder and piston ran downward to a pair of beams, one on each side, and the opposite end of the beams actuated rods working upward to the crankshaft. The arrangement reduced the height of the engine and the center of gravity of the machinery.

Each of the cylinders of the *Mississippi* was 75 inches in diameter, with a 7-foot stroke; and the engine occupied 31 feet of the hold. Even to the twentieth-century beholder, these were massive machines: each of the four side frames was a single casting over 18 feet high, 20 feet wide, and a foot in breadth; and each of the four side-levers was about 20 feet long.[67] The weight of such castings can be judged by similar engines in the steamer *Southerner* of 1846, which had side-levers weighing five-and-a-half tons each. A typical iron bedplate for such engines weighed 15 tons and was secured to the ship's keelsons by bolts 5 inches long and 2 inches in diameter.[68]

The complete original plans for the engines of the *Mississippi* are in the Bureau of Steam Engineering records in the National Archives. They depict an architectural approach to engine design reflecting the mid-Victorian view of engineering as a monument to human progress. Therefore the lofty frames became fair objects for arched fenestration and fluted pilasters "in the Gothic style."[69] The paint scheme has not been left to us, but with gleaming brass and a majestic ten to twelve strokes per minute, these machines would truly have approached Victorian ideals of the sublime.

The performance of both of these frigates was exemplary, within the limitations of paddle-wheel warship design. No long-term comparison of the two ships is possible, of course, because of the early loss of the *Missouri*. The one attempt to run the pair in tandem snagged when the *Missouri* grounded and her sister vessel developed overheated bearings.[70]

The *Missouri*'s engines were described by journalists as "scarcely jarring a timber of the ship" in their "noiseless accuracy." On her trials Charles Copeland reported she reached 12½ to 14 knots, and on a measured course, 11⅔ knots. On her passage to Gibraltar, where she was lost, she ran under steam for 280 hours at an average speed of 8.02 knots, consuming 1.43 tons of coal per hour.[71] This passage, one of the first powered crossings by a steam warship, was followed eight days later (23 August 1843) by an accidental fire that destroyed the new vessel.[72]

Had the *Missouri* survived and emulated the *Mississippi* in her performance and longevity, she would no doubt have been another eminently successful vessel. Her short career was marked by one rather eccentric experiment. Her engineer, Gilbert Thompson, theorized that the rotation of the paddle wheels would create a useful draft for the engines. Therefore, her funnel was replaced by two, which angled outward to the wheel housings. The idea was as ineffective—and odd looking—as it sounded and the original stack was soon replaced.[73]

The *Mississippi*'s engines were described, with poetic license, as "iron earthquakes" and the vessel was "beautiful indeed," "an American sea steamer in the strict sense of the word, with materials and manufacture being American throughout."[74] The writer ignored her English pattern engines for his American readership.

On her trials the *Mississippi* ran up the river at "11 miles against the current, per ground log." From October 1845 to March 1847, she averaged 7.06 knots under steam at 10.4 revolutions and 10.5 pounds pressure, consuming 36 tons of coal per day.[75]

She became known as a paragon of reliability, and newer steamers were hard pressed to match her. In 1853, Commodore Perry wrote from Hong Kong: "Our Mississippi is as staunch and fit as when she was in the Gulf, beating the Susquehanna, making better weather and consuming one third less coal. But I shall nurse the lame ducks." (He was referring to the *Powhatan* and *Susquehanna*.)[76]

By the time she was lost, in 1863, the vessel had circumnavigated the globe twice. In the first instance, she was sent home from Japan via Cape Horn, a route Perry did not trust to the newer *Susquehanna*.[77]

The drawbacks of the *Mississippi* were only those inherent in paddle-wheel warships of the era. She was a voracious coal eater, much as the *Fulton II*

Sail and Outboard Profile of the Missouri, *Short-Lived Sister to the* Mississippi. *(NARS 40-11-3A, National Archives)*

had been but with the saving grace of larger bunkers. In December 1842, the secretary of the navy called her "unsuited to cruising in time of peace" because of the expense of keeping her in coal.[78]

Furthermore, she was such a poor sailer that for practical purposes her sails were auxiliaries. A report by Jesse Gay, one of her engineers, described the problem: "The sails are auxiliary to her steam; with her sails unaided by her engines, she is helpless; on the other hand, her engines are sufficient to handle her without the assistance of sails." Gay advocated reducing her spars to decrease her resistance to the wind when steaming. He continued, "The mainsail cannot be carried—the main topsail is seldom used—steering sails have been useless—fore topsail useful—top-gallant sails seldom—fore topmast stay sail and jib useful. The useful sails are fore and main trysails, fore topmast stay sail, and jib, and occasionally, the spanker, with effect." In moderate head breezes the topgallant masts were taken down; in heavier winds, topmasts and lower yards were also taken in. All the masts and spars were sent up in good weather, to "improve the appearance of the ship." Gay also observed that her sailing qualities were not correctable: the mainmast was abaft the center of motion, making "its sails of little use except with the wind astern, and the fore mast was too far forward. . . . The fact that the paddle-wheel ship's machinery was restricted to the areas where the main mast should have been is a great part of the explanation for the poor sailing qualities of such ships."[79]

Gay's recommendations were not implemented. His complaint, however, pointed up the inherent problems of paddle-wheel war vessels: inefficient engines precluded lengthy cruising under steam, and poor sailing qualities likewise limited their efficient operation under canvas.

Few modifications and little maintenance was required by the *Mississippi* during her career. New iron boilers were installed in 1856, and her funnel was shortened by ten feet and hinged to allow use of the mainsail. During the war, she carried as many as nineteen 8-inch guns and one 11-inch pivot.[80] In the Mississippi River campaign, her topmasts were taken down and iron-shielded fighting tops were substituted.

Before the war she had been in the Japan expedition and the engagement with the Pei Ho forts in China. During the war, at New Orleans, she was instrumental in the destruction of the ironclad *Manassas*. At Port Hudson in 1863, she grounded under Confederate batteries and was set on fire by her crew. Burning from end to end, the abandoned ship floated free, with guns discharging and crashing through collapsing decks. When the flames reached her magazine, she blew up in a "tremendous tongue of flame." The *Mississippi* was the only prewar steamer lost to hostile fire during the conflict.[81]

The Mississippi *As She Appeared during the River Campaign in 1863. Her top masts had been sent down and iron-shielded fighting tops are in place. A later painting by R. G. Skerrit, based on this photo, shows an alligator figurehead. (U.S. Army Military History Institute)*

CHAPTER 2

Experiments in Construction and Propulsion, 1841–1846

Between the launching of the *Missouri* and the *Mississippi* in 1841 and the congressional authorization of four steamers in 1847, the list of ships added to the inventory reflects an ambiguous blend of progressivism, stasis, and reaction. In the latter instance, fourteen sailing vessels were launched before 1844, three of them frigates—an impressive number for any three-year period. Not only were new sailing warships completed, the department continued its policy of "rebuilding" or extensively modifying existing sailing warships.[1]

Despite the signal success of the "sea steamers" authorized in 1839, no conventional paddle steamers were constructed (with the exception of the *Michigan,* which flouted convention with her iron construction). In this five-year period, the British added more than twenty side-wheelers to their fleet.[2]

Yet another paradox, in view of the Navy Department's reluctance to build conventional steamers, was the emphasis placed on the innovative and even the eccentric. The *Princeton,* the first screw-propelled warship, placed the navy in the forefront of naval steam technology. The three attempts to legitimize W. W. Hunter's horizontal paddle-wheel aberration, however, virtually negated any progressive momentum begun by the *Princeton.* Hunter's wheel was not the sole experiment contemplated in the era. There was a high level of official interest in novel engines and propulsion systems, particularly those seen as alternatives to the side-mounted paddle wheel.

These contradictions become less puzzling in light of a few background factors. First, by this date the most hard-boiled of the old sailing leadership conceded that steam propulsion was indeed essential, if for no other reason than to parry potential enemies who had adopted it. Second, the *Mississippi,* which was comparable to the best foreign paddle-wheel vessels, fell far short of the navy's needs. Her coal consumption limited her to two weeks at sea, and she was a clumsy sailer.

Lack of economy was not the sole drawback of the side-wheelers. First, the drag of their paddles when not in use was excessive. Second, the huge wheel housings created a windage problem—a tendency to catch the wind beneath the windward paddle box. Third, their fighting qualities were hampered by the thirty-foot gap in the broadside created by the paddle boxes and the resulting reduction in the ships' batteries. The most frequent objection was to the paddles' vulnerability in combat, creating the specter of disabling the vessels in action. (The last objection was somewhat discredited in the Civil War, when it was found that the very size of the paddles made disabling them difficult, and only extremely lucky shots would find the paddle shafts.)

Another significant factor at work in this era was the advent of alternative steam propulsion systems. The underwater screw propeller was coming into use, in England with the *Archimedes* in 1838 and the following year in the United States. Simultaneously, W. W. Hunter proposed a horizontal application of the paddle wheel, an idea that died a lingering death but was considered feasible at its inception.

To the era's technological problems was added the element of the unexpected: the explosion of one of the experimental shell guns aboard the *Princeton* in 1844. This detonation would indirectly inflict its own cost on the development of the steam navy.

The Medium Steamers

One episode of this era stands out as an example of the pressures resulting from these factors. In secretary of the navy Abel P. Upshur's annual report for 1841, he noted that three steamers were being built, "of medium size, under the act of 3rd March 1841, one at New York, one at Philadelphia, and one at Norfolk."[3] This was one of the few official acknowledgments that these "medium steamers" were to be built.

The majority of the information on these ships is found in correspondence among the naval constructors, the engineers, and the navy commissioners, beginning in September 1841 and terminating abruptly on 2 June 1842. The dimensions of these paddle-wheel steamers were to be 152 feet 6 inches by 27 feet, with a 16-foot depth of hold and a displacement of 500 tons; their armament would be two 8-inch pivot guns and six 32-pounders. The New York vessel was to have inclined engines; the Norfolk ship, "English marine engines" with side-levers; and "Norris vertical direct action" (oscillating?) machinery was to power the steamer building at Philadelphia. Engine proposals from three firms indicate 220 horsepower was expected from the side-lever machinery. Of the three vessels, the Norfolk ship was apparently the farthest along and was given priority for completion on 2 June 1842. One half-cross-section labeled "medium steamer" remains in the National Archives, annotated with the dimensions noted as above. (Also, the iron lake steamer begun at this time was to have the same length and beam as the medium steamers but was to have a shallower draft.)[4]

With this evidence, we are left with the question of the fate of these never-built vessels, for indeed, there were no warships of these dimensions ever in the navy inventory. The only subsequent official acknowledgment of the ships is an oblique reference in the secretary's report of 1842, which indicates the "propriety of assigning two or three medium steamers to beat up the Atlantic coast."[5] (It has been suggested that these conventional steamers may have been "replaced" by the *Princeton* and *Union,* but Upshur's report of 1841 clearly indicates that the latter two were being constructed "in addition" to these paddle steamers.)

It is likely that the Norfolk-built "medium steamer" was completed as a sailing storeship, the *Southampton.* Howard I. Chapelle noted in his volume on the sailing navy that there was some doubt about whether the vessel was "purchased or built" at Norfolk, and that there was reason to believe she was "built for government use." According to Chapelle, she was laid down in October 1841, her dimensions were 152 feet 6 inches by 27 feet by 16 feet, and she was originally a paddle steamer but had her machinery removed. The cross section of

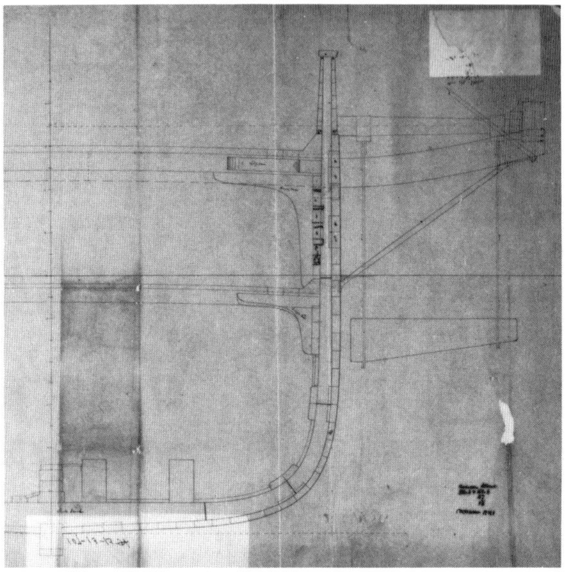

Cross Section of the Medium Steamers. Three of these vessels were projected, but none were completed as steamers. Plans for the sailing storeship Southampton, *apparently the only one of the three completed, can be seen in H. I. Chapelle's* History of the American Sailing Navy, *1949. (NARS 107-13-12H, National Archives)*

the *Southampton*'s hull corresponds with that of the medium steamer section found in the archives, but there is no evidence that engines were ever erected in the vessel. She was launched in 1845 and was active as a storeship in the Pacific until sold in 1855 or 1856.[6]

The Philadelphia and New York steamers were never completed and we can only speculate as to the reasons. In these last years of the sailing navy, as Chapelle relates, there was much pressure to use available funds for sailing vessels immediately, before inexorable factors forced the final turn to steam.[7] Thus the budgetary problem was the most likely key to the fate of the ships.

In September 1841, however, board member Lewis Warrington wrote to Humphreys that since these ships were to have steam as "the principal contemplated moving power, the masts and spars will not be so large as they would be, if sails were to be mainly relied on."[8] Such a statement and its implications for the sailing navy may well have made these proposed ships anathema to those yet unconvinced of the reliability of steam as the primary motive power, and this opposition may have been a factor in preventing their completion.

Michigan

In this era, the department was simultaneously involved in many diverse projects, the most conventional of which was the iron Great Lakes steamer *Michigan.* The genesis of the *Michigan* can be found in the increasing tensions along the lakes in the late

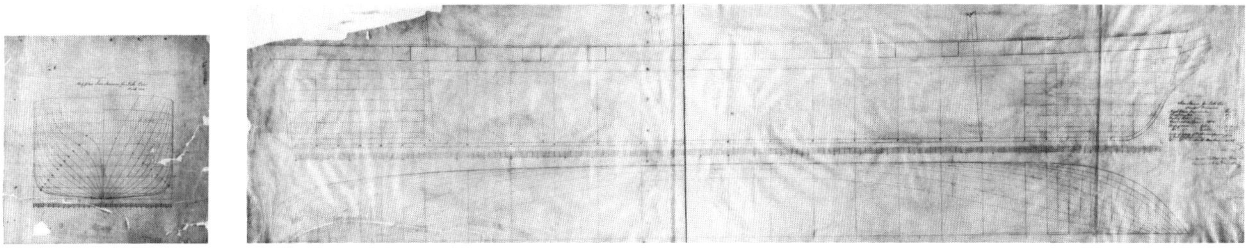

Lines of the Iron Lakes' Steamer Michigan. *(NARS 28-14-45, National Archives)*

1830s, when rebellion broke out in Quebec and pressure began to build for increased protection for American interests and trade.

Sentiment for the construction of a naval steamer for the Great Lakes reached a boiling point when it was learned that two war steamers were being built on the Canadian side. One, the *Minos,* was described somewhat hysterically as having nine ports on each side, with an additional 68-pounder pivot gun forward. Her sides were said to be 2 feet thick with iron bars 2¾ inches by ½ inch strengthening her planking, "rendering her perfectly impervious to small cannon shot."[9]

Finally, an amendment to a fortification bill called for a steamer "for the defense of Lake Erie." She was to be comparable to the British steamers that it was feared would cruise the American coast, "prying into its exposed parts."[10]

By February 1842, Samuel Hartt had begun the hull design, and the decision had been made to pattern the vessel on the medium steamers already planned, with a maximum draft of nine feet. The letter from the board on this subject also indicates that the decision to build the vessel of iron had already been made.[11]

The decision was courageous considering the state of the American iron shipbuilding industry at the time. As early as 1825 small iron vessels had been built for river use, but the first iron ocean-going steamer (the *Bangor,* by Harlan and Hollingsworth of Wilmington, Delaware) did not appear until 1845.[12] The difficult transition of American shipbuilding from an art suited to hand tools and half models to a technology of machine tools and engineering drawings had not yet occurred.

The source of this decision has been debated, but a letter from Secretary of the Navy Upshur, replying to congressional criticism settles the question adequately: "I determined to build this vessel of iron instead of wood for two reasons. In the first place, I was desirous to aid . . . in developing and applying to a new use the immense resources . . . in that most valuable metal; and in the second place . . . to ascertain the . . . utility of building vessels . . . of so cheap and indestructible material."[13] Upshur's unwillingness to waffle or evade responsibility for the decision to use iron, even when under congressional fire, effectively removes any doubt concerning the source of the decision.

The unbid contract for the vessel went to Stackhouse and Tomlinson of Pittsburgh and marked the first instance where the same firm was to build both the engines and hull of a naval vessel. The contract price for the engines was 24 cents per pound; for the hull, 13 cents per pound. The firm fabricated the iron parts in Pittsburgh. The vessel's iron hull was assembled to assure proper fit, then disassembled and transported by rail and drayage to Erie, Pennsylvania, for completion.[14]

Construction of the vessel was, necessarily, an experiment in structural strength and was typical of the day's technology. Welding was unknown, and ¾-inch rivets, spaced no more than three times their diameter, center to center, were more than adequate for the ship. Structural members were T-beams, angle iron, and wrought iron plates.

The keel was made up of plates that also formed a drainage trough. These were ⅝ inch by 8 inches and in 8-foot sections, protruding 4 inches from the bottom. The primary longitudinal strength of the hull was in seven substantial box keelsons. The largest, over the keel, was formed of 18-inch vertical and horizontal plates bolstered by half-inch diagonal bars riveted to the floor and the top member. The smallest keelsons were 12-inch boxes minus the diagonal bars.

The frames were of T-iron, 4 by 4½ inches, ¾-inch thick, spaced 24 inches apart. Some of these were single units running rail to rail. The deck beams were also T-iron, measuring 7 inches by 4 inches.[15]

The hull plating was ⅜ inch to ⅝ inch thick (the thinnest was at the level of the sheer) and ranged from 13 inches to 30 inches wide, narrowing from midships to the extremities of the hull. These were in 8-foot sections, the ends of which were riveted to vertical ribbands. Longitudinally, the plating was "clinker-built," overlapping in a manner similar to house shingling. (Hartt patterned his iron structure after the British armed steamer *Nemesis* and the merchant steamer *Troubadour.*)[16]

The superstructure was of wood. Pine planking in 45-foot sections formed the deck and 4-inch bronze spikes secured the planks to the iron frame-

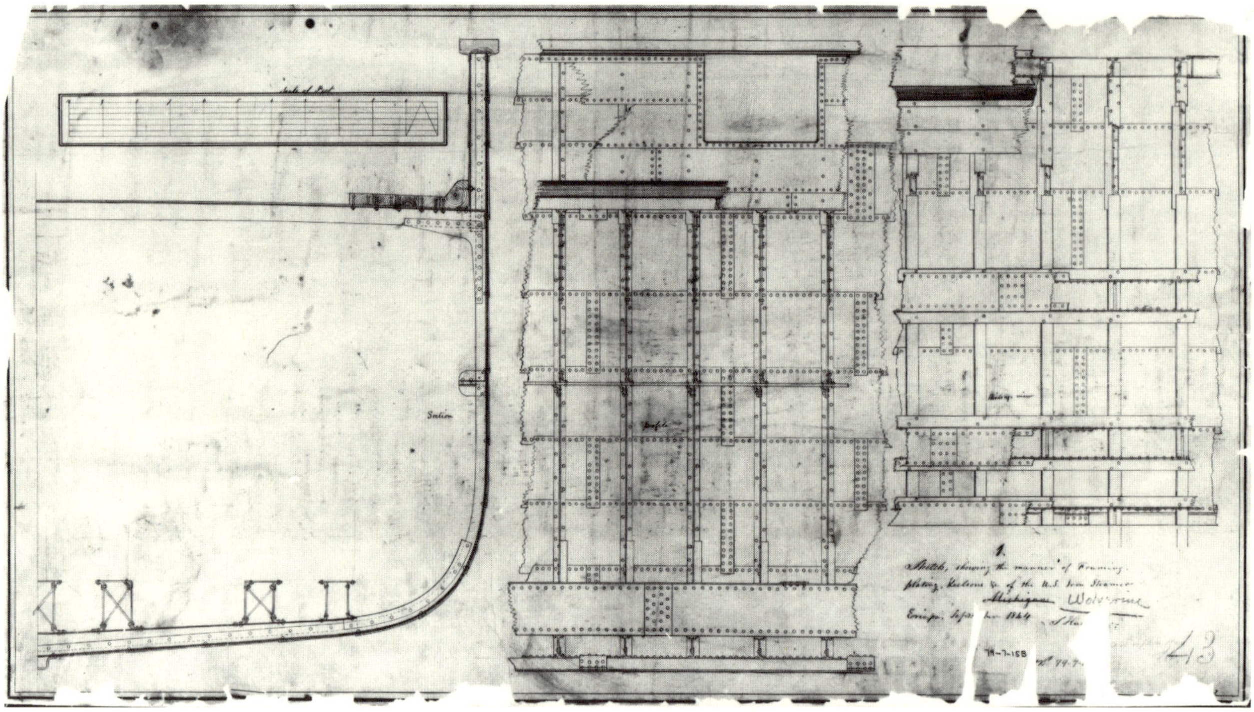

Iron Framing and Hull Structure of the Michigan. *A cross section of her keelsons shows diagonal rods within each box. (NARS 79-7-15B, National Archives)*

work.[17] Watertight bulkheads were used to subdivide the interior into three compartments. Especially designed doors completed the integrity of these divisions. Coal bunkers ran the entire length of the engine spaces and from the turn of the bilge to above the waterline.[18]

Other than her iron hull, the *Michigan* was strictly conventional. The inclined engine was of two cylinders, 36 inches diameter by 8-foot stroke, driving 21-foot paddle wheels. Live-oak members, 14 by 14 inches, formed the frame of the engine. A braking arrangement allowed the manual removal of the paddle buckets to eliminate drag when the ship was under sail. Two boilers of the iron flue type were installed, and bunkers that held 120 tons of coal completed the ship's steam propulsion plant.[19]

She was rigged as a barkentine though she rarely moved under canvas alone. She was originally supposed to carry two pivoting Paixhans guns fore and aft and up to twelve broadside cannons. To conform to treaty specifications, she was commissioned with a single 64-pounder on her forward pivot circle. This was deemed sufficient for her duties, which would include surveying, aiding vessels in distress, and maintaining a symbolic naval presence on the lakes. During the Civil War, the treaty was politely disregarded and she was armed to the teeth with one 30- and five 20-pounder Parrotts, two light 12-pounders, and six 24-pounder smoothbores.[20]

The Michigan *Midway in Her Eighty-year Active Service, before the Enlargement of Her Pilothouse. (Herbert Reynolds Spencer, Jr.)*

A Later, Turn-of-the-Century View of the Michigan. *Her pilothouse is now a chart house and her rig has been reduced. She rarely relied on her sails, in any case. (Herbert Reynolds Spencer, Jr.)*

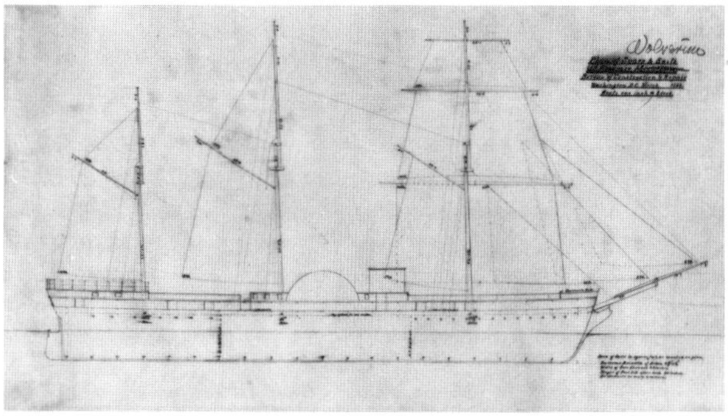

Spar Plan of the Michigan, *1884. (NARS 79-7-15S, National Archives)*

As completed, the *Michigan* measured 162 feet 6 inches between perpendiculars, had a 27-foot beam, and a mean draft of 7 feet 7 inches. Her machinery required 60 feet of hull space and the total weight of her hull was over 500,000 pounds. Her displacement was 604 tons.[21]

The *Michigan*'s iron structure was not her sole distinction. Her longevity and reliability were equally remarkable. Her launch, however, could not have been seen as a positive augury. With a large and reportedly sceptical crowd in attendance, supposedly wagering that the iron ship would immediately sink, she stuck fifty feet down the ways. Local historians tell us that Hartt returned the following dawn to find the ship afloat on the lake; she had settled on her ways and launched herself. An alternative but more likely account has it that Hartt and his crew adjusted the angle of the incline and she was launched successfully the following day.[22]

Her performance was always satisfactory, and inordinately reliable. Such characteristics were generic to many of the early, simply designed, low-pressure reciprocating steam engines. In the 1840s she averaged 10.4 statute miles per hour with 18 revolutions of the paddles per minute, developing 333 horsepower. A technical report of 1909 indicated age had not materially retarded her. After being reboilered in the 1890s, and having had considerable weight added in the form of a poop cabin and framing for stowing steam launches, she was still able to make "ten knots on twenty revolutions in smooth sea with a favorable wind."[23] Her relatively shallow draft and flat bottom made her somewhat leewardly and uncomfortable in heavy weather. She tended to corkscrew from side to side as one paddle entered the water and the opposite wheel was in midair.[24]

By the 1890s the venerable steamer had survived much of her useful life without major mishap or modification. Her rig had been reduced to pole masts and her black hull with white stripe above the ports had been repainted white. Her closest brush with enemy action had been in the abortive, seriocomic Confederate attempt to seize her and to liberate the prisoners on Johnson's Island, on Lake Erie.

Seemingly the *Michigan*'s sole mechanical mishap was her last. In August 1923, the steamer (renamed *Wolverine*) broke one of her connecting rods, sending the freed piston through the head and nearly penetrating the bottom of the hull. She limped six hundred miles to port on the remaining cylinder and was laid to rest on a mud bank.

In 1942 her name was applied to a paddle-wheel aircraft carrier built for training pilots, and her abandoned hulk was considered for the wartime scrap drives. Attempts to raise funds for her restoration were futile and she was broken up in 1949. Her iron prow can still be seen as a monument in Erie, Pennsylvania. She had been in active service eighty years.[25]

Of course her longevity was in part due to her habitat, fresh water, which does not have the corrosive effects of salt. Furthermore, she was iced in each winter, effectively reducing her active career by nearly half. At either eighty or forty years, however, she was a credit to her designers, builders, and Secretary of the Navy Upshur.

Princeton

The navy's intention to construct a screw steam warship first surfaced in the secretary of the navy's report of 1839: "It being in contemplation to adopt a model presented by a distinguished officer of the navy to be propelled by a different description of machinery." As in the decision to use iron, this marked rather advanced thinking on the part of naval leaders, because the successful use of the screw was a very recent development. John Ericsson had built a small screw steamer in England in 1836 using his patented counter-rotating propellers (both screws rotating in opposite directions on the same shaft), and an American naval officer,

Robert F. Stockton, had been impressed to the extent that he ordered a second vessel built for use in the United States. This ship, the *Robert F. Stockton,* arrived in the United States in April 1839. Stockton then began to prod the Navy Department to adopt the Ericsson screw for use in a warship. His case was strengthened by the success of the bark *Clarion,* which used the Ericsson propeller. Records indicate the board directed representatives to attend and report on the trials of the vessel. The ship became the first screw steamer to ply an ocean route.[26]

Construction of the screw steam sloop-of-war *Princeton* began in 1841 and she was launched on 9 September 1843. She was the world's first warship designed and built as a screw steamer. The first British naval screw steamer, the *Rattler,* famous for her tug-of-war with the paddle-wheel *Alecto,* was originally designed as a sailing sloop and launched in April 1843.[27] The *Princeton*'s place in naval history is secure not only for her propeller but also for her unusual machinery and for the disaster that occurred on her deck, an event with repercussions that plagued the development of the steam navy for a decade.

The engine of the ship was described as a semicylinder or a pendulum engine. The pendulum was a flat rectangular plate swinging much as a door on a hinge, but in this case, it was hung from above, allowing gravity to provide additional momentum to its movements. The plate was therefore a piston swinging in a half-round cylinder, powered both by gravity and steam introduced on alternate sides of the plate. Power was transferred to a connecting rod that was an extension of the "hinge" itself. Two semicylinders worked in conjunction to provide the complete rotation of a single driving shaft mounted between and below the engines. These unique pistons were 3 feet from hinge to cylinder wall, by 8 feet fore and aft, as mounted in the vessel. The entire engine could therefore be located beneath the waterline, and safely below danger from shot. The engine was rated at 250 nominal horsepower.[28]

She was given three iron return-flue boilers, and, for the first time on a naval vessel, blowers for forced draft operation. Two other innovations were incorporated in the vessel, the use of anthracite coal, and a telescoping smokepipe. When the latter was lowered to below the rail, the blowers were to compensate for the reduction in draft. Ericsson, the compleat inventor, designed the boilers, blowers, and smokepipe.[29]

The original Ericsson propeller was an ungainly contraption, though much less so than the earlier counter-rotating versions. Six arms radiated from a bronze hub 20 inches in diameter, surrounding by a circular copper band to which were riveted six blades. The extreme diameter was 14 feet, the blades were 4 feet in length, and the entire assembly weighed 6 tons. In 1845 Commodore Stockton replaced this propeller with another, designed by the inventor Robert L. Stevens, who had been experimenting with screw propulsion since 1805. This Stevens "scull" was six inches larger in diameter and weighed nearly two tons more than Ericsson's. Each blade of the Stevens screw was a single piece, along with the corresponding one-sixth of the hub. The *Princeton*'s screw shaft was designed to allow the propeller to be uncoupled and rotate freely when under sail.[30]

The *Princeton*'s hull lines, as well as general dimensions, displacement, and costs, were set down by John Ericsson in October 1841 and sent to Stockton. Stockton then passed them on to John Lenthall, who completed the detailed working plans for the vessel's construction.[31]

The *Princeton* was a beautiful ship, easily identified by her sharp raking stem and stern. Below water, she was of great sharpness in the bows, and

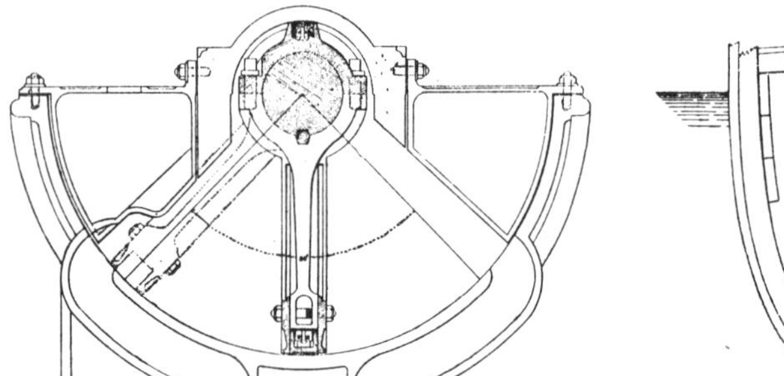

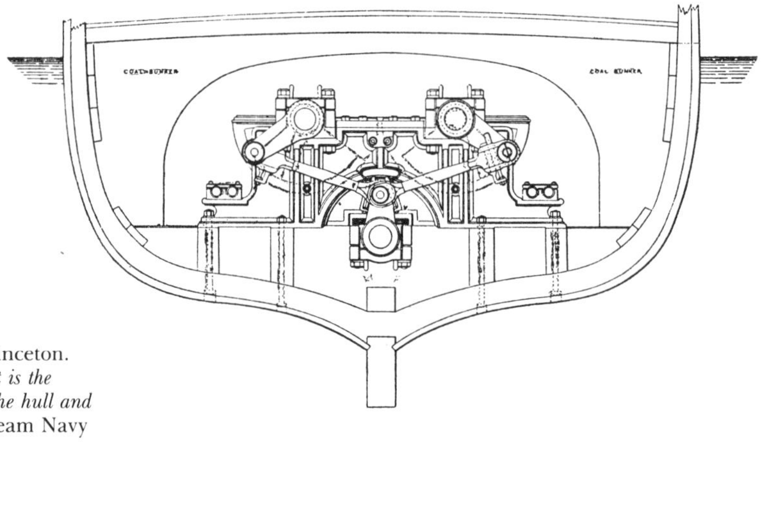

Ericsson's Semicylinder ("Pendulum") Engines for the Princeton. *Cutaway at left shows the swing of the piston; on the right is the vessel's cross section, showing a low profile of engines in the hull and the drive mechanism to the crankshaft. (From Bennett,* Steam Navy of the United States, *1896)*

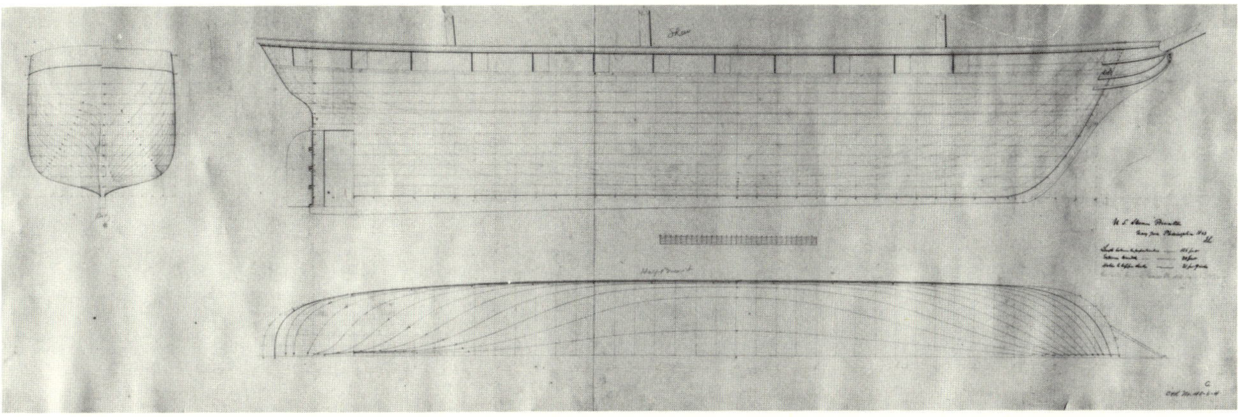

Lines of the Princeton, *Drawn by John Lenthall to a Design by Ericsson. Note the sharpness of her hull. (NARS 40-6-4C, National Archives)*

her run was "remarkably fine." (A long and fine run was requisite for screw-driven vessels to facilitate flow to the propeller.) She measured 156 feet between perpendiculars by 30 feet 6 inches and displaced 1,046 tons at a draft of eighteen feet. She was built of white oak and there is no evidence of diagonal iron strapping in her hull.

The addition of a propeller to the stern required the positioning of a "false" sternpost on which to mount the rudder, leaving six feet open for the screw. Brass flanges attached the post to the counter and to a 14-inch solid oak keel extension. The rudder was of pine planking framed by wrought iron and covered with 3⁄16-inch copper. At the center of the propeller shaft, the sternpost measured an unusual but necessary 26 inches wide, tapering above and below the 13-inch aperture for the shaft itself. There is no record of the method or material used for shaft bearings through the aft deadwood.[32]

The *Princeton* was ship-rigged, spreading 14,400 square feet of canvas, carrying royals. Her armament at commissioning consisted of two 12-inch wrought iron pivot guns and ten 42-pounder carronades. In a letter extolling "his" ship, Captain Stockton stated that all the guns "may be used at once, on either side of the ship," since Ericsson also invented an instrument to automatically calculate the range of any given target, as well as "self-acting" locks, which automatically fired a cannon at a predetermined angle.[33]

The two wrought iron guns were the "Oregon," designed by Ericsson, and Captain Stockton's imitation of Ericsson's design, labeled "Peacemaker." Both fired 225-pound projectiles; the major difference was in the larger breech banding of Stockton's design.[34] As events proved, the quality rather than quantity of metal in the "Peacemaker" was its weak point.

In commission, the screw sloop-of-war *Princeton* was a triumph for Ericsson as an inventor and for Stockton as mentor, patron, and general publicity director. Stockton was not reluctant to wax excessive in his praises of the vessel. On 21 October 1843

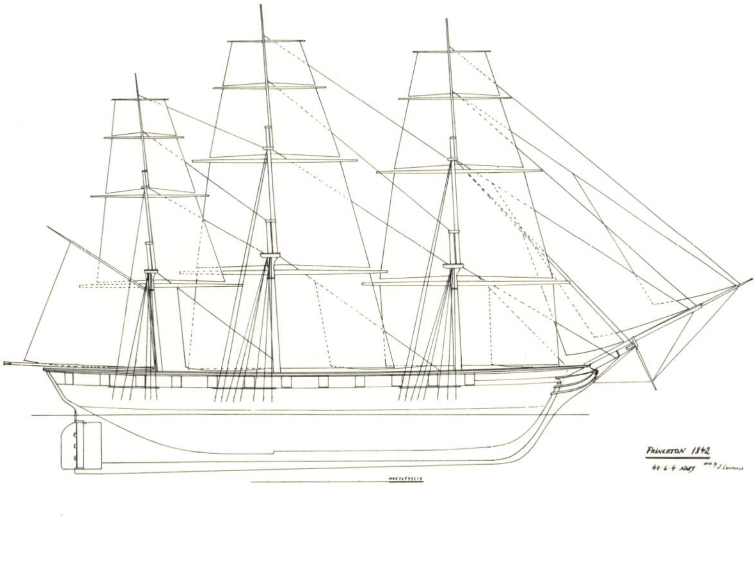

Sail and Spar Plan of the Princeton. *(Tracing by author of NARS 40-6-4, National Archives)*

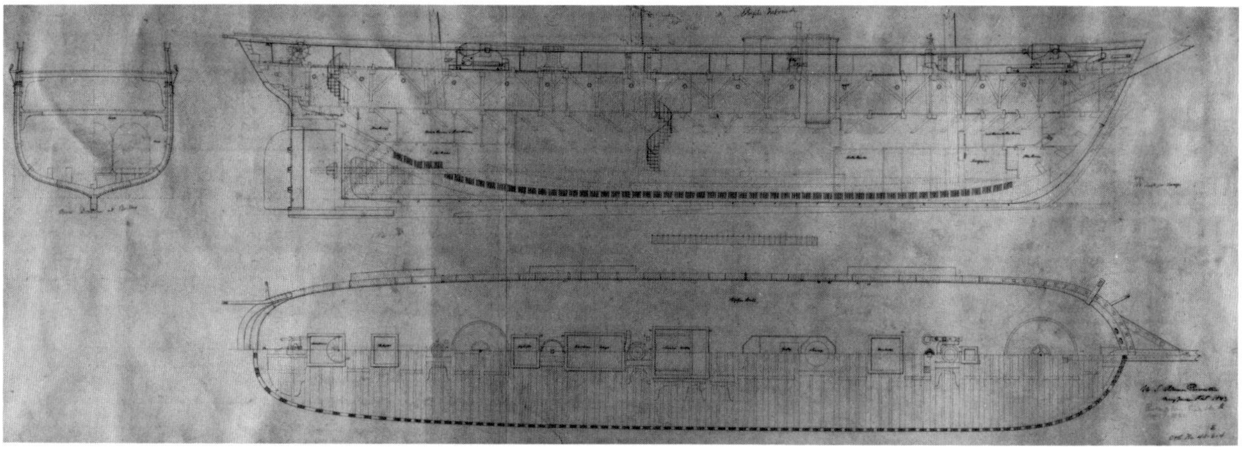

Inboard Profile of the Princeton. *Note the lowered smoke pipe—another Ericsson innovation—and the two 12-inch shell guns. The gun designed by Ericsson may still be seen on the grounds of the U.S. Naval Academy. (NARS 40-6-4B, National Archives)*

he wrote of an early trial race with the British steamer *Great Western* off New York (the British steamer seems to have been a favorite target for the Yankee naval steamers of the day): "The trial took place from the battery to the sea, in which we gained a most glorious triumph, in the presence of many thousands." Stockton continues: "The Princeton immediately started her engine, gave chase . . . and soon passed her with no sails set and the yards square." The American vessel ran twenty-one miles at "more than fourteen miles per hour, and that against flood tide, and proving her to be the fastest steamer in the world."[35]

Hyperbole aside, the ship was indeed an impressive performer, under sail as well as with auxiliary steam, though speed under steam was never her strong point. A report from Captain Engle, her commander in late 1845, describes her performance: "As a sailing vessel the Princeton is equal to many of our sloops and no doubt from the trial we had with the Potomac, is also superior to many—under double reefed topsails and whole courses the Potomac was no match for her. She can run round her 4 times in a watch with ease." He complained she heeled easily to "two strakes" and that more beam would improve her carrying sail, but that she was "the sweetest ship in a gale of wind I ever saw. . . . No wind can hurt her."[36]

Under steam alone, regardless of the claims of Captain Stockton, the ship was no speed maker, with a mean of 6.9 knots with the Ericsson screw and 7.6 with the Stevens propeller. New boilers later in her career did not materially effect these figures.[37]

The *Princeton*'s metier was in her performance as an auxiliary steamer. In May 1845 a trial was held with this steamer, the corvettes *St. Marys* and *Saratoga,* and the brig *Porpoise,* to determine the steam pressure and weight of coal necessary to beat the sailing vessels. It was found that with 10 pounds of steam, 17½ revolutions per minute, and 900 pounds coal per hour she could "easily beat them all." The second part of the trial was to determine the *Princeton*'s towing capabilities. She took the 224-ton brig in tow with the *St. Marys* three miles ahead and the *Saratoga* one and a half miles ahead. In approximately three hours the *Princeton* was abeam of the *St. Marys* and the *Saratoga* was the same distance astern. By noon the following day the *St. Marys* was twelve miles behind. In this performance, the *Princeton* averaged 8.8 knots and consumed, 1,656 pounds of coal per hour. Her maximum speed was 10 knots.[38]

Her auxiliary power was particularly useful in the blockade during the Mexican War. Off Vera Cruz, she lay under easy sail, with banked fires on one boiler until a quarry was spotted. Then fresh coal was spread and the fan blast started, allowing use of her steam in fifteen minutes. With the combination of sail and steam she was able to overhaul any vessel encountered. Her engineer, John Faron, reported that on the blockade the screw was "hard to beat," particularly because of the ease in changing from sail to steam and vice versa.[39]

In another imminently practical situation, her steam power was a critical asset, described in a contemporary magazine: "Caught on a lee shore during the violence of the gale, the Princeton got up steam, and 'crawled off' against a tremendous sea, at the rate of two knots per hour. On her return into port she picked up a dismantled brig . . . passed through the immense fields of floating ice . . . without being impeded." The article concluded that these proved the advantages of steam and the submerged propeller.[40]

Another point in her favor was her economical use of coal. Two examples suffice: at 4 knots with a head wind under steam alone, she burned 1,170 pounds per hour; at 5.9 knots she consumed 1,253 pounds. For a rough comparison, the *Mississippi* used 2,172 to 4,829 pounds per hour at 6.2 to 7.9 knots.[41] Even taking into account the difference in displacement, the screw-propelled ship was more economical—and a vastly better sailer at that.

Her machinery was generally trouble free throughout her career and was sufficiently serviceable to be reused for the second version of the vessel in the early 1850s. The least satisfactory portion of her steam plant was her boilers. The original units were badly corroded and were replaced in 1847, and by her decommissioning in 1849 the second set was beyond repair. This trouble was attributed to the high temperatures resulting from the use of her blowers.[42]

Despite the creditable performance of the semicylinder engines, no other naval vessels were powered by such engines. Ericsson himself first modified the semicylinder configuration, then discarded the idea altogether in favor of "complete" cylinders. Circular cylinder heads maintained their seal more consistently than the semicircular ones.[43]

Though a successful vessel, the *Princeton* had a short career, marred of course by the explosion of the "Peacemaker" on 28 February 1844. The blast killed Abel P. Upshur, by then secretary of state; Thomas Gilmer, who had taken Upshur's place as navy secretary; and three others. At that juncture, Captain Stockton quickly (and very disingenuously, it seems) denied any connection whatever with Ericsson, the *Princeton,* and, of course, his gun. He then gladly proclaimed Ericsson as the man who was responsible for the defective weapon. Relations between the navy and Ericsson—who held patents on his screw-propelling system—then fell on hard times, retarding the navy's progress in adopting the screw propeller for some years afterwards.[44]

The delay was critical, for the *Princeton* was not only the first screw steam warship, she was the first successful auxiliary steam sailing man-of-war—a ship with the advantages of steam in addition to the economic and strategic necessity of sail. Captain Engle, her commander, summed up the *Princeton*'s achievements: "Steam in this ship is secondary. Com'd Stockton . . . insisted this ship being styled the U.S. Ship Princeton in consequence of sails being the primary propelling power. I candidly think . . . that she is what the inventor desired she would be—a successful experiment."[45]

In 1849 she returned from a Mediterranean cruise and was found to be too rotten to repair. Her white oak timbers were said to have been unseasoned when she was built. She was broken up and her machinery was stored until 1851, when a slightly larger vessel was constructed for the engines. This was the *Princeton II,* discussed in a later chapter.[46]

Union

If the reputation of the steam navy of the 1840s had been based on the *Mississippi, Michigan,* and *Princeton,* posterity's judgment would have been eminently favorable. The navy would have been shown as excelling both in conventional and in technologically innovative vessels, despite the continued building of sailing warships, a practice not unique to the American navy—the last British sailing frigate was launched in 1850.[47] The unprofitable and protracted saga of Lieutenant Hunter's wheels, however, marred the navy's progressive luster.

Lieutenant William W. Hunter, USN, was not an inventor or engineer, even by the unregulated standards of the time. He had a seemingly practical idea and influence, however. Early in 1841 his scheme was tested in the 52-foot vessel *Germ,* built at Gosport but financed by Hunter and an associate. It was powered by a 6-horsepower engine and was said to have attained 9 knots, using Lieutenant Hunter's horizontal wheels.[48]

The rationale for the wheels was simple: rather than mounting the paddles on the side of the ship, they were located horizontally within the hull, exposing only the number of paddle buckets that would effectively exert forward motion. In principle, this would solve two of the side-wheeler's handicaps: the machinery and propellers would be beneath the waterline, and the broadside would be uninterrupted by paddle housings.

Based on the success of the *Germ* and recommendations by various constructors and naval officers, the navy authorized construction of the *Union,* a 900-ton vessel, to test the idea. It was built at Norfolk, commencing in 1841.[49]

The vessel, measuring 185 feet 6 inches by 33 feet with an 11-foot draft, was launched on 12 May 1842 and towed to Washington Navy Yard, where the machinery was erected on board. Possibly because the wheels' small diameter required a relatively short driving stroke, machinery of a type generally found in locomotives and stationary power plants was used: two high-pressure noncondensing cylinders with 28-inch bore and 4-foot stroke, supplied with steam at 100 pounds pressure from three iron boilers. The cylinders were independent and drove two horizontal wheels 14 feet in diameter with paddles 4 feet high by 10 inches wide. Each paddle wheel was enclosed in a tightly fitting case, watertight except for an aperture at the side of the hull, between bilge and waterline where the paddles protruded from the hull.[50]

The unique propulsion system required an unusual hull, designed by naval constructor Francis Grice. To keep the paddles low for effective operation, a nearly flat floor was used. To prevent the paddles from interfering with docking or other

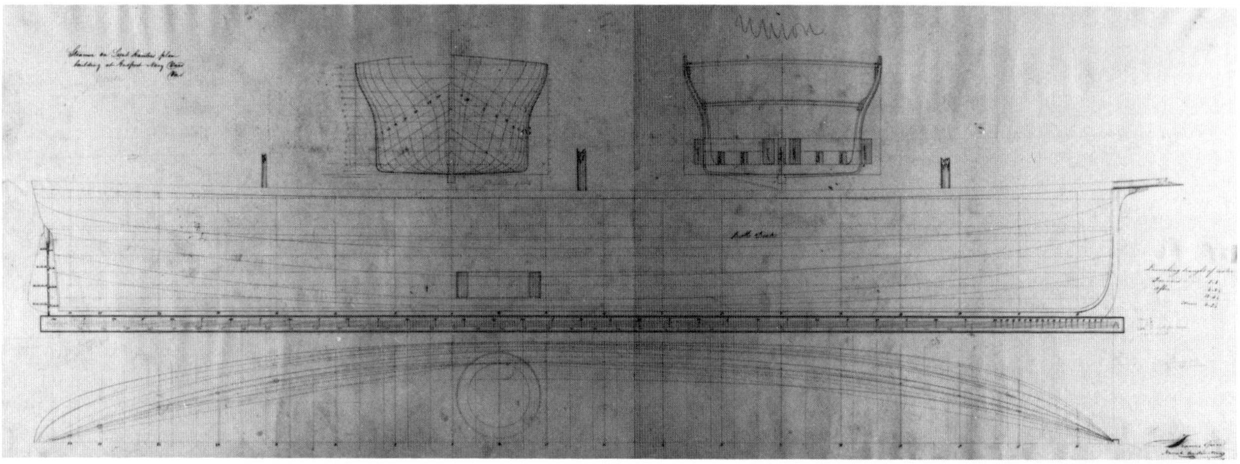

Lines and Cross Section of the Hunter's Wheel Ship Union. *The plan shows her problematic inverted-bell hull form as well as the arrangement of horizontal paddle wheels. (NARS 41-4-1E, National Archives)*

broadside approaches, the hull was given what might be termed "inverted tumblehome," becoming narrower below the waterline, though not in the usual convex curve: from about the waterline down to the flat floor, the sides were *concave*. The *Union*'s beam at the level of the wheels was 25 feet; at about 8 feet above the keel line, the hull began to flare out to the full 33 feet. To complete the break from the traditional hull form, she was sharp on both ends, to the extent that her widest point was only at the midship line, at the center of the paddles.[51]

She was constructed of white oak and according to Lieutenant Hunter quite solidly built: "Her frame is of heavy oak timber, sided fourteen inches, solid and caulked for eighty feet, in her midship sections on the bottom and sides, up to her berth deck. She is planked to her waterline with heavy six-inch oak plank, and ceiled with four-inch oak and pine, and caulked to the berth deck." This solidity was apparently to counteract the weakness inherent in frames with such radical curves in opposite directions.

Hunter also proposed a curved iron protective "shield deck," which was to abut the vessel's sides below the water line. The deck was intended to deflect any shot from the vessel's paddles and machinery, limiting damage to nonvital areas of the vessel. None of the Hunter's-wheel ships was equipped with this feature, though Hunter considered it part of his system, and the idea reappeared in warships in the last half of the century.[52]

Once launched and equipped, the *Union* mounted four 64-pounder guns pivoted on the centerline. She was rigged as a topsail schooner with just over 5,000 square feet of sail.[53] With a nearly straight sheer, vestigial knee-bow, short bowsprit, and fat funnel riding uneasily, well forward of the main mast, she reminded one of a locomotive.

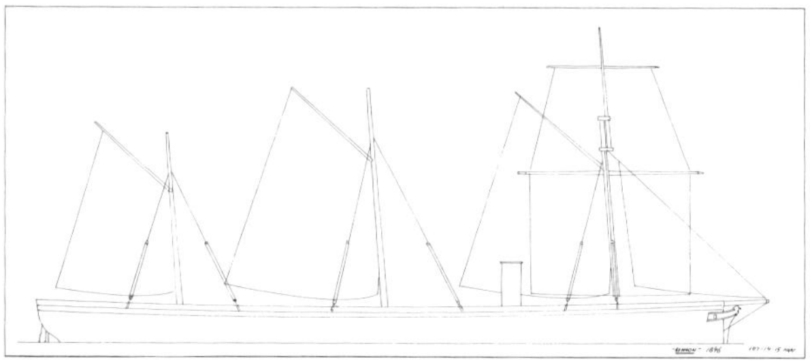

A Proposed Sail Plan for the Union, *1846. (NARS 107-14-15, National Archives)*

In operation, most of her career was off the coast and she averaged 5 knots for her first year, according to Stuart. Lieutenant Hunter reported that with sail, engines, and a favorable wind, she could make 9 or 10 knots.[54] Leaving aside Lieutenant Hunter's reports as necessarily biased, according to an assistant engineer's log she made only 4 knots under ordinary conditions and consumed nearly 20 tons of coal per day. It was calculated that the slip of the paddle (the differential between the mathematically calculated distance moved by the paddle and the actual movement of the vessel) was from 50 to 70 percent, a horrendously large figure. In comparison, with Ericsson's original screw the *Princeton*'s mean slip was 23 percent, and the screw's greatest slip was 46 percent in unfavorable conditions). The *Union*'s poor economy was an obvious result of the design of the propelling system.[55] The engine was not only propelling the ship, it was in essence pumping seawater through the paddle casings and overcoming the resistance inherent in that process.

The high-pressure boilers installed in the ship were exceedingly short lived: they were reported "burnt out in the course of one cruize." They accumulated proportionately more scale than low-pressure boilers, and because they were designed for use on land, they were not fitted for extensive scaling. At the end of her first year, new, larger boilers were put in the vessel. These endured nearly eighteen months and similarly deteriorated.[56]

The inverted bell configuration of the hull was also a detriment to the ship's performance. Her flat bottom was not conducive to smooth rolling in a seaway and her commander considered her "dangerous under sail," showing a dangerous "want of stability." Humphreys reported she rolled deeply, "taking water on one side and discharging it on the other." Haswell and Copeland reported that the "form of the vessel [is] so ill-adapted for sea going purposes that we deem her hull unworthy of the expense to render her a safe & efficient cruiser."[57]

Despite such criticism she was modified in 1846, receiving condensing engines and having her paddle buckets reduced from twenty to ten. (The reduction in number of buckets was a tacit admission of the excessive water resistance within the casings.) There was no significant improvement in her performance. Her paddle shafts were then found worn, and this required docking the vessel to remove the casings. She was then laid up and subsequently had her machinery removed. In 1849 she was made a receiving vessel at Philadelphia.[58]

Water Witch

The second Hunter's wheel vessel built for the navy, though not originally intended for war, must be included here for a complete delineation of this episode. The *Water Witch* was constructed at Norfolk and launched in 1843, specifically for the transportation of fresh water to the vessels at the yard, via the Dismal Swamp Canal. She was of galvanized iron, 100 feet by 21 feet, with the same inverted bell cross section as the *Union.* Again, high-pressure, noncondensing machinery was used, with 22-inch cylinders and a 48-inch stroke.[59]

At her completion she was 5 feet 10 inches forward and 8 feet 10 inches aft, without water or coal. The depth of the canal was six feet. Of course, this problem could not necessarily have been foreseen. Incredibly, however, she was also "too long for the first lock" of the waterway she was designed to use. Her speed was not in excess of 6½ knots.

Alternatively, it was suggested she be used to tow vessels at Hampton Roads. This came to nothing when it was found she was inefficient for towing any vessel larger than a sloop-of-war. An *ad hoc* committee compared her coal consumption to the side-wheel vessel *Engineer* and found that the latter used "10/35ths" as much fuel as the *Water Witch.* The committee concluded: "We do not consider the Water Witch as she is now is efficient for any naval purpose whatever." They recommended she be lengthened by thirty feet, fitted with side-wheels and used as a tow boat.[60]

At Philadelphia, the first portion of the recommendation was carried out. Her new propelling force was not paddle wheels but a pair of Richard F. Loper's screw propellers, powered by new engines with a 24-inch stroke and 22-inch diameter cylinders.[61] Loper's screws had cylindrical hubs and were simpler in design than Ericsson's. They had been used on commercial river vessels, and one authority has stated that Loper's pattern was more influential on later screw development than Ericsson's. In trials under the auspices of the Franklin Institute, the *Water Witch* made 6.6 to 8.9 knots. This apparently was not satisfactory and the navy again rebuilt her in 1847, with side-wheels.[62] For a short time she had been the first American naval vessel with twin screws.

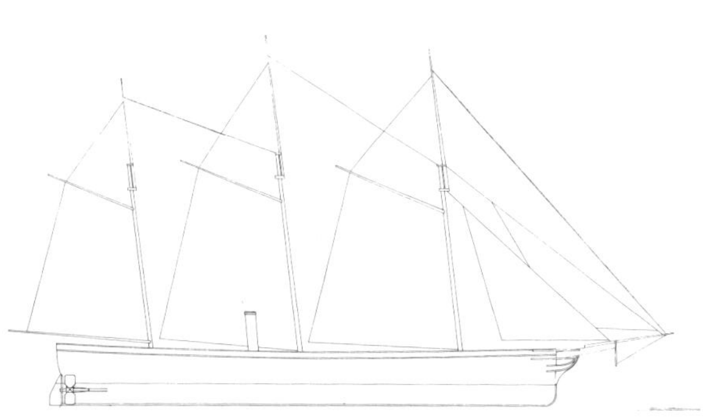

Plan of the Water Witch, *1845. She is fitted with twin Loper propellers. (Drawn by author from NARS 107-14-13A, National Archives)*

From 1847 to 1851, the ship was powered by a single-cylinder engine with stroke of 72 inches and bore of 37½ inches, with 17-foot paddles. She was armed with one 64-pounder pivot gun and two 32-pounders, and averaged five knots. Her boiler and hull were found defective in 1851 and the latter was then a target for testing armor plate at Washington Navy Yard.[63] Later in the decade her name was reused in a wooden vessel described in a later chapter.

Allegheny

The final installment in the Hunter's wheel story was the construction of the *Allegheny,* the largest vessel to use that form of propulsion. The navy was not alone in wrestling with Lieutenant Hunter. Both the Revenue Marine and the Army Topographical Engineers were having ships with Hunter's wheels built in these same years: four for the former service, one for the latter. As far as is known, only one of these was completed with her Hunter's wheel; the remainder received side-wheels before being completed or shortly thereafter.[64]

The contract for the *Allegheny* was dated October 1843. She was to be built of iron by Stackhouse and Tomlinson of Pittsburgh, the builders of the *Michigan.* The dimensions of the vessel were 185 feet by

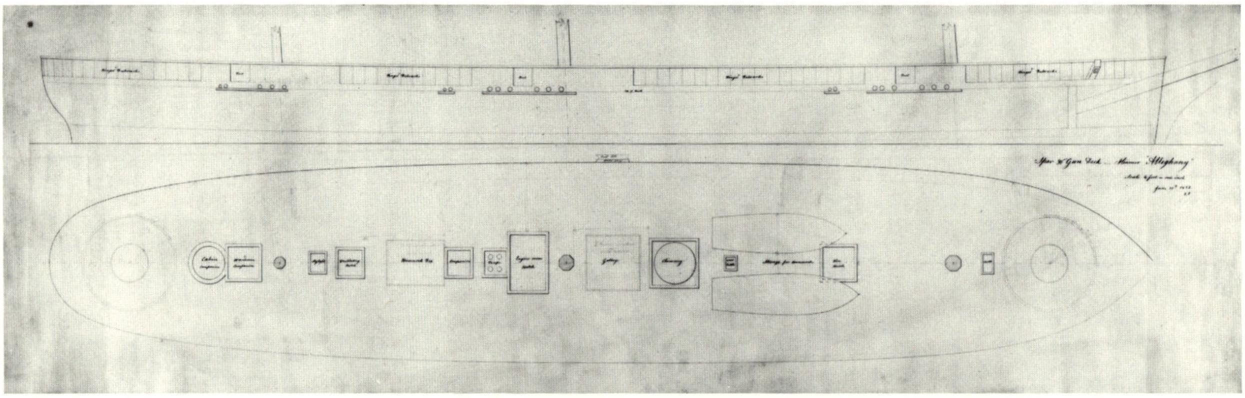

Allegheny, *1852, Showing Four Center-pivot Gun Ports. (National Archives)*

33 feet by 13 feet 6 inches, with a displacement of 1,026 tons, therefore slightly larger than the *Union,* with a deeper draft.

Hunter himself designed the hull of this vessel but the only available half breadth (NARS 107-14-12E) indicates there was little difference between the lines of the *Allegheny* and those of the earlier Hunter's wheel ships. Hunter attempted to ameliorate the effects of the flat bottom by decreasing the height of the paddles, thus allowing a deeper V from the keel to the lower edge of the paddle apertures.[65] A half-hull model labeled *Allegheny* (shown) seems to show much more convex bilges than the other Hunter's wheel ships. The dimensions of the model, however, do not coincide with any of Hunter's ships, raising the possibility that the model was a generic rather than specific vessel.

She was supplied with two iron boilers and a two-cylinder engine, this time of the condensing, low-pressure variety. These were designed by Charles Haswell, and the engine had a stroke of 4 feet and cylinder diameter of 5 feet.[66] She was rigged as a bark and armed with four 8-inch Paixhan guns mounted on centerline swivel carriages. This armament was subsequently reduced by half. From the waterline up, she was indistinguishable from conventional screw steamers.[67]

In this vessel, Lieutenant Hunter strove to eliminate two of the major objections to his ships: the odd hull cross section, and the short-lived high-pressure boilers. This may account for the navy's willingness to undertake a second such ship despite the poor performance of the *Union.* (At the time of this contract, the *Water Witch* had not been completed.) Furthermore, conventional engines and hull would furnish more direct comparisons with vessels such as the *Princeton,* in this competition between rival propulsion systems.

The final resolution of the contest was deferred until the completion of the *Allegheny,* in April 1847, some three years after her keel was laid. No explanation has been found for her protracted construction time. Possibly, Lieutenant Hunter surmised

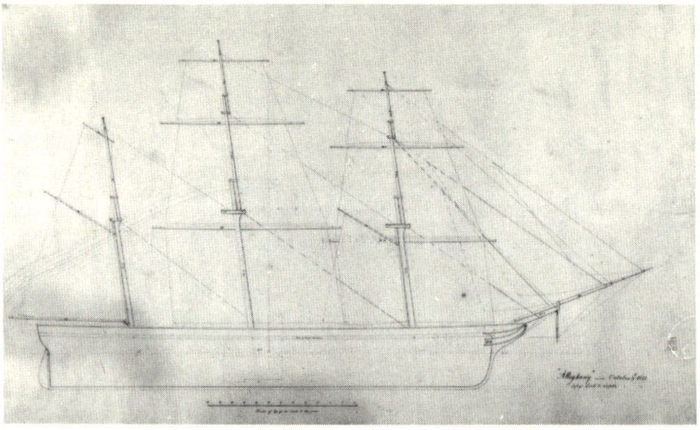

Sail Plan of the Allegheny, *1843, with Gaff Topsail on the Mizzen. (NARS 40-15-1B, National Archives)*

that this vessel would be his concluding argument for his invention and temporized to insure all was being done to make it a success.

After an expenditure of more than $242,595 ($10,320 of which covered the use of Lt. Hunter's patent), the *Allegheny* began her initial cruise: the descent from Pittsburgh on the Ohio and Mississippi rivers.[68] From New Orleans she steamed to Norfolk, where she was immediately docked and modified, having four of the eight paddles removed from each wheel. (One of the irremedial drawbacks of the horizontal wheel was the necessity of drydocking the vessels for any maintenance on the paddles.)

Her performance on this cruise, a great deal of which was in calm river water, was not encouraging: she burned a mean of 2,000 pounds of coal per hour and averaged 4.92 knots. After removing her paddles, her speed increased to 5.9 knots, but her coal consumption also increased slightly (2,096 pounds per hour).[69]

She was first assigned on the Brazil station, then transferred to the Mediterranean. Her Atlantic crossing was the first made by an American iron vessel.[70] Her performance on station from 1847 to September 1849 remained remarkably inefficient:

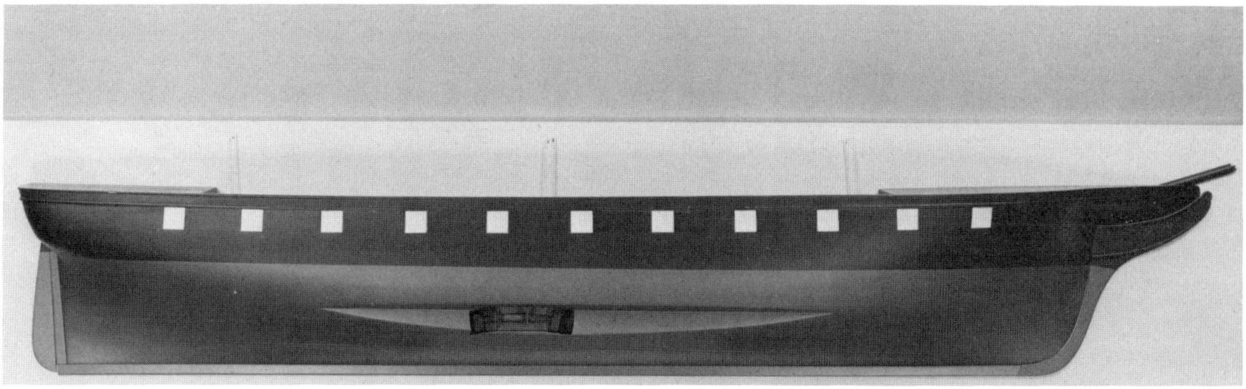

Half-Hull Model of a Hunter's Wheel Vessel, Showing the Location of the Wheel below the Waterline. Though labeled the Allegheny, *the model's dimensions do not coincide with any known vessel equipped with Hunter's wheels. (Courtesy Smithsonian Institution)*

consuming 1,940 pounds of coal per hour and maintaining an average of 5.89 knots. (For comparison, the *Princeton* used approximately 1,300 pounds and the *Michigan,* 1,500 pounds of coal per hour.)[71]

In 1850 she was the object of a board of inquiry and the result was a final condemnation of the Hunter's wheel.[72] The justification for this was the system's inefficiency and consequent lack of economy, aggravated by the negative sailing qualities of the unusual hull form. An infinite number of propelling systems could be devised, from Fitch's oars to jets of water, all of which would accomplish the basic task of moving a floating vessel. The limiting criteria, however, is the relative efficiency of the method used. Apparently the Navy Department was at the outset prepared to sacrifice much efficiency to achieve the goal of a warship with motive power safely beneath the waterline. When it became apparent, however, that no amount of modification would eliminate the inherent inefficiency of Hunter's scheme, they conceded the field to the submerged screw propeller.

The board recommended that the *Allegheny* be fitted with side-wheels, but it was found that her short-stroke cylinders were more suited to screw propulsion. Consequently, Benjamin F. Isherwood was directed to design suitable engines. These used many parts from the original installation, but the cylinders were arranged to operate athwartships rather than fore and aft. To obtain sufficient stroke of piston within the confines of the ship's beam, the connecting rods worked back from crosstails to the propeller shaft. This was the first of many back-acting engines designed by B. F. Isherwood.[73]

New boilers, three in number, were installed, and of course the bilges were filled to eliminate the wheel inlets. Several of her iron frames were found to be buckled inward by the stresses of ocean seas and were replaced. Altogether, an area of forty-five feet amidships received new iron and strengthened bracing. Her new battery consisted of two 8-inch weapons on centerline pivot carriages and eight 32-pounder guns in broadside.[74]

The first trial of the refurbished *Allegheny,* in 1853, added another failure to the vessel's log. The new boilers were inadequate for the engines, and the engines' bedplates broke in several places. An investigating committee concluded that the "known weakness" of the ship's bottom had not been rectified in her rebuild, and that the engine frames ought to have been more substantially built to prevent their destruction by the racking of the hull.[75] The *Allegheny* was then laid up, converted to a receiving ship, and sold in 1869.

EXPERIMENTAL PROPOSALS

The Hunter's wheel interlude has its ludicrous aspects, particularly the simultaneous building of seemingly useless vessels by three separate government agencies and the suspicion that influence peddling had a heavy hand in the proceedings. Those events, however, become less incomprehensible (barring a few of the more obvious debacles) when seen in the context of the era and the goals of the navy. The emphasis placed on Hunter's invention is a measure of the determination on the part of the navy and in particular Secretary Upshur to see that the "ordinary mode" (side-wheels) was replaced by propulsion invulnerable to shot and compatible with sail.[76]

Furthermore, this was an era of experiment in the field of steam engineering, and it was by no means clear that the screw propeller would be dominant. In fact, there were several alternatives to Hunter's plan being studied by the department.

The earliest alternative mentioned was "Keller's submerged wheel," which appears in official letters in 1841. This contrivance was a variation on Hunter's wheels but could be vertical or horizontal; the key difference was that the individual paddle buckets remained retracted into the circumference of the wheel except when allowed to extend by the apertures in the vessel's hull; when the paddle bucket passed the hull opening, it would again be retracted. This plan eliminated much of the dead space between the individual paddle buckets, which caused the inefficiency of Hunter's paddles. In 1846, this plan was still considered "well worthy of the attention of the department" by a committee of engineers studying the various alternate systems.[77]

A second variation on Hunter's wheels was the Everett "vertical shifting wheel." This was to be mounted inboard and raised into the ship's hull and enclosed for sailing. No further comments were found on this invention.[78]

Unlike the Everett wheel, the Aldrich vertical wheel did not shift. It was also mounted within the hull, with only the paddles extending into the water. Therefore, according to the engineers' report, it would be easier to maintain and would squander less energy than Hunter's wheels. A merchant vessel, the *Virginia,* was reported to have this system in 1846, though no further information has been found on that ship. An unidentified plan in the National Archives may well be the Aldrich system: two wheels are shown, each installed vertically midway between the centerline and sides of the vessel.[79]

Two other plans mentioned during this era were those of Havens and Peter von Schmidt. The former involved modified side-wheels, possibly a type of feathering wheel.[80] The von Schmidt plan was examined and rejected in 1844 by Chief Engineer Haswell and consisted of a rotary engine and submerged propeller. The concept of the rotary engine was a favorite with inventors of the era and was attractive because of its simplicity: it usually consisted of a disk mounted directly on the paddle or screw shaft, fitted with arms or other appendages around its circumference. The arms became the "pistons," which were forced, whirligig fashion, around in a circular doughnut-shaped cylinder. (In principle, the concept has seen modern use in the "Wankel" automobile engine.) Despite the number of patents granted (103 from 1831 to 1859) none proved exceedingly practical.[81]

Thus Lieutenant Hunter had much company in advancing variations on the paddle wheel in competition with the screw propeller. It may also be noted here that the engineers' report of 1846 rated Loper's propeller "fully equal to all others," commenting that it presented less resistance and less weight than Ericsson's screw.

A final comment from this engineers' report brings us back to Hunter's wheel: "It fails to merit further consideration." This report was dated 14 February 1846, over a year before the completion of the *Allegheny.*[82] The conclusion is obvious: the fate of Hunter's plan was sealed by the *Union* and *Water Witch,* and the *Allegheny* became an unwelcome stepchild, the product of a premature contract.

Possibly the most significant impact of the Hunter's wheel episode on the navy was an altered attitude toward experimentation. None of the propulsion plans studied were attempted by the navy and three of the four new vessels that were authorized in 1847 retained side-wheels, a system by then palpably obsolete. The secretary of the navy, in December 1845, advised in his annual report: "Should it be determined to increase [the steam navy] . . . the best experience should be consulted . . . and that doubtful novelties, especially such as conflict with the known laws of mechanical forces, should be disregarded."[83]

By 1845, activist leadership of the Navy Department was moribund. Abel P. Upshur, in his short tenure, had encouraged iron shipbuilding, the screw propeller, Hunter's wheels, and the study of alternative propulsion systems. Additionally, he supported congressional funding for an experimental ironclad warship proposed by Robert L. Stevens of Hoboken, New Jersey. This project, which predated the first armored floating batteries by over a decade, was never completed. It was representative, however, of what one authority describes as the "energetic, open-minded leadership" of Upshur.[84] Unfortunately, such progressive leadership would be the exception rather than the rule in the age of the steam navy.

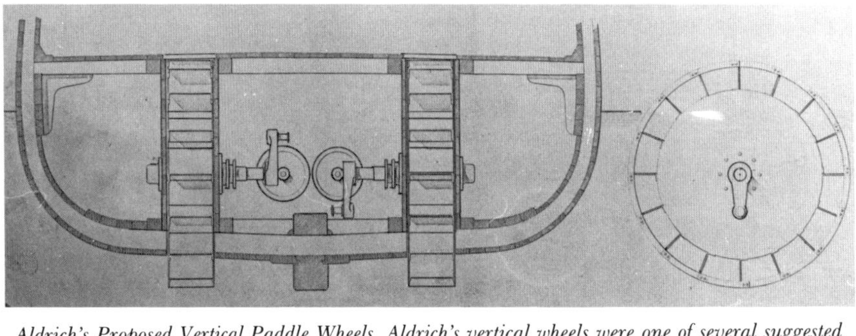

Aldrich's Proposed Vertical Paddle Wheels. Aldrich's vertical wheels were one of several suggested alternatives to Hunter's and Ericsson's propulsion systems. (NARS 140-1-5B, National Archives)

CHAPTER 3

Conservative Expansion, 1847–1853

The Mexican War both encouraged the expansion of the steam navy and discouraged further dalliance with "doubtful novelties" in the design of American naval ships. Steam proved its utility in diverse wartime roles, the most evident being the blockade and the shelling of targets on the Mexican coast. The light-draft, purchased steamers (*Vixen, Spitfire,* and *Scorpion*) were particularly effective in river operations and in the landings at Vera Cruz, the latter being the largest American amphibious operation undertaken to that date. While the smaller vessels towed surf boats, in at least one instance a larger steamer towed a sailing frigate into range of her targets, this off the mouth of the Papaloapan River in 1846.[1] Further proof of the steamers' usefulness was provided in November of that year by M. C. Perry and the *Mississippi.* On the 16th he was dispatched from Tampico to Matamoros and thence to New Orleans to obtain troops and supplies, returning to his starting point on the 29th.[2] That was considered a record turnaround in its day and pointed up the steamers' capability of acting independently of wind and weather conditions.

Congress was not blind to such practical evidence and the naval appropriations bill of March 1847 called for the construction of four steamships. A board of line officers, constructors, and engineers was directed by Secretary of the Navy John Y. Mason to determine the specifics of the vessels. Minutes of their meetings, later published as part of a congressional inquiry, outline the design process.[3]

The *Mississippi* and *Princeton* were patterns for the planned vessels. The former was cited for her ability to contend with heavy weather but was deemed lacking in sufficient capacity for long-range operations. The *Princeton*'s shortcoming as a prototype was her inadequate steam power. A second objection was the necessity to dock her for any maintenance to her screw. Basing their actions on these considerations, the board first elected to build three side-wheel vessels and postpone a decision on the propulsion for the fourth. Their final decision was in favor of a screw vessel. Two ships were to be larger than the *Mississippi,* and two were to be somewhat larger than the displacement of the *Princeton.* Also deferred was a question on the building material for one of the ships, though this was shortly settled in favor of wood.[4]

The suitability of iron for warship hulls was the subject of testing by the British from 1846 to 1850 (the *Simoom* tests). These showed the metal had poor resistance to shot as well as having the property of shattering into shards more lethal than wood splinters. The tests discouraged the use of iron alone and resulted in the development of "composite" construction: iron framing with wood planking or, in some instances, wood sheathing over an iron hull. No such vessels, however, were constructed for the U.S. Navy until the 1890s.[5]

The model for the larger American vessels was also a point deferred by the committee. Constructor Lenthall preferred the expansion of the lines of the *Mississippi,* while Hartt and Francis Grice favored new lines. Eventually, Lenthall designed one of the frigates, the *Susquehanna,* along lines similar to the older vessel, and Hartt drafted new plans for the *Powhatan.* The committee noted that new lines would be necessary if the screw steamer was built.[6]

Copeland and Haswell evidently had agreed earlier to replace side-lever machinery with inclined engines in the side-wheel vessels, and they affirmed that these engines would not exceed the weight and cubic space of the *Mississippi*'s engines in the

The Susquehanna *Fitting Out at Philadelphia, July 1850. This is believed to be the oldest photograph of a U.S. naval vessel. (Library of Congress)*

new ships. Explanations for not repeating the side-lever machinery were not discussed by the board, but the February 1846 engineers' report on various types of machinery indicated that direct-action engines were preferred for their cheapness of maintenance and repair. And, it was no doubt still high on the engineers' priorities to use engines of American design. In fact, Copeland had a patent on the inclined engine arrangement used on the *Susquehanna.*[7]

Once the building of a screw steamer was agreed upon, Copeland suggested an oscillating engine, while Haswell and John Faron, the third engineer on the board, desired stationary cylinders and crossheads. At this juncture, Ericsson offered his patented engines and propeller. Nevertheless, the board opted for a navy-designed engine and propeller that would not infringe any patent rights.[8]

The report of the committee was certainly not radical. Three of the vessels would be propelled by side-wheels and the fourth would use a screw. None would be of iron. To put these decisions in perspective, the Royal Navy launched ten screw sloops or frigates on or before 1847 and by 1850 had sixteen screw vessels in their inventory. Nine paddle-wheel vessels, however, were built in the same general era. Only five iron vessels were built for the British navy up to 1846.[9]

Susquehanna and *Powhatan*

Most contemporaries referred to the *Susquehanna* and *Powhatan* as frigates because of their size, but technically they were sloops (what the British termed corvettes), because the battery was on a single deck. The dimensions of these vessels made them among the largest yet completed in the United States. At 18 feet 6 inches mean draft, the *Powhatan* measured three inches shorter than the *Susquehanna*'s 250 feet; and at the same waterline, the latter displaced 3,550 tons, the former, 3,600 tons. At a foot deeper draft, the *Powhatan* then displaced more than the *Susquehanna* (3,824 tons for the *Susquehanna,* versus 3,865 tons for her sister). Both were 44 feet in beam. For a comparison, in 1849 the merchant steamer *Ohio* was called the largest American vessel ever built, measuring 246 feet by 46 feet with 2,432 tons displacement. These records were short-lived; in 1850 the first of the Collins liners surpassed them in length by 30 feet.[10]

The reversal of the two ships' relative displacements between 18 feet 6 inches and 19 feet 6 inches was a result of their contrasting hull lines. Lenthall modeled the *Susquehanna* on the *Mississippi,* a traditional hull with the fullest lines forward and finest lines aft, and fullest midsection forward of the midlength. The *Powhatan* entered the water with finer lines, and her fullest midsection was at midlength.[11]

The length of these hulls made great strength imperative. Live oak formed the major part of their structure, with white oak planking. The bottom, between frames, was filled in solid and caulked. Five 7-inch thick planks were stacked and fastened with $1\frac{1}{4}$-inch copper bolts to each frame to form the keelson. A series of diagonal iron braces, 4 inches by $\frac{3}{4}$ inches, ran from the gundeck clamps down to the heads of the first futtocks.[12]

Inclined condensing engines powered both vessels, with 70-inch cylinders and 10-foot stroke. Differences existed in the type of valve mechanism and in the placement of the air pump (this was in effect a water pump, to draw the condensed water from the condenser for reuse). Engineer Copeland's patented air pump, used on the *Susquehanna,* was inclined; that of the *Powhatan* was vertical. The advantage of either position is not clear. The framework for the *Powhatan*'s engine was an innovation, with a box girder arrangement of cast and wrought iron rather than a wooden foundation.[13]

Both vessels had four copper-flue boilers each. The *Powhatan*'s bunkers, however, stowed 100 tons less than the *Susquehanna*'s 900. Engines, boilers,

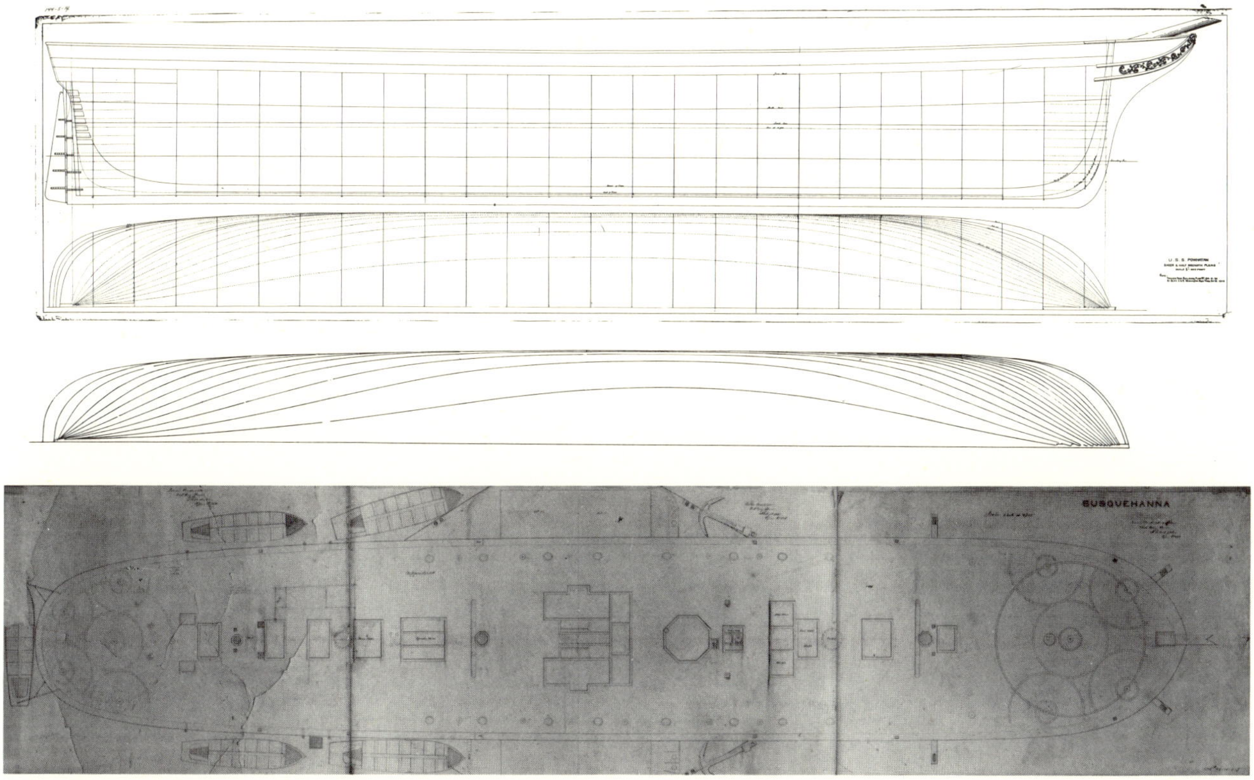

Top to Bottom: Sheer and Half-Breadth of the Powhatan, *Half-Breadth of the* Susquehanna, *Deck of the* Susquehanna. *The broadest point of the* Susquehanna *is forward of the center of her hull length. (NARS 144-4-14, 40-14-4, 40-14-46, National Archives.* Susquehanna *lines traced by author.)*

and coal occupied 102 feet 9 inches in each hold. Both vessels were bark-rigged, spreading 21,230 square feet of plain sails. The height of the wheelhouses prevented the use of mainsails on these vessels.[14]

Armament of the ships as commissioned was three 10-inch shell guns on pivot circles fore and aft (two on the forecastle) and six 8-inch guns in broadside. This was increased considerably during the Civil War. By 1865, the *Official Records* show the *Powhatan* with three 100-pound Parrott rifles, one 11-inch and sixteen 9-inch Dahlgrens. The *Susquehanna* was reported as carrying twelve 9-inchers and two 150-pound rifles in 1863.[15]

These two ships proved to be among the most durable and long-lived in the fleet. Their initial breaking-in period, however, was fraught with difficulties, causing at least one commodore to cast scurrilous comments their way and compare them unfavorably with the old *Mississippi.* In September 1853, Commodore Perry wrote from Hong Kong complaining of the frequency of repairs on both ships: "She [the *Powhatan*] is as bad as the *Susquehanna* and that is saying enough to damn her as a war steamer." He then compared the *Susquehanna* to the *Mississippi,* the latter described as "beating the Susquehanna, making better weather and consuming one-third less coal. But I shall nurse the two lame ducks, until I can finish my Japan business." Perry then sent the older vessel—the *Mississippi*—home via the tempestuous Cape Horn route, not trusting the newer side-wheeler to that route.[16]

Published reports substantiated Perry's claims and more. Some of the statistics were made possible by, and given unusual credence in, an unprecedented cruise of the three vessels to Japan in 1854. The three steamed side by side, within hailing distance, for an entire week in February 1854. Their voyage must have been a magnificent sight, and it yielded pertinent figures. The *Mississippi,* which had over thirty thousand miles to her credit, burned an average of 2,336 pounds of coal per hour while the *Powhatan* and *Susquehanna* consumed 3,248 and 3,310 pounds, respectively. The calculated slip of the paddles for the newer steamers was 18 percent; for the veteran frigate, 11.79 percent.[17]

On the subject of maintenance and repair, the *Mississippi* was reported "in perfect order . . . and at no time since leaving Norfolk . . . out of order." The *Susquehanna* had suffered a series of mishaps, and the *Powhatan* had required ten weeks' of repair after arriving in Chinese waters.[18] Both ships, however, clearly reversed this unfortunate trend and became favorites in the service. Their strength of

The Powhatan *during or after the Civil War. She served until 1887. (Naval Historical Center)*

construction was phenomenal, as witnessed by the large batteries placed on them in wartime and their survival in the vicissitudes of weather and climate. In 1851, the *Susquehanna* was reported to have survived unharmed in seas that "buried" one paddle wheel to half its depth, while raising the other ten feet in the air.

The *Powhatan* was reported "strong and in good condition" in commanders' reports as late as 1875. Bennett related an instance in which she dipped her foreyard in stormy seas three years afterwards, and she remained another nine years on active service, in many cases towing vessels in distress.[19]

The performance of the two ships was uneconomical but reliable after their early troubles ceased. The *Susquehanna* on her first cruise met with fine sailing conditions, and proceeded for a time using sail alone, with her paddle floats removed to prevent dragging. With the wind directly aft and all sail set her mean speed was 7.3 knots with a moderate breeze. With the wind on the port quarter, this figure declined to 6.5 knots. The time required to remove the paddle was two hours, removing eleven from each wheel.

A portion of the same cruise was under sail alone but with sufficient steam to turn the paddles and prevent their dragging. With winds from abaft to abeam, she made 8.2 knots. Under steam alone, in winds from ahead to abeam, her velocity ranged from 6 to 8.3 knots, with a mean of 7.4. During the war, she was credited with 10 knots maximum but averaged 8.[20]

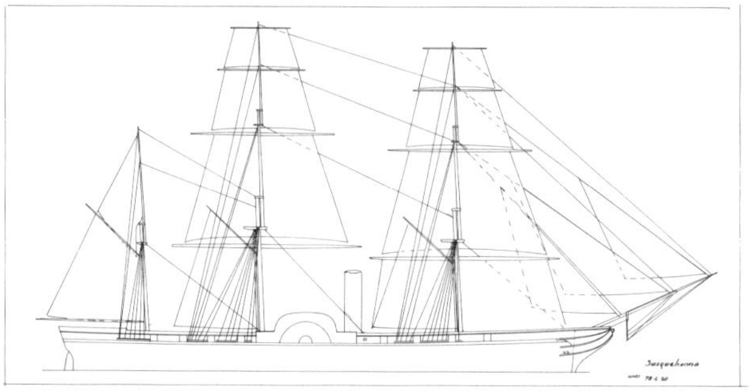

Sail Plan of the Susquehanna *and* Powhatan. *More efficient spacing of the mainmast improved the sailing of these vessels over the* Mississippi*'s poor performance under sail. (NARS 78-6-20, National Archives)*

The *Powhatan* was a slightly faster vessel, making a mean of 9.6 knots steaming without sail; her maximum speed recorded in cruising in 1852 was 10.4, in light to moderate head or beam winds. With sail assistance, the mean rose to 10.47 knots. With the minimal differences in their engines, this higher speed is attributable to the *Powhatan*'s hull lines, with her fullest portion further aft than the *Susquehanna*'s. Both ships received iron boilers later in their careers, but few other modifications were made during their service life.[21]

One of the few reports on the sailing qualities of side-wheel steamers was on the *Powhatan* in 1858. Her commander, A. T. Pearson, related that she "performed admirably . . . under sail, and worked to windward against wind and current far better than I had supposed it possible for any of our side-wheel steamers."[22] He did not compare her with screw steamers or sailing vessels, however, and, as

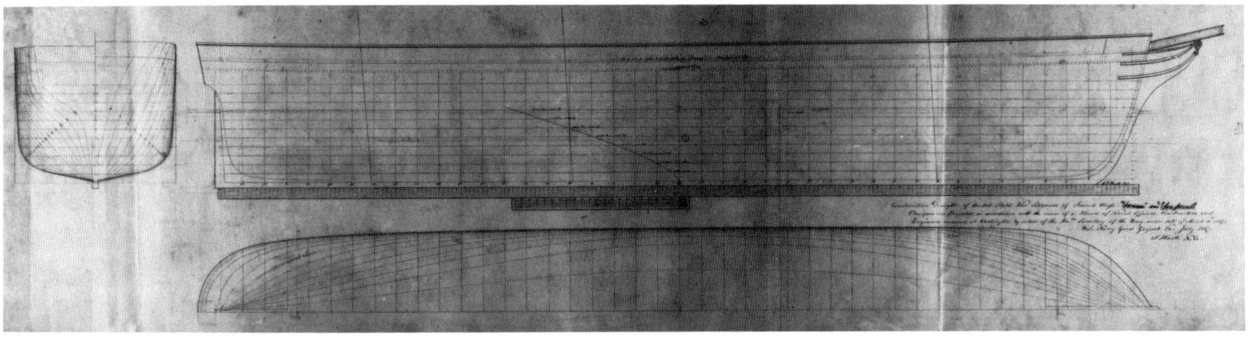

Sheer and Lines of the Saranac *and* San Jacinto. *(NARS 79-7-14A, National Archives)*

can be judged by his phraseology, he did not harbor great expectations for the *Powhatan* or her type in general. Therefore, what was "admirable" performance for the *Powhatan* may have been less so for vessels other than side-wheelers. One explanation for this satisfactory performance was in the placement of the mainmast of the *Powhatan,* much further forward than that of the *Mississippi.*

Figurehead and Cutwater Carving of the Susquehanna *and* Powhatan. *(NARS 108-1-7A, National Archives)*

Model of the Powhatan *Early in Her Career. During the Civil War she carried up to sixteen broadside guns (9-inch Dahlgrens), three 100-pdr rifles, and one 11-inch pivot gun. Her funnel was later made telescopic, and she gained a quarter deck. (Courtesy Smithsonian Institution)*

The careers of the pair were successful and of course long. Both accompanied Commodore Perry to Japan, then the *Susquehanna* assisted the *Niagara* in the Atlantic cable operation of 1857, participating in an informal race with the *Niagara* and the British screw battleship *Agamemnon* in the process, and placing second behind the Steers-designed ship.[23] During the war, the heavy armament of these paddle frigates made them useful for shore operations, though their draft prevented close-in work. The *Powhatan* was a favorite ship, according to Bennett, and rendered useful, though auxiliary, service in the postwar years.[24]

Both vessels were considered for conversion to screw propulsion after the war. In 1870, the *Powhatan* was to be converted while under repairs, but a pressing need for her as a flag vessel prevented this. (In the postwar years there was a great shortage of vessels suitable for flag duties.) She was condemned and sold in 1887.[25]

The *Susquehanna* was in the process of being converted in 1869. Her engines were removed, and a complete set of plans in the National Archives show her as a two-funneled sloop carrying eighteen 9-inchers, two 11-inch Dahlgrens and two 100-pound rifles. In that era, miniscule appropriations slowed all such projects, and she was never completed. She was sold in 1883.[26]

Saranac

The two smaller ships of the authorization of 1847 were the *Saranac* and *San Jacinto.* Other than their hull form, the two were virtually opposites in every way. The most evident difference was their propulsion, with the *Saranac* employing side-wheels and the *San Jacinto* screw propulsion. Moreover, while the *San Jacinto* was in the thick of Atlantic wartime cruising and became virtually a household word in the *Trent* affair, the side-wheel sloop remained in the Pacific, never saw hostile action, and thus remained anonymous to the general public. Mechanically, the two had nothing whatever in common: the *Saranac* was phenomenally reliable and mechanically sound, while the *San Jacinto* was a mechanical albatross that plagued the navy virtually from her inception.

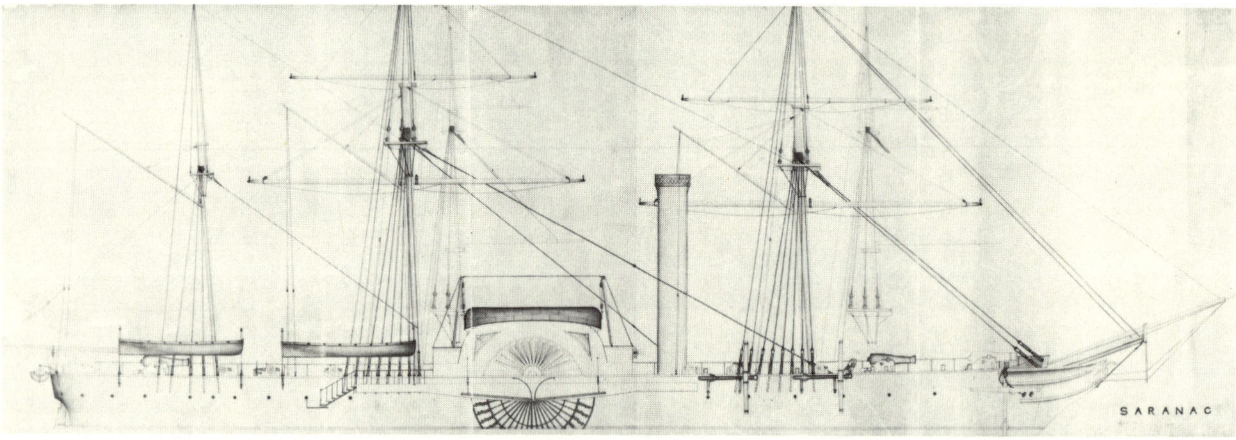

The Saranac, *1849. The draftsman has drawn topmasts low and in front of lower masts. Fore and aft shell guns are shown both stowed and run out (bulwarks have been cut away for clarity). Note metal boats, which doubled as tops for paddle-wheel housings, and the early use of turnbuckles on shrouds. The masts of the* San Jacinto *were somewhat forward of the* Saranac*'s. (NARS 35-8-2, National Archives)*

The *Saranac* was such a success that little can be found in the records of the Bureau of Construction and Repair regarding her, indicating she had few mechanical or structural maladies requiring official attention. This lack of information is compounded by her noncombatant role in the Civil War.

The sloop was built at Portsmouth Navy Yard to hull lines by Samuel Hartt, and the same draft was used for the *San Jacinto.* She measured 210 feet between perpendiculars and had a beam of 38 feet (extreme), with a displacement at 17 feet draft of 2,100 tons. Her hull form was similar to that of the *Mississippi,* having her fullest form forward of the center of her load length; however, her bilges were slacker and she had longer but less fine lines aft.[27]

Her construction was of typical naval solidity. She was for the most part live oak, with iron diagonal bracing. The vessel had, additionally, timber bracing running diagonally opposite to the iron supports. Two watertight bulkheads divided her machinery and coal spaces from the fore and aft holds.

Her engines were smaller versions of those of the *Susquehanna,* designed by Charles Copeland, though with wrought iron frames. Her cylinders measured 60 inches by 9 feet and were rated at 605 horsepower. Steam was supplied by three copper return-flue boilers, and her bunker capacity was 400 tons.[28]

She was rigged as a bark and spread 12,800 feet of canvas. Her original armament was two 8-inch pivot guns, fore and aft, and four 8-inch shell guns in broadside. During the war, she carried one 11-inch Dahlgren on pivot and eight 8-inch 55-hundredweight guns in broadside.[29]

She was launched 14 November 1848 and commissioned 12 October 1850. On trials in April 1850, her best speed was 12 knots, in smooth seas with light winds. Her commander, Josiah Tatnall, however, limited her engines' revolutions because of the minor engine defects prevalent in new machinery and particularly the need to "wear in" bearing surfaces.[30]

After commissioning, Tatnall reported her first "real trial": with 400 tons of coal, three years' stores, four months' provisions, 39 days' water, and 235 men on board. Tatnall called this a "most unfavorable position in which she could have been placed for speed and efficiency, and I am gratified to say that highly as my expectations were raised, her performance exceeded them." In smooth seas without canvas, she ran 9 knots, consuming 17 tons of coal per day; at times she made 12 knots under sail and steam. He continued: "When therefore it is considered that her frame is live oak, and that she has no treenails, but is bolted throughout, with a scantling of great size and strength and the masts and spars of a first class sloop, with which she can circumnavigate the globe without the aid of steam, I think I should be justified in saying that the Saranac is as fine a war steamer as can be found in any service."[31]

Late in the 1860s her commander reported her maximum speed as 10 knots with an average of 7. She rolled easily, deep and quick, and answered her helm promptly.[32] Her engines rarely malfunctioned and her only major alteration was the replacement of her copper boilers with iron and the shortening of her funnel.

Stuart referred to her as particularly well finished and an "ornament" to the service, and this is reinforced by her plans. Her proportions were not even spoiled by her early tall, flared funnel. All three of these side-wheelers were distinguished looking vessels, with their wheelhouses deemphasized to prevent the ugly midship hump typical of paddle-wheel ships.

After a career unsullied by hostile action or mechanical dysfunction, in 1875 the *Saranac* ran aground and was wrecked, en route to Alaska.

San Jacinto

Though the keels of both the *Saranac* and *San Jacinto* were laid in August 1847, the launch of the screw sloop was nearly a year and a half after that of the *Saranac,* a delay not only portending future problems but indicating that the ship's afflictions were well under way long before she reached active service.

The ship's preponderant difficulty was mechanical, because her hull form and structure corresponded to that of her semisister. Given the divergence in the two propulsion systems, the use of identical hull lines became the hatchery for many sins. The first was the location of the propeller shaft.

Screw propulsion in wooden ships engendered long-standing problems with the shaft's exit through the hull. One was leakage around and through the bearing into the hull. A second, more critical problem was the vibration of the shaft against the deadwood of the stern, which exacerbated any leakage and weakened the vessel's stern structure. Furthermore, placing the screw forward of the rudder weakened the rudder's security.

To prevent these problems, the design board decided to avoid penetrating the stern post altogether and to place the *San Jacinto*'s propeller shaft twenty inches to the port side of the keel. The shaft was then extended five feet beyond the rudder. To prevent the rudder from turning and striking the propeller shaft, an appropriately shaped slot was made in the rudder. Though asymmetrical and awkward, this arrangement was not unusual in 1848.[33]

Inexplicably, despite the design board's stated desire to avoid any patent-right difficulties, this arrangement duplicated in most respects a plan owned by John Ericsson. It had been used on the 1,400-ton packet *Massachusetts* in 1845, in conjunction with a propeller mounted on a swinging arm, which allowed it to be hoisted for sailing. This ship went into federal service during the Mexican War.[34]

Another source of difficulty on the *San Jacinto* was her propeller, which was designed by Charles Haswell specifically to avoid infringing on Ericsson's patent. As with the *Princeton*'s first screw, the Ericsson prop retained an inner ring, on which the blades were mounted. To compensate for the strength lost by not using this inner ring, Haswell increased the weight of the screw. This, with the use of six blades with a diameter of 14½ feet, re-

A Postwar View of the Saranac, *during her Long and Uneventful Career. (Naval Historical Center)*

sulted in a burden of 10 tons on the already overhanging shaft.[35]

Unfortunately, the propeller and rudder arrangement was not the greatest lack in the *San Jacinto.* According to F. M. Bennett, the design of the engines was the "object of ridicule" and was termed a "fearful botch" on the part of their designer, Charles Haswell. The "hue and cry" was such that Charles Stuart, former engineer for the Erie Canal, displaced Haswell as engineer-in-chief of the navy in December 1850. At this juncture, the engines were complete, but the propeller had yet to be cast.[36]

No plans of these engines exist, but written descriptions tend to confirm contemporary disparagement of the machines. Two inclined 62½-inch cylinders worked their 50-inch pistons outward and upward to crossheads, which worked connecting rods that ran back alongside the cylinders to two shafts, one for each cylinder. Drag links joined these shafts, one of which was extended to the screw.[37] The whole was termed "very complicated" and "unequally balanced, thereby involving great irregularity in their motion," characteristics "highly objectionable" for high-velocity engines. In fact, Haswell explained that his engines were "wholly novel, and not being symmetrical (from the eccentricity of the shaft), a double set of drawings are necessary." Other criticisms were of their frames, which were called too light, and of the difficulties that arose in maintaining the engines within the cramped space they occupied far aft in the hold.[38]

Immediately on taking Mr. Haswell's position, Mr. Stuart ordered a board to survey and recommend changes to the still incomplete *San Jacinto.* The engines and rudder-and-shaft arrangements were roundly criticized by this board, though the point where engine modifications could be accomplished was past. The propeller was redesigned by Benjamin F. Isherwood, a relatively new naval steam engineer, and was reduced to four blades and 7 tons.[39]

This screw was then mounted "next to the stern post" of the vessel, to eliminate the excessive leverage that would have worked upon the stern in the original plan. Given the diameter of the screw (remaining at 14 feet), "next to the sternpost" was actually immediately behind that structure. A new rudder was then necessary, "curved over and abaft the propeller, being attached to the stern post above and below the propeller."[40]

The *San Jacinto* was rigged as a bark and carried 16,500 square feet of sail. Two 8-inch pivots and four broadside 8-inch guns made up her battery. In 1863 she carried ten 9-inch Dahlgrens and one 100-pounder Parrott rifle.[41]

Trials of the ship in October 1851 pointed up the general inefficiency of the engines. Though she ran 9.95 statute miles per hour against a strong wind, calculations revealed a slip of the screw of 30 percent. Using a dynamometer, a figure of 375 horsepower was indicated as actually propelling the vessel. Total horsepower developed was 782, and the remainder above the actual propelling power was absorbed by screw slip and the friction developed in the working of the engines.[42]

It required actual sea service to prove or disprove the efficacy of Haswell's "botched" machinery. On her trial cruise, one engine was disabled. Once repaired, she was sent to the Mediterranean for eighteen months, "much of it repairing," and returned to the U.S. with engines "crippled." A survey was ordered and her engines and propeller were removed and sold.[43]

New machinery was then contracted to Merrick and Sons of Philadelphia, with the contractor guaranteeing the performance of the engines for a specified time. This arrangement called for the contractor (not the navy) to design the details of the engines.[44]

The new machinery, which would remain in the vessel for the balance of her service, consisted of two horizontal cylinders of 70-inch bore and 48-inch stroke. The piston rods rotated four 8-foot-diameter wooden-toothed gears, which in turn operated a pinion-geared propeller shaft. The ratio

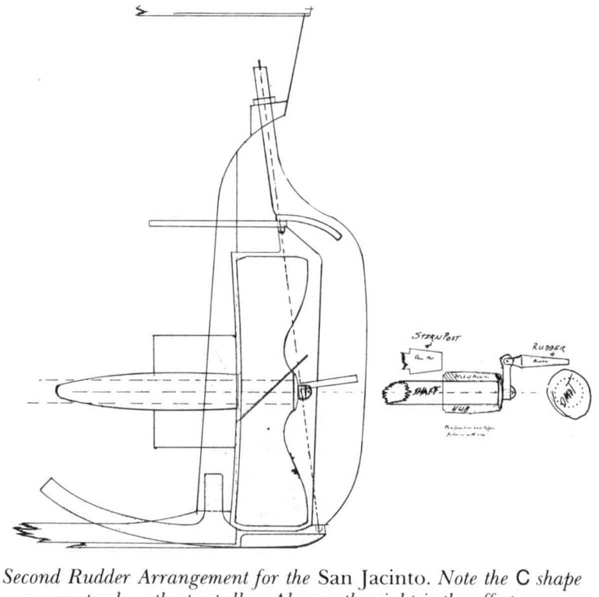

Second Rudder Arrangement for the San Jacinto. *Note the* C *shape necessary to clear the propeller. Also on the right is the offset propeller, unique to this naval vessel though used by Ericsson in at least one merchant ship. (NARS Bureau of Steam Engineering Plan, National Archives)*

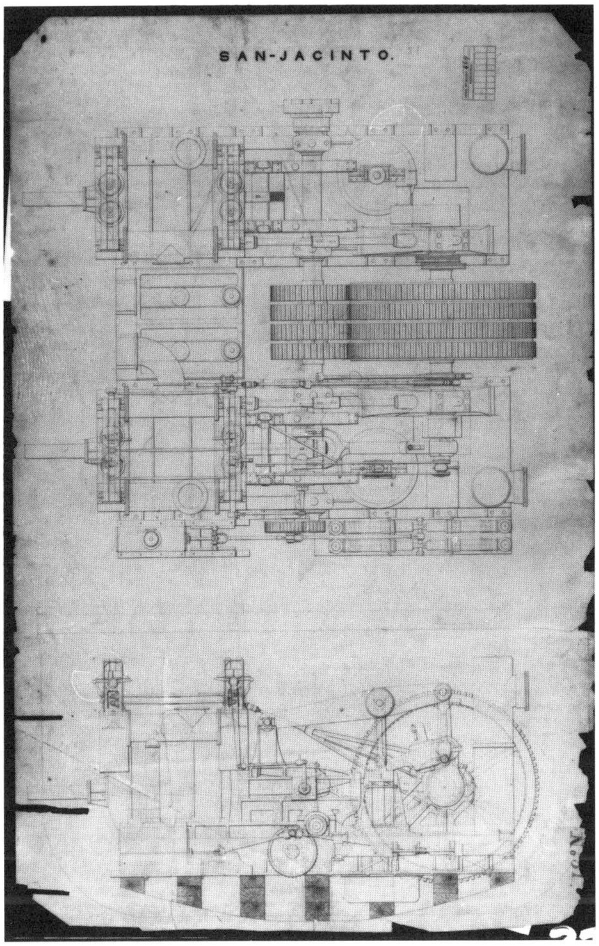

Engines That Replaced the Disastrous Originals in the San Jacinto. *Geared engines were not unusual in early screw vessels. Overhead beams operated air pumps. (NARS BSE Plan, National Archives)*

between the large and small gears was approximately 2 to 1. This geared engine was unique to this vessel but became a pattern for engines used in the *Wampanoag*-class ships after the war.[45]

As a centerline propeller shaft was installed, a 4-foot space was inlet into the hull below the waterline for a three-bladed screw. The propeller weighed 15 tons and was fitted with a clutch coupling, allowing the screw to be disengaged for operation under sail.[46]

Performance of the renovated *San Jacinto* on her trials yielded a speed of 8 knots, with screw slippage of 18 to 21 percent. Her uncoupled propeller was found to be of "trifling" hindrance, and, under sail, she steered well and tacked easily.[47]

The subsequent career of the *San Jacinto* was anticlimactic to the stir created in her first years. H. H. Bell, who commanded her for nearly three years, reported in 1861 that she was "always defective in propeller and shaft, is slow, and . . . has a battery of the lightest class of VIII inch shell guns (55 cwt.)" and that she was "a very inefficient vessel . . . as a cruiser or for bombardment."[48]

Her Civil War notoriety was as the vessel that halted the British steamer *Trent* with the Confederate commissioners Mason and Slidell on board. She was Charles Wilkes's flagship for his "flying squadron" in the West Indies and was lost on No Name Key in the Bahamas in 1865.

In sum, the tally for the four vessels authorized in 1847 seems straightforward: three successes and one lame duck. A counterpoint, however, can be found in a letter from B. F. Isherwood to the chief of the Bureau of Construction and Repair, Shubrick, in 1852. First Isherwood criticized the hull designs: "Now nothing in Naval Architecture is better understood than that a totally different model is required for a screw propeller to what is required for a paddle wheel." He then dismissed their copper boilers as more expensive and excessively soft. He considered the size of the engines to be excessive, citing 49 feet of space needed for those of the *Susquehanna,* whereas the side-lever installations of the Collins line's *Arctic* and *Baltic* required 36 feet (36 percent more space than engines of twice the cylinder size). Finally, Isherwood reminded Shubrick that the *Princeton* had been a "signal success," and with her machinery well below the waterline, she was "as perfect a war steamer as could be a model of her size." He therefore characterized the use of paddle wheels for three of these vessels as a "retrograde" step. He concluded: "The government has expended in round numbers on the three . . . $2,000,000 and has obtained in exchange three very good first class towboats." On the *San Jacinto,* which he had earlier termed a "monument of Mr. Haswell's incompetence and folly," Isherwood added comments about her "absurdly contrived machinery" and "injudiciously modeled hull." He concluded, however, that she was a "good war steamer" and a good sailing vessel, because of her underwater screw propulsion.[49]

The replacement of Charles Haswell in connection with the engines of the *San Jacinto* raises another point concerning the early years of steam in the navy: steam engineering was an uncertain career in this era. Shifting and uncertain technology made technical competence a very insecure basis on which to build a reputation, and the nonexistence of technical schools or standards organizations resulted in the rise of individuals in the profession on the basis of self-proclaimed expertise, self-promotion, and, not uncommonly, political pull. "Every man his own engineer" would apply for many years in the field of steam engineering and bring predictably uncertain results in the machinery of U.S. naval ships.

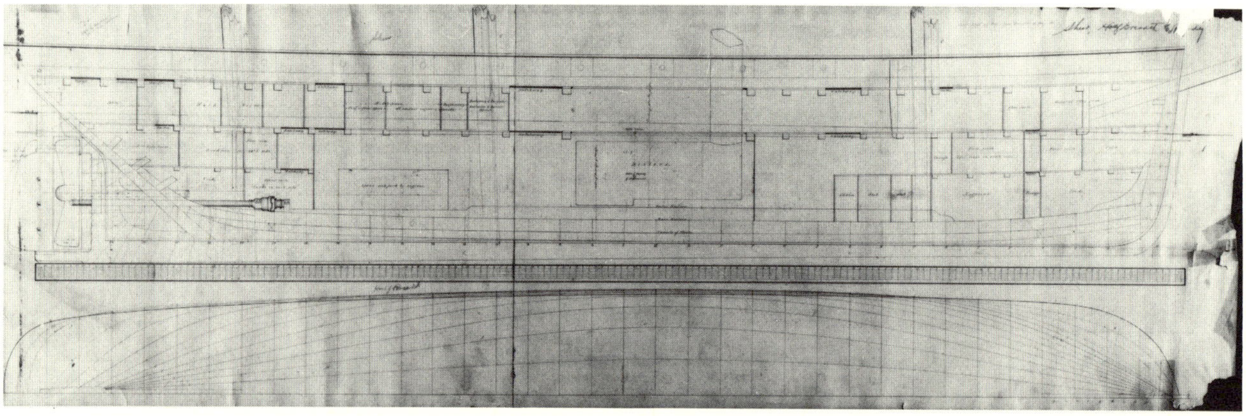

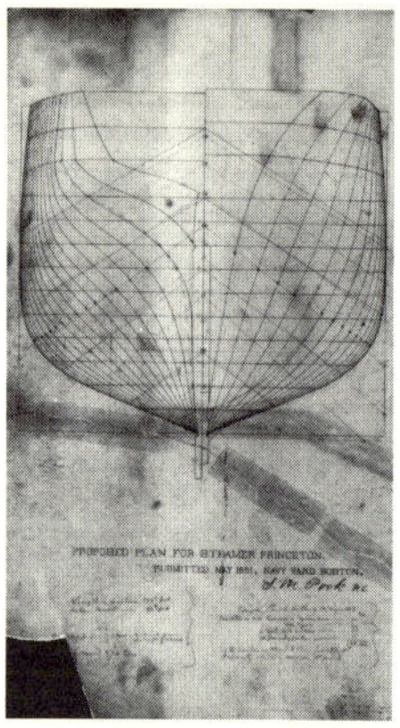

Inboard and Lines of the Second Princeton, *Designed by S. M. Pook. He was noted for his fast vessels. (NARS 40-8-9C, National Archives)*

THE REBUILT SHIPS

The post–Mexican War era brought back the budgetary constraints traditional for the American armed services. The navy, however, was not without stratagems to circumvent these cuts. The "administratively rebuilt" ship was one method of obtaining a new vessel without irritating a sleeping Congress for construction appropriations.

The method was simple: dismantle a worn-out vessel completely, then "rebuild" it with new materials, with or without the former dimensions and rate. This could be a lengthy process, though, because funds were from the annual repair budgets. The name of the vessel remained, and possibly some of the older ship's timbers or fittings, but in essence an entirely new vessel was the result. The process was repeated many times in the era of wooden ships when the building material was easy to modify.[50]

Before the congressionally authorized vessels of 1854, two new vessels emerged from old ships, and a third received a massive overhaul. Yet another was taken in hand but would not emerge complete for another ten years.

Princeton II

The first of the new vessels, the second *Princeton,* incorporated Ericsson's engine, which was in good order, only substituting the Sickles cut-off.[51] (The cut-off mechanism regulated the point in the stroke of the piston at which the supply of steam would be cut off—a subject that later became the source of much controversy.) Three boilers on the English Lamb and Sumner patent were installed, known as "sheet water space" boilers, in which vertical rectangular "envelopes" were used in place of tubes or flues. The supposed advantages of these boilers were in their compact size, compared to their grate surface, and their expected greater economy.[52]

The hull of the vessel was for the most part new material (a survey of the original hull had reported four-fifths of her timbers rotten and all of her planking) and was 177 feet in length by 32 feet (the original was 156 feet by 30 feet). She was designed by Samuel M. Pook, who was responsible for the sailing sloops *Saratoga* and *Plymouth,* the latter considered by some the finest such vessel in any navy. The *Princeton*'s hull was referred to as "clipper built" by Stuart, and the plans indeed show such lines: a sharp, long entrance and fine run, with much deadrise. Her deadrise was similar to that of the vessels of the British navy designed by William Symonds, which were noted for their sailing qualities rather than their steadiness as gun platforms.[53]

The *Princeton* was built of live oak and displaced 1,385 tons at a mean draft of 19 feet 2 inches. She was ship-rigged and spread 13,282 square feet of sail, exclusive of royals.[54] Her armament was four 8-inch guns and six 32-pounders. Pivot rails were emplaced fore and aft.[55]

The new *Princeton* was launched on 29 October 1851 and departed in November 1852 for the Japan expedition. The 150-mile passage from Annapolis to Norfolk revealed that the boilers were "absolute and unequivocal failures" and that "incessant effort was used without effect to keep steam up." In fifteen minutes pressure dropped from twenty-five pounds to eight.[56] Her place with the Japan expedition was taken by the *Powhatan*. Commodore Perry, not one to be trifled with, had postponed his departure nearly a year awaiting the promised vessel. He was not pleased and later referred to the errant vessel as an "abortion" and a "miserable" failure.[57]

Inevitably there was an investigation but with much more to feed upon than the *Princeton*'s boilers. The *Allegheny* and *San Jacinto* fiascoes had occurred nearly simultaneously, certifying that there was enough blame to spread around evenly and widely.

Both the *Allegheny* (now with screw propulsion) and the *Princeton* suffered the same boiler problem, which was corrected to some extent by replacing in both vessels "sheet water" spaces with standard tubes. The investigators' report laid the blame for the failure on Charles Stuart, who had recommended the "experimental" boilers, and on unknown parties who had "departed from in a very extraordinary degree" the "approved arrangements" for these boilers. A hint of impropriety leavened the blame-seeking: the American patentee (who received 45 cents per foot of heating surface, on a total of ten boilers used in various naval vessels) was William Sewell, Jr., "late chief engineer in the navy."[58]

With restructured boilers, the *Princeton* went to sea in September 1853. Her performance was not outstanding, with speeds ranging from 8.6 knots under steam and sail, down to 4.7 knots, with a mean of 6.68. She was considered less efficient than her forebear, but this was blamed in part on leaking cylinder packings. Her Sickel's cut-off mechanism was also considered an "injudicious" addition to the engine, because it did not allow sufficient adjustment. Furthermore, the vessel's coal consumption attained a mean of 2,009 pounds per hour, which compared poorly to the original vessel's 1,226-pound consumption.[59]

The Water Witch, *Far Different from Her Hunter's Wheel Origins—a Completely New Vessel. The light color may be wartime gray or the cream color used in the South American squadron. (Courtesy Peabody Museum)*

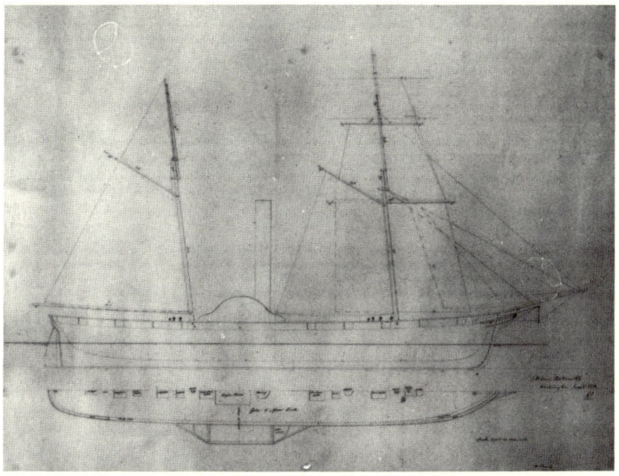

Sail and Deck Plan of the Water Witch. *(NARS 108-11-8G, National Archives)*

The vessel was used on the North Atlantic and the Gulf of Mexico for two years, then was laid up, later becoming a receiving ship in Philadelphia. She was broken up in 1866.

Captain Stockton agreed that she was, in her second life, "an abortion in the service," though, according to Bennett, he had long suspected "his" ship had been badly treated by those in the department who were jealous of his championship of steam propulsion. Stockton's insistence and influence were the sole reasons the *Princeton* was rebuilt, asserted Bennett, giving further cause for resistance to the vessel on the part of many line officers.[60]

Water Witch II

In contrast to the *Princeton,* the second "rebuilt" vessel, the *Water Witch,* benefited from her transformation. The earlier patchwork conversion of the Hunter's wheel vessel had outlasted her Mexican War service but had broken down in 1851.

The new wooden *Water Witch* measured 150 feet by 22 feet with a displacement of 450 tons at 7 feet 10 inches draft. She was rigged as a topsail schooner and lightly armed; during the war she mounted one 30-pounder rifle and three 12-pounders.

She was a paddle-wheel ship, with a single cylinder of 36-inch stroke and diameter of 37½ inches. Two Lamb and Sumner–pattern boilers supplied her steam.[61] This kind of boiler was apparently satisfactory on a smaller scale.

For the first time in a U.S. naval vessel, feathering paddle wheels were used. Designed by B. F. Isherwood, these incorporated eccentrics and levers to cause the paddles to enter the water perpendicularly rather than at the angle of the radius of the wheel.[62] This more efficient design had seen service in Europe and can still be seen there today.

The Strictly Conventional Paddle-Wheel Steamer Fulton II *of the 1850s. The only known photograph of the vessel shows her nearly down to her frame, rebuilding at Pensacola early in the Civil War. (Engraving from* Gleason's Pictorial*)*

The *Water Witch* showed commendable early performance. Even when in poor trim, she ran 8.7 knots, using 631 tons of coal per hour. No problems were noted with her water space boilers, although these were considerably smaller than those of the *Princeton*.[63]

She was a useful vessel, especially in service in shallow South American rivers. While surveying the Río de la Plata in 1855, she was fired upon, resulting in an American punitive expedition against Paraguay. During the Civil War she saw duty on the Atlantic, until she was captured in June 1864 by the Confederates. She was burned to prevent her recapture in December 1864, near Savannah, Georgia.[64]

Fulton II

The third vessel recast in a new form was the old *Fulton II,* which had been laid up since 1842, still encumbered with her massive and ill-placed bulwarks. As with the *Water Witch,* this reconstruction salvaged a previously hopeless vessel.

In this rebuild the ship retained the earlier hull, though Charles Stuart had again recommended she be lengthened. The old bulwarks were cut down and she was given a conventional sheer, knee-bow, and a topsail schooner rig. More than 90 tons were removed in eliminating the bulwarks.[65] New machinery of the single-cylinder, inclined variety was installed, with a 50-inch bore and 10-foot, 4-inch stroke. Two iron boilers replaced the original copper units.[66]

The renovated vessel, armed with a 64-pounder pivot forward and four 32s in broadside, went into service early in 1852 and immediately reestablished a reputation for speed. On trials she averaged 13.34 miles per hour under steam and (supposedly) reached 20 miles per hour. The latter figure was promulgated by Charles Stuart, who also supervised her construction. Statistics included in a congressional report are more likely to be accurate: a maximum of 11.75 knots under steam and sail and 10.5 under steam alone. Though she was still uneconomical, burning over 1,800 pounds of coal per hour, she performed useful service as part of the Home Squadron, until running aground in 1859 near Pensacola.[67]

Even then, her hull remained solid enough to warrant rebuilding, and the work was in progress when the yard was captured early in the war. Her captors continued the reconstruction but were forced to burn the vessel on the stocks to prevent her recapture by federal troops in May 1862.[68]

CONVERSION OF SAILING SHIPS

The idea of converting existing sailing vessels to steam ("mixed") propulsion first surfaced in the records of the Navy Department in 1840. This was a proposal to add an engine to the frigate *Raritan.*

The engine, propeller, and rudder arrangement were by Robert F. Stockton, and, though no plans or specific descriptions remain, it was to have a screw propeller similar to that of the *Princeton.* A letter to the board notes that the proposal was rejected because there had been "no known experiments" with such an engine and propeller, and that the after part of the ship would be injured. Furthermore, the report continued, the action of the propeller would unfavorably affect the rudder, and weakness would result from the propeller and rudder being attached to the sternpost. The board was, however, impressed by the low position of the engines and propeller.[69]

The next such scheme, had it come to fruition, would have been virtually sacrilegious: converting the frigate *Constitution* to a paddle vessel. The entire cost for the project, dated 22 July 1845, was to be $135,500. Records do not indicate why this plan was shelved, but it would not be difficult to surmise the reactions to it among the sailing officers.[70]

The overall concept of converting or adding steam power to sailing vessels remained and was encouraged by the success of the screw propeller and the British policy of converting their line-of-battle ships to auxiliary screw vessels in the late 1840s. In 1851, Francis Grice presented a plan for converting frigates to screw propulsion, but the plan was rejected because of the need to increase the length of these vessels to support the engines and coal spaces. Another plan to convert the *Constellation* to steam was called uneconomical because an entirely new vessel would have been less expensive.[71]

The American navy did not follow the example of the British (or the French) for several reasons. First, the conversion of frigates was overly expensive and involved extensive lengthening of the hulls. Second, the few ships-of-the-line in the inventory had been found to be excessively expensive to operate and had been replaced on station by frigates. Consequently, there was little need to convert these vessels to steam. Finally, there was much resistance on the part of the sailing navy leadership to weakening the hulls of perfectly good sailing frigates by adding screw propellers to their sterns.[72]

The conversion of the ship-of-the-line *Franklin* is sometimes considered the single pre–Civil War instance in which an existing sailing ship was reconstructed as a steam vessel. This rebuilding, however, was yet another instance of the replacing of an old ship by an entirely new one. Moreover, when considered solely as an isolated example of massive rebuilding, the significance of the vessel is vastly underestimated, as will be seen in the next chapter.

The conversion of the old battleships to steam was considered anew in 1860, when a committee surveyed the existing liners and made recommendations according to their condition and suitability for conversion. The committee concluded that lengthening these ships to retain them as steam ships-of-the-line would be injudicious and the resulting vessels would be "very expensive to maintain in commission." The proposed alternative was to razee the vessels and thus reduce their rate. (The counters of the vessels would have been extended to accommodate the additional rudder posts.)

The huge *Pennsylvania,* which required new planking in any case, would have been capable of carrying a battery of 9-inch Dahlgrens equal to that of the *Wabash*-class frigates, and the *North Carolina* and *Ohio* would mount some ten fewer guns each. Seventy-fours such as the *Alabama* and *New York,* which would retain their original ports, would receive 40-gun batteries composed of 32-pounders and 8-inch shell guns. Finally, the *Columbus,* of slightly smaller displacement than the others, would have become a sloop, mounting fewer than 35 guns. The committee strongly advocated such conversions in view of the relatively modest cost (approximately $383,000) of the modification compared to that of constructing new steam frigates ($725,000 each). The National Archives contains a hold plan of the "steam frigate" *Ohio,* no doubt done as part of this study, but the outbreak of the war prevented the implementation of these recommendations, particularly when it was found that the vital need was for shallow-draft vessels. Furthermore, the conflagration at Norfolk destroyed four of the nine liners in question.[73]

Pilcomayo

In 1852, Daniel Ammen, an officer on the Paraguayan survey expedition, was ordered to build a small flat-floored steamboat. Using native boat-carpenters, he soon had a vessel of 65 feet by 14 feet, with a draft of 8 inches, powered by a two-cylinder high-pressure engine (6 inches by 18 inches) with two locomotive boilers, and 12-foot paddle wheels. The hull was apparently rectangular with one deck, the sides for the deck house were cedar, and the roof was canvas. It was used successfully, though its boilers were never considered particularly satisfactory, according to Ammen, in his memoirs.[74] The vessel was considered an auxiliary to the *Water Witch* and was quite an attraction in the small villages of the Paraguayan interior. She was possibly the only "foreign built" vessel constructed for the navy in this era.

The Minnesota *with Smokepipe Extended. (Naval Historical Center)*

CHAPTER 4

The Steam Frigates of 1854

Possibly the single most significant date in the development of the United States steam navy was 6 April 1854. On that day, Congress authorized the building of six first-class steam frigates "to be provided with screw propellers." This marked the end of the era of the paddle wheel for major warships. As Secretary of the Navy J. C. Dobbin phrased it, steam power could then be reserved "for emergencies when the greatest speed is required, or when, in a calm, a desirable position can . . . be taken." Thus the screw propeller had supplanted the paddle wheel and the era of the auxiliary screw steamer had arrived.[1]

Ironically, the adoption of the screw actually extended the life of the sailing navy. The arguments set forth by Secretary Dobbin against the paddle system were three: vulnerability in combat, poor economy, and objectionable sailing qualities. Setting aside the issue of vulnerability, the lack of economy can be in part blamed on the navy's insistence on full-sail rig. The *Mississippi* has been given as an example in which a reduced rig was recommended, to remove excess weight as well as to decrease her resistance to headwinds. (That vessel's rig weighed just short of 100 tons.)[2] Nevertheless, eventually the screw would have triumphed, though screw vessels were also hampered for decades by increasingly unnecessary sailing paraphernalia.

The building of these six vessels marked a second major departure for the navy: the adoption of the large-caliber shell gun for the entire broadside and pivot battery of the ships. The shell gun was not an innovation in itself, the first having been introduced in the United States in 1841. By 1843, 8- and 10-inch Paixhan guns were in the inventory, used as fore and aft pivots.[3] The standard broadside gun remained the 32-pounder.

In 1850, John A. Dahlgren designed a shell gun intended to throw shot as well as shell and to do so with greater range and accuracy than the earlier weapons. By 1854, 9-, 10-, and 11-inch versions of Dahlgren's system had been successfully tested. The most significant outcome was the increased weight of broadside possible: the 9-inch shell weighed 72.5 pounds; the 11-inch, 136 pounds. The weight of the gun also increased considerably, with the 9-inch tube at 9,000 pounds and the 11-inch at 15,700 pounds, compared to the typical 32-pounder, which at most weighed 6,400 pounds for a 57-hundredweight gun. The small 32-pound weapon weighed 3,000 pounds. The new frigates were to carry complete broadsides of 9-inch shell guns, thus nearly tripling the weight of projectiles fired over that of an equal number of 32-pounders. Of course, the larger size of the Dahlgren guns, as well as their weight, would dictate design factors for the new frigates.[4]

Five of the six ships were frigates, with similar dimensions and armament: the *Colorado, Roanoke, Merrimack, Minnesota,* and *Wabash.* The *Colorado* and *Roanoke* were built at Norfolk, the *Merrimack* at Boston, the *Minnesota* at Washington, and the *Wabash* at Philadelphia. The sixth, the *Niagara,* though larger, was a sloop, according to her armament arrangement. She was designed and built by a civilian contractor at New York.

Merrimack-Class Frigates: *Merrimack, Colorado, Roanoke, Wabash,* and *Minnesota*

The five sister frigates' similarity of design, as well as their hulls' resemblance to sailing ship lines, has been attributed to outmoded and conservative thinking among the naval constructors. Much of the hull design, however, was imposed by their superior, Secretary Dobbin, for economic reasons. In June 1854, Dobbin wrote the constructors reminding them of the verbal instructions given immediately after the congressional act. The frigates were to be "from the live oak frames of frigates which have been cut for ships of the length of 179 feet with a moulded beam of 45 feet, that the whole of the oak frames be used and the additional quantity . . . made from promiscuous timber." Consequently, the basic hull was to be on the lines of the *Congress*-class frigates of 1839.

Dobbin's instructions to the constructors of these vessels called for "not less than 15 ports on the gun deck," and a "corresponding number . . . on the spar deck," with pivots fore and aft, clearing fore and mizzen masts. (The *Congress* carried 15 ports other than bridle ports.) Ports were to be "14 2/12" feet from center to center, an increase of some three feet over port spacing for conventional broadside guns. The frigates were to carry five months' provisions and draw 23 feet. The machinery was to not exceed 380 tons, plus 500 tons of coal, and take up "55 to 60 feet" of the hold. Finally, the spars were to be "the same as the present frigates of the first class" with "lower masts the same height as those ships," and carry 21,000 square feet of canvas.[5]

The completed design for these five vessels, however, was in existence before both the congressional directive and Secretary Dobbin's instructions to the constructors. In August 1853, a committee of constructors and engineers submitted a plan for a "substitute" for the old 74-gun ship *Franklin*. This was to be a "frigate-built ship of war . . . [with] . . . in addition to her sails, an auxiliary steam power." She was to have the Dahlgren shell guns, mounting twenty-eight 9-inch weapons on the gun deck and twenty of the older design 8-inch shell guns on the spar deck, in addition to three pivot guns. She was to attain seven knots with auxiliary power and have a hoisting screw.[6]

John Lenthall's plans for the vessel's lines were completed in February 1854. The hull was to be 265 feet by 53 feet with a 27-foot 2-inch depth of hold. (These dimensions bore no relation to those of the original ship, which was 187 feet between perpendiculars by 50 feet.) When it was suggested that more hull length was required for machinery, Lenthall wrote that she was already 36 feet longer than the British 90-gun screw vessels and 54 feet beyond their screw frigates. Secretary Dobbin limited her engine and coal space to 70 feet, though by the time engines were ordered the length alloted to machinery had increased.[7] The *Franklin* remained under construction until 1867 and will be examined at the close of the chapter.

At this point the plans for two of the five congressionally authorized vessels should be considered. The *Roanoke* and *Colorado* each measured 262 feet 10½ inches by 51 feet 4 inches with a depth of hold of 26 feet 2½ inches. While the similarity in dimensions is noteworthy, the resemblance in hull lines is remarkable and therefore the relationship between the *Franklin* and these two frigates of 1854 is undeniable. Taking into account the small disparity in dimensions, one can virtually trace the lines of the *Franklin* over those of the new pair.

The *Franklin*'s resemblance to the hull lines of the other three frigates is less marked. All three had more deadrise and were fuller in their waterlines fore and aft. Dimensionally, the *Merrimack* was the smallest, at 256 feet 10½ inches by 50 feet 2 inches; and the *Minnesota*, at 264 feet 8½ inches,

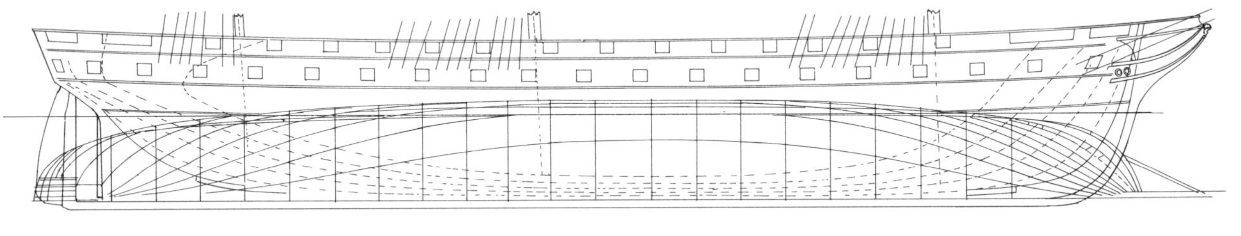

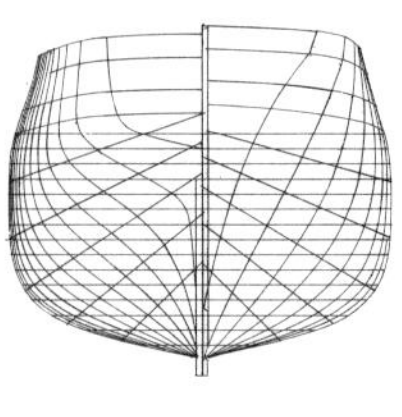

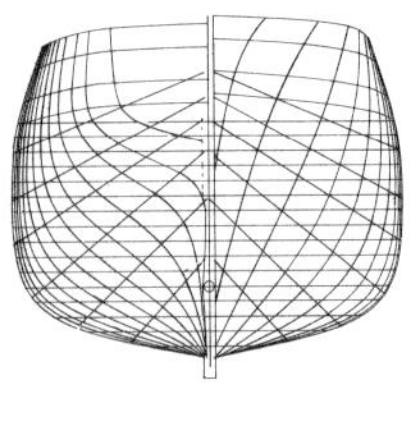

Top and Left: Sheer, Half-breadth and Body Plans of the Roanoke *and* Colorado, *Traced from a Plan Dated July 1854. To Right, Body Plan of the* Franklin, *February 1854. The similarities of these plans indicate the* Franklin, *though completed over ten years later, was the prototype of the* Merrimack *and class. (NARS 107-10-13A, 53-12-2, National Archives)*

Lithograph of the Inboard Plan of the Merrimack, *D. Van Nostrand Company, 1857. Note the propeller well and provision for hoisting. (National Archives)*

the longest of the five. The beams of the *Wabash* and *Minnesota* were identical to that of the *Merrimack.* As with the *Franklin,* however, the design for all five was credited to John Lenthall, and this final factor secures the fact that the plan of the *Franklin* was the prototype for the five government-built frigates of 1854.

These dimensions and plans are all of early dates (the *Merrimack*'s lines are the oldest for the five vessels, dated June 1854), and therefore there exists the possibility that some variations may have been introduced in the actual building of the ships. For the purpose of illustrating the relationship of the *Franklin* to the other five ships, however, the earliest plans are obviously more pertinent than lines of a later date.

Despite the date and origin of the design of these frigates, Isherwood stated that the old frame timbers were the "only material available" and were "thoroughly" used, to the extent that "the whole of these valuable frames, without waste" was worked into the construction of the five frigates. Isherwood used the phase "worked into" advisedly, because the existing frame timbers were for significantly narrower vessels. The same sort of timber use must also have gone into the *Franklin,* because congressional appropriations were never designated for that vessel.)[8]

The frigates' structural strength was imparted in part by two sets of diagonal iron braces set into the inside of the timbers, running from the turn of the bilge to the spar deck clamps. The stem and stern were likewise supported by braces to the outside of the timbers. There were three straps, 5 inches by ⅝ inches, on each side of the stern to bind the deadwood below the shaft to the frame timbers above it. The floor timbers, each 14 inches by 17 inches at the keel, spaced approximately 20 inches between centers, were filled from stem to stern to the turn of the bilge. The deadwood at the propeller shaft was 20 feet of solid oak.[9]

Three types of engines were incorporated in the vessels, all with equal area and stroke of piston but differing in arrangements and types of cylinders. One engine was to be an Ericsson "vibrating shaft" engine, probably for the *Merrimack,* but this did not materialize. The *Merrimack*'s two horizontal cylinders were back-acting, with two piston rods driving each crosshead, which in turn drove a connecting rod to the shaft, the latter being placed between the upper and lower piston rods. The cylinders were 72 inches in diameter, with a stroke of 36 inches, and were located on each side of the keel on opposite corners of the cast-iron bed plate. Simple jet condensers were used, which sprayed cold water into the exhaust steam to reduce it to water for boiler feed.[10]

The *Wabash*'s machinery was unique to the navy: a horizontal steeple engine. In this design, a sliding triangular yoke transferred the power from a single piston rod to two connecting rods, the latter working back to the shaft, which rotated within the yoke or harp itself. The engines weighed over 420,000 pounds, of which more than 212,000 pounds was cast iron.[11]

The other three vessels were powered by a version of the trunk engine much used in British line-of-battle ships. The trunk was a method of saving the precious athwartship space. In this case the connecting rod ran from the crankshaft into a tubular piston rod. This piston rod, rather than connecting to the top of a solid circular piston, ran through the piston, the piston then resembling a large collar surrounding the tube. Thus both the tube and piston reciprocated within the cylinder, and the entire assembly pushed and pulled the connecting rod and shaft. These cylinders were 79½ inches in diameter, but their area equalled that of the 72-inch conventional cylinders of the other frigates, and the stroke was the same 36 inches. The characteristic defect of trunk engines was the tendency of the packings around the large tubular rod to leak where it moved through the cylinder head.[12]

The propellers of all the frigates were 17 feet 4 inches in diameter, with two blades, though that of the *Merrimack* was of a different pattern. A mechanism was provided to allow hoisting the propeller when under sail. The screw hub was slotted to accept the shaft, and the propeller was contained in a yoke or frame; the whole screw and yoke assembly was raised by capstan and gearing.[13]

Each frigate had four Martin's vertical water-tube boilers and an 8-foot diameter smokepipe. The latter could be lowered to rail level to provide clearance for use of the main sail.[14]

The frigates were rigged identically, with 28,008 square feet of canvas in the ten principal sails, which included jib and topgallants. Incorporating all sail—including royals, studding sails, and storm sails—the total measured 48,757 square feet. The minimum figure for the ten principal sails exceeds Secretary Dobbin's total considerably, just as the ships exceeded his other original specifications. Only the dimensions of the lower masts of the steam frigates approximated those of the *Congress* class of 1839. The mainmast measured 106 feet 5 inches and from deck to truck was an impressive 222 feet 2 inches. The main yard was 110 feet 4 inches and its sail covered 5,100 square feet.[15] Those who are impressed by figures should consider the possible weight and area of such a vast piece of canvas, 50 feet long and 100 feet wide—larger than the square footage of a large suburban home.

The foremast was stepped on the keelson, the usual practice. The mainmast on these ships was over the shaft, however, and therefore was stepped on a live-oak beam 10 feet from the floor, measuring 3 feet wide by 15 inches. This in turn was supported by 10-inch diameter iron columns. The mizzen was stepped on the orlop deck.[16]

The original battery of the *Merrimack* was forty guns, but she could accommodate sixty. On the main deck were twenty-four 9-inch shell guns; on the spar deck were fourteen 8-inch guns in broadside with two 10-inch pivot guns, fore and aft. In wartime, the two heaviest batteries were on the *Colorado,* which listed forty-six 9-inchers, one 150-pounder Parrott, and one 11-inch Dahlgren (1865); and the *Minnesota,* with forty-two 9-inchers, four 100-pounder rifles, one 150-pounder, and one 11-inch shell gun (October 1863).[17]

Once in service, these ships, along with the larger *Niagara,* created more public interest than any U.S. naval vessels since the *Constitution* and her sister ships of 1797. Contemporary discussions of the frigates usually began with their great size, then moved to their innovative batteries. Once the dry facts and statistics, or distortions thereof, were aired, the character of their engines was brought into question. At this point, comparisons with the British would arise, and rational thought would be supplanted by an updated version of the earlier scenario of "the upstart Yankee tweaking John Bull's nose with their two-deckers disguised as frigates"—a discussion entirely appropriate for these ships but with a less than complimentary outcome for the new American attempts to emulate "Old Ironsides" in steam.

The controversy began, unfortunately, with the appearance of the *Merrimack,* commissioned in December 1855. The first of the vessels to be completed, she spent several months on the Atlantic coast, then visited England in the fall of 1856.

In her early trials, the usual exaggerated claims were made: greatest speed of 9½ knots under steam alone—exiting Boston Harbor with fair wind and slack tide. Against the wind the claim declined to 7½ knots. A published abstract of her steam log for the cruise cited above belies these figures, indicating the maximum she attained under steam was 6.1 knots. With sail assistance, she reached 10.5 knots with a strong quartering breeze. Under steam alone she would reach 8.8 knots, but the mean figure was 5.2. With sails, her

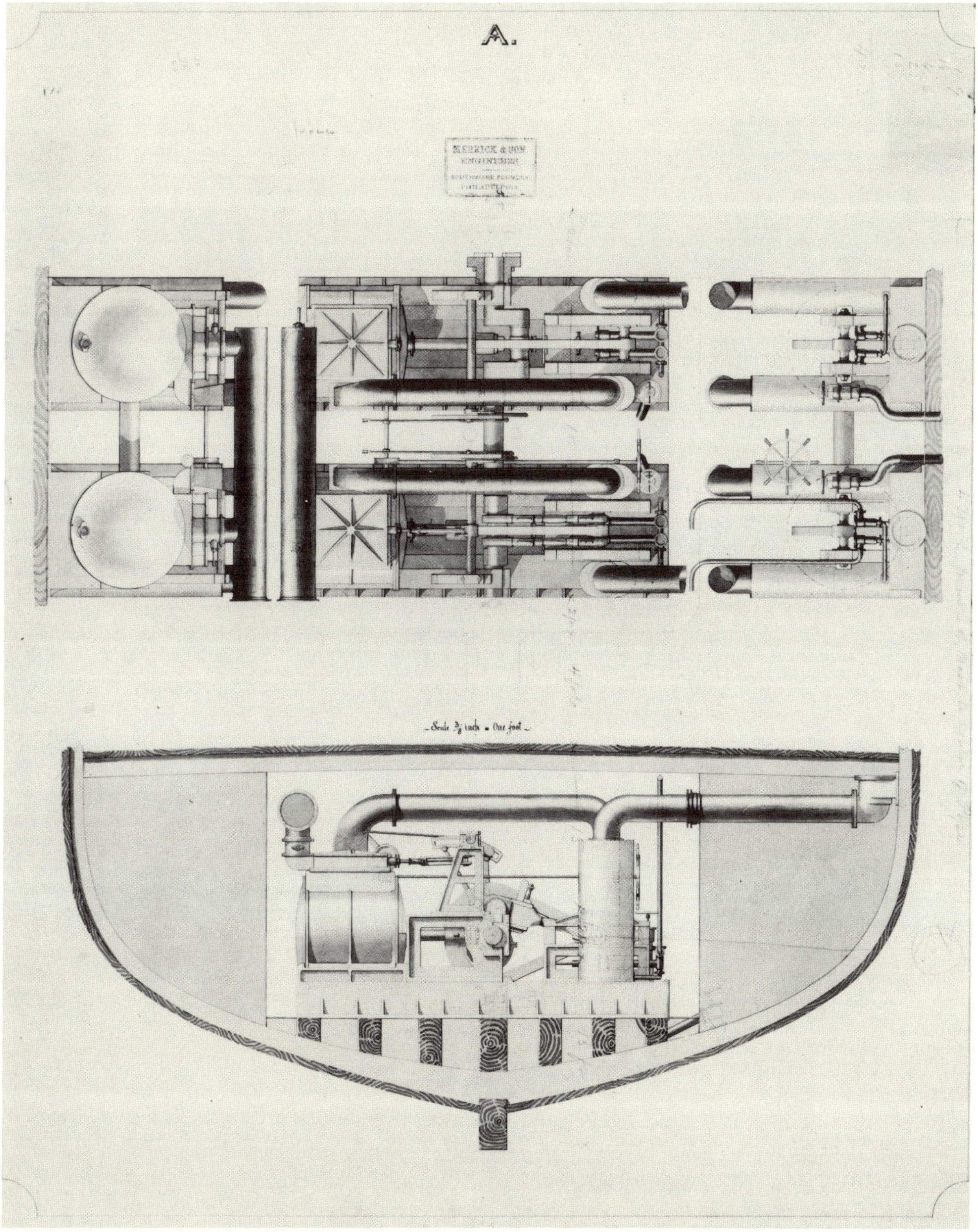

Horizontal Steeple Engines of the Wabash. *The cylinders are on the left, with piston rods connected to the large end of the triangular "harp"; the connecting rod is between the small end of the harp and the propeller shaft. The harp slides on a horizontal bed. The condensers are on the right of the lower drawing. The upper left drawing is a side view of the cylinders; the upper right is a side view showing the ends of the harps. The horizontal steeple engine is one type of back-acting engine. (NARS BSE plan, National Archives)*

mean speed was 7.6 knots. These figures covered 1,900 hours of steaming, from February 1856 to February 1860. The slip of her screw ranged as high as 73 percent, but with a mean of 38 percent; fuel consumption was approximately 3,400 pounds of anthracite per hour.[18]

Her trial passage from Norfolk to Havana set a poor precedent: she broke her propeller four days out and made Havana in twenty-four days under sail alone. Her next port was Key West, where she arrived with rudder unhung, towed by four boats. From thence she was hauled by the *Susquehanna* to Boston "in a disabled condition."[19] The propeller malfunction was due to the wearing down of the brass bearings and bushings of the shaft. These were replaced, following a British example, by lignum vitae bearings, rectifying the problem.[20]

A lengthy public debate ensued on the "failure" of the *Merrimack.* A series of articles and letters appeared in *The U.S. Nautical Magazine and Naval Journal,* a publication that was not loath to criticize the navy for its perceived failure to keep pace with developments in the merchant service. Among the many criticisms of this vessel were three that struck home. First, her draft was excessive and, indeed, was beyond the 23-foot limit set by Secretary Dobbin. Even as originally armed with 40 guns, the *Merrimack* drew 23 feet 9 inches, which was sufficient to prevent her operating from "nine-tenths of the harbors of the nation's entire sea-coast." Of course this would prove more serious when war came: most of those shallow harbors were in the seceded states.[21]

The second criticism was of her lack of speed. In this instance, the fault was found in the nautical magazine's editorial opinion that the navy had been "humbugged" into accepting the "hermaphrodite" idea of auxiliary steam propulsion—desiring "full power" be applied to naval vessels for pursuit and capture of "one of Collin's [*sic*] or Cunard's steamers."[22]

A third defect noted was in the model of the hull. Her reported heavy rolling was blamed on the great deadrise and high center of gravity of the vessel. By the 1850s extreme deadrise was being discarded in favor of flat floors on merchant vessels, but Lenthall chose not to follow this example.[23]

Compared to this embarrassment at home, the *Merrimack*'s reception in England in October 1856 was a triumph. On the opposite side of the Atlantic, she was a cudgel to wield at the British government. In this case, her positive qualities were emphasized to point up deficiencies in policies of the Royal Navy. *The Engineer,* a British publication, described her armament as "of the heaviest and most terrific description." Her length and "transept bracing" were pointed out as well as her ease of management compared to "our three deckers." The piece concluded, "The practice of a nation so shrewd, go-ahead and brave . . . ought not to be despised."[24]

Before her arrival, the *Merrimack* had been mentioned in the House of Commons by Sir Charles Wood, First Lord of the Admiralty, who lamented the Royal Navy's lack of vessels "of that description" (mentioning the *Niagara* also). Their existence was seen as sufficient rationale for ordering "one or two of this description built."[25]

In fact, two classes of screw frigates, a total of eleven vessels, were begun from 1855 to 1859, all of which had broadside batteries of 8- and 10-inch shell guns. Two others, the *Euryalus* and *Shannon,* were completed with such batteries in this period. The similarity of all these to the *Merrimack* class was emphasized by their dimensions, ranging from 240 feet for the *Diadem* to 336 feet for the *Mersey* and *Orlando.* The five vessels of the *Immortalité* class measured approximately 250 feet between perpendiculars. The latter ships carried thirty 8-inch shell guns, twenty 32-pounder smoothbores, and one 68-pounder. The *Orlando* and *Mersey* had main batteries of twenty-eight 10-inch shell guns.[26]

The key shortcoming of the *Merrimack* in British eyes was also her lack of speed, compared to that of some of the newest frigates, as well as many of her line-of-battle ships. Some of the latter steamed in excess of nine knots. Thus the destructive power of the American frigate meant a great deal less if she could not escape a larger foe.[27]

The *Merrimack* was on the Pacific station until 1860 and returned to Norfolk for extensive machinery repairs. Though her early career was relatively unmarred by engine failure, she became increasingly unsatisfactory, and her engineers reported many "efforts to overcome inherent defects of design."[28]

At the onset of the Civil War, she was still under repair and the department sent B. F. Isherwood to expedite sufficient measures to get steam up and remove her before the Confederate forces took the yard. Isherwood found the machinery in "a wretched state" but had her ready to fire up in three-days time. The yard commandant, despite the preemptory nature of the orders to save the vessel (the most valuable warship in the yard) temporized, reasoning that the ship's battery might be used to protect the yard. The decision was made to scuttle her and fire the yard. As the burning vessel settled to the bottom, the *Pawnee* arrived and succeeded in towing one vessel from the conflagration, the *Germantown.* The story of the armored incarnation of the steam frigate as the Confederate *Virginia* is beyond this book, but her machinery remained as unreliable for the Rebels as it had been for the Union.[29]

The *Colorado* and *Roanoke,* with identical engines and hulls, attained overall, under steam and sail

Wabash *Fit for Inspection, as a Receiving Ship at Boston after 1875. (Naval Historical Center)*

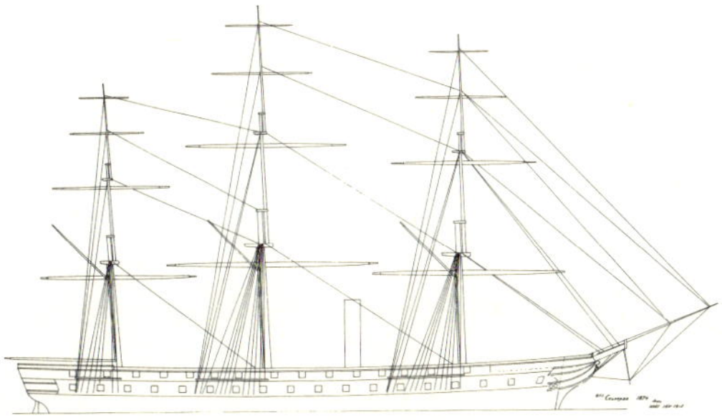

Plan of the Colorado, *1874. (Drawn by author from NARS 152-14-1, National Archives)*

combined, 6.3 and 6.4 knots respectively, slightly better than the *Merrimack*'s 6.2 knots. Compared to the *Merrimack*'s average figure of 5.2 knots for steam alone, the *Colorado* made 5.5; the *Roanoke,* 5.7 knots. The maximum that could be maintained under steam alone (in smooth water and calm conditions) was 8.8 knots for the *Roanoke* as well as the *Merrimack.* The *Merrimack* and *Colorado* burned similar amounts of coal (2,775 versus 2,678 pounds), while the *Roanoke* was less economical, burning a mean of 2,957 pounds. The Norfolk-built vessels recorded about 10 percent less screw slip than the *Merrimack*'s.[30]

In 1861 an unidentified engineer on the *Roanoke* commented in a letter on the wide disparity between the speeds of the vessel in smooth water versus its poor performance in adverse conditions. She was credited with 7½ knots in good weather, but with headwinds of about force 3, the speed dropped to 3.55 knots. He blamed this on the "very small power of the engines compared with the tonnage of the ship." Similarly, in an official report in 1864, the *Colorado* was reported to struggle at 2 to 4 knots in a seaway but yield 6½ maximum under steam.[31]

The latter report gave sketchy details of other aspects of the *Colorado*'s performance. She worked under sail "slowly" but could attain 10 to 13 knots. Her rolling was described as "easy," and she was probably stiffer than the three other frigates because of her fuller midsection. Her performance in a gale was succinctly described as "good." Later in the war she ran from New York to Fayal in 12½ days under sail alone, averaging 11.4 knots on her best day, with wind "about a point free" and moderate enough to carry royals.[32]

The *Wabash* and *Minnesota* were the best of the lot, the *Wabash* having the largest gross effective horsepower of all the frigates (1,038). The *Merrimack* was listed at 972; the *Roanoke,* 996. The *Minnesota* developed 995 horsepower.[33] The maximum speed in smooth water, under steam for the *Minnesota* was 8.9 knots; the *Wabash,* 9.1. The *Minnesota* had the highest mean speed under steam and square sails (when in service) at 8.7 knots, with the *Wabash* capable of 8.5 knots. Under steam alone, the latter vessel had a mean of 6.7 knots, the *Minnesota,* 5.9 knots. Under all conditions of combined sail and steam and steam alone, the overall figure for the *Minnesota* was 6.9 knots, using 2,994 pounds of coal per hour. The *Wabash* made 6.99 knots overall and consumed 3,290 pounds of coal per hour.[34]

Tabulated statistics for the vessels are from B. F. Isherwood, *Experimental Researches in Steam Engineering* (1863). Of course, tabulations using averages or means necessarily overlook a vessel's performance in any specific circumstance, when in particularly favorable conditions she may well have performed better than was reflected in published figures. Thus the only record of such performance would be the hour-by-hour log and the perceptions, however faulty or accurate, of the men aboard. For objectivity and comparison purposes, however, the tabulated figures are requisites. (Note that Isherwood's tabulations do not include performance under sail alone.)

Impressions of the performance of the *Wabash* in 1864 by her commander, Melancton Smith, for instance, do little to reinforce the statistics above. She made 5 knots maximum under steam, according to Smith, and less in a seaway. Furthermore, she worked under sail "very badly" and was "weak" and "rotten" structurally. Of course, this was after months of continual service on the blockade.[35]

A similar report made in the same year on the *Minnesota,* however, carries a much more positive picture. Her captain, Joseph Lanham, reported 5½ knots under steam and 12½ with sail. She worked "well with propeller up" and behaved well in gale conditions. Her steering was satisfactory, and she rolled "long and easy." Nevertheless, the vessel had not been repaired since striking a torpedo.[36]

Finally, a letter written by an obviously enthusiastic officer on board the *Minnesota* in 1858 serves to further dispel the negative reputation of these vessels. In the China Sea, the officer related, "Dupont tried the ship every way, including a terrific tay-foons" and she had gone "17 knots, 16 several times, 14 and 15 without a struggle & what I think more remarkable—13 under royals mizzen included, no stud'ge sails. She has not discovered yet that she has a battery." To complete his side of the implied argument, he concluded: "Nothing in the British or French fleet compares with her."[37]

The careers of the four were all long but generally uneventful. The *Roanoke* was cut down to a top-heavy three-turret ironclad, which was found to roll too seriously to be of much use. She was condemned in 1877 and sold in 1883.

The *Wabash* participated in the taking of Port Royal and both the *Colorado* and *Minnesota* were in the Fort Fisher expedition of 1864. At Hampton Roads, on 8 March 1862, both the preturret *Roanoke* and the *Minnesota* were present when their erstwhile sister ship, the *Merrimack,* began her short but effective ironclad career. The latter was intent on sinking the grounded *Minnesota* after claiming both the *Cumberland* and the "model" for the steam frigates, the *Congress,* when the day's action subsided. All in all, the big frigates saw much less action than the lighter draft vessels of the fleet.

The *Colorado* was flagship of the Asiatic squadron in the Korean punitive action of 1871, then was the flagship of the Atlantic squadron in 1875, and was sold in 1885. The *Minnesota* was housed over and used as a stationary training ship. She was sold in 1901. All three participated in the preparations in wake of the *Virginius* affair in 1873, at Key West. Longest lived was the *Wabash,* flagship for the European squadron until 1874, then for many years receiving ship at Boston, until she was finally sold in 1912.

When these five steam frigates were planned, the navy no doubt intended to re-create in them a steam version of the classic American frigate design first seen in the *Constitution* and her consorts. The essence of the success of the earlier vessels, however, was not only size of battery, but sufficient speed to outrun any more formidable opponent. Unfortunately, achieving half of this recipe did not suffice. The slowness of these vessels can be attributed to the misapplication of the auxiliary steam idea—that steam would be available for movement in and out of ports and in calms, as well as for tactical maneuvering. The dilatory crossing of a bar in a calm was of little import, but the same dullness when attempting to get the advantage of a hostile opponent would have been fatal. Fortunately, much of the Civil War combat duty these vessels performed was in bombarding short fortifications, which moved not at all.

The great structural strength of all five frigates was their most remarkable quality. They were solid long after any need for them existed. If any comparison is worthwhile here, only two of the comparable British frigates survived beyond 1885 and structural weakness showed early in the longer vessels.[38]

Finally, a comparison of the combat strengths of the British and American frigates can be easily made. Again, speed was the key weakness, but in size of battery the *Merrimack*s would have had a distinct advantage. A comparison of the broadside throw weight of the *Euryalus* and *Shannon* to the American gave the British vessels 1,066 and 1,167 pounds respectively, compared to the *Merrimack*'s 1,424 pounds with her original 40-gun battery. Of course, against sailing vessels and 32-pounder broadsides, there would have been no real contest, but such a contretemps was never likely.[39]

Niagara

The sixth vessel authorized in 1854 was an anomaly from the outset. This was the *Niagara,* designed by George Steers, whose reputation was made by such fast vessels as the yachts *Gimcrack* and *Moses H. Grinnell,* the extreme clipper *Sunny South,* and the schooner-yacht *America.* The heterodox nature of the *Niagara* is reflected in the terminology applied to her. This confusion, by extension, implied some uncertainty concerning the purpose and role of the vessel—as designed by Steers and as interpreted by the navy.

As part of the *Merrimack* class, she was generally referred to as a frigate. She was, however, as Bennett says, "an exceedingly large sloop-of-war and not a frigate at all." This was technically true, in view of her dimensions and battery. In size she was more like a frigate: 328 feet 10½ inches on the load line, 345 feet overall, and 5,540 tons displacement. In fact, she was over 700 tons and 50 feet larger than her nominal sister frigates. On the other hand, her armament for most of her career—twelve 11-inch Dahlgren smoothbores on her upper deck, on pivot rails, allowing a maximum broadside of seven guns—could hardly be

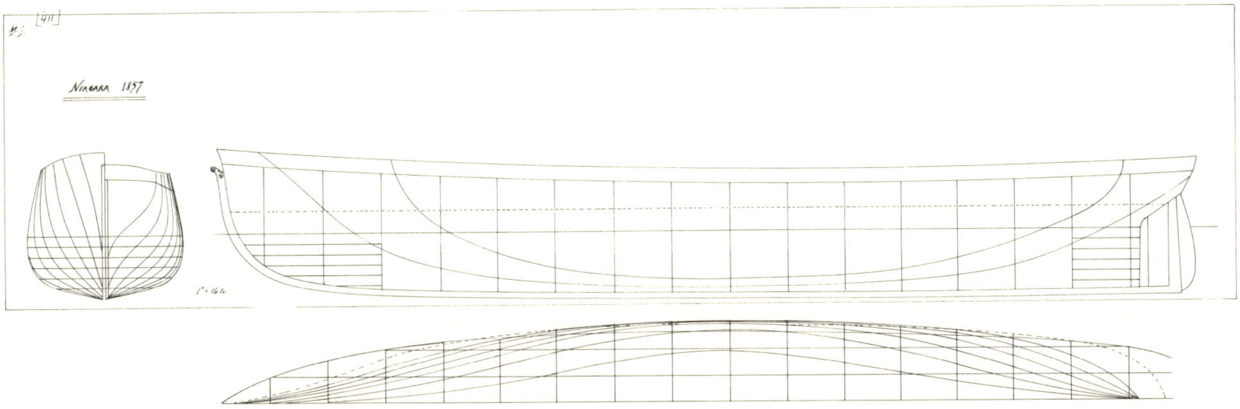

Lines of the Niagara. *No other original lines of the vessel exist, though a half hull is in the Naval Historical Center. (Traced from* U.S. Nautical Magazine and Naval Journal, *1857)*

considered that of a frigate from any standpoint—numbers, throw-weight, or deck arrangement.[40]

The term "frigate" was acceptable simply because of her size. The true issue, however, was the practical one: what rationale resulted in the department's acceptance of a twelve-gun sloop in lieu of the congressionally mandated gundeck frigate carrying forty or more guns? The answer to the question concerning her battery is not clear-cut and cannot be isolated from the other design characteristics of the vessel.

The selection of George Steers as the vessel's architect implies a major expectation by the department: considerable speed. A contemporary commentator described Steers's methods: "With the exception of the propulsory power, in the quality of the canvas, the ground tackle, in the kind of anchors, and one or two other unimportant things [Steers] has been allowed to exercise his own judgement, both in the model and manner of construction." The department's only criteria were a draft of 23 feet and a hoisting screw. With such freedom, it should have not been surprising that Steers's hull design was, in effect, that of a clipper ship modified to accept auxiliary screw propulsion and a battery.[41]

In fact, it appears that the *Niagara* was a deliberate exercise by the navy to determine the compatibility of extreme clipper lines and naval purposes. (The other question, concerning the compatibility of steam power and sailing lines, apparently was not raised, because all of the vessels authorized in 1854 were officially only "auxiliary" steamers.) A letter from John A. Dahlgren to A. H. Foote written shortly before the *Niagara*'s completion elucidates this point: "Present notions do really proceed on the basis that clipper lines and clipper speed are incompatible with the carrying of a heavy battery. I have believed otherwise, with the proviso that the ends be not loaded with guns or other freight. Now if the Niagara have the speed her builder claimed, and will preserve her form as well as other ships, the main point is settled."[42] Steers's essential problem was to prevent a long, narrow clipper hull from hogging under the weight of the battery—a substantial order, particularly in view of the high placement of these weights.

The resulting hull was described by Isherwood as "excessively sharp fore and aft, [with] the appearance and indeed the qualities of a first class clipper ship."[43] The *Niagara*'s lines were not simply "clipper-like" but compared favorably with the extreme clippers such as Donald McKay's *Lightning*—a vessel that had earlier in 1854 averaged 18 knots for a twenty-four-hour period, making her arguably the fastest sailing ship afloat.

Both vessels exhibited extremely long and fine entrance lines with the widest point aft of the center point of the load line. Steers's *America* had this characteristic to a greater extent and it was considered of great significance in her speed. The *Lightning*'s widest point was eight feet aft of her center, and the *Niagara*'s, according to Isherwood's published description, was seven feet, six inches, although the *Lightning*'s was a slightly larger percentage of her length than the *Niagara*'s.[44]

The typical hollow bow of the classic clipper hull, as seen on the load entrance line of the *Lightning*, is described by Arthur Clark in *The Clipper Ship Era:* "A chord from her cutwater to just abaft her fore rigging showed a concavity of 16 inches." A comparable test on Steers's vessel yields a hollowness of 12 inches.[45]

The early clippers were known for their V-shaped bottoms, a configuration gradually discarded and superceded by flat floors in this era. The deadrise on Steers's *Sunny South* was 20 degrees at the midships section, and on the *Niagara,* 12 degrees. The *Lightning*'s was 6 degrees.[46]

The design of the forefoot on the *Niagara* was characteristic of Steers's ships: a single curve from the waterline at the stem to the horizontal of the keel, measuring some 35 feet. The stems of the *Lightning* and McKay's huge *Great Republic* were similarly curved, though in the former its length was about 20 feet.

A further criterion for inclusion in the ranks of the clippers was the ability to carry acres of canvas. The masts of the *Niagara* were impressive, with the main measuring 195 feet to the truck; the fore, 173 feet; and the mizzen, 155 feet. The main yard was 106 feet, and the total sail area was calculated at 58,756 square feet, of which 18,000 square feet was fore and aft sails. An early sail plan shows sky sails and Isherwood's dimensions include them, but they are not mentioned in the vessel's logs. This square footage was comparable to such vessels as the 266-foot *James Baines,* one of the larger clippers, and no doubt represents virtually the largest square footage possible on a three-masted vessel with wooden masts. The only wooden clipper with comparable tonnage had been the *Great Republic,* which originally had four masts.[47]

The *Niagara*'s sail power was "supplemented" by an auxiliary steam engine, which was in itself large for the time. Although the *Merrimack* and class had two-cylinder engines, some of which were notoriously temperamental, that of the *Niagara* had three cylinders and proved relatively problem-free. The 72-inch pistons worked athwartship with double piston rods directly to the crankshaft. Four water-tube boilers had a total grate surface 50 percent larger than those in the smaller vessels yielding 1,955 horsepower, compared to 1,294 for the *Merrimack.*[48]

The 50-ton propeller shaft was over 100 feet in length and in four sections, connected by couplings each weighing 18 tons. To prevent the shaft from working against and weakening the stern timbers, it passed through three concentric bronze bearings each weighing two tons. The outer bearing was hammered solidly into the twenty-four feet of stern deadwood. A four-ton thrust journal, or block, was mounted "in a most substantial manner" on the keelson.[49] The purpose of this block was to transfer the power of the propeller to the ship, rather than back to the engine itself.

The propeller was 18 feet in diameter, with two adjustable-pitch blades. The 15-ton screw could be hoisted into a well below the spar deck, and was mated to the propeller shaft by means of a slot in the end of that shaft.[50]

In the vessel's hull structure, Steers saw to it that no method of preventing hogging was overlooked. Two sets of iron diagonal straps were inset into the outside of the frames and ran from the turn of the bilge to the gun deck. Similar strapping ran across the upper deck beams as well. Two iron braces or stays ran from the upper deck through the lower decks and stepped on the sternpost and keelson. These were 40 and 48 feet long and kept taut by means of turnbuckles. Between her frames, which were on 40-inch centers, the bottom of the hull was filled in solid with yellow pine to a level six feet above the base line.[51] Two iron bulkheads separated the engine and coal spaces from the remainder of the hull, and an iron coal bunker floor also formed the ceiling of the engine room.[52]

Lack of detailed plans leaves much of the deck arrangements to speculation, and the unique assignments of her service career further muddied these waters with temporary deck structures. When she was first commissioned, a newspaper illustration shows a hurricane deck extending forward from her taffrail to shelter the helmsman, but little further. An illustration of 1858 shows a bridge just forward of the funnels, and a topgallant forecastle was fitted. The spar deck bulwarks were originally

Conjectural Sail Plan of the Niagara *before Her Midwar Rebuild. Note the high bulwarks, location of long ports for pivot guns and raked stem, and the absence of a cutwater knee. (Based on plans in* U.S. Nautical Magazine and Naval Journal *vol. 3, October 1856–May 1857, and NARS 79-13-31B, 79-13-31D, National Archives.)*

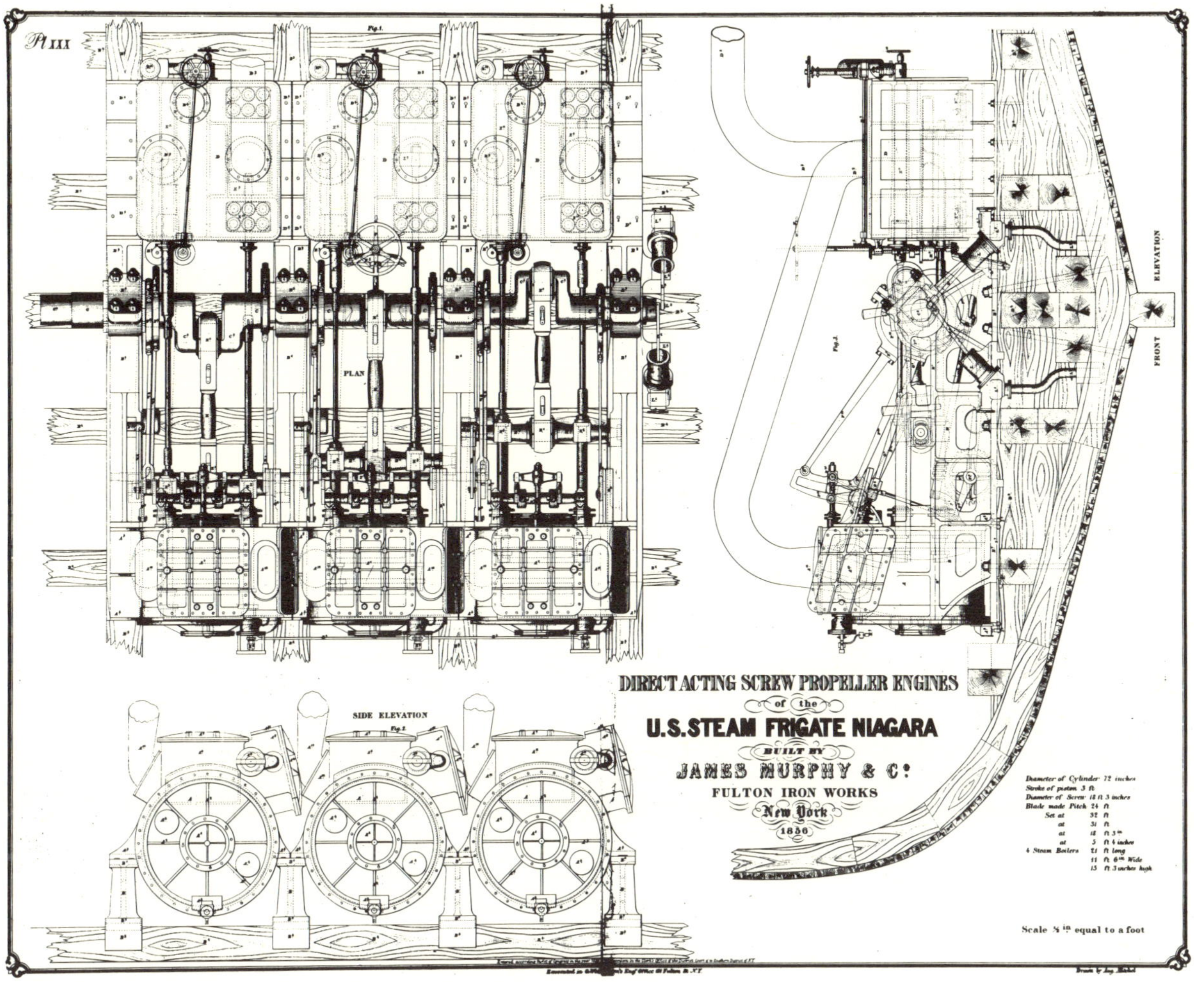

Unique Three-Cylinder Machinery of the Niagara, *the largest prewar screw engines. (Courtesy Smithsonian Institution)*

8 feet high, and the port shutters opened below the rail. The height of the bulwarks was later reduced to 5 feet, and the rails and stanchions were removed to allow greater elevation for the guns.[53]

Questions concerning the size of the *Niagara*'s battery will be dealt with later. She was not given her guns until May 1860, however, when she received twelve spar-deck-mounted 11-inch Dahlgrens on pivots. Her "gun" deck (main deck) though a spacious 7 feet in height, had neither guns nor ports in her original configuration. The fore and aft guns could be used with either broadside, and the ten midship weapons were stowed in fore and aft positions. The position of the wheel prevented fire directly astern, but ports were placed within six feet of the ship's centerline, and on her quarters.[54] The funnels were telescopic and 7 feet in diameter. When lowered, they stood 12 feet above the deck; when extended, 32 feet.[55]

The crew of the *Niagara* numbered 514 before the war and would reach a "wartime complement" of 750. Her paint was standard black, relieved only by a gilt figurehead and stern decoration, both of which depicted spread eagles.[56]

In her original state, before she was rebuilt in 1862–63, her plain raked stem and two stacks served to punctuate and emphasize her already great sheer, to the detriment of her overall appearance. An English journalist commented on her awkward appearance: "The Niagara is without exception the ugliest ship of war we have ever seen. . . . her bow one great plane, and her side another, breaking into each other with a harsh sudden curve. . . . Her sheer is enormous, and impresses one . . . that her constructor expected her to break or 'hog' greatly, and made allowance for the change."[57]

Her steaming performance data for her early years were tabulated extensively in Isherwood's *Engineering Precedents.* Her maximum speed "in

Smooth water, Uninfluenced by Wind or Current" at 22 feet draft is given as 10.9 knots at 45 revolutions per minute and screw slippage of 21.38 percent. This speed is described as that which the vessel could maintain "permanently" with good quality coal. Under actual sea conditions, before 11 December 1858, her logs showed one thirty-two-hour period where she *averaged* 13.5 knots under steam and sail combined—recording a 6 percent *negative* slip of her screw. (She was actually "outrunning" her propeller.) With her head into a "moderate gale," she only managed 2.227 knots.[58]

With a coal bunker capacity of 825 tons, at 7 knots she was capable of seventeen days steaming and over 2,500 miles. For a comparison, British capital ships of the 1860s could only achieve this distance by maintaining speeds below 6 knots.[59]

The vessel's deck log records her speeds under sail alone and shows that her best days occurred on her return from the Atlantic cable attempt in November 1857. This was the first opportunity for sustained runs to try her qualities. On November 7, 8, and 9, she logged 228, 297, and 303 miles, respectively. On the first day, in the noon to four watch is this notation: "The vessel ran 16 knots at different times . . . in puffs." Two hourly figures on the 8th and 9th show 19 and 20 knots, but no further comments confirm these. She was running without her battery, in force 4 to 6 winds and crowding on all canvas. She was averaging 12.6 knots when 303 miles were logged on the 9th. (Deck log figures must not be taken as exact; however, it appears that at an early date the *Niagara* had a patent log in addition to the chip log.)

Such was the *Niagara*'s performance in her early years. She was by far the largest vessel in the navy and for a short time the largest wooden ship in existence. The Collin's liner *Adriatic,* also designed by Steers, shortly overtook her, measuring 345 feet on the load line, and the Royal Navy's *Mersey,* built in 1859 as a response to the *Merrimack* class, was 336 feet in length.[60]

Because of her size, origins, and peaceful, internationally important missions, the *Niagara* became quite a favorite with the American people. Even her engine room merited a full-page illustration in Frank Leslie's nationally known paper, and a great deal of nationalistic hyperbole was expended on her.[61]

Her highly visible place in the public eye began with her launch, on 23 February 1856. Literally thousands viewed the proceedings in New York with some trepidation. The launches of other large ships in this era had not been unmarred; the *Roanoke* had suffered serious frame damage, for example. No such incident marked this event, and more than one journalist noted that Mr. Steers literally leaped into the air when she floated free.[62]

She was commissioned on 6 April 1857 and made passage to Great Britain for the first attempt to lay the Atlantic cable. The passage set no records and was hindered by a four-day stop to make taut rigging set up in cold winter temperatures.[63] Off Gravesend, she was opened to visitors, and the press noted her proposed armament with awe, exaggerating both its range and shot weight (7,000 yards and 270 pounds).[64] The tenor of such comments reflected a lingering wariness of Yankee frigates.

Officially, naval experts also expressed similar misgivings concerning her speed and firepower vis-à-vis slower British three-deckers. Sir Charles Wood, First Lord of the Admiralty, responded to criticism by ordering "one or two of this description built."[65]

The cable operation required extensive gutting of the *Niagara*'s 'tween-deck spaces to allow stowage of five 40-foot wide coils of cable, weighing 1,250 tons. Also, a substantial trestle framework was constructed on the spar deck to carry the cable aft to be paid out.[66]

The cable attempt failed when the *Niagara*'s cable parted about three hundred miles out. The exercise resulted, however, in an impromptu contest involving the *Niagara, Susquehanna,* and ship-of-the-line *Agamemnon,* one of the faster British steamers, with a reputation for surpassing 11 or 12 knots. After eight hours the *Agamemnon* was more than hull down astern of the *Niagara,* and the *Susquehanna*—no slouch in her own right—was seven to eight miles behind the *Niagara.* The writer of the report estimated the latter's speed at 12 knots, with smooth seas and a light wind astern, loaded with 1,150 tons of cable.[67]

The cable effort in 1858 was in itself uneventful, though the telegraphic connection failed in less than a month. At the Newfoundland terminus of the cable, the crew of the *Niagara* celebrated by naming a hamlet in the vicinity after their ship, though it cannot be found on today's maps. They were then met with great festivities in New York.[68]

The *Niagara*'s next prewar tasks were the return of 280 blacks to Liberia after the capture of the slaver *Echo* off Cuba and the return of the first Japanese embassy to their homeland in 1860. She received her battery between the two assignments.[69] In April 1861 she completed her circumnavigation of the globe and the temporary embassy cabin was immediately dismantled and replaced with the displaced 11-inch Dahlgren. On 12 May 1861 she captured the *General Parkhill* off Charleston, the first victim of the blockade of that port.[70]

The ship's first combat was the shelling of Fort McRae at Pensacola in November 1861. To bring her within two miles of the target, Captain W. W. McKean removed spare spars, boats, and topgal-

The Niagara *as a Thirty-Two-Gun Frigate Shortly after Her Rebuilding at Boston. Note the width of the gundeck ports, to provide training room for 11-inch Dahlgrens. The port stripe emphasized the ship's extreme sheer. The frontispiece shows the vessel after the removal of her gundeck battery. (Courtesy Peabody Museum)*

lant masts, reducing her draft to 21 feet 10 inches. To gain elevation, he ran sheet and bower anchors over the port side, attaining about 16 degrees. The fort's guns were silenced on the first day, but adverse winds and current negated these efforts on the next, and the Confederates had found their range. The contest was called off with two minor hits on the ship and no casualties. The engagement was an example of the difficulties meeting the deep-draft frigates off Southern shores during the war.[71]

On 16 June 1862 she was decommissioned at the Charlestown navy yard for overhaul. Captain McKean used the opportunity to express his opinion of the vessel to Secretary Welles: "She is but a sloop of war, mounting twelve guns, and not efficient as a man of war. . . . she is, however, a noble ship, and can . . . be made equal, if not superior to any frigate we have. She sails well, and as a steamer is far superior to them. . . . She has great stability, and would bear any weight . . . put upon her, and is decidedly the best seaboat I have ever seen. With her present battery she could not be fought under canvas, and at close quarters would not be equal to a ship mounting a broadside of twenty 9-inch guns. . . . With a proper broadside battery . . . she would be equal to any frigate afloat."[72]

During the refit, her engines were overhauled and she received new boilers. Externally, her civilian heritage was disguised by the addition of a cutwater knee and planked-in head.

Her fifteen-month stay at Boston was largely for a major modification of her armament, the fitting of a "proper broadside battery" in accordance with the recommendations of a board of survey. Gunports were cut for a battery of 11-inch guns on her gun deck. These were to be on pivots with ports more than six feet wide to allow considerable leeway for training the guns. Twenty 11-inch weapons were mounted, weighing over 260 tons, and the spar deck Dahlgrens were replaced by twelve 150-pound Parrotts. She now was a true 32-gun frigate, with the most formidable battery of any American vessel, with a total throw-weight of 4,460 pounds of shells from all guns and 2,385 pounds in each broadside (seven Parrotts and ten Dahlgrens). The *Colorado*'s broadside guns (twenty-three 9-inch Dahlgrens and two pivots) threw 1,936 pounds of shells.[73]

When she departed from Boston on 17 October 1863, the *Niagara* was a traditional American frigate, with cutwater knee and wide port stripe. Though the former may have softened her angular forward profile, the port stripe served only to draw unneeded attention to her sheer, and the stripe's precipitous descent toward the waterline at midships foreshadowed problems in the offing.

At this juncture, her commanding officer, Thomas T. Craven, wrote Secretary Welles: "The batteries are entirely too heavy for the ship. . . . her midships port was 5 feet 6 inches above the water line. . . . On our passage here, although there was little swell and the ports were lashed in—the gundeck was awash with water—demonstrating that in a gale of wind she would be exceedingly uncomfortable if not a dangerous ship and that under the most favorable circumstances, only two or three of her XI inch guns could be used. . . . I would suggest that her main deck battery be taken out."[74] She then was dispatched to Nova Scotia in search of the Confederate-held vessel *Chesapeake,* arriving only after the vessel had been taken by the *Dacotah.*

She was then ordered from New York to search for the raider *Tallahassee,* but at this point her immense armament betrayed her. She attempted to stand out of the harbor under steam against force 6 winds. Her log states: "The wind being too strong to handle the ship [we] returned to anchorage." At precisely this point, Secretary Welles's telegram ordering the removal of her gun deck battery arrived and the guns were unshipped immediately.[75]

After this ill-advised episode, she sailed for Europe in June 1864. In August, off Portugal, she captured the former Confederate raider *Georgia,* by then a British merchant vessel.[76]

The final incident in her career occurred off Corunna, Spain, in March 1865, where she and the *Sacramento* located the Confederate ram *Stonewall.* On the 24th, the ram steamed out and away, without interference by the federal vessels. Captain Craven had refused combat, as his earlier reports had indicated he would: "If she is as fast as she is reported to be, in a smooth sea she would be more than a match for three ships as the Niagara." The threat of the *Stonewall* was negated by the close of the war.[77]

The *Niagara* returned to the United States and was decommissioned on 29 September 1865. Commander Craven was subsequently court-martialed for allowing the escape of the *Stonewall.* He was convicted, but Secretary Welles overturned the decision. At the proceedings the performance of the *Niagara* was scrutinized.

At the time of the confrontation, the *Niagara* had been at sea for about eighteen months, and her machinery and boilers were in poor condition. She could make about 8½ knots under steam alone in smooth water. This was not a constant, however, because her chief engineer testified that her engines were inadequate for her tonnage, and head seas or "even a swell" could advance or retard her by a full knot. She was still capable of 12 to 13 knots under sail and canvas, and in a run into Flushing, Netherlands, she had made 25 miles in 93 minutes—about 16 knots. On the negative side, her turning capability was typical for such a long vessel: about 12 to 15 minutes and ⅝ mile to come about.[78]

After the war, she remained structurally sound, so much so that a serious scheme for armoring her was undertaken. Her decks were to be raised two feet and twenty 11-inch guns were to be on her gun deck. One proposal called for an 8-foot armor belt along her waterline; a second idea was to extend the plating over the four midships ports.[79] Bennett points out that these plans were prosecuted for a time but never brought to fruition. On 5 May 1885 her hulk was auctioned to a Boston junk dealer, and she was burned to recover the metal in her structure.[80]

Evaluating the career of the *Niagara* leads to one immediate conclusion: she was not an unqualified success, particularly as an overgunned frigate. But her performance should be considered in light of the original intentions of both the department and George Steers regarding her armament and their expectations of the vessel. Two sources do much to shed light on the design of the ship: an article in the *U.S. Nautical Magazine and Naval Journal,* and the letter by John A. Dahlgren mentioned earlier; both were written before the completion of the vessel.

According to *U.S. Nautical Magazine and Naval Journal,* Steers presented three proposed models, or plans, for the ship to the department for their consideration. The Ordnance Bureau was then consulted to determine which would best carry the proposed armament: twelve 11-inch Dahlgrens on the spar deck. Steers later proposed that more powerful engines be supplied and that she be given the "*same battery as the other five steamers . . .* yet the heavy spar deck battery was preferred" [Italics in the original]. Steers, with some perspicacity, "then adapted her decks and sides to the needs of a gun deck, so that if it was deemed necessary, her spar-deck battery could be reduced in weight, and a gun-deck battery be mounted, by simply cutting ports in the sides." The article lends credence to the idea that the naval authorities had little faith that Steers's clipper design would support a frigate's battery. Indeed, the article implies that the naval constructors feared she would not support even the twelve spar-deck guns.[81]

Dahlgren's letter to Foote completes the equation: "She requires much to perfect her as a man of war . . . I . . . did more to remedy the deficiency of the battery, and the result was only prevented by the fact that the original plan had been too far carried out to introduce an armament on the gun deck. . . . With thirty 9-inch guns below, and the twelve 11-inch above, she will have a broadside of 2000 pounds—nearly equal in weight, and superior in all else to any three decker in the British Navy."[82]

Therefore, it appears that the navy was responsible for two errors: the first was in underestimating the capabilities of Steers's design and assigning her an inadequate battery. Second, when the department chose to take advantage of Steers's provisions for a gun-deck battery, they unnecessarily overburdened the vessel by adding 11-inch guns on the gun deck without substantially reducing the spar deck armament. In fact, the twelve 150-pounder actually mounted Parrotts weighed more than the Dahlgrens.

Though the *Niagara*'s midwar rebuild was technically ill advised, it was in keeping with the thrust of the navy's building programs late in the war: the creation of a fleet of ocean-going warships to counter the threat of foreign intervention (see chapter nine). The *Niagara*'s huge hull was an obvious candidate for transformation into a respectable two-decker, and in fact her broadside throw-weight as a frigate was actually heavier than that of the formidable HMS *Warrior,* though of course the armoring of the British vessel invalidates further comparisons.

Thus the *Niagara* had the potential to demonstrate the successful combination of clipper lines and warship needs, but in practice she was radically misused. As will be seen, however, this pattern of sharp lines, long hull, and relatively few large guns would be emulated extensively during the war. Thus her influence was possibly of more importance than her career.

The Long-a-Building Frigate Franklin *at Boston. Note the elaborate stern decoration, befitting her flag status. She was the show ship of Farragut's postwar European tour. (Naval Historical Center)*

Franklin

The construction of the *Franklin,* begun in 1853, continued at a desultory pace for ten years at the Portsmouth Navy Yard, Kittery, Maine. Before the war, small appropriations and higher priorities kept her on the stocks. Secretary Toucey was informed by Lenthall that she was in that status because she would "be preserved better than when afloat."[83] Wartime demand for such huge vessels was small, further delaying her progress. Her machinery was not ordered until November 1863, and she was launched on 17 September 1864.

The machinery for the vessel was designed by Benjamin F. Isherwood and consisted of two 68-inch by 42-inch cylinders in the back-acting configuration. The machinery was built at the Charlestown Navy Yard. Four vertical boilers and two superheaters were provided. Early plans indicate only one funnel was planned, but a second was incorporated in the completed ship, and both could be lowered below the level of the rails.[84]

The *Franklin* was the last traditional frigate with broadside guns on two decks. On her main deck were twenty-six or twenty-eight 9-inch Dahlgrens, with six additional on the spar deck. Also on the spar deck were four 100-pounder Parrott rifles and on 11-inch Dahlgren on pivot. The latter was on the forecastle and fired through ports on each bow.[85] The location of the rifles is not certain. The majority of the vessels denominated "frigates" in this era were more accurately spar-decked sloops—with broadside guns only on the gun deck and bow and stern pivot guns above.

The new frigate was faster than her predecessors, making 10¼ knots under steam in her early cruising.[86] With the remainder of the *Merrimack* class, she was always officially described as an auxiliary steam frigate. Her commanding officer remarked on the satisfactory performance of her engines as well as her buoyancy and steering. Before the wind in gale conditions she maintained 11½ knots under steam and sail.[87]

The frigate had a short but eventful active service life. Her first assignment was as the flagship of the European squadron under the command of Admiral Farragut—showing the flag of the reunited nation in a European tour in 1867 and 1868. At the end of her third cruise on the European station, she was detailed to "escort" the infamous "Boss" Tweed from Vigo, Spain, to the United States for prosecution. An enterprising journalist estimated it cost about $5,000 for the coal necessary to make the passage, "more than Tweed is worth dead or alive."[88]

In 1877 the *Franklin* became a receiving ship at Norfolk. She was sold in October 1915 and was one of the last of her kind in the service.

The Hartford, *Farragut's Flagship during the Mississippi River Campaign. Tiers of chain cable can be discerned on her sides next to her engine spaces. (Naval Historical Center)*

CHAPTER 5

Hartford-Class Screw Sloops, 1857

With the adoption of both the screw propeller and the concept of the auxiliary steam-powered warship, the navy discarded the pure sailing ship as a man-of-war. This transformation was underscored by the launching of the final three pure sailing vessels in 1854 and 1855—the frigates *Sabine, Santee,* and the rebuilt corvette *Constellation.*[1] Though the sailers would continue to be active for many years, their roles would be secondary.

The transition to steam now moved at a more orderly pace, to the construction of vessels less grandiose than the unwieldy super frigates. The new ships were the steam sloops of the *Hartford* class, which with the subsequent *Mohican*-class vessels, became the mainstays of the cruising fleet for the remaining decades of the wooden steam navy.

The five *Hartford*-class steam sloops were to be steam-powered continuations of the line of large corvettes begun with the converted frigates *Cumberland* and *Macedonian* and the rebuilt *Constellation.* All these maintained their battery on a single deck, except for pivoted shell guns on the forecastle and quarter decks.[2]

Factors that influenced the design of the *Hartford, Brooklyn, Richmond, Lancaster,* and *Pensacola* were both foreign and domestic in origin. A navy design board suggested they were to "cope with new ships of the same class in foreign navies" in their armament and mount fourteen to eighteen guns on a single gun deck, with one vessel to have fore and aft pivot guns on a complete spar deck. These sloops would be comparable to the British *Cadmus* and *Pearl* corvettes of 1856, which mounted twenty-one guns each. The board also suggested a maximum draft of 18¼ feet for the largest vessel and 16 for the smallest. This would allow these ships access to most of the American ports that were too shallow for the *Merrimack*-class frigates.[3]

The five sloops were authorized on 3 March 1857. Four, the *Hartford, Richmond, Pensacola,* and *Lancaster* were built at the navy yards in Boston, Norfolk, Pensacola, and Philadelphia, respectively. The fifth was contracted to Jacob Westervelt of New York City and named *Brooklyn.* According to the secretary of the navy's report of 1857, all were to have watertight bulkheads, for the safety of the crews.[4]

The five vessels were sister ships only in classification, differing entirely in dimensions. The disparity between the two largest, *Pensacola* and *Lancaster,* and the others was sufficient to justify such a division for this study. The *Pensacola* was 230 feet 8 inches in length by 44 feet 6 inches and 3,000 tons; the *Lancaster,* 235 feet 8 inches, 46 feet, and 3,290 tons. The *Hartford* and *Richmond* were the nearest to being alike dimensionally, at 225 feet by 44 feet and 2,550 tons for the former, 225 feet by 42 feet and 2,604 tons displacement for the *Richmond.* The *Brooklyn* was least likely to approximate any of the navy-built ships; she measured 233 feet by 42 feet and 2,686 tons. Her lighter displacement and narrower beam places her more closely with the two smaller vessels.

Hartford

The most famous and longest lasting of the five was the *Hartford,* designed by B. F. Delano and laid down in January 1858. Her hull was of standard naval construction, white oak keel and live-oak frames, the latter filled in solid to the bilge. No watertight bulkheads are shown on an 1858 plan, but an 1882 inboard profile appears to show three: one forward of the mainmast, the others on each

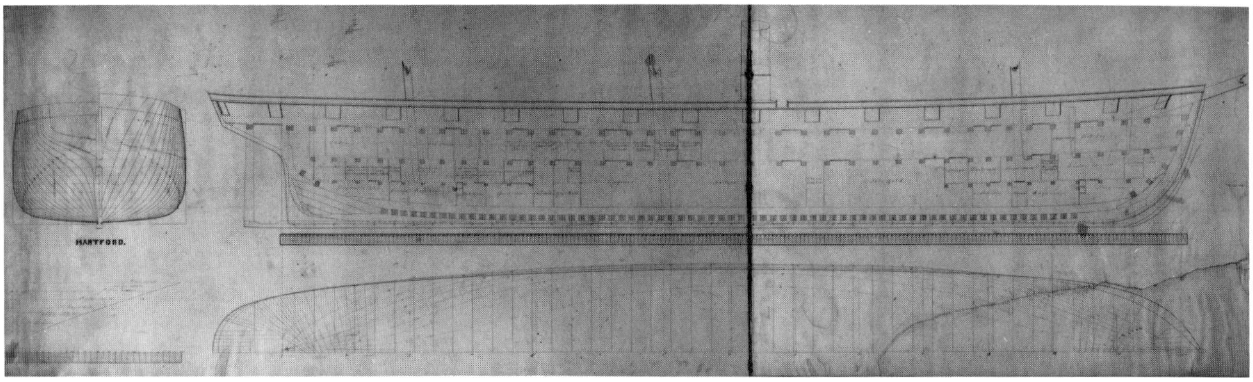

Lines and Inboard Plans of the Hartford *As Originally Built. Her forward lines were sharper than those of any of her sister vessels. (NARS 80-14-11, National Archives)*

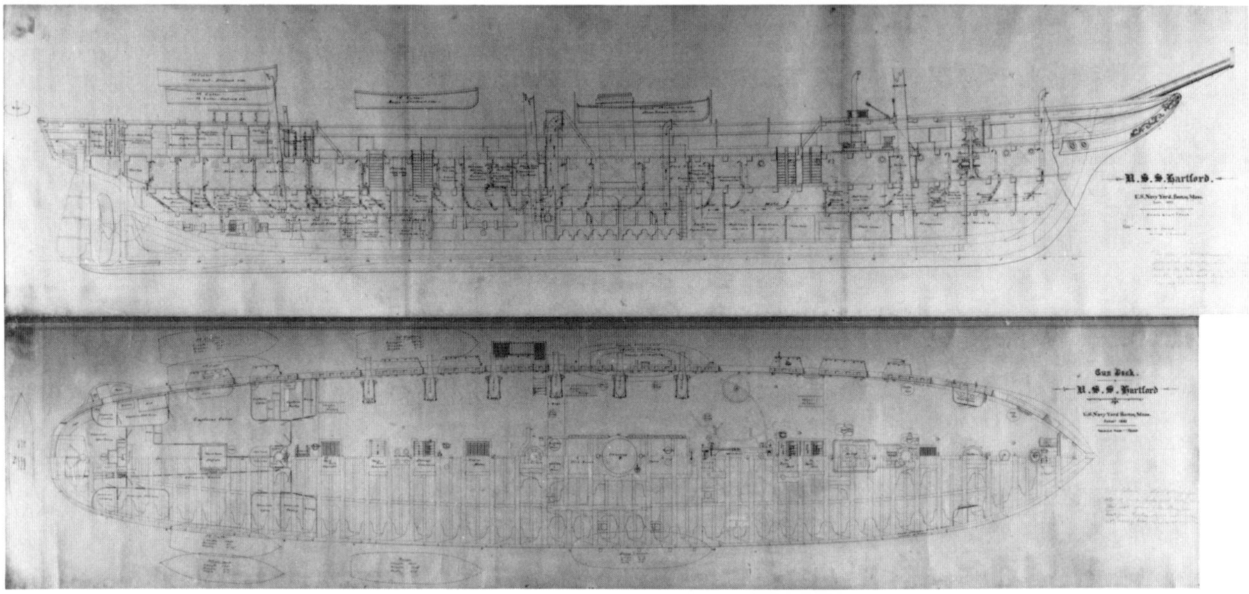

Gundeck and Inboard of the Hartford, *1882. She is fitted with a waist 8-inch converted rifle on pivot rails, steam capstan, and ventilation system. (NARS 27-13-4, 27-13-5, National Archives)*

end of the engine spaces. Cross-strapping of iron was inlet into the inside of the timbers.[5]

In form, the hull was unusually sharp, with an entrance angle at the load line of approximately 50 degrees. This was complemented by a 60-degree angle at the stern, reflecting a long, fine run. The *Hartford* was also the sharpest of all five, thus approaching civilian clipper practice in hull form more closely than did the Westervelt-designed *Brooklyn*. Furthermore, the *Hartford*'s buttock lines were nearly straight diagonals, while the Brooklyn's were quite convex. Thus the *Hartford*'s lines reflected a considerable interest in speed.

The steam sloop's engines were horizontal direct-acting with jet condensers and a stroke of 34 inches and bore of 62 inches. The two-cylinder powerplant drove a 14½-foot, hoisting, two-bladed propeller. Two Martin vertical water-tube boilers were provided and a single hoisting funnel.[6]

She was ship-rigged, with 19,000 square feet in her principal sails. With royals and other minor canvas, this total, according to a newspaper account, exceeded 37,000 square feet.[7] Her lower standing rigging was set up with iron turnbuckles rather than deadeyes. This was not standard navy practice, although turnbuckles (rigging screws) had been applied as early as 1849 to some U.S. naval vessels. She may have received these in her wartime refit.

The broadside battery of the vessel was twenty 9-inch Dahlgrens. In June 1862, she carried in addition two 20-pounder and one 30-pounder rifle. In her 1863 refit, two 100-pounder rifles replaced two of the 9-inch Dahlgrens. Peacetime brought some reductions in her battery, as shown by an 1882 deck plan showing sixteen 9-inch smoothbores. Forward of these, between the funnel and foremast, a single 8-inch converted rifle was mounted on a centerline pivot, to fire through long ports on each side. Because of the length of the *Hartford*'s career, other postwar modifications will be covered in a later chapter.[8]

In her first commission, the *Hartford* gave "entire satisfaction" according to her commanding officer, H. K. Stribling. He commented that the engines appeared to be "perfect" and performed well. An endemic weakness in these early horizontal screw engines, however, was that against a head wind and sea, the sloop did not "possess the power to give her much speed." Her maximum speed under steam alone was 9.5 knots. Under steam and sail, she averaged 7.3 knots. In favorable circumstances under steam and sail, however, she made 13½ knots.[9]

Her Civil War reputation put the *Hartford* on a par with the *Kearsarge* as the two most venerated unarmored vessels of the conflict. She was Farragut's flag vessel at New Orleans, Vicksburg, Mobile Bay, and Port Hudson and survived them all relatively intact. Her sturdiness was enhanced considerably by the addition of armor in the form of chain cables arranged on her sides to protect her machinery spaces.

Additionally, the *Hartford* and many of the larger vessels of Farragut's command were fitted with rope cutters on their bows. These were forward-curved, saw-toothed iron contrivances attached to the cutwater of the vessels, intended to sever rope obstructions at Mobile Bay. Farragut later recommended that two revolving rings be placed around the ships' propellers to prevent fouling, but this idea was not implemented.[10]

Richmond

Though the same length as the *Hartford,* the *Richmond* was two feet narrower (42 feet) and had a slightly greater displacement, 2,604 tons. Her hull was designed by Samuel T. Hartt and was much like the *Brooklyn* in entrance and clearance angles. Her draft was 15 feet 6 inches. Of the three ships, the *Richmond* had the fullest section, hardest bilges, and straightest sides.[11]

The ship's machinery consisted of two horizontal back-acting engines, of 58-inch cylinder and 36-inch stroke. The cut-off mechanism was of the Sickels's pattern, which was objectionable because of the "quantity of machinery required, the complication, and the number of moving parts."[12] The Sickels's cut-off was also adopted for the *Pensacola* and became an element of the controversy surrounding the machinery of that ship.

The boilers of the *Richmond* were the Martin water-tube type. There were three, two with six furnaces each and the third with a single furnace auxiliary unit. It could be connected to the main boilers if needed. A single 14-foot screw was used, weighing 11,820 pounds.[13]

Her original armament was sixteen 9-inch Dahlgrens. During the war she carried as many as eighteen, plus single 80-pounder Dahlgren and 30-pounder Parrott guns. After the introduction of the 8-inch rifled Dahlgren, she mounted twelve of the smoothbores and one of the converted rifles, the latter on a pivot mount between fore and main masts.[14]

After her launch in 1860, the *Richmond* was the flagship of the Mediterranean squadron. Her run from Gibraltar to Sardinia was made in "four days and three hours—making an average of 9 knots an hour. Under steam alone 8 knots, but with steam and sail, with a moderate breeze, 11 to 11.5 knots."[15]

This was a creditable performance but apparently under easy circumstances, because the passage from Sardinia to Messina was the subject of the following critical letter by Commodore C. H. Bell to Secretary Toucey in January 1861:

> During the week we were at sea between Spezia and this place, we had a better opportunity of testing the qualities of this ship, than at any period

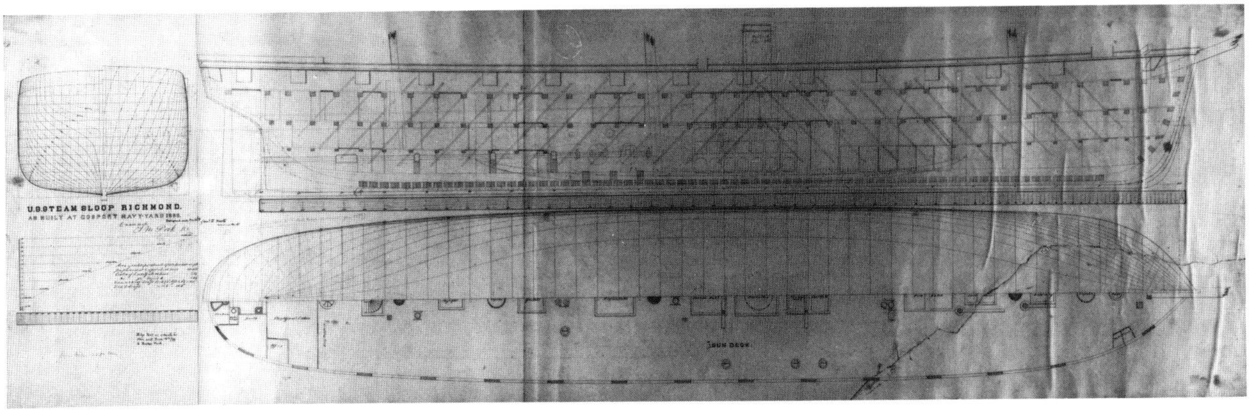

Inboard and Lines of the Richmond, *the Smallest of the* Hartford *Class. (NARS 78-4-3B, National Archives)*

A Postwar View of the Richmond. *Note long port for waist-mounted pivot rifle. The* Richmond *can be distinguished from the* Hartford *by her more angular stem and wide gap between first and second ports. She also had less rake to her stern. (Naval Historical Center)*

> since we left the United States. . . . The wind being ahead all sails were furled and we steamed against a slight head swell. As the swell increased her speed was lessened to two knots. She pitched heavily, and when her stern lifted, which raised the propeller partly out of the water, the vibration was so much increased that the whole stern frame appeared to be shaking to pieces. . . . As the wind increased to a full topsail breeze she lost her steerageway. I then set the fore and aft sails and tried turning to windward with staysails and steam, but we made from four to six points leeway, and the ship pitched as much as ever.

After stopping engines, the ship was put under square sails and an attempt made to turn windward, "which any fair sailing vessel in the Navy could easily have . . . gained not less than two miles an hour on her direct course. This ship sagged off to leeward, making so much leeway that if there had not been plenty of sea-room, she would probably have gone ashore." The commodore considered her "unsafe" at sea in such "bad weather" and concluded that her malady was in the full midsection, sharp-ended hull form used in an attempt to achieve both light draft and speed: "In going head to a swell, when her main body is on the top of the wave, as soon as the center is passed she comes down with full force, having no floor to catch her—this is undoubtably the cause of her heavy pitching."[16]

Mechanically, the *Richmond* was also unsatisfactory. Her Sickels's valve gear mechanism was the primary source of her malfunctioning. Her engineer complained that the complication of the mechanism prevented keeping it in order, and Commodore Bell added that a three-day cruise resulted in "weeks" of repairs.[17]

Bell considered the steam sloop a "failure" and after her return to the United States wrote that her condition was "unsafe." He thought her appropriate for the Chesapeake Bay, however, where she could anchor in a gale.[18] Her stern was strengthened subsequently. Bilge keels were added in 1878 in an effort to reduce her rolling.[19]

The *Richmond*'s Civil War career paralleled the *Hartford*'s at New Orleans, Vicksburg, Port Hudson, and Mobile Bay. Before those, however, she was the war's first victim of an ironclad, having been rammed on the port bow on 12 October 1861 by the *Manassas*. The Confederate vessel's machinery was partially disabled by the shock of the collision and she withdrew. The sloop sustained a two-foot gash.

In 1866, she was given new 60-inch by 36-inch engines and remained in the inventory until sold in

1919. She had been an active cruiser until being made a receiving ship in the late 1880s.

Brooklyn

Compared earlier to her navy-built sisters, the *Brooklyn* was eight feet longer than the *Richmond* and *Hartford,* although she was narrower and about 180 tons larger in displacement than the latter. Her hull was described as "full but easy" in her waterlines, with "well rounded bilges." From her 56-degree entrance angle, her sharpness can be deduced, and a reasonably fine run is reflected by the 80-degree clearance angle. Her rounder bilges were one factor in reducing her displacement to approximate the lighter sloops, rather than equaling the *Lancaster* and *Pensacola*'s 3,200-ton mark. Her "easy" lines indicated less fullness in her midsection than that of the *Richmond.*[20]

Her relatively small displacement for her length was blamed on the lighter construction methods used by her civilian constructor. Contract-built vessels in general, however, met with considerable negative criticism among naval officers of the era.

There is little evidence to support any charges of weak construction on the *Brooklyn.* First, her plans show that in many ways she was more substantially constructed than the *Richmond,* for example. The length of the after deadwood, including the stern post, of the *Richmond* was 8½ feet, while the *Brooklyn*'s measured 10 feet. On a horizontal line extending forward from the top of the keelson to the cutwater, the *Brooklyn* measured 9 feet of deadwood and stem, while the *Richmond* was 8 feet at this point. Furthermore, the deck beams, frames, and keel of Westervelt's vessel were all larger in cross section than those of the *Richmond.*[21]

The *Brooklyn* was diagonally strapped, using 4-inch by ¾-inch iron. On the *Richmond,* however, the straps of the fore part of the hull ran upward and aft, and those of the after hull ran upward and forward; none extended farther than a line seven feet from the base of the keel. Westervelt exceeded this considerably and installed two complete sets of straps crossing each other, extending to within five feet of the base line and terminating at a head strap running nearly the length of the vessel. Though not shown on the plan, this strap may have also encompassed the stem and stern.[22]

Finally, the *Brooklyn*'s hull was subdivided into four compartments by watertight bulkheads. These consisted of two thicknesses of yellow pine, each 4 inches thick, crossing at right angles and fastened to the keelsons with ⅞-inch iron bolts. It is not known whether the *Richmond*'s two engine-space bulkheads were as substantial.[23]

Despite the structural strength shown by the vessel's plans, in 1864 her commander complained that she was "not as strong as naval vessels usually are."[24] This pointed up a long-standing and significant difference between civilian and naval shipbuilding practices—a subject that was a sore spot in relations between the navy and contractors. The civilian constructors complained that navy vessels were "over built," particularly in their fastenings; they contended that the navy's use of through bolts unnecessarily weakened the butt ends of the hull and deck timbers. They felt that spikes of sufficient length would suffice and reduce the likelihood of splitting the ends of the timbers. Naval constructors countered that the weight of the battery and its high placement required the extra strength rendered by bolting. The *Brooklyn*'s first major rebuilding began in 1869, while the *Richmond* went into the docks as early as 1865 and the *Hartford,* 1868.

The Brooklyn, *Dressed and Firing a Salute at the Naval Review of 1889. (U.S. Navy)*

Mechanically, the ship was not remarkable, having a two-cylinder powerplant with cylinder diameter of 61 inches and stroke of 33 inches. Each piston worked two piston rods, with the connecting rod to the shaft operating from a crosshead. The engine developed 705 gross effective horsepower.[25]

She carried 22,480 square feet of plain sails and had a complement of 417 officers and men. The vessel originally mounted sixteen 9-inch Dahlgrens plus two 10-inch Dahlgrens, the latter on pivots fore and aft. Her heaviest battery was twenty 9-inch guns, two 100-pounder Parrott rifles and two 60-pounder Parrotts (December 1864).[26]

At her commissioning on 26 January 1859, she had cost the government $417,921. This was $83,000 less than the least costly navy-built ship, the *Hartford.* The *Richmond* totaled $566,259—

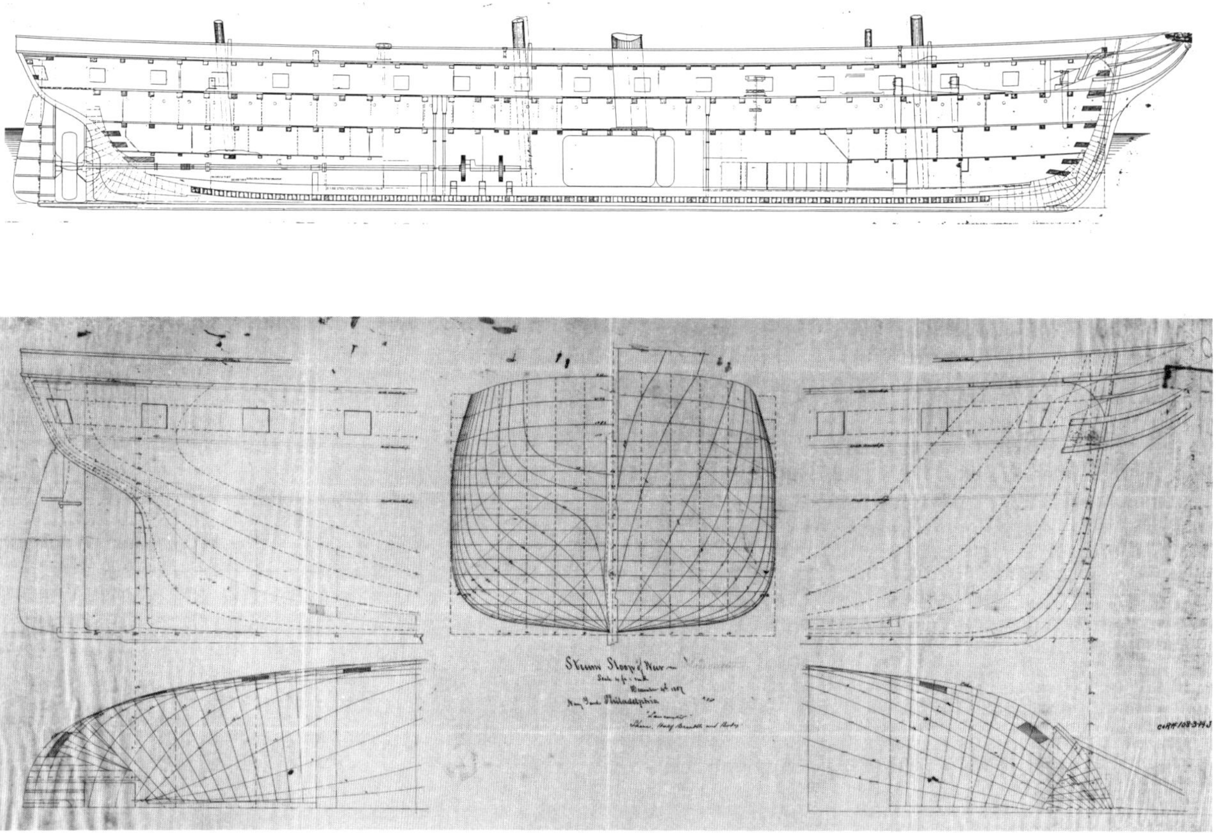

Lines and Inboard of the Lancaster. *The only vessel of the group to have a complete spar deck as originally built, she carried sixteen gun ports, excluding bridle and stern ports, while the others of the class carried either fourteen or fifteen. (NARS 108-3-14G, 108-3-14J, National Archives)*

nearly $150,000 more than the *Brooklyn*—and the performance of the civilian-built vessel did not negate the fact that the navy had gotten a bargain for its money.[27]

Her first commanding officer, D. G. Farragut, called her a "fine ship," steaming "10 knots and a little upwards." Directly against a heavy head swell, with furled sails, she made 6 miles per hour "to the astonishment of all on board." She performed all her evolutions with "ease and certainty" and was stable and a good steerer. Negatively, her mizzen mast was "almost useless . . . except with the wind directly astern," and she was poorly ventilated.[28]

Other reports gave her a maximum of 11 knots with sail assistance. She rolled easily and "very deep" when light.[29] She was, therefore, on a par with the *Richmond* in speed though a bit slower than the *Hartford.* In seaworthiness and mechanical performance, however, she was certainly beyond comparing with the *Richmond.*

Her active career was similar in length to her sister ships, but she was sold earlier, in 1891. Structurally, she must have been sound even at that date, because the secretary of the navy's report of December 1888 gave her life expectancy as an additional six years (the *Hartford* only rated five in the same report).[30]

Her Civil War career was also similar to the *Hartford*'s, although she did not pass the guns at Vicksburg. Like the *Richmond,* she was also rammed by the *Manassas* (April 1862). Unlike the *Hartford* and *Richmond,* she participated in the expedition against Fort Fisher later in the conflict.

Like the *Hartford,* she was later rearmed—in 1876—and for a short period had a spar deck. She remained in the service long enough to receive many fashionable improvements, such as steam capstans and steering as well as electric lighting.[31]

Lancaster

Of the two larger ships of this class, the *Lancaster,* though less well known, was by far the more successful. She also had the distinction of being the only one of the class to become a model for a later vessel.

Unfortunately there is little information available on the ship before her extensive rebuilding of 1879, a reconstruction that recast her in every aspect except basic hull lines. The vessel's lines were the fullest of all her class, reflected by her 3,290-ton displacement and dimensions (235 feet 8 inches by 46 feet). Her clearance angle at the load line was over 80 degrees. Her entrance angle at the load line was some 10 degrees sharper than the *Pensacola*'s. She had considerable tumble home topside, and a slight rake to her stem. She was no doubt strapped diagonally, and iron bulkheads are mentioned in reference to her in 1858. However, watertight compartmentation is not borne out by her plans. Her designer, John Lenthall, was obviously emphasizing carrying capacity rather than speed in her lines. Her engines were identical to the direct-acting installation of the *Brooklyn*. Her boilers, however, were given 12 percent more heating surface.[32]

The *Lancaster* was the only one of the five to have a complete spar deck, though others of the class received them in post-war rebuildings. With her great length, and spar deck pivot rails, she carried twenty-four 9-inch Dahlgrens and two 11-inch Dahlgrens, plus two 30-pounder Parrott rifles. This battery varied little until after the war.[33]

She was credited with an average speed of six knots and a maximum of ten. An engineer on board wrote that she was capable of obtaining "high rates of speed with a small amount of slip of screw, and under all circumstances as an auxiliary powered steamer her performance under steam is above average."[34] There was little reason, however, to test her to extremes. As flagship of the Pacific squadron from her commissioning to 1867, she was not involved in the war except for unfruitful forays in search of Confederate raiders.

Evidently, however, her uneventful career was overshadowed by her positive qualities as a warship. In the 1870s, when Congress reluctantly dispensed appropriations for new construction, one of the new vessels, the *Trenton*, was designed on the hull lines of the *Lancaster* but given one-sixth more displacement. Also, in the *Lancaster*'s rebuilding from 1875 to 1881, she emerged very much like the *Trenton*. The details of this transformation will be presented in chapter eleven.[35]

The Lancaster *before 1875, the Most Substantial of Her Class. (Courtesy Peabody Museum)*

The Pensacola, *with Yards Manned for Inspection by President Lincoln, November 1861. Her Dickerson engines were as yet incomplete. (NARS 28-1-46, National Archives)*

Pensacola

Of the five steam sloops authorized in 1857, the *Pensacola* gained the most notoriety. She became the center of a long-lasting controversy involving steam engineering theories, personal animosities, and many taxpayer dollars.

Her hull design was not the source of contention, however. She was 230 feet 8 inches by 44 feet 6 inches and displaced 3,000 tons. Her deadrise was greater than that of the *Lancaster*, and she was not as sharp in her entrance lines as that ship. Her run was longer and finer than her sister's, however, and she proved to be an uneasy roller in a seaway.[36]

Her armament ranged from sixteen 9-inch smoothbores and one 11-incher, early in the war, to twenty-two of the 9-inch guns in broadside and one each of the 11-inch Dahlgrens and the 100-pounder Parrotts. All her guns were on the gun deck, including pivots.[37]

The controversy concerned the engines of the Pensacola, specifically involving differing theories on the expansion of steam. One school of thought held that steam expanded exactly as other gases. The opposition view was that it expanded much less. The practical application of these theories was found in the "cut-off" valve, which regulated the amount of steam allowed into the cylinder. The "short cut-off" advocates expected a small amount of steam to be sufficiently expansive to drive the piston its full stroke. The "long cut-off" people disagreed and expected much less expansion from a given amount of steam; thus they would allow the valve to be open for a longer portion of the piston's

The Controversial and Inadequate Dickerson Engines of the Pensacola. *Three of her four cylinders can be seen, as well as her massive journals and counterweights. This machinery weighed 540 tons—twice that of the* Lancaster*'s engines. (National Archives)*

stroke. Of the two theories, the "short cut-off"—if true—would result in the most economical engines.

The opposing leaders were quite a contrast. The long cut-off men looked to Benjamin F. Isherwood, chief engineer of the navy during the war, a man with much practical experience and a penchant for exhaustive experimentation. He was bluff and outspoken and had little patience with politics and politicians. On the other side was Edward N. Dickerson. To the disgust of men like Isherwood, he was a New York lawyer with a hobby: steam engineering. Even worse, he was smooth talking and politically influential.[38]

Dickerson, allied with Frederick E. Sickels, the inventor of one type of cut-off mechanism, proposed that one of the five steam sloops be provided with an engine of their design. He claimed his engine would be more economical and weigh less than comparable steam powerplants. The prospect of these desirable characteristics, plus a heavy dose of influence (Dickerson was on good terms with Senators Mallory and Yulee of Florida, both of whom were on the committee on naval affairs), resulted in their obtaining a contract for the *Pensacola*'s engines.

The completed engine exhibited characteristics appropriate to the short cut-off theory. First, the boilers were relatively small in grate surface and heating surface. Normal practice, of course, would call for increased boiler dimensions, commensurate with the larger size of cylinders and the increased displacement of the vessel. The key difference between Dickerson's machinery and standard practice, however, was in the larger cubic capacity of the cylinders. Rather than two, Dickerson and Sickels used four cylinders, with a total capacity twice that of the cylinders of the *Richmond*. Dickerson expected such economical use of steam that boilers smaller than those of her sister ships would be sufficient to supply steam for twice the cubic space as that of the cylinders of the other vessels. Conversely, if the short cut-off theory was faulty, it is equally obvious that the result would be a powerplant with an immense shortfall in steam-making capacity—literally half as powerful as her competitors.

To facilitate making the engine economical, the weight of the *Pensacola*'s machinery ought to have been kept at a minimum, and several factors militated against this goal. First, using twice the number of cylinders meant doubling the number of valves, valve gears, valve linkages, air pumps, and other mechanical parts. The weight of these necessities on the *Pensacola*'s engines was further augmented by the employment of Sickels's cut-off, which has been described earlier as exceedingly complicated and composed of a large number of working parts. Finally, according to F. M. Bennett, the design of the engine abounded in amateurish and weighty mechanical redundancies.

The condensing apparatus of the *Pensacola*'s engines was also peculiarly designed. First, surface condensers were used, unusual at this early date because of leakage problems with the internal tubing. (The surface condenser used pipes through which cold water flowed, causing the temperature drop necessary for condensation.) The *Pensacola*'s condensers were provided with small circulating pumps and water scoops on the ship's bottom. It was expected that the great speed of the vessel would force sufficient water into the system.

In the end, the total weight of the engines was 1,080,000 pounds (540 tons). In comparison, those of the *Lancaster* scaled 246½ tons and those of the *Wabash* weighed 235 tons. Inevitably, the weight implied cost, and this machinery cost the taxpayers $328,460—nearly as much as the entire steam sloop *Brooklyn*.

To the intrinsic problems of the engines was appended a series of other mechanical as well as constructional misadventures. The screw, for instance, was redesigned in midstream, increasing its diameter, pitch, weight, and number of blades (from two to four). This necessitated docking the vessel and modifying her stern to accommodate the larger screw. In the process, the already completed two-bladed screw and its now useless hoisting apparatus were discarded.[39]

Construction of the engines dragged on for two years and nine months, during which time, according to a Senate document on the affair, there were "long intervals" in which neither drawings nor directions were furnished by the designers. During this period, the Bureau of Construction and Repair's efforts to expedite the building process were hampered by "openly" political pressures, "even to the extent of menaces" by Senators Yulee and Mallory. Sickels's dilatoriness was construed as disloyalty late in 1861, and Welles ordered Henry W.

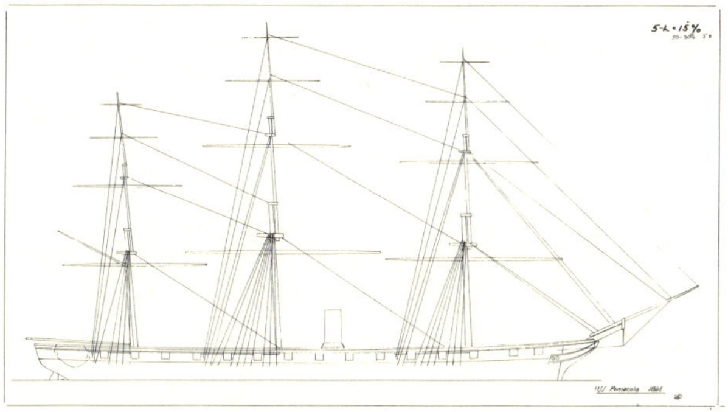

The General Arrangement of the Pensacola, *1861. Plan drawn from one of the few existing plans of the original vessel. The funnel and quarter galleries have been reconstructed from photographs. (NARS 8-46-50, National Archives)*

Morris to "retain Mr. Sickels on board and permit him no communication with the shore except through the Navy Department."[40] In the end, six months after the secession of Florida (home state of both Yulee and Mallory), the machinery was taken from the hands of the designers, and another engineer, Edward Faron, was designated to complete the engines.

The building of the *Pensacola* was an unusual process in any case. The hull was launched at Warrington Yard, Pensacola, on 15 August 1859, and she was commissioned, without engines, on 5 December. She then sailed for Washington Navy Yard, where her engines were being built. On this passage without engines and battery her commanding officer reported she "actually beat to leeward" because of her shallow draft. She was commissioned again 16 September 1861, but the engines were not completed and tried until 3 January 1862.[41] After commissioning she was sent to Farragut's gulf squadron. On her arrival Farragut wrote Assistant Secretary Fox that she had arrived shortly after a severe norther, and he continued: "God knows when she would have arrived" if she had encountered the storm. "They represent the engines as perfectly worthless" was his final remark on the vessel.[42]

Her trial had shown her to attain a maximum of 8.8 knots, at the expense of 25 percent more coal than the *Hartford* had burned to attain 9.5 knots. Moreover, the engines weighed and cost two-and-a-half times more than those of her smaller sister ship. The causes of this failure were connected to the faulty design: "There is scarcely a piece of machinery that has not been made twice over," because of "numerous blunders in design," read the congressional report of 1863 on the vessel. The only specific portion of the engines not tied to the general design, yet deserving of condemnation, was the Sickels's valve mechanism. The *Richmond*'s machinery also used this contrivance, and she was called "the slowest . . . in the Navy, and is wholly unreliable on account of continual breakdowns."[43]

Finally, it was also revealed that Sickels and Dickerson had designed and begun construction of a pumping engine for the city of Detroit in 1858. They had not completed the project, and legal action was being taken against the two "engineers."[44]

The failure of his engines in the *Pensacola* did nothing to discourage E. N. Dickerson. He continued his fulminations against the department and Isherwood until he again finagled second—and third—vessels to test his theories. His persistence and what might be termed engineering quackery later became the subject of a priceless bit of satire called "Uncle Samuel's Whistle and What It Cost."

After participating in the battle at New Orleans, the *Pensacola*, her machinery as always in a state of "semi-collapse," became in effect a floating battery.[45] New engines were ordered for her in 1864. These were 60-inch by 36-inch back-acting cylinders of a standard type designed by B. F. Isherwood weighing about 320 tons including boilers—a considerable decrease from those designed by Dickerson and Sickels.

On trials she averaged 8.56 knots (slightly less than the 8.8-knot maximum speed of the vessel with Dickerson's engines). Statistics published in 1875 show that her new engines produced 1 horsepower per 3.494 pounds of coal consumed, compared to 5.044 pounds per horsepower required by her original engines. The new machinery was also reliable and durable, characteristics unknown in the earlier engine.[46]

After this rebuilding she began a second, more useful career. She sailed "fairly with the wind free, but on the wind with her yards braced sharp . . . she makes rapid leeway," reported her commanding officer, John Worden, in 1866. Her funnel, which prevented the use of her mainsail, was later made telescopic. In 1878, in yet another major overhaul, her boilers were replaced by those of the short-lived *Benicia* (seen in a later chapter) making her the only vessel of this class to have twin funnels. By the same year, she had received a complete spar deck, altering her appearance greatly.[47] She remained on the inventory until 1912, when she was sold. She was later burned to recover her metal parts (the expedient method of disposing of wooden ships because live-oak vessels were as difficult and time-consuming to dismantle as to build).

This entire class of vessels were long survivors in the service because of the quality of their construction and their usefulness. During the war, four of the five ships had reasonably satisfactory machinery and were among the most versatile large steamers in the Union navy, with that particular combination of large battery and relatively shallow draft appropriate for both river and coastal operations. After the replacement of the *Pensacola*'s machinery, all five were on a par mechanically and became virtually ubiquitous on the navy's cruising stations for the remaining years of the wooden navy. Thus, as a class, these were the finest steam warships produced since the inception of the steam navy.

CHAPTER 6

The Sloops of 1858

The steam navy had begun with large sailing cruisers rather than the shallower draft vessels. To fill the latter need, in 1857, Secretary of the Navy Isaac Toucey requested funds for ten such ships, costing $2.3 million, pointing out that smaller vessels were as "effective as larger vessels and often more so" for coastal work. The requirements of all ten "light draft, great speed, and heavy guns." In his report the secretary observed: "The time has gone by when steam can be regarded in other light than as the principal motive power on the water for war purposes." The concept of the auxiliary screw steamer was being set aside for these smaller vessels.[1]

Great Britain provided an effective additional impetus to the congressional approval of funds for these vessels by detaining American ships thought to be engaged in the slave trade. Southerners who chaired the naval committees in both houses of Congress consequently approved the department's request, though paring it to eight vessels, one of which would be a side-wheel steamer. The authority was by an act of Congress dated 12 June 1858.[2]

Of the seven screw sloops, three were to draw 10 feet, and the others, 13 feet. One of the former, the *Pawnee,* was contracted to John W. Griffiths, a civilian shipbuilder of considerable repute. As in the case of the *Brooklyn,* the contract-built ship varied considerably from the others. The four 13-foot-draft ships built by the government were named *Mohican, Iroquois, Wyoming,* and *Dacotah.* Three of these were duplicated at the outset of the war and will be discussed in this chapter also. The *Iroquois* was repeated in two sloops, the *Oneida* and *Wachusett;* the *Wyoming* was repeated in the *Tuscarora;* and the *Mohican* in the *Kearsarge.* The other two light draft ships of the authorization were the *Narragansett* and *Seminole.*

These vessels were the first of many sloops in which the requirement for heavy armament was met by using one or two large shell guns, usually 11-inch Dahlgrens, mounted on pivot circles in the waist. These were stowed on the center line, in a fore-and-aft position, and supplemented by up to six 32-pounders in broadside. This battery was certainly small in numbers, particularly when the length of these ships was noted. At 198 feet for the 13-foot draft vessels, they were comparable to the length of 40- and 50-gun sailing frigates.

This disparity between size and armament was a consequence of several factors. Increased length was necessary to gain sufficient displacement within the required light draft, as well as to accommodate the engines and boilers. A third factor was the result of an effort to combine a large battery with speed in a steam-powered vessel. Secretary of the Navy Welles explained these considerations in a letter in 1863, which, though it applied directly to vessels of the longer *Sacramento* class, was in principle applicable to the *Mohican* and her sisters: "The heavy pivot guns can not be carried on the sharp bows of a steam vessel. The vessel will not sustain them, and there is not room to train them out of the direct line, which must be done by sheering the vessel. For practical reasons, in seagoing vessels of this form the pivot guns must be placed nearer the middle of the length of the ship . . . so that it can be worked on either side and be trained to 10 to 15 degrees with a fore-and-aft line." Henry A. Wise, head of ordnance at the time, added that the center mounting was "in accordance with the views of Mr. Steers," a revelation that coincides with the views of John A. Dahlgren (see chapter 4) that speed was possible, provided the ends of the vessels were not overladen.[3]

Therefore, much length was indispensible to allow the fine transition from sharp entrance and clearance lines to sufficient beam amidships for working the pivot and broadside guns. The excessive weight of the 11-inch Dahlgren could only be handled on pivot carriages with recoil control mechanisms, and these carriages required over 18 feet of deck space, from the ship's rail to the end of the carriage slide. The final justification for this entire arrangement was the Dahlgren gun itself, a gun that in its 11-inch variant fired a projectile five times the weight of the shot of the standard 32-pound broadside gun. This gave a vessel such as the *Kearsarge,* with two such guns, the theoretical equivalent of a ten-gun broadside.

Secretary Welles had written in response to Admiral Farragut, who complained at some length concerning the drawbacks of this reliance on large pivot guns in lieu of smaller and more numerous broadside guns. The substance of Farragut's remarks and the navy's subsequent deemphasis of this system will be found in chapter 9.

The method used in contracting for the engines of these vessels was also an innovation, though it had been tried with the second engines for the *San Jacinto.* The contractors were to guarantee their machinery would meet the department's preset performance requirements. First, the weight of machinery, boilers, and coal for five days' steaming were not to exceed 406 tons. Second, the engines were to attain 80 revolutions per minute and develop 1,000 horsepower. Third, coal consumption was not to exceed levels predetermined for the individual vessels.[4]

The hulls of the deep-draft vessels measured within inches of each other: just short of 199 feet in length and 33 feet in breadth. However, there were four distinctive hull forms. The *Iroquois* and her two later sisters (*Oneida* and *Wachusett*) were designed by B. F. Delano; the *Wyoming* and *Tuscarora,* by Francis Grice; the *Mohican* and *Kearsarge,* by William L. Hanscomb; and the *Dacotah,* by S. T. Hartt.

Wyoming and *Tuscarora*

Of the eight, the *Wyoming* was the first to be completed. She and the later *Tuscarora* were slightly narrower and shorter than all the deep-draft vessels with the exception of the *Dacotah.* Her entrance lines show a slight hollow at the load waterline, but the angle itself is slightly greater than those of the other 13-foot draft vessels. Though her angle of deadrise is slightly more than that of the *Iroquois,* her bilges are much harder and squarer, resulting in a nearly flat floor and virtually no tumble home.

Her machinery, which occupied some 50 feet of hull space between watertight bulkheads, consisted of two horizontal direct-acting cylinders, built by Merrick of Philadelphia, with 50-inch diameter pistons and a stroke of 30 inches. A surface condenser was provided, made up of 3,000 brass 5/8-inch tubes, with a total surface of 3,000 square feet. The

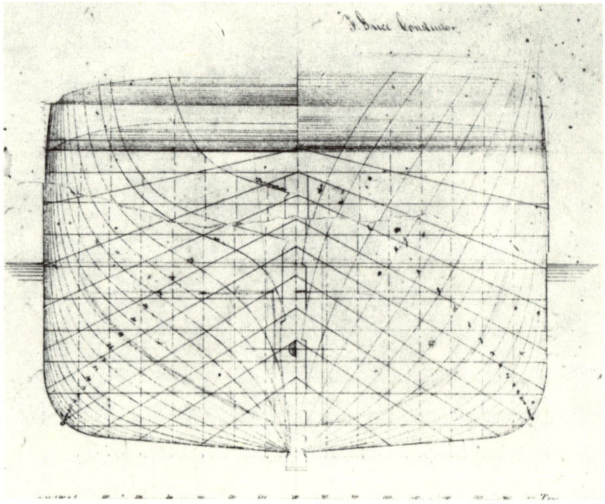

Body Plan of the Wyoming, *1859. The damaged portion of NARS 79-10-5A shows the vessel's nearly flat bottom, hard bilges, and nearly straight sides. Both* Wyoming *and the later* Tuscarora, *built from the same plans, seem to have had much less tendency to roll than others of this class. (National Archives)*

engine itself occupied only 16 feet longitudinally and approximately 8 feet vertically.[5]

Three Martin boilers were installed, one of which was a single-furnace donkey for auxiliary power. Exhaust was through a two-section, telescoping pipe. A four-bladed nonhoisting propeller was used with a clutch coupling to allow its free rotation when under sail. She was bark-rigged, carried 9,705 square feet of canvas, and was armed at the outset with two 11-inch Dahlgrens and four 32-pounders.

On the *Wyoming*'s engineering trials she made the run from the Delaware capes to Charleston against head winds and sea, averaging 9.3 knots. On the return, with favorable winds for twenty-four hours of a total of forty-seven, and a moderate adverse gale for the last ten hours, she averaged 10.8 knots. The highest speed for six consecutive hours was 11 knots, and the maximum for a single hour was 11.5 knots.[6] She gained a reputation for fast steaming early on, but in the average wooden screw vessel the working of the hull tended to rob the vessel of the critical engine and shaft alignment necessary to maintain optimum performance. Such dislocations may explain why her commanding officer later in the war reported he was "at a loss" to explain how she gained a reputation for speed and cited an average of 6 knots.[7]

The *Tuscarora* generally maintained average speeds similar to her sister. T. A. M. Craven, her commanding officer at commissioning, in 1864 recalled her as capable of 11 knots at 60 revolutions and recounted an informal race with nine vessels of the Spanish navy. She outdistanced all the ships save one, a side-wheeler, the *Isabella II.*[8]

The Wyoming, *or* Tuscarora, *during the Civil War, with Bark Rig. Note the prominent cutwater knee. (Naval Historical Center)*

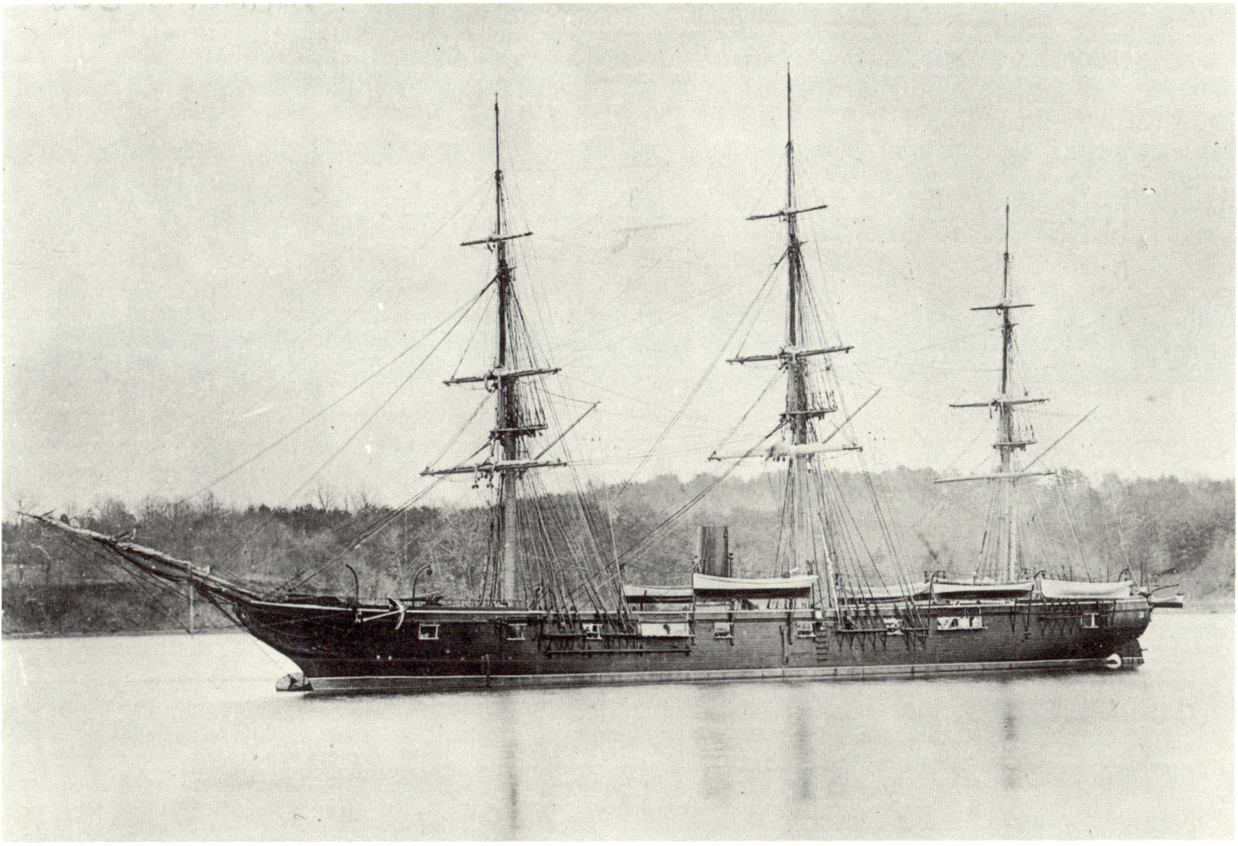

The Wyoming, *Postwar View, with Quarter Galleries and Ship Rig. (Reproduced with the permission of The Huntington Library, San Marino, California)*

The *Tuscarora* was, however, armed more heavily than the *Wyoming,* carrying six rather than four broadside guns. For about half of the war these were 8-inch, 55-hundredweight shell guns.[9]

Little has been found on the sailing and seakeeping qualities of either the *Wyoming* or *Tuscarora.* The commanding officer of the latter employed the stock phrase "behaved well under sail" for her and added the equally overused "proved to be a fast sailer."[10] In some cases, the only information available on the performance of some vessels is on preprinted forms, in particular those of the North Atlantic Blockading Squadron, or the sailing quality reports of the postwar years. Such forms encouraged only short phrases and only when the commander felt strongly concerning the vessel's qualities would he detail his comments.

Most of these sloops were atrocious rollers, however, and reaped generally harsh words from harried and wet commanding officers. No such commentary has been found for these two ships. This can be attributed to her flatter floors, resulting in greater stability and stiffness. Also, the vessels exhibited less sheer and one to two feet greater freeboard amidships than the *Iroquois* and *Mohican* and sisters, making them drier vessels in heavy weather. Their straighter sheer made them more attractive than the *Mohican* and *Kearsarge,* but their profile was not enhanced by the heavy and deep curve of their cutwater knees.

The careers of both sloops were typical for cruisers of this class: the majority of their wartime existence was spent searching for but not finding Confederate raiders. The *Tuscarora,* however, was instrumental in forcing the abandonment of the raider *Sumter* at Gibraltar in 1862. She maintained a typically peripatetic career in the post-war years, including Pacific sounding duties in 1874. She was decommissioned in 1880 and sold three years later.

The *Wyoming,* assigned to the Pacific at the outset of the Civil War, applied her offensive weight to upholding trade privileges with Japan in 1863; in the process she became the first American vessel to sink a Japanese ship. She completed her Pacific wartime duties with a circumnavigation of the globe. The quality of her machinery can be deduced by the fact that her world circling was only the final segment of a two-year commission spent in the far reaches of the Pacific. Her boilers finally reached their nadir when she reached home. Despite her broken-down condition, she was immediately sent in search of the C.S.S. *Florida,* only to return after five days of nursing worn-out machinery and boilers in adverse weather conditions.[11]

As with most of this class she was rerigged as a ship in the postwar era and cruised extensively in that period. She was decommissioned and sold in 1882.

Mohican and *Kearsarge*

These two vessels, one forgotten, the other virtually a naval icon after sinking the *Alabama,* were designed by William L. Hanscomb and built at the Portsmouth Navy Yard (Kittery) to the same hull plan. Other than their lines, the most significant variation from the *Wyoming* and *Tuscarora* was the use of back-acting, rather than direct-acting, engines. In this case, the stroke remained 30 inches, but the piston diameter measured 54 inches, slightly larger than the *Wyoming*'s. Woodruff and Beach of Hartford, Connecticut, built the machinery for both the *Mohican* and *Kearsarge.*

The hull lines of these two vessels show entrance lines similar to those of the other sloops, and as such they were sharper than any other American naval screw steamer before that time, with the notable exception of the *Niagara.* Their stern lines were considerably sharper than others of this deep-draft class. With nearly perpendicular sides and much rounder bilges than the Wyoming, the potential for excessive rolling was inherent in this design, while their sharpness brought expectations of good speed.

The original rig of the vessels was a reduced bark, carrying only two yards each on fore and mainmasts. No main or fore courses or gaff topsails are shown on early sail plans and the total sail area was therefore similar to that of the *Wyoming* (at 9,705).[12] This was an exceedingly small spread of canvas for ships of this size (198 feet). The *Princeton,* for instance, which displaced some 500 tons less, carried nearly 50 percent more sail, and 100-foot sailing brigs of the 1840s pressed around 10,000 square feet. This deemphasis on sail area, which was increasingly characteristic of wartime vessels, reflected the discarding of the auxiliary steam concept in these ships.

In appearance, the *Kearsarge* in the war years was far from graceful, with her tall stack serving to emphasize the vessel's considerable sheer. This ungainly aspect was particularly noticeable forward, where the sheer was exaggerated by a heavy topgallant forecastle deck angling upward and into the pronounced 16-foot cutwater knee. This was handsomely rectified when her sheer was straightened in one of her rebuilds in the 1870s.[13]

The main armament of the *Kearsarge* was two 11-inch Dahlgrens, supported by four 32-pounders of 42 hundredweight each. An 1859 deck plan of the *Mohican* shows pivot rails on the forecastle, as well as amidships. At commissioning, however, she was armed as the *Kearsarge.* As early as 1862, one 100-pound rifle was added on her forecastle, and by late 1864, the 11-inch pivots and 32-pounders had been replaced by six 9-inch Dahlgrens. After the war, she was reduced to four 9-inchers in broadside and gained one 11-inch pivot in 1869.[14]

The Kearsarge *in 1864, Shortly after Sinking the* Alabama. *Note boxed-in areas on her sides next to the engine spaces where chain cables were hung for protection. (Naval Historical Center)*

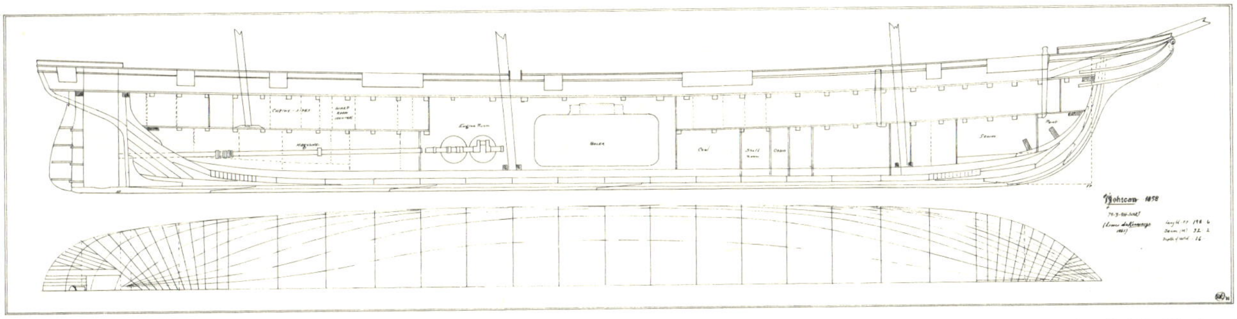

Lines and Inboard Plan of the Mohican, *1859. The* Kearsarge *was built to these lines. Note the sharpness forward. (NARS 79-3-9H, National Archives)*

Performance of these two ships was comparable to the *Wyoming* and *Tuscarora,* though the *Kearsarge* was possibly the speediest of the lot. T. A. M. Craven claimed that the *Kearsarge* could make 13 knots. Her first commander, C. W. Pickering, wrote that her greatest speed without canvas was 8½ knots, though this report was made within a month of her commissioning, hardly a broad sample on which to make a definitive judgment.[15]

Under sail alone, Pickering wrote that she could scud under close-reefed topsails with propeller disconnected at 10 to 11 knots. Late in her career, after two extensive rebuilds, she could attain over 13 knots in moderate weather, under sail and steam. By the 1870s her rig had been significantly increased, however, as shown here.[16]

Her other sailing characteristics were also described by Pickering: "With her present weight of armament, she is only adapted to river and harbor defense. Her bulwarks . . . are so extremely low, and she rolls so deeply, as to force . . . battening down the hatches even in moderate gales. . . . There has not been a day in which it would have been safe to cast loose the pivot guns." Unfortunately for the Confederate cause, the fight with the *Alabama* was on calm seas.[17]

By the 1880s, before her engine was replaced, the *Kearsarge* was called by Admiral Porter "the best vessel of her class in the Navy," and he credited her with 12 knots under sail or steam. He continued: "She is a good sea boat and could go around the world without using coal, and do much better in time of war than a faster steamer with small sail power."[18]

The *Mohican*'s sailing qualities were adversely affected by the forecastle-mounted 100-pounder, which her commander complained "destroyed all her good sea and sailing qualities." It brought her down by the head to the extent that she labored heavily in gales and he considered her unsafe. Later in the war, with the 100-pounder still aboard, and six 9-inchers replacing the 11-inch pivots and 32-pounders, Ammen credited her with 10 knots maximum under steam ("probably").[19]

The Kearsarge, *1888. Contrast her sail area with the 1861 plan. (NARS 79-9-34G, National Archives)*

The *Mohican* served initially off Africa, on anti-slave trade patrol; then early in the Civil War she was on the Atlantic coast, in the Port Royal expedition and the blockade. For a short period she cruised in search of Confederate raiders, then returned to the Atlantic blockade and the attacks on Fort Fisher. She served her remaining years in the Pacific, with the only significant incident the successful chase, boarding, and capture of the Mexican pirate steamer *Forward* in 1870. She was decommissioned at Mare Island in 1872 and for several years lay on the mud flats before being broken up. Administratively, however, she did not cease to exist, becoming one of the many new rebuilt ships added to the navy in the 1880's. Her namesake would become, as seen in a later chapter, the last wooden vessel added to the fleet.

The *Kearsarge* outlasted the first *Mohican* and had the distinction of fighting the last significant single-ship action in the age of the wooden warship. At the beginning of her career the *Kearsarge* and others blockaded the *Sumter,* under Raphael Semmes, then fought and sank Semmes's second command, the *Alabama,* off Cherbourg on 14 June 1864. In a war in which the adversaries were totally mismatched, both in types and numbers of ships, it could hardly be credited that two nearly matched vessels should come to blows. The advantage in the battle, however, went to the *Kearsarge*'s better gunnery and fresher powder, with assistance from chain armor on her hull abreast the engine spaces. The significance of the chain armor was minimal considering that of more than 350 Confederate projectiles fired, fewer than 20 hulled the *Kearsarge.*[20]

An 11-inch shell to the hull of the *Alabama* sealed her fate and marked another significant change in naval warfare brought about by steam propulsion: no longer could an enemy be defeated by dismasting her. Only when the engines were disabled or the hull opened to flooding was the battle over, and, in consequence, it was now virtually a necessity that the adversary be sunk.

No more than 173 projectiles were fired in sinking the *Alabama.* The percentage of hits is unknown, but the increased firepower of Civil War ordnance is evident in the number of rounds and

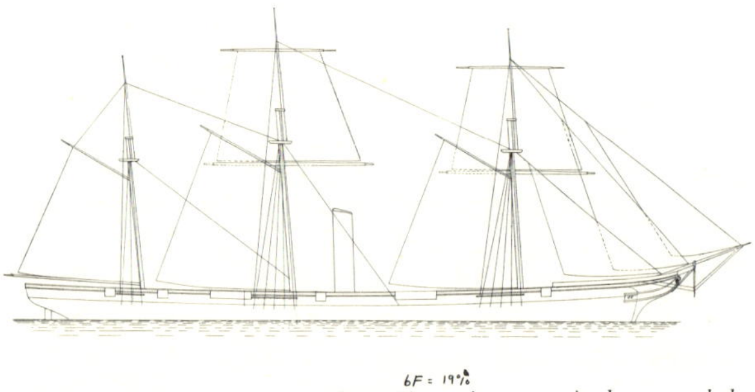

Sail Plan of the Kearsarge, *1861. No main course is shown and the sparsity of canvas is typical of U.S. naval sloops of the war years. (NARS 79-9-34R, National Archives)*

Decks and Outboard of the Kearsarge, *1888, As She Was Fitted When Lost in 1894. She had reverted to bark rig and had iron carriages for 9-inch smoothbores as well as converted pivot rifles. (NARS 79-9-34D, 79-9-34E, 79-9-34F, National Archives)*

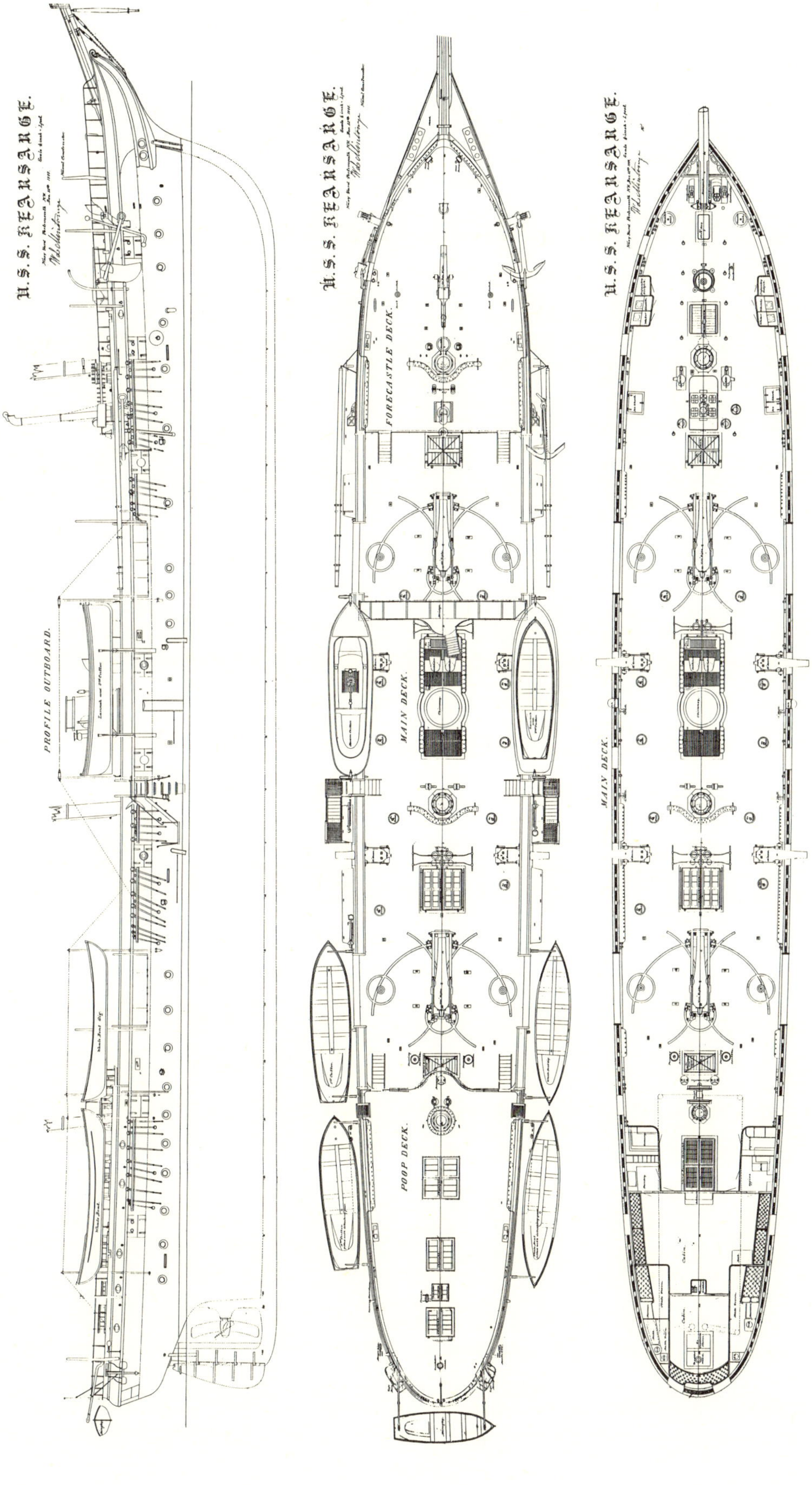
U.S.S. KEARSARGE.
PROFILE OUTBOARD.
U.S.S. KEARSARGE.
FORECASTLE DECK.
MAIN DECK.
POOP DECK.
U.S.S. KEARSARGE.
MAIN DECK.

The Kearsarge *in the Postwar Era, after Her Sheer Had Been Raised and Straightened. (U.S. Army Military History Institute)*

guns used in 1864 compared to the number required in earlier conflicts fought with 24-pounder or smaller cannon. Captain Winslow later pointed out that he was able to force the order of battle on the *Alabama* and prevent the raider from escaping to the three-mile limit and safety. Thus the steam engine was as decisive a factor in 1864 as sailing qualities had been three decades before.[21]

After an unsuccessful search for the CSS *Florida,* the *Kearsarge* ended her war career, then was stationed in the Pacific, North Atlantic, and West Indies for the balance of her long service life. In the postwar years, she went into refit on five occasions. In 1871 to 1873, her sheer was straightened and in her final refit she was given new engines. Her original engines were scrapped in 1891. Her armament in the later years was two converted 8-inch rifles and four 9-inchers on iron carriages in broadside.[22]

She was wrecked on Roncador Reef in the Caribbean on 2 February 1894 and a salvage team, sent at congressional expense, found that she had been burned by local scavengers. Four years later a second *Kearsarge* was launched, the only battleship ever built that was not named after a state.

Iroquois, Oneida, and *Wachusett*

The third of the 13-foot draft sloops authorized in 1858 was the *Iroquois,* designed by B. F. Delano at New York Navy Yard. Her hull design was again used in 1861 for the *Oneida* and *Wachusett.* These vessels were 8 inches longer than the *Wyoming* and 10 inches longer than the *Mohican.* The resulting ships were also slightly larger in displacement than any of their sister vessels, 1,488 tons.

The machinery of the *Iroquois* was back-acting, with cylinders of 54 inches and stroke of 28 inches, built by Pease and Murphy of New York. The *Wachusett*'s engines were also back-acting, 50 inches by 30 inches, duplicating those of the *Seminole,* built by Morgan Iron Works of New York. The *Iroquois* was originally built with a hoisting screw, unlike the remainder of the 13-foot draft vessels, which had uncoupling propellers.[23]

In hull design, the *Iroquois* and her sisters showed entrance angles on the load waterline slightly greater than the others of the class, and the lines were not as fine forward as the other vessels. Their bilges were the slackest of all the sloops, with slight tumble home topside. They had the lowest freeboard of these vessels and a moderate sheer amidships, which flared noticeably forward. The cutwater knee of these vessels was higher and more pointed than those of the other vessels of the class, giving them a less prominent stem profile. A plan of the *Oneida* shows that vessel with a perpendicular stem and no cutwater knee—surely a wartime expedient not seen on any of the other sloops of this class. In appearance, their long, low freeboard, with rather abrupt rise forward and comparatively

The Iroquois *in the Late 1860s. She had the least prominent cutwater knee of the class. (U.S. Naval Institute)*

small upturn aft, resulted in a rather unbalanced, down-at-the-stern appearance that was rectified somewhat by higher bulwarks added later.[24]

As originally built these ships were rigged as barkentines. A plan dated 1861, however, shows the *Oneida* with a schooner rig, unique to this class of sloops. In their later service, all were rigged as barks.

Their armament differed somewhat from the remaining ships of the class. The *Iroquois* was commissioned with a conventional battery of two 11-inch pivot guns and four 32-pounders. In 1863 a 50-pounder Dahlgren rifle was added. In 1864, however, two 9-inch Dahlgrens were substituted for the larger pivot guns, and a single 100-pounder rifle replaced the 50-pounder. Her original deck plan shows three pivot tracks, with long ports immediately aft of the topgallant forecastle, and it is assumed that this fore pivot circle was occupied by the 50- and 100-pounder rifles in succession. In the 1880s she received four 8-inch smoothbores, one 8-inch rifle, and one 11-inch pivot. She received a complete battery of 60-pounder rifles and 8-inch converted Dahlgrens in 1889.[25]

The *Oneida* was armed with two 11-inch pivots and at least one 30-pound rifle in 1862, at the time of her encounter with the blockade-running *Oreto* (*Florida*). The *Official Records of the Union and Confederate Navies in the War of the Rebellion* credits her with three 30-pounders in addition to four 32-

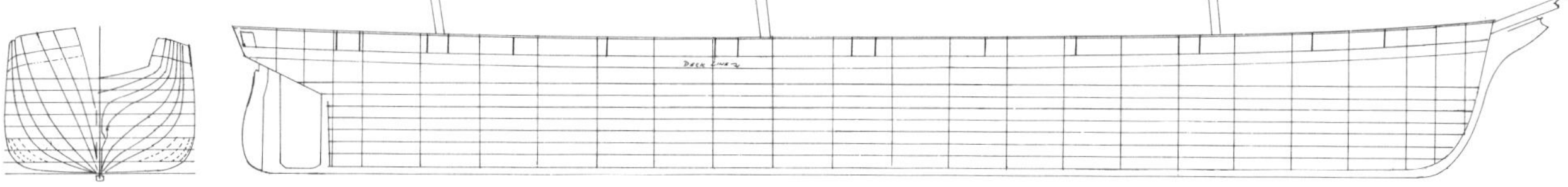

Lines and Sheer of the Iroquois, Oneida, *and* Wachusett. *Note the three pivot parts. (NARS 78-3-2L, National Archives)*

The Iroquois *in the 1870s, with Quarter Galleries, Ship Rig, and Higher Bulwarks. (U.S. Army Military History Institute)*

pound, 33-hundredweight smoothbores and two 9-inch Dahlgrens. By war's end she carried six 32s and one 11-inch pivot.[26]

The earliest record of the *Wachusett*'s guns (March 1862), refers to 11-inch pivot guns, in addition to four 32s and two 30-pounder rifles. In 1864, three 100-pounder Parrotts replaced the Dahlgrens. Two of the pivot rifles used the aft ports, with one gun on each side of the vessel. After her refit in 1869 to 1871, the battery reverted to two 11-inch and four 9-inch Dahlgrens, an arrangement that continued until her decommissioning.[27]

The steaming and sailing characteristics of all three ships unfortunately must be based on those of the *Wachusett.* This vessel seemed to be a magnet for aggressive commanders such as Charles Wilkes, who were none too reticent in airing their criticisms. Wilkes's particular complaint was with the ship's machinery, citing twelve breakdowns cruising from Washington to Havana in 1862. He criticized the vertical water-tube boilers, which required twelve hours for any leaks to be repaired, because they needed to be completely cooled and empty before maintenance could be performed.[28] (Horizontal tube boilers needed only to be drained far enough to empty the defective tube.)

The excessive rolling of the *Wachusett* was the subject of an effective complaint by J. S. Missroon, her first commander: "Her rolling . . . is so unusually sharp, quick and deep as to make it doubtful if her battery, especially the XI-inch guns, can be worked . . . in an ordinary seaway. . . . she seems to be entirely without the buoyancy essential . . . with her present battery."[29]

Whether Commander Missroon's complaint was the sole catalyst for the alterations that ensued is not known. In 1863, however, the vessel was docked and received bilge keels, possibly the first U.S. naval ship to be so equipped.[30] This apparently remedied the excessive rolling. The keels were removed in 1865, however, and then her commander, Robert Townsend, wrote that she sailed "at least one third better" than before, reaching 9½ knots under sail. He did, however, admit that he had "never sailed on a craft that rolled so much, and with so little provocation." His conclusion was that the extra speed compensated for the vessel's rolling.[31]

Possibly the change in her armament from the 11-inch Dahlgrens to 100-pounder rifles was also an attempt to alter the weight distribution and rolling problem. Each 100-pounder rifle tube weighed approximately 6,000 pounds less than an 11-inch

Dahlgren tube. Thus with two 100s stowed parallel to the midline for the aft pivot ports and one on the rails between main and foremast, the aggregate weight would be somewhat reduced, but the net effect would be to bring this weight nearer to the ship's center of gravity. In any case, commander Townsend's letter of 1865 shows that the problem was not eliminated by the change.

The *Iroquois* also was subject to excessive rolling. Her commander in 1864, however, wrote that she was "a good sea boat, although very wet and uncomfortable." She also had been given a new battery by that date: 9-inch in place of the 11-inch Dahlgrens, and a 100-pounder in lieu of the 50-pounder rifle. Commander C. R. P. Rodgers continued: "I am led to believe that the change in her battery has made her much easier at sea—that she rolls less and with a decreased jerk."[32]

For speed, the *Iroquois* averaged around 7 knots under steam alone at 60 revolutions per minute. Under the best circumstances, her commander estimated she could exceed 12 knots under sail and steam, "only for a short time," but he feared that the resulting vibration would strain the vessel.[33]

Little has been found on the rolling problem for the *Oneida*. Her speed, however, was of much interest late in 1862, when her commanding officer, George H. Preble, allowed the raider *Florida* to escape the blockade. He reported the *Oneida*'s "usual good weather speed" was 10 to 10½ knots. On the day in question, however, with one boiler out, her maximum was 7 knots and 38 to 40 revolutions. The *Official Records* credits the vessel with a maximum of 12 knots and an average of 8.5.[34]

The careers of the three ships varied widely. The *Wachusett* gained the most notoriety when her commander, Napoleon Collins, took it upon himself to ram the Confederate cruiser *Florida* while in a neutral harbor. The remainder of the *Wachusett*'s wartime service was divided among the North Atlantic squadron, Charles Wilkes's "flying squadron" in the West Indies, and a stint in the Far East in search of the raider *Shenandoah*. She cruised on various stations in the postwar years and made one ascent of the Mississippi as far as Vicksburg on recruiting duty in 1879. She was decommissioned in 1885 and sold two years later.

The *Oneida*'s close but inglorious encounter with the *Florida* was in September 1862, when the raider slipped past George H. Preble and his vessel into Mobile in broad daylight, using the age-old ruse of showing British colors to run the gauntlet. Only the *Florida*'s speed saved her from the pounding administered by the *Oneida* and gunboat *Winona* in the course of the chase. Preble was summarily cashiered, though he was later reinstated by a reluctant Lincoln.

While part of the gulf squadron, the *Oneida* was in the line at New Orleans, Vicksburg, and Mobile Bay; she was then attached to the Asiatic station in the postwar years. Her fate was tragic; she was run down by the British merchant steamer *Bombay* in 1870. The merchant vessel failed to render assistance to the sinking vessel and many lives were lost. The salvaged wreck was sold in 1872.

The *Iroquois* was also a participant at New Orleans and Vicksburg during the Civil War and began the conflict patrolling the Caribbean. She ended the war with a search for the *Shenandoah* and remained on the Pacific for the balance of her service. From 1892 to 1898 she was part of the Marine Hospital Service, then in commission for six months during the Spanish-American conflict. Subsequently, she was renamed *Ionie* and was removed from the navy list in 1910.

Dacotah

Of the four 13-foot draft ships, the *Dacotah* is the least well known and was decommissioned first, in 1869. She also participated in none of the major coastal or river operations of the Civil War.

Her design, however, was in no way inferior to her sisters. She was built at Norfolk to the plan of Samuel T. Hartt and measured 198 feet 5 inches by 32 feet 9 inches—slightly narrower than her consorts. She was nearly 100 tons lighter in displacement than the smallest of these sloops, measuring 1,369 tons.

Her lines were the sharpest of all the sloops, both fore and aft. Her fine run is evident in her buttock lines, which were nearly straight for a great deal of their length on her quarters. She had little rise of floors and her bilges approached the angularity of the *Wyoming*'s. Of all four ships, her lines sacrificed the most carrying power to speed. She was given a bark rig with substantial rake to her masts. These features, combined with a graceful sheer, without the pronounced forward flare of the *Iroquois* or the heavy-handed cutwater of the *Tuscarora*, made her a decidedly handsome vessel.[35]

Her engines were unique to the class, with gearing employed to drive the propeller shaft. Gearing had been used previously only on the second engines of the *San Jacinto*. Two cylinders, of 63-inch diameter and 36-inch stroke, drove an 8-foot diameter wheel with wooden gear teeth. This turned a pinion gear of 42 inches, resulting in a ratio of 9 to 4. Thirty-six engine revolutions gave eighty-one turns to the three-bladed propeller. Despite the large diameter of the main gear, the machinery was below the waterline of the vessel.[36]

Her two boilers were of a type new to the service: the fire-tube boiler, in which the water surrounded the heating gases rather than vice-versa. Such boilers had the advantages of simplicity and a steadier

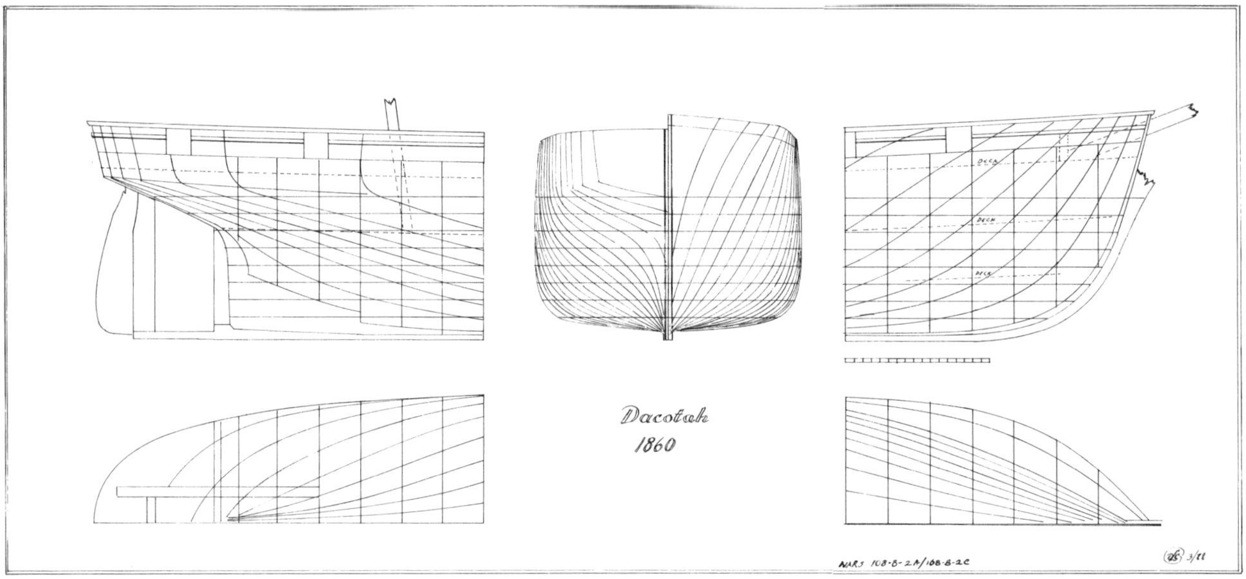

Lines of the Dacotah, *One of the Lighter Draft Sloops of 1858. (Traced from NARS 107-15-20, National Archives)*

supply of steam. Their larger water capacity, however, resulted in increased weight and required more time to build up steam.[37]

The *Dacotah* was originally armed with a pair of 11-inch Dahlgrens on pivots and four 32-pounder, 42-hundredweight broadside guns. In 1862 one of the Dahlgrens was replaced by a 100-pounder rifle, and by 1866 a 30-pounder rifle had been added.[38]

The performance required of the vessel by contract was a minimum of 14 statute miles per hour, with an additional premium paid to the builder for 15 miles per hour, for six consecutive hours. Fuel consumption was not to exceed 2.9 pounds of coal per hour. In her week-long trial at sea, the sloop bettered both figures, maintaining 15.24 statute miles (13.2 knots) per hour and consuming 2.81 pounds of coal per hour. In service, she could maintain 7 knots at two-thirds boiler pressure.[39]

The vessel's war record was less exciting than those of some of her sister sloops, who spent the duration of the conflict pursuing elusive Confederate cruisers. She was part of the North Atlantic Squadron, then the James River flotilla, and participated in the search for the *Chesapeake* late in 1863. She was out of commission for repairs for the last eight months of the war, then was assigned to the Pacific for the last three years of her service. She was inactive from 26 July 1869 to her sale on 30 May 1873, at Mare Island Navy Yard.

Seminole and *Narragansett*

The two lighter-draft, government-built sloops of the 1858 authorization were the *Seminole* and *Narragansett.* These two were equal in dimensions, at 188 feet by 30 feet. They displaced 1,230 and 1,235 tons, respectively, and were therefore about 150 tons lighter and 10 feet shorter than the remainder of the group (excepting the *Pawnee*). The hull lines of the two differed in all aspects except length and breadth. The *Narragansett* was designed by E. H. Delano and resembled his lines for the *Iroquois* in sharpness forward and angle of deadrise, though the *Narragansett* had harder bilges.

The *Seminole* was designed by John L. Porter, an assistant constructor at Warrington Navy Yard at Pensacola. According to her plans (NARS 108-7-8B), she was sharper forward and aft than the *Narragansett* and possessed slightly greater deadrise. Her bilges, however, were more pronounced, making her fuller in the lower waterlines.

Two types of engines were employed, with the *Seminole* receiving 50-inch by 30-inch back-acting steeple machinery and the *Narragansett* having direct-acting engines, 48-inch by 28-inch. Each had two Martin boilers and a third auxiliary. Grate surface of the boilers for each was 200 square feet and their heating area was about 6,000 square feet. Therefore, all the major engine specifications were proportionally smaller than those of the larger sloops.[40] Both were bark-rigged and armed with single 11-inch Dahlgrens on pivot. The *Narragansett* had four 32-pounders, and six were shipped on the *Seminole.*[41]

Reports of the performance of the *Seminole* are contradictory, especially speed. Early in the war she was ruefully referred to as the "old wagon," and Captain Dupont made the acid comment, "The Seminole is next to nothing because she can catch nothing." Yet, after a short refit in 1863 her commanding officer wrote: "The Seminole has a speed of 11 knots per hour with 60 revolutions, and can be driven faster."[42] Though the refit may have improved her speed, it appears she began her career with a reputation for plodding, and the facts

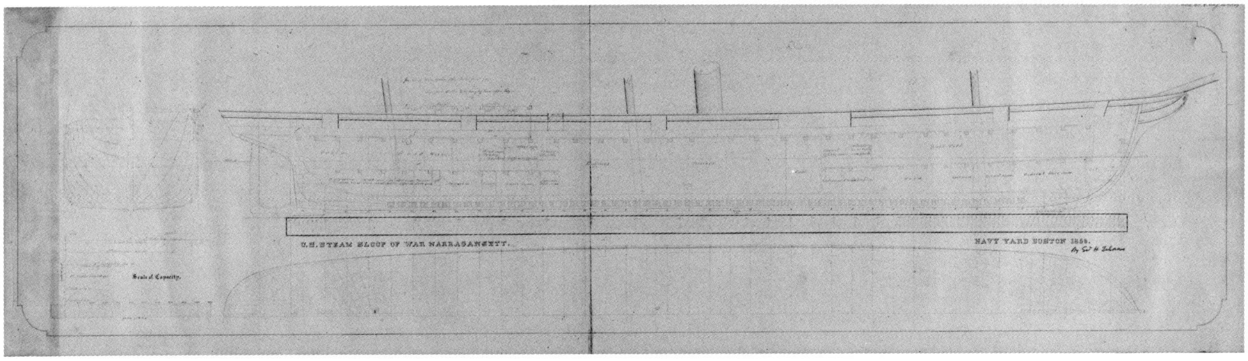

The Narragansett, *Designed by E. H. Delano at Boston. (NARS 79-12-12, National Archives)*

of the matter carried less weight than the accepted stories about the vessel.

The negative reports on the ship may have been the result of some complaints on her alleged poor construction shortly after commissioning. A survey, however, found that the defects were not serious. Otherwise, she proved to be a satisfactory ship. After giving her speed, her commanding officer in 1863 summed up the performance of the *Seminole:* "In all respects I am pleased with the vessel, and particularly with her steadiness, as most vessels of her class roll so as to interfere with fighting their pivot guns."[43]

On her trial trip the *Narragansett* made 7¾ knots with favorable conditions, including a 1½ knot tide, at 77 revolutions. With sail and wind on the quarter she reached 11 knots. Under canvas alone 7 knots was recorded. Like the *Seminole,* the *Narragansett* was not an excessive roller. The relatively flat floors and hard bilges can be credited with minimizing that problem, which plagued many of the larger sloops.[44]

There was a wide disparity between the wartime careers of the two ships, a natural result of the *Narragansett*'s station in the Pacific. Following the war, she served in both the Atlantic and Pacific, surveying steamer routes while in the Pacific. She was decommissioned in 1875 and sold in 1883.

Sail Plan of the Seminole, *Built at Pensacola. Note the long lower masts. (NARS 108-7-8D, National Archives)*

The so-called old wagon was active on river service in Virginia, shelling Confederate emplacements, and participating in the assaults on Port Royal and Fernandina, Florida—assignments thought appropriate for her slowness. After the 1863 refit, she was part of the West Gulf blockade and had three captures to her credit. She was part of the fleet action at Mobile Bay and was decommissioned after the war and sold in 1870.

In the sloops of war of 1858, the navy obtained the most versatile and reliable ships of the entire wooden steamer era, and among the longest lasting. The key to their success was not in perfection of engine or hull but in a reasonable combination of capacity, firepower, speed, and mechanical reliability. Moreover, their draft was sufficient for the open sea but shallow enough for coastal and river operations. These characteristics, combined with the solidity of live-oak construction, enabled their use in many roles and guaranteed their continued utility well after the conflict.

One important caveat must be made, however. The reputation of these ships may have been much different in any kind of war other than with the South, essentially not a naval conflict. If they had had to cope with modern vessels, their defects would have been disastrously evident, particularly their excessive rolling and consequent inability to use their main offensive armament, the 11-inch Dahlgren, in any kind of seaway.

Finally, the *Kearsarge* must be summed up separately. This vessel, with the *Monitor* and possibly the *Hartford,* symbolized the entire naval effort in the Civil War, and the *Kearsarge* stands out distinctively because she alone fought and won a classic single-ship engagement.

The consequences of this victory and the elevation of the *Kearsarge* to her preeminent status are still with us. To generations of Americans, the perception of the navy's role in the war was limited to the defeat of the *Alabama,* the Battle of Mobile Bay, the *Monitor* and *Merrimack,* and some acknowledgment of the blockade. Thus the wooden steam navy as a whole, along with its strategic functions, was overshadowed by dramatic moments and memorable quotations.

The *Kearsarge*'s longevity reinforced her status as a legend, and she became virtually an embodiment of the old wooden steam Navy. The timing of her loss in 1894, when the war had become a heroic national trial by fire, simply ennobled her further. In effect, an entire era of U.S. naval history became the fief of one sloop-of-war, one ironclad, and Farragut's determined "Damn the torpedoes!" at Mobile Bay. Consequently, the majority of the ships were relegated to obscurity.

Pawnee

In the last screw vessel of the authorization of 1858, the navy found itself with the most peculiar design since that of the unlamented Hunter's wheel ships. The *Pawnee* was designed by John W. Griffiths of New York and built under his supervision at the Philadelphia Navy Yard.

Griffiths, who was famous for his clipper ships *Rainbow* and *Sea Witch,* was also noted for rather unusual light-draft merchant steamers. The strangest was the *Ocean Bird,* of 1854, which featured an 8-foot draft with a flat bottom on a length of 225 feet and a breadth of 37 feet. She was lightly built, but Griffiths compensated for this with diagonal strapping in the hull and beneath the deck beams, and with longitudinal as well as transverse watertight bulkheads.

A second ship, the *North Carolina,* was built to enter that state's shallow ports and consequently had a 10-foot draft. She was screw propelled with geared engines allowing the propeller to turn at twice the speed of the engine. She was noted for poor steering and excessive rolling.[45]

In June 1858, Griffiths and an associate wrote Secretary Toucey with ideas for both side-wheel and screw vessels for use in Chinese waters where marauding pirates and civil strife were threatening American interests. (This had been one of the fac-

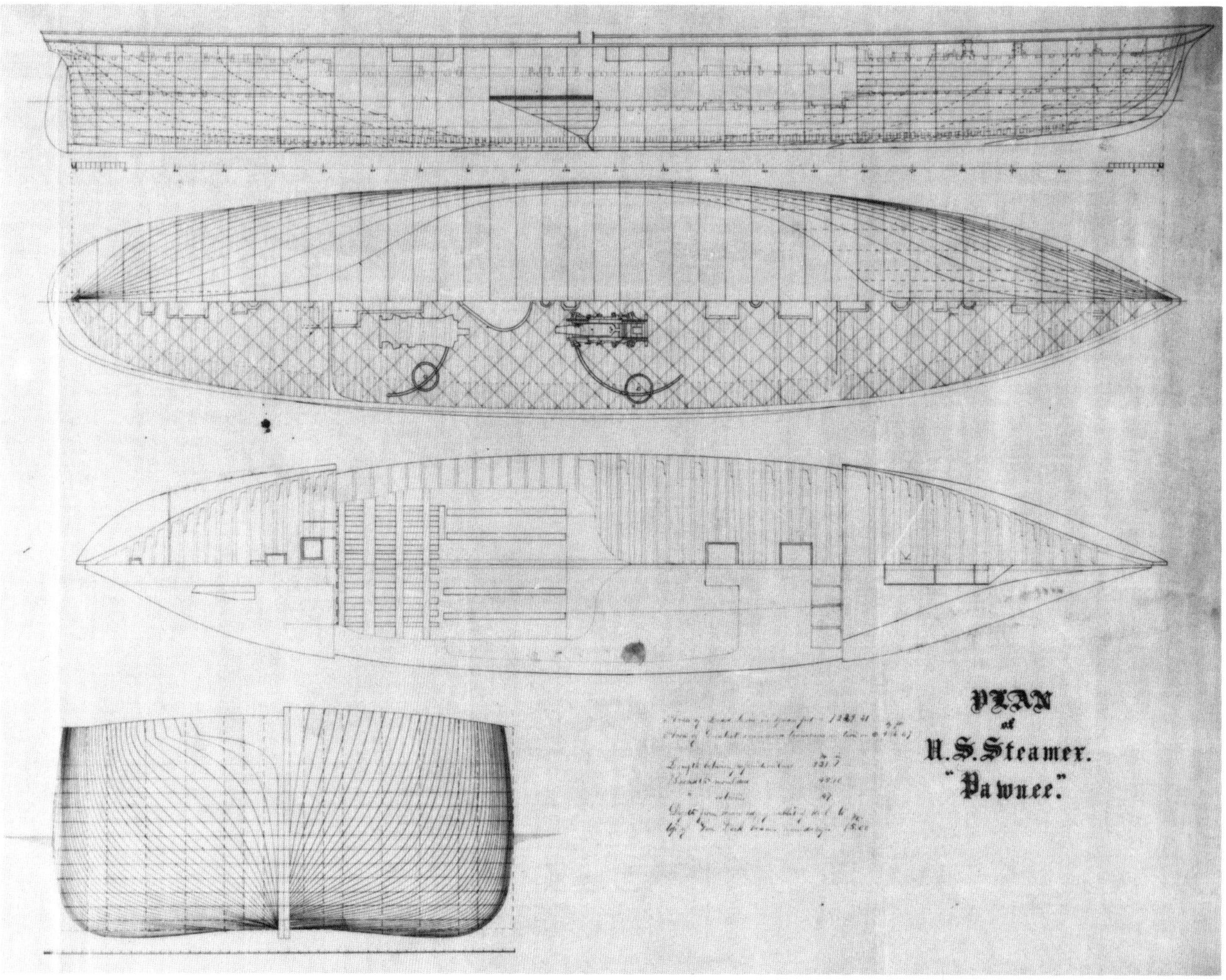

Sheer and Lines of the Pawnee. *The design by J. W. Griffith shows a unique concave hull form, designed to allow increased displacement without commensurate deepening of the draft. (NARS 79-4-5A, National Archives)*

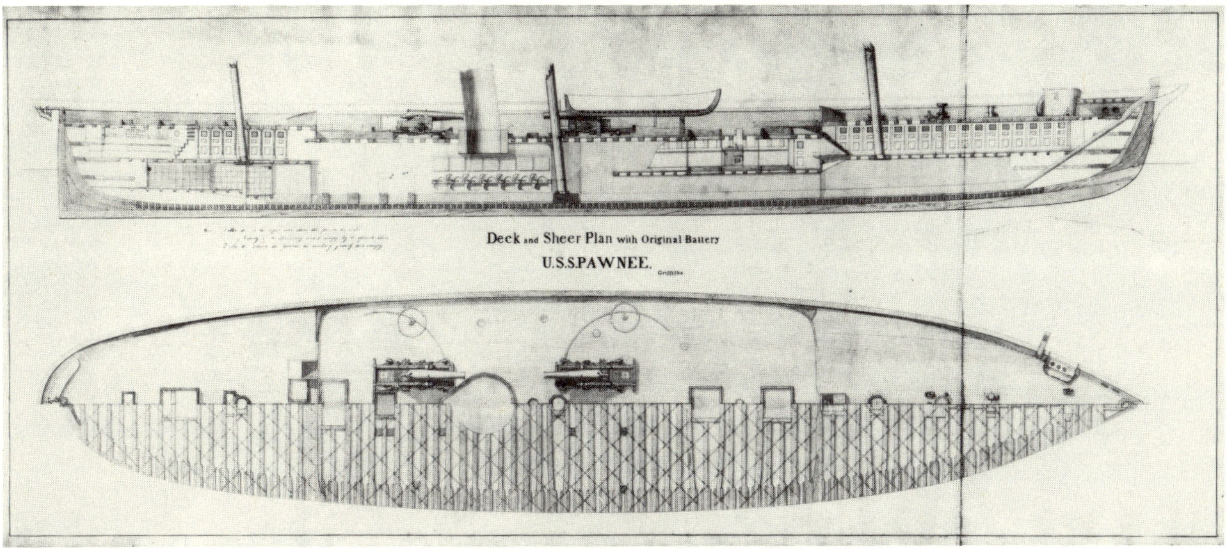

Griffith's Inboard Plan of the Pawnee, *with Deck and Her Original Four Pivot-Gun Battery—All 11-inch Dahlgrens. Note the diagonal iron bracing under the decks. The original plan is hand-colored. (NARS 35-7-6A, National Archives)*

tors in bringing about congressional approval of the shallow-draft sloops.) Griffiths offered to build the screw steamer at 14-, 12-, or 10-foot draft, to carry eight, six, or four 11-inch pivot guns respectively. The guns were to be mounted "to bring all the guns into action on either side at the same time." Twin screws would provide propulsion.[46]

In the end the 10-foot draft offer was accepted, though without the capability of using all guns on each side. The resulting vessel, which measured 221 feet 6 inches by 47 feet (extreme) was the largest in displacement (1,533 tons) and burden (1,289 tons) of the entire group, with the latter measurement reflecting her capacious hull. The wide beam was essential to reach the tonnage necessary for such substantial weapons on a light-draft vessel.

Some characteristics of the ship reflect Griffiths's earlier merchant ships, while others were unique to the *Pawnee.* The building instructions for her called for live-oak frames filled in solid with yellow pine to a point four feet above the base line. The keelsons were to be of 1/4-inch and 3/8-inch iron plates forming a cross section like an inverted V, riveted to horizontal 4-inch-by-6-inch angle iron. These triangular beams were seated on yellow pine strakes, bolted to the floors.

Diagonal strapping was composed of 5/8-inch copper and galvanized rods running from the floor heads to the deck line. Two complete sets were used, with each set crossing and bolted to the other. The frame timbers were grooved to accept the rods. Another feature virtually unique to the *Pawnee* was additional strapping, consisting of 1/4- by 2 1/2-inch bars, run diagonally on top of the deck beams. Two sets of these criss-crossed the entire deck and were riveted at each crossing point.

This already unusual amount of ironwork was supplemented by two 3/16-inch-plate watertight bulkheads with watertight door passages, fore and aft of the engine and boiler spaces. The engine-space ceiling was 3/16-inch galvanized iron, riveted, caulked, and bolted to the timbers.[47] Without a doubt, more iron was used by Griffiths in this ship than had been used before in any other wooden U.S. Navy vessel. With the ship's live-oak framing, the ship must have been among the strongest afloat.

Yet another construction technique was unique to this vessel: the use of bent live-oak frames. Griffiths had developed his own method for bending water- or vapor-soaked frames and had used such timbers in several of his merchant vessels. Bending the frames eliminated the need to find suitably shaped natural knees. The process also cured the timbers.[48]

The hull design itself was predicated on the need to reconcile large burden with shallow draft. Fore and aft the water lines were extremely sharp and hollow, with this concavity extending aft to a very full midship section. Aft, the concave lines were required to allow clearance for the screws between the counter and line of the keel.

The most obvious characteristics of the hull were the bilges, which in the midship section descended to the level of the bottom of the keel, making the bottom concave parallel to the keel for some 45 feet amidships. This unorthodox arrangement was employed in order to increase her displacement without exceeding the designated draft.[49]

The machinery of the *Pawnee* was complementary to her unique hull. A two-cylinder direct-acting engine with 65-inch cylinders and 36-inch

The Pawnee, *a Wartime View, with Blockade Gray Paint and Torpedo Rigged Out. (U.S. Army Military History Institute)*

stroke, built by Reanie and Neafie of Philadelphia, drove a gear 87 inches in diameter, set slightly to port. This gear turned two pinions 35 inches in diameter, one of which was keyed to one of the two propeller shafts; the other 35-inch gear turned a third gear of the same diameter, keyed to the second propeller shaft. Without the action of the third 35-inch gear between the main and pinion, both propellers would have rotated in the same direction, with obvious consequences to the vessel's steering.

The two screws were four-bladed and supported by a horizontal strut mounted on the sternpost. A clutch allowed disconnecting the propellers, but the single drive gear arrangement prevented operating the screws independently for steering purposes.[50] The *Pawnee* was the first operational U.S. Navy ship with twin screws, though the original *Water Witch* was so fitted experimentally for a short time.

Completing this unusual picture was a reduced bark rig: "the sail being the auxiliary," as designated in Griffiths's building instructions. The single most outstanding visual feature of the *Pawnee,* however, was a clipper bow without a bowsprit. A sliding jibboom could be moved "at pleasure to take its place." Her clipper bow, without bowsprit, jibbooms, and flying jib, was an incongruity on a vessel whose masts and yards were dwarfed by her hull length.

The finish of the woodwork on the *Pawnee* may have been of a higher grade than that of navy-built vessels. When Griffiths requested funds to apply expensive veneers to her appointments, however, Lenthall would have none of it: white pine was cheaper—there would be no paying passengers on the *Pawnee.*[51]

The *Pawnee* was launched in October 1859 and commissioned 11 June 1860. Her battery consisted of four 11-inch Dahlgrens mounted on pivot rails, stowed in pairs parallel to the centerline of the deck, an arrangement similar to that of the *Niagara.* Two 12-foot pivot ports were cut in each side. After a trial trip, however, the secretary of the navy had the big Dahlgrens replaced by eight 9-inch guns, mounted in broadside.[52] The rationale for this significant alteration is not known. The aggregate weight of the eight smaller guns was greater than that of the larger weapons by at least four tons, with a gain of only 22 pounds in throw-weight. Furthermore, the eight would require a larger crew. The deciding factor may have been the longer firing intervals for the 11-inchers and a preference for more continuous fire.

The ship's structural strength was such that in 1863 she was given 100-pounder and 50-pounder rifles. By war's end, twelve 9-inch Dahlgrens were shipped in addition to the two rifles and two light howitzers. This was an aggregate weight of over 62 tons of ordnance (considering the weight of the tubes alone). As can be seen, the *Pawnee,* though a product of the same authorization, was far from being another "sister" ship to the *Mohican* and others.

The only test of the *Pawnee*'s sailing qualities came after the war, though she was already known as a "great roller." As might be expected, her shallowness made her excessively leewardly. Her commanding officer reported that with a fair wind forward of the beam she made "as much to leeward as ahead." Under sail alone with screws uncoupled, she made 7 to 9 knots; under steam, 8. Her battery at the time was ten 9-inch guns and two 60-pounder rifles.[53]

Her leeward wandering was hardly a factor in her war record, which began with the attempt to rescue the vessels laid up at Norfolk before the conflagration. She participated in the Hatteras and Port Royal expeditions, then in various coastal operations for the remainder of the war. She was active all but six months of the conflict, when she was under repair at Philadelphia. Though the operations she was involved in were smaller in nature, she sustained a great deal of damage. In a sortie on the Stono River in 1863, for instance, she received thirty-three hits in the starboard hull and twelve elsewhere, and only chain cables prevented damage to her boilers. In a survey in July 1865, she was reported "penetrated with shot and shell in eighteen places and some of the shot are still embedded in the timbers; the timbers are but little injured, but the plank are badly shattered."[54]

Griffiths's peculiar hull design was put to the test in preparation for an unidentified "special service" off Morris Island in 1863, when her entire battery (eight 9-inchers and two rifles) was hauled to one side. The ten guns, plus more than two hundred fathoms of protective chain cable, brought the affected side down only twelve inches.[55]

After the war, she was stationed with the South American squadron for a short time. In 1869, her engines were removed and she was converted to a hospital ship for Key West. She was decommissioned in 1872 and sold in 1884.

Saginaw

The side-wheel vessel called for in the 1858 authorization was designated *Saginaw* and was the only naval paddle-wheel ship built between the 1847 authorization and the wartime double-enders. Though this side-wheel vessel may appear to have been a retrograde development, in the merchant service the widespread use of screw propulsion came somewhat later than its naval predominance. As late as 1864, the French transatlantic mail company Cie. Generale Transatlantique inaugurated their service with two paddle steamers.[56] The use of screw vessels by American firms was tried, then discontinued, in the early 1850s. Two major problems plagued the early screw vessels: the working of the wooden hulls, an ill that would only be resolved satisfactorily with the use of iron and steel, and the unsuitability of available materials for propeller shaft bearings.

Given the *Saginaw*'s intended mission, the suppression of piracy on the coasts and rivers of China, the paddle wheel was a logical choice. She would not be involved in the full-scale naval warfare considered so inappropriate for side-wheel ships.

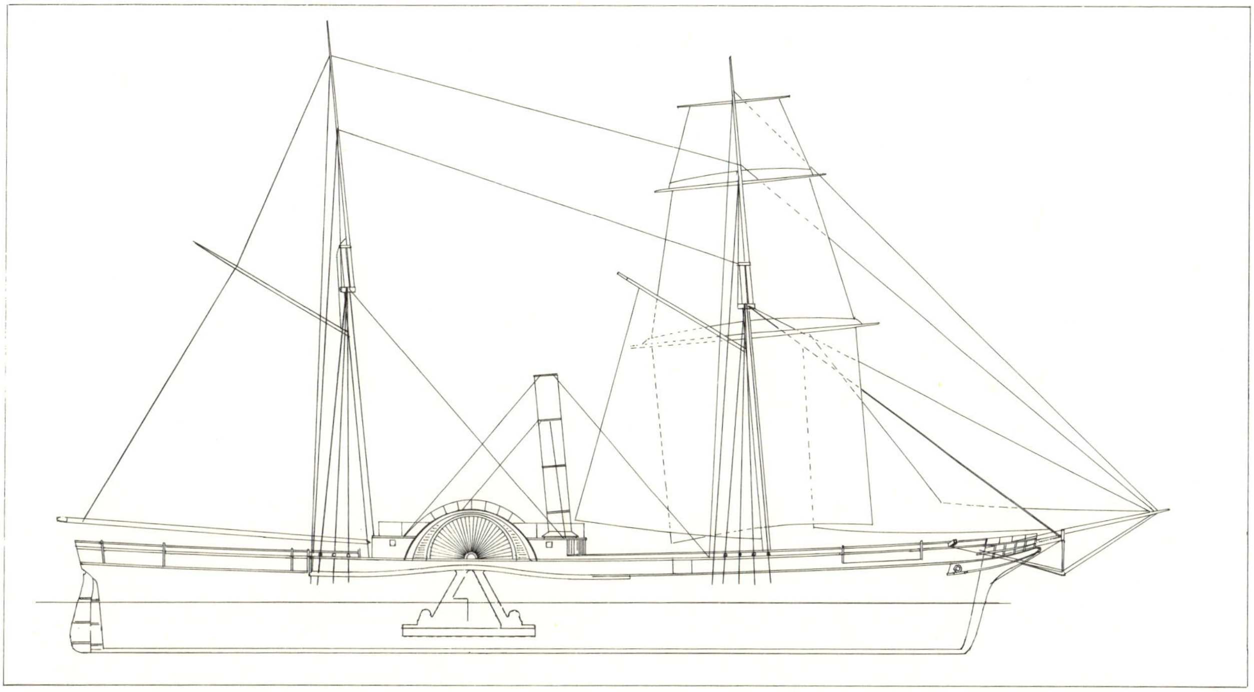

The Saginaw, *the Last Prewar Paddle Steamer. She was built for work in Chinese coastal waters and was the first vessel built at the Mare Island Navy Yard. The* A*-frame shown is for her oscillating cylinders; the cylinders were mounted on trunnions, and her piston rods worked upward to the paddle shaft. (Drawn from NARS 40-7-7B and 40-7-7F, National Archives)*

She was laid down 16 September 1858 at Mare Island Navy Yard, the first ship constructed there as well as the first naval vessel built on the West Coast. She was 155 feet by 26 feet (453 tons) and built, according to the *Official Records,* of laurel wood.[57]

Although her hull design was conventional, her engine was unique to American warships. She had oscillating cylinders, a type used previously only on the storeship *John Hancock* of 1850. Oscillating engines were known both for compactness and simplicity. In the *Saginaw,* the machinery occupied 23 feet longitudinally but only 16 feet athwartships, allowing considerable stowage and bunkerage on either side.[58]

The engine was composed of two 39-inch by 49-inch cylinders, with piston rods working upward to the shaft. As in the typical oscillating engine, no separate connecting rod was necessary: the piston rod attached directly to the crankshaft. In conventional engines, the connecting rod was necessary to translate the straight reciprocating piston rod motion into the circular arcs required to rotate the throws on the crankshaft. In the oscillating engine, the cylinder itself was mounted on trunnions, allowing it to move in sympathy with the piston rod as it cranked the shaft. In many oscillating engines, the intake and exhaust valves were incorporated into the trunnions, further simplifying the engine.

One of the main theoretical objections to this type of engine was the supposed effect the movement of the cylinder had on the vessel in heavy seas. It is noteworthy, however, that the *Great Eastern,* I. K. Brunel's outsized iron ship, had four oscillating cylinders, each of which weighed 38 tons, including piston and rod.[59] One suspects that the true objection to these engines was based on a general uneasiness about such great weights being allowed considerable movement within the hull.

The *Saginaw* appears to have been relatively trouble free mechanically. She averaged 8 knots in a career spent in the Pacific where cruises could be extraordinarily long. She was rigged as a topsail schooner, and her armament was one 50-pounder Dahlgren rifle, one 32-pounder, and two 24-pounder rifles.[60]

Her first years were on the coast of China, suppressing piracy. She was found to be quite rotten at Whampoa in January 1862 and was decommissioned and repaired sufficiently to allow her return to Mare Island that July. After recommissioning in December, she remained in the Pacific for the remainder of her existence.[61]

The *Saginaw*'s gig is no doubt more famous than the side-wheeler. Returning from Midway in 1870, the *Saginaw* grounded and broke up on Ocean Island. Five of her crew survived 1,500 miles and thirty-one days in the gig and reached Hawaii only

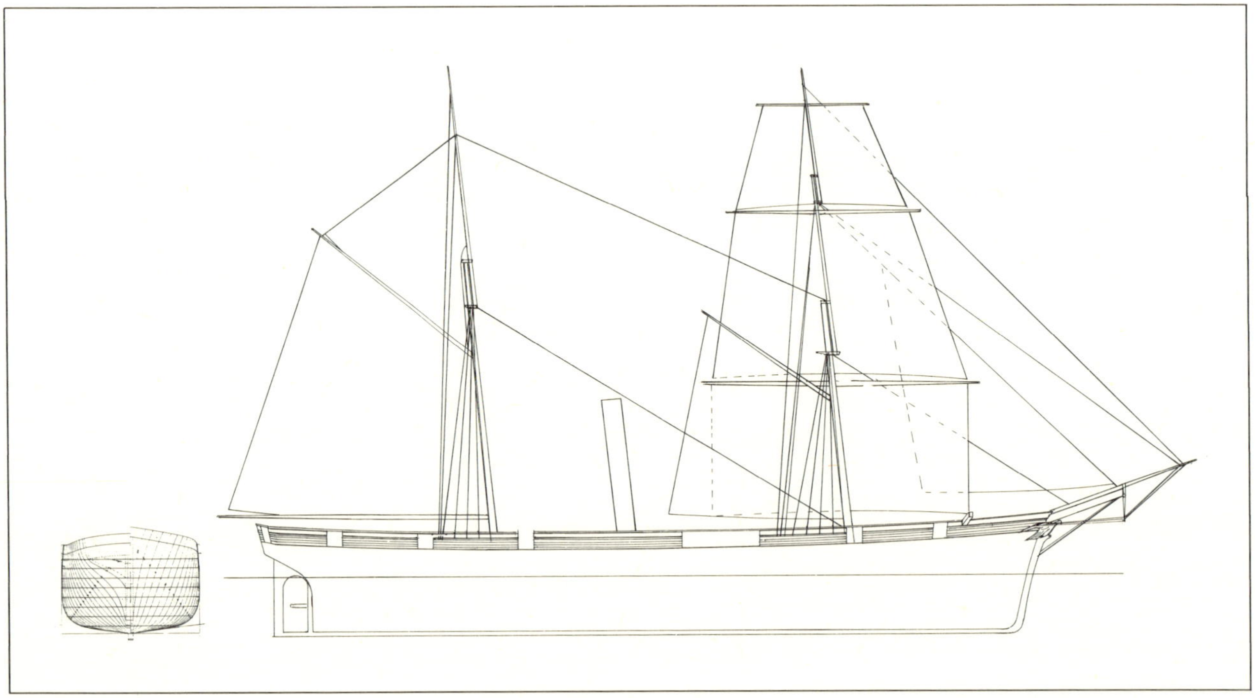

The Pocahontas, *Formerly the* Despatch, *As She Was Rebuilt by the Navy. Her general arrangement and size became the pattern for the ninety-day gunboats to come in 1861. (NARS 40-13-3C, 40-13-3D, National Archives)*

to lose the boat on the breakers. Four of the five died there. The only survivor, William Halford, then walked to civilization and obtained rescue for the remainder of the crew still on the island.[62]

Pocahontas

The last warship built before the Civil War was another example of administrative sleight of hand: the *Pocahontas,* earlier known as the *Despatch,* or *City of Boston.* As *Pocahontas* she entered the navy list in 1859. She had originally been purchased as the *Despatch* in 1855 at Boston, having been the *City of Boston* in merchant service. This small steamer, though active in the war, was much more important for her design influence than for any combat duty.

The *Despatch* was purchased as a tender for Pensacola (Florida) and had a displacement of 558 tons. In 1859 the vessel was rebuilt at Gosport to a design by S. M. Pook, emerging at 694 tons and 154 feet by 30 feet 4 inches. The draft of the vessel, now named *Pocahontas,* was 12 feet, and she was powered by a two-cylinder vertical engine with 33-inch cylinders and 30-inch stroke. Two Martin boilers were installed.[63]

She exhibited considerable sheer and flared clipper bows with a two-masted fore-and-aft rig. She was armed with one 10-inch Dahlgren on a waist pivot and four 32s in broadside. During the war she received heavier (57-hundredweight) 32 pounders, and a 100-pounder Parrott replaced the Dahlgren.[64]

On her trial at sea she made 8 knots, and some modifications were suggested subsequently. Her commander described her as an "excellent sea boat, steams very well indeed, considering the little power (60 horses) she has, and might be made a very fast vessel under canvas." He considered her an inefficient sailer, however, due to her small spread of canvas.[65]

She served throughout the war with no major modifications, though the placement of her vertical engines gave her commanders some cause for alarm. The only barrier between her cylinder heads and open air was a grating; one of her commanders recommended covering the engines with sheet iron, and another suggested piling one hundred bags of coal around the openings.[66]

The *Pocahontas* was sold out at the end of the war and generally was categorized with the hundreds of anonymous vessels purchased for the blockade. She was, however, indeed built by the navy. More important, however, was the influence her design would have on the ninety-day gunboats at the outset of the war.

The Pocahontas, *a Wartime View. Note the 10-inch Dahlgren on pivot and the field piece on the ship's boat astern. (Southern Historical Collection, Wilson Library, University of North Carolina at Chapel Hill)*

Festivities for the Launch of the Ninety-day Gunboat Marblehead, *19 October 1861. One of the first launched, she was not commissioned until March 1862. (Courtesy Peabody Museum)*

CHAPTER 7

Gunboats and Cruisers, 1861–1862

The firing on Fort Sumter in April 1861 found the U.S. Navy unprepared for the conflict. Although the steam vessels of the fleet were for the most part technologically viable, both in armament and propulsion, they were few in number. Twenty-four steam war vessels were in active service in March 1861—not including the *Michigan,* which was on the Great Lakes, and the five steam frigates, which were out of commission. Of these twenty-four, but three were in northern ports at the outbreak of hostilities.

Rectifying this shortage of vessels would involve procuring ships for roles ranging from river service to blockade duty and ocean cruising. Many vessels were purchased and converted, particularly for blockade and river duties. Blue-water cruisers and vessels that would be involved in the bombardment of coastal fortifications, however, were not likely to be found on the civilian market. These had to be built, in many cases by contract, specifically for these roles.

Second only to the monitors, the "90-day gunboats" were the most publicized class of ships built for the navy early in the war. The sobriquet was not accurate and seemed to function more as a morale-boosting catch phrase than a description of the actual construction of these vessels. The title conjured up images of legendary Yankee ingenuity at work bringing the agrarian South into submission.

Although the completion of these vessels was not as swift as the title implied, the initial design process was expeditious. The earliest pencil sketch of the vessels' general arrangement was dated May 1861 and initialed by Lenthall, setting forth a general sail and spar plan.[1] The same month, Lenthall summoned S. H. Pook (the son of S. M. Pook), who arrived in the capital along with a delegation of other shipbuilders, including R. B. Forbes. This group urged the construction of a large number of shoal-draft, maneuverable steamers with heavy armament for their size. Designed to be useful in coastal, river, and blockade duties, they were also to be inexpensive and to require little construction time. The idea was accepted, and assuming *ex post facto* congressional approval, keels for twenty-three such ships were laid, all contracted to civilian shipyards. The naval yards were occupied with the construction of larger warships. The number of ninety-day gunboats laid down was said to have been determined by the total number of available slips in civilian yards.[2]

Definitive plans for the vessels were completed in June, from the hand of Pook, "under chief constructor Lenthall." Contracts were let from 29 June through 10 July and called for delivery from 90 days for the first four to 148 days for the last. The first completed was the *Unadilla,* commissioned 93 days from contract date. The last commissioned was the *Marblehead,* on 8 March 1862.[3]

The completed design called for a vessel 158 feet 4 inches by 28 feet with a 12-foot depth of hold (from gun deck to keelson) and a displacement of 691 tons. Since there is no record of variations in hull design among the vessels, a description of one, the *Chippewa,* should serve for the class.

The *Chippewa* was framed in white oak with the usual iron strapping from bilge to 6 inches below the planksheer. An additional horizontal head strap secured the vessel's stem. A 16-foot section of bulwarks in the waist was hinged for the pivot gun.[4] Early photos of the vessels show a stationary rail, the supporting stanchions in place, and no evidence of bottom-hinged port shutters. Later images indicate the hinged bulwarks folded in their entirety, after the rail was unshipped.

The hull form was marked by a moderate deadrise and nearly straight sides. The entrance angle was 52 degrees and the clearance angle measured

120 degrees. Thus the gunboats were slightly sharper than the *Hartford* but not as sharp as the *Kearsarge* and *Iroquois.* The clearance angle of the gunboats, however, was considerably fuller than any of those ships. They had a bit of a sheer and were given round sterns and cutwater knees. The bowsprit, fashioned of metal, was vestigial, measuring approximately 15 feet. The vessels were rigged as fore topsail schooners with gaff topsails.

A two-cylinder back-acting engine of 30-inch cylinders and 18-inch stroke was installed. The first four engines were built by Novelty Iron Works, duplicating machinery built for gunboats for the Russian navy, and the remaining nineteen were built from designs of Benjamin F. Isherwood. The two cylinders drove a 9-foot disconnecting screw and could be operated independently. Two bearings supported the shaft through the stern deadwood, with a bearing surface 7 feet in length. In use, the lignum vitae bearings were provided with a constant flow of water to prevent heat build-up. The cylinders had a single surface condenser located between them.[5]

Two boilers were installed and connected so that each one could be operated with either cylinder. An independent oscillating engine provided forced draft for the boilers and operated auxiliary bilge and feed water pumps. The sole known variation in all the vessels was in the initial four ships (the *Unadilla, Pembina, Ottawa,* and *Seneca*). These had some 60 percent less boiler power than the other nineteen ships, whose boilers were designed according to Isherwood's ideas on steam expansion.[6]

With a few exceptions, the gunboats were commissioned with a battery of one 11-inch Dahlgren on the waist pivot, two 24-pounders further aft, and a 20-pounder Parrott on the forecastle. They were crewed by 100 officers and men and carried 112 tons of coal, sufficient for five and a half days of steaming with the blowers, or ten days without.[7]

In 1863, B. F. Isherwood outlined the performance of the *Chippewa* in his two-volume *Experimental Researches in Steam Engineering.* The figures serve to illustrate the significant impact of the blower on the speed of the vessel. Without the forced draft, the ship averaged 8.5 knots, burned 900 pounds of coal per hour and developed 218 horsepower. This was 3.43 pounds of coal per nominal horsepower. Using the fan system, the speed was 9.98 knots and the engines consumed 2,148 pounds per hour and reached 382 horsepower—4.68 pounds per horsepower. The tradeoff was a reduction in economy, with more than

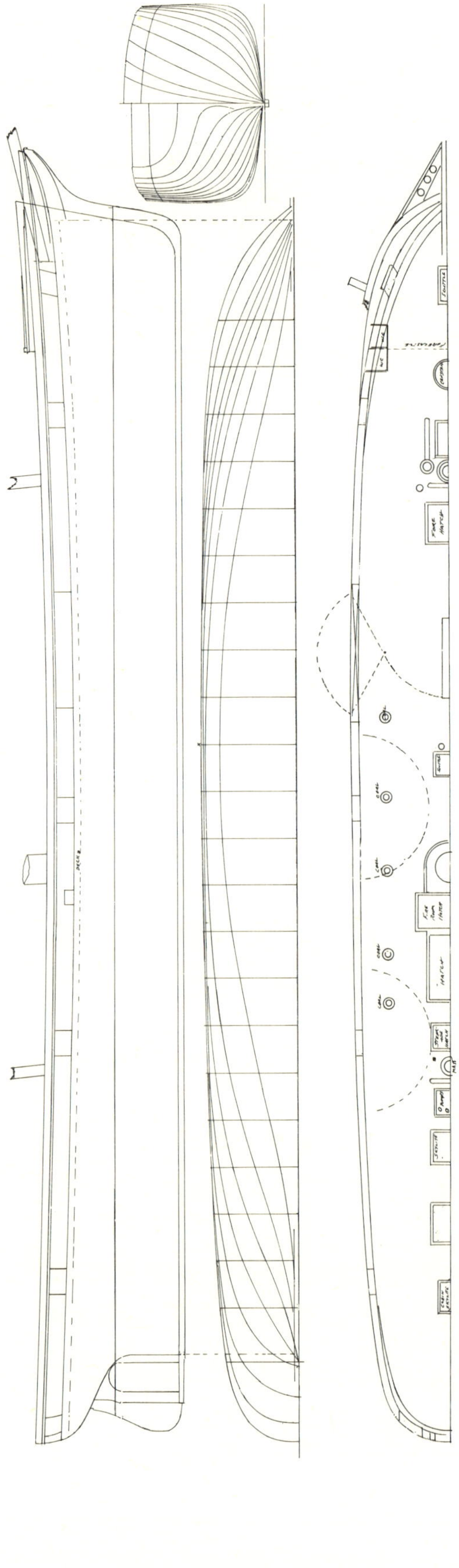

Lines, Sheer, and Gundeck of Ninety-day Gunboats. Both plans and specifications for these vessels—officially called "gunboats of 1861" —were copied in sufficient numbers for each of the twenty-three contractors. Note general similarities to the Pocahontas. *(Drawn from NARS 79-5-19, 79-5-21, 79-5-22, National Archives)*

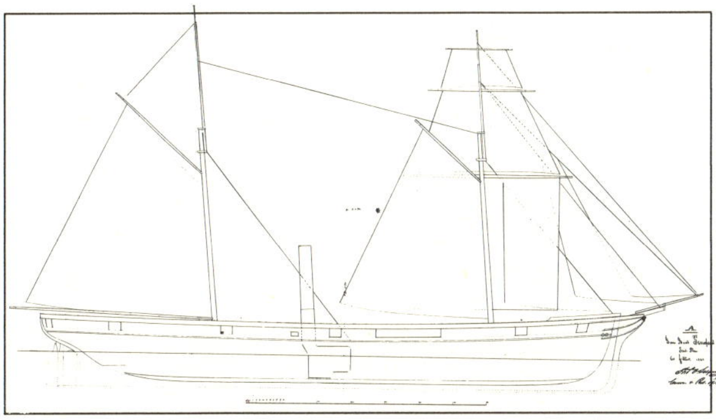

Sail plan of the Penobscot, *1861. (NARS 80-12-6A, National Archives)*

twice the coal consumption begetting only a 1½-knot augmentation in speed; however, for short periods, over 100 revolutions of the engine was possible, yielding 12½ knots.[8]

An example of a ninety-day gunboat in action was the chase of the *Harriet Lane* by the *Katahdin* in May 1864. By this late date in the war, the little ship had long passed her prime, but she maintained an average of 8½ knots and reached 10 in the course of the pursuit, beating against a head wind and rough seas. Her engineer reported her engines ran "perfectly" and they had never "run so fast for so long," yet remained in good repair subsequently.[9]

When they were in good repair, there seemed to be uniformity in the steaming performance of these ships. Wide discrepancies existed in their repair records, however, even from their first appearance on the blockade. For example, the *Chippewa,* despite Isherwood's laudatory descriptions, almost immediately arrived at such a broken-down state that in February 1862 her engineer requested a survey on machinery and boilers and asserted that he would not "be held responsible for any damage caused by bad workmanship, or carelessness on the part of the contractors." His complaints included leaking boilers, a crankshaft out of line, poor fitting parts and defective valve gear.[10]

Two others, the *Wyandotte* and *Seneca,* were objects of concern as early as July 1862. The *Wyandotte* was sent to New York with the comment, "She cannot be put together for any purpose whatever." The *Seneca* was described as "disabled" in the same month by S. F. Dupont. Blockade duty was constant and unyielding, however, accomplished with constantly banked fires and rare opportunities to give engines and boilers the attention necessary. In August 1862, Dupont wrote to Fox of the poor condition of the *Pembina*'s engines: "Her fires have been out seventy hours since October 1861."[11] Given this rigorous duty, the machinery of these vessels held up extraordinarily well.

Under sail the ships were less satisfactory. Comments on their working qualities under sail ranged from "poorly" to "miserably." Generally, comments on their steering were positive.[12] George H. Preble, commander of the *Katahdin* early in the war, was not impressed with the ship: "[She has] not the speed to chase or maneuver nor escape from superior foes. . . . [and because of] excessive rolling they can not use with effect or safety, except in smooth or very moderate weather, their XI-inch pivot gun which is their main dependence. . . . [She is a] safe and buoyant sea boat. Under steam and a close reefed topsail, with the wind a little on the quarter, we were all charmed with her scudding before a very heavy N.W. gale and sea." He concluded that the vessels were "complete failures" as "cruising men of war" but efficient for "special service in smooth shoal water."[13] Blockade duty in many cases, however, required only the threat of force to cause the quarry to heave to. In such situations, the effectiveness of heavy ordnance was of little moment, though speed was. Therefore, as cruisers, these vessels were inefficient. On the other hand, their relatively heavy battery was an asset in close-in, set-piece bombardment roles.

Despite Preble's comments it appears that the vessels' large pivot guns could be used with some accuracy, though without great rapidity, in a seaway. As early as June 1862, the *Cayuga* was considered sufficiently steady to warrant adding another two 24-pounders to her battery. Similarly, the *Kineo* received two 32-pounders in December 1862, and others of the class were also given extra guns during the course of the war.[14]

The careers of these ships were remarkable, beginning with the attack on Port Royal in November 1861, in which the first four participated, barely four months from their keel-laying. Ten were with Farragut at New Orleans, and the *Cayuga* led the fleet past Vicksburg, sustaining forty-two sizable

The Unadilla *and a Second Ninety-day Gunboat on River Duty during the War. Topmasts have been sent down. (U.S. Army Military History Institute)*

hits in that battle. All survived the war with the exception of the *Sciota,* which was sunk twice. The first instance was the result of an accidental collision in 1863. She was then raised and put back into service. Five days after Appomattox she struck a mine and was auctioned for $16,000 where she lay. This was a sizable sum for a sunken and no doubt worn-out vessel. Three gunboats remained in the service until 1869, the *Huron, Penobscot,* and *Unadilla.* The latter was sold as a war vessel to the government of Annam and was sunk in a collision with an American merchant ship in 1870.[15]

Though these gunboats did long stints of service on the blockade, it should be noted that the *Official Records* inadvertently misrepresent their endurance between repairs by implying that the ships' actual active service is represented by their commissioning and decommissioning dates. In August 1862, Secretary Welles wrote to Commandant Paulding at New York Navy Yard to "not allow these out of commission . . . or the internal organization to be broken up" but to make repairs quickly, and thus expedite their return to their stations.[16] Consequently, though the *Unadilla* was in commission from 30 September 1861 to 4 May 1865, only a study of her logs would reveal the actual number of those days when she was on duty. Since the *Official Records* also reported that her repairs amounted to about $20,000 in this period, it is unlikely that these were all performed at sea. Welles's directive was aimed at the four original gunboats, but it could be safely assumed that at least the remainder of the ninety-day gunboats were also so treated.

On the blockade, the ninety-day ships were credited with 146 captures. The highest number for a single vessel was 19 for the *Sagamore.* The *Kennebec* took over $1.5 million worth of prize vessels and cargo.[17]

Commenting on the vessels designed so hastily in mid-1861, Alexander Laing, in his book on American ships, observes that when S. H. Pook arrived in Washington in response to Lenthall's summons, the chief constructor "must have had a gunboat design in an advanced state of readiness," and Pook's chore was to "make it foolproof in detail."[18] It requires no great insight to deduce that the pattern Lenthall had in mind was the *Pocahontas,* which had been designed by S. M. Pook (the father of Samuel Hartt Pook).

In general arrangement, rig, and dimensions, the earlier vessel is visibly the prototype of the gunboats. The major internal change was the wartime necessity of engines with a lower profile and greater power. The former requirement was met by using horizontal engines rather than the vertical machinery of the *Pocahontas.* Greater power was accomplished with the use of forced draft and larger boiler capacity. The *Unadilla* and class were somewhat fuller in their stern lines. Their 10-foot draft was a necessary reduction of the *Pocahontas's* vessel's 12-foot draw and resulted in 18 inches less depth of hold. Externally, the clipper bow of the *Pocahontas* was replaced by the conventional naval cutwater knee.

In light of the probable use of the *Pocahontas* as a prototype, the swift production of a suitable and reasonably successful design for these vessels is less astounding but no less important. It also serves to credit S. M. Pook as well as John Lenthall and Samuel Hartt Pook for the design of the vessels.

Although honors for the hull design go to the Pooks, the key to the vessels' success was their engines, which withstood literally years of constant use on the blockade. B. F. Isherwood designed these installations, and his descriptions of the machinery indicate the governing rationale for the designs: simplicity of operation, ease of maintenance, and heavy structural components. For example, one of the most troublesome aspects of early engines was in their journals and bearings—the surfaces that received and redirected the power of the pistons. Isherwood, despite the extra weight involved, made such parts "unusually large," and therefore more durable.[19] Because this machinery was placed in the hands of inexperienced operators, all of these features coalesced to form a reliable engine for wartime use, contributing significantly to the success of these gunboats.

Even this early in the Civil War, in 1861, the ninety-day gunboats can be seen as a necessary advance from the auxiliary steam concept. Their primary mission ensured that their steam engine was indispensable. Gone were the days when the blockader and the blockaded were subject to the same winds and conditions at sea, and the blockader was forced to adopt a source of power comparable to his steam-driven opponents. As the war progressed, the constant demand made by the commanders of the blockading squadrons was not for better sailers but for vessels of greater speed under steam. Therefore, by the end of the conflict, the U.S. naval vessels being constructed were for all practical purposes auxiliary sailing ships. Consequently, though the sail-versus-steam controversy had been papered over with the auxiliary steam compromise before the war, it would again rear up in epic proportions shortly after wartime necessities ceased, when the relative importance of cruising endurance and economy regained its prewar position.

Ossipee Class

A congressional authorization in February 1861 for the construction of seven screw steamers was not implemented until May 1861, after the firing

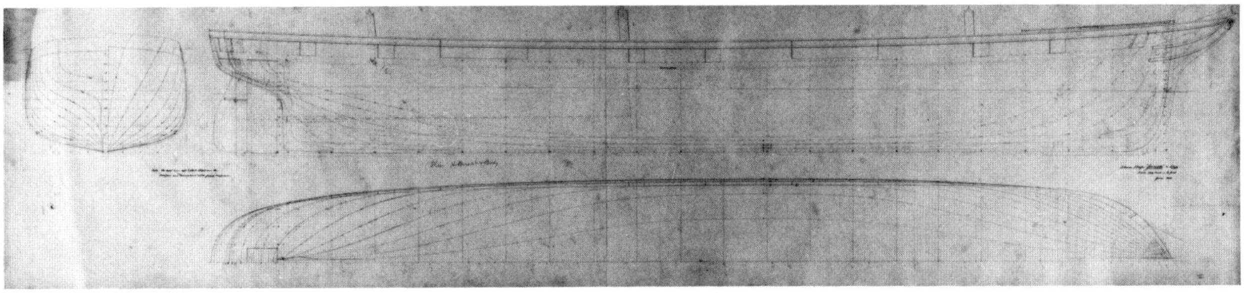

The Juniata *and Class as Originally Built. The* Housatonic *was sunk by the submersible* H. L. Hunley *in 1864. (NARS 77-15-4P, 77-15-4V, National Archives)*

on Fort Sumter. On 27 May, the department ordered the Bureau of Construction and Repair to direct the building of these ships, which were to have "full steam power . . . [and] combine heaviest armament and greatest speed compatible with their character and tonnage."[20] Three of these were repeats of the *Mohican*-class vessels, with a fourth ship, the *Oneida,* added subsequently. The remaining four were to be classed as second rates and have increased beam and displacement. These were the *Ossippee, Housatonic, Adirondack,* and *Juniata.*

These four vessels were considerably greater in tonnage (at 1,900 tons displacement) than the *Kearsarge* and others, though only five feet wider and six feet longer: 38 feet by 205 feet. Their 16.7 feet of draft reflected their intended use as cruisers on the high seas.

The hull lines of these vessels also belie any idea that they were mere enlargements of the earlier ships. The most obvious difference here was in the angular forefoot of the *Ossippee* class compared to the curved forefoot of the earlier vessels. Though having entrance lines similar in degree to the *Kearsarge,* the decreased rake forward allowed a much fuller midsection and increased tonnage. The buttock lines of these four were also somewhat more convex than the earlier ships. At midships, their cross section was equal in deadrise to the *Mohican* and *Kearsarge* but with slightly rounder bilges and floors.

The engines of the *Ossipee* and her sisters marked the first instance in which all the machinery of a single class of ships was designed by Benjamin F. Isherwood, then the navy's chief engineer. Consequently, his ideas on steam expansion were quite evident in the engines and boilers and in particular the relative proportions of these two components of the installations. The two cylinders measured 42 inches by 30 inches and were back-acting, with the piston rod connected to the large end of a harp, or steeple, the small end of which actuated the connecting rod to the shaft.[21] The harp moved athwartships acting much as would two piston rods, over and under the crankshaft. This was the first use of this type of machinery since the successful engines of the *Wabash.*

Isherwood's theory that smaller cylinders and larger boilers were required for greater power is evident in a comparison of the engines of previous screw steamers with those of the *Ossipee* class. First, in the *Mohican*-class ships, the smallest cylinder was 50 inches in diameter, the largest (the *Dacotah*'s), 63 inches. The latter had the longest stroke at 36 inches, and the remaining vessels had 30-inch or 28-inch strokes. Compare those to the 42-inch cylinders and 30-inch stroke of the *Ossipee* and others in her class.

Heating surfaces of the boilers of the *Ossipee* measured 8,950 square feet, while the largest surface of the *Mohican*-class boilers was 8,700 square feet, with four of the vessels' boilers having 7,800 square feet in surface area.[22]

Therefore, in the *Ossipee* class, with some 500 more tons of displacement than the earlier sloops, the cylinders were smaller in cubic capacity but the boilers were some 14 percent larger in heating surface. Identical Isherwood engines and Martin water-tube boilers would also be used in larger sloops yet to come, among them the 2,500-ton *Lackawanna* and *Ticonderoga.*

The *Ossipee*-class sloops were bark-rigged, carried a complement of 200 and stowed 220 to 235 tons of coal, some 50 tons more than the *Mohican*-class. Their original armament was similar to that of the earlier vessels: two large pivot guns, one of which might have been a 100-pound Parrott rifle. The *Adirondack* had four 32-pounders in addition to the 11-inch Dahlgrens. On the *Housatonic,* which had one 11-inch Dahlgren and one Parrott rifle in pivot, there were three 30-pounder rifles and two 32-pounder smoothbores.

By the end of the war the *Ossipee* and *Juniata* had batteries more suitable to their capacities. The former carried six 32-pounders (57 hundredweight) in addition to 11-inch and 100-pounder pivot guns. Six 9-inch Dahlgrens replaced the 32-pounders in the late 1860s, and the Parrott was removed. On the *Juniata,* a broadside armament of ten 8-inch Dahlgrens and a pivot rifle (100-pound Parrott) composed her battery in July 1864, the most imposing armament of any of these ships. Later, six 9-inch and one 11-inch Dahlgren were standard.[23]

The Juniata *As Configured from 1869 to 1872. (Naval Historical Center)*

Judging the performance of these ships as a class is hampered by the loss of the *Adirondack* in 1862 and the *Housatonic* in early 1864. Furthermore, both the *Ossipee* and *Juniata* had engine problems early in their careers and the latter was constantly under repair as a result.

The *Adirondack* was cited as achieving 11⅔ knots without the use of her forced draft blowers. In a House of Representatives report on marine engines, all four ships were listed as 12-knot vessels, though this may have been somewhat exaggerated. The *Juniata* was listed as reaching 10 knots under maximum steam late in the war, and the *Ossipee* also rated the same figure.[24] Given the considerably better performances by the later, larger vessels with identical machinery, however, 11 knots should not have been unlikely with engines in proper order.

Both the *Ossipee* and *Juniata* suffered engine defects, the former breaking down on her initial cruise to take her station on the blockade. The *Juniata,* by September 1863, was noted for being "more than half the time repairing her engine."[25] The explanation given for these problems was that the contractors had never built marine steam engines and therefore did not have the proper tools for the project. Each, however, had been the low bidder for the respective contracts.[26]

The careers of these ships ranged from two months to thirty years. The *Adirondack* was wrecked on Man-of-War Cay in the Bahamas on 23 August 1862, after joining the South Atlantic blockade in July and taking one prize. Her crew was rescued but the vessel was battered too severely to be salvaged.

The sole member of this quartet known outside of naval circles is the *Housatonic,* which had the

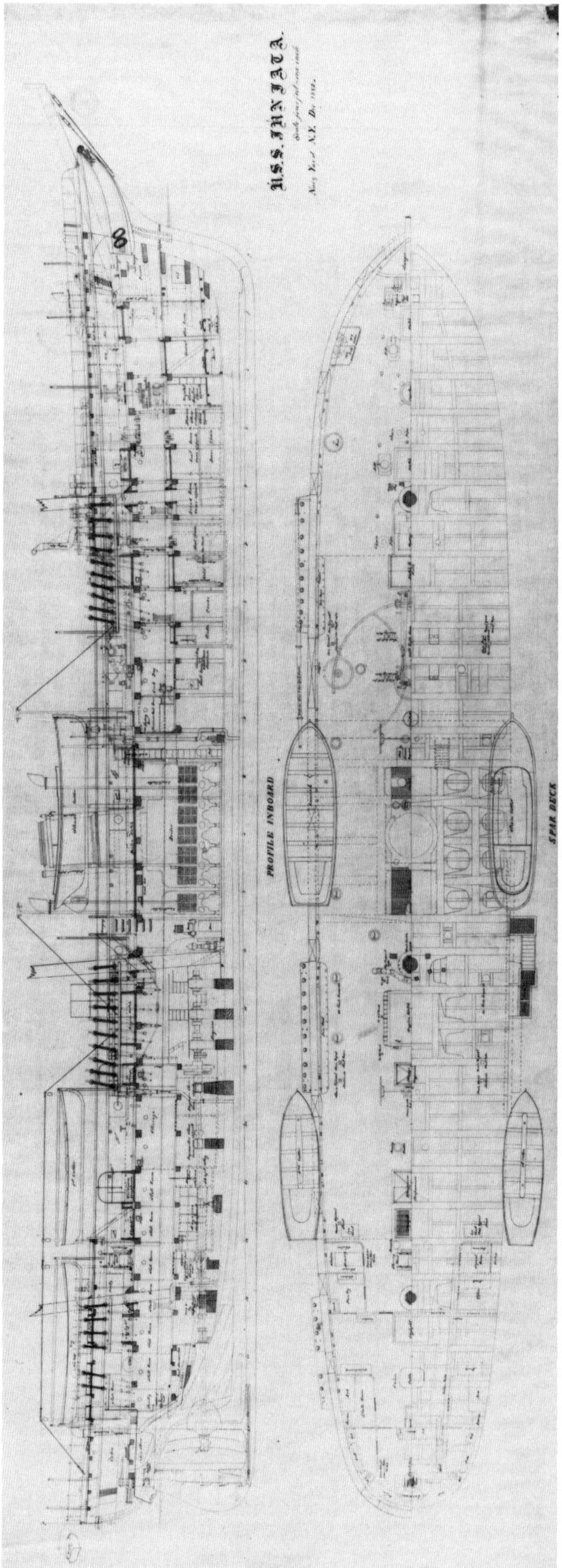

The Juniata, *1882. Her armament by that date was one 8-inch pivot gun and six 9-inch guns in broadside. (NARS 109-6-3B, National Archives)*

The Ossipee *in the 1880s. Note the close correspondence to the* Juniata *plans. (Naval Historical Center)*

unenviable historical distinction of being the first warship sunk by a submarine, or submersible. She was part of the South Atlantic Blockading Squadron and was involved in one encounter with the Confederate rams *Chicora* and *Palmetto State,* as well as the capture of the important blockade runner *Princess Royal.* In the cargo of the latter were two marine engines intended for Confederate war vessels, and the ship itself was taken into federal service. On 17 February 1864, the Confederate spar-torpedo-armed submersible *H. L. Hunley* sank the *Housatonic,* with the loss of five lives.

The *Ossipee* was in the North Atlantic and Gulf blockading squadrons and in 1864 was one of the vessels that rammed the ironclad *Tennessee* in the attack on Mobile. She was active until decommissioned in 1889 and was sold two years later.

The *Juniata* was commissioned 4 December 1862 and was active in the West Indies and the North and South Atlantic squadrons, participating in the two attacks on Fort Fisher. She was under repair for some thirteen months of her wartime service. She cruised on various stations after the war and was extensively repaired from 1876 to 1882. She was decommissioned in 1889 and sold in 1891.

Sacramento Class

In August 1861, a board was set up to examine plans for a class of "fast screw steamers" for ocean cruising. The board was chaired by Commodore Joseph Smith and included John Lenthall, Henry A. Wise of the ordnance bureau, John Dahlgren, and others.[27] According to later recollections by Wise, Assistant Secretary of the Navy Gustavus V. Fox was instrumental in determining the armament of these six vessels, submitting the plan to provide them with three 16,000-pound pivot guns and an additional 50-pounder Dahlgren rifle forward. Other than boat howitzers (four), this was to be the entire armament of these ships.[28] Although the third pivot gun can be seen as a logical extension of the battery of the *Mohican* class, the absence of broadside weapons was unusual. The sole precedent was in the *Niagara.*

The hulls of these vessels were 225 feet for the *Monongahela* and *Shenandoah,* 226 feet for the *Canandaigua,* 229 for the *Sacramento,* and 232 feet for the *Ticonderoga* and *Lackawanna.* Their beams were about 38 feet each, with planned draft of 16.7 feet.[29] They were dimensionally extended versions of the *Ossipee*-class ships.

The *Monongahela* and *Shenandoah* were built at Philadelphia and had very nearly the same lines, with the *Monongahela* marginally fuller amidships. Above water the stern of the latter was fuller and had two stern ports as originally built, while the *Shenandoah* had four ports aft and her stern had considerable rake. The *Shenandoah* displaced 2,030 tons and the *Monongahela,* 2,078. They were designed by H. Hoover.[30]

The *Canandaigua* was built with a cutwater knee and her stern had less rake than the *Monongahela*

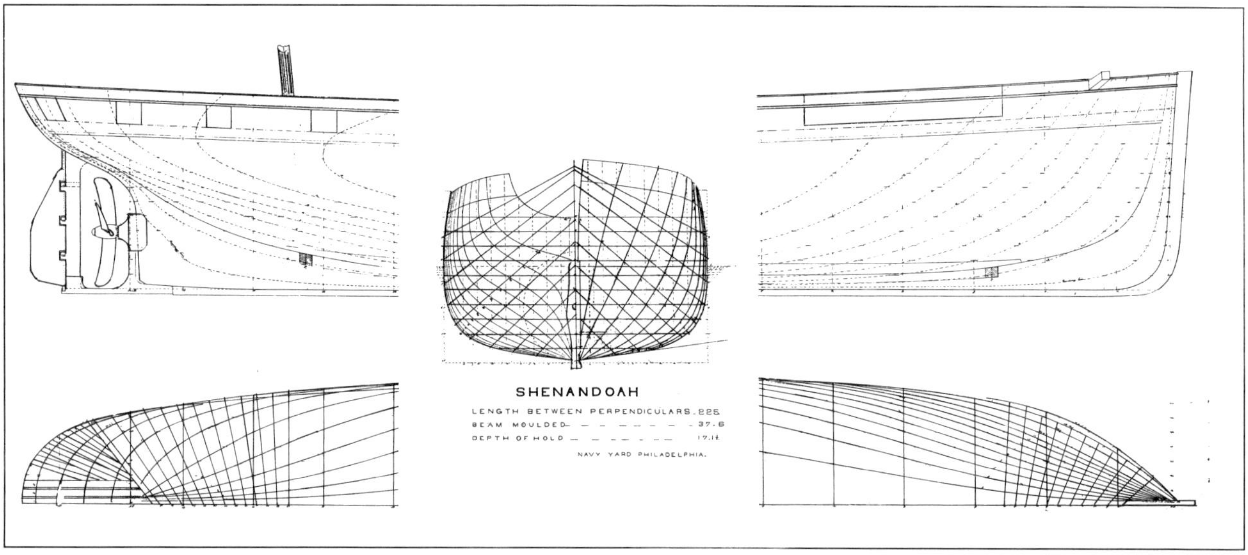

Fore, Aft, and Body Plans of the Shenandoah *As Originally Built with Plain, Nearly Plumb Stem. This class of vessels represented the extreme in all-big-pivot batteries. (NARS 78-7-14D, partial tracing by author, National Archives)*

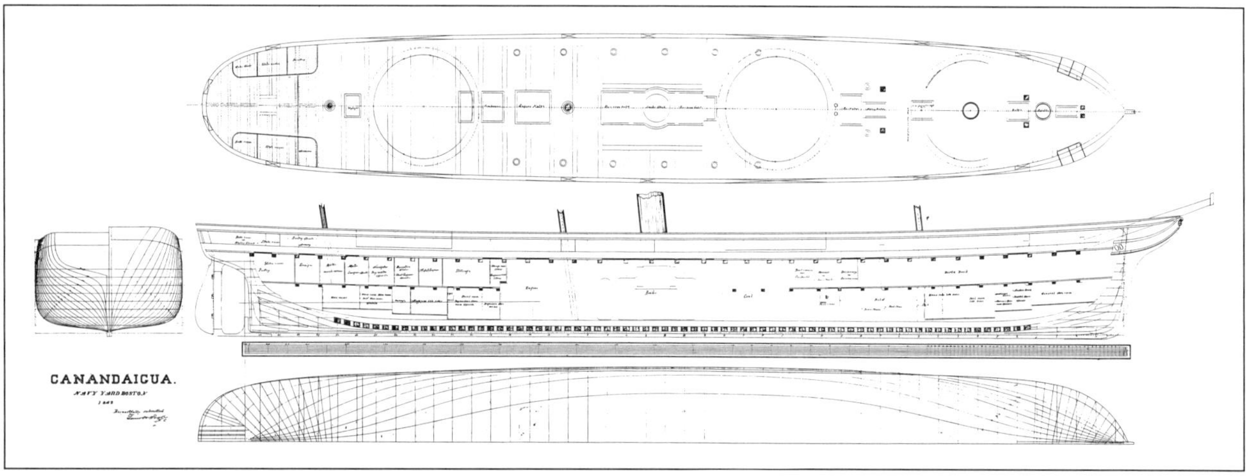

Lines and Sheer of the Canandaigua. *She had the fullest midsection of these ships. (NARS 107-9-3A, National Archives)*

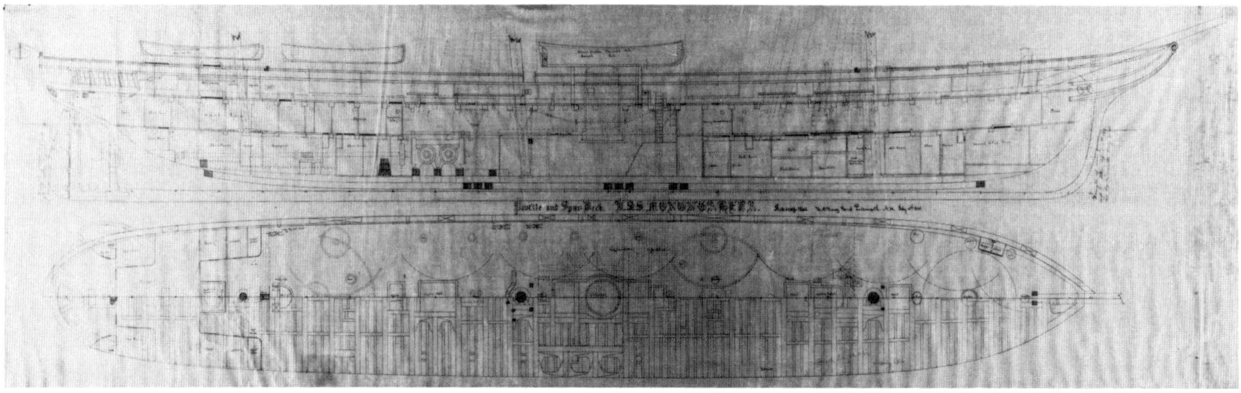

The Monongahela, *Inboard and Deck Plans, 1874. (NARS 78-3-8H, National Archives)*

and *Shenandoah*. She also had the longest forecastle deck and had no pivot port forward. Below water, she was the fullest amidships and had a noticeable hollow in her garboard strakes.

The hull designs used for these vessels are a matter of some speculation, because all the original plans have not been found. No plans of the *Sacramento* have been found, and the lines of the *Ticonderoga* may have been modified significantly. Photographs of the *Sacramento* show little except a straight stem, no bowsprit, and a full stern similar to that of the *Monongahela*.

Both built at New York, the *Lackawanna* and *Ticonderoga* were at 2,526 tons and 237 feet the largest of the class. The only lines for these vessels are dated November 1861 and exist in two copies, one for each vessel. The accuracy of these lines can be questioned on several counts, at least in the case of the *Ticonderoga*. First, the date of the lines is some nine months before the launch of the ship. This, along with the plans' lack of detail indicates they were preliminary designs. Second, a cross section of the *Ticonderoga* taken off her in 1874 is quite different from that in the 1861 plan. Third, both the stem and stern on an 1878 plan of the *Ticonderoga* differ in profile from those of the early plan. Finally, photographs of the *Ticonderoga* do not coincide with the 1861 draft.[31]

Differences between the early plan and the vessel as built may be explained in part by a letter written in February 1862 by G. V. Fox to B. F. Delano, designer of both the vessels, in which this obviously very influential assistant secretary expressed "certain points of beauty" regarding the profiles of American naval vessels. He suggested a "perpendicular stem, very light oval stern. . . . and rounding sides" with little sheer.[32] Fox's influence is also evident in the 1887 annual report of the secretary of the navy: the *Shenandoah*'s "nearly plumb" stem was attributed to Secretary Fox, who "intended her to be a ram."[33] The latter phrase smacks of hearsay, but although the November 1861 plans show 15 degrees of rake and a cutwater knee on the stem, and an angular knuckle on the stern, the

The Sacramento, *1865. No plans have been found of this vessel. (Naval Historical Center)*

The Monongahela *at Portsmouth, Configured As in the Plans of 1874. (U.S. Army Military History Institute)*

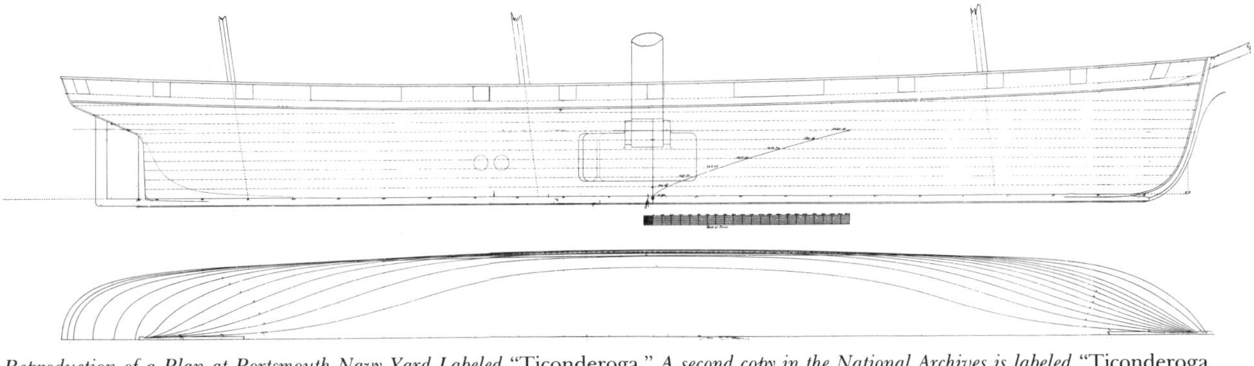

Reproduction of a Plan at Portsmouth Navy Yard Labeled "Ticonderoga." *A second copy in the National Archives is labeled* "Ticonderoga and Lackawanna" *(NARS 79-7-11). Plans of the* Ticonderoga *as built show a plumb stem in place of the raked stem shown in this plan, as shown in the photograph taken in Venice (see p. 100). Photos of the* Lackawanna *confirm her raked stem as well as cutwater knee. (Portsmouth Navy Yard)*

The Ticonderoga *at Venice, with pivot ports open. The bowsprit was added in 1865. (U.S. Naval Institute)*

later plans and photographs of the *Ticonderoga* reveal the plumb stem, no cutwater knee, and rounded stern. A cutwater knee was added in a postwar rebuilding.

Plans and photographs of the *Lackawanna* indicate she was built according to the November 1861 plan. The only available cross section of the *Ticonderoga,* however, shows she had rounder bilges and more curvature in her topsides than the *Lackawanna.* Also, the *Ticonderoga* exhibited some hollowness in her garboard strakes, a characteristic not seen in the hull of the sister ship.

It appears that Assistant Secretary Fox was responsible for a great many aspects of this class of vessels. Furthermore, the plumb stem used on the *Ticonderoga* became virtually a standard feature of U.S. naval ships built during the war years.

While the *Ticonderoga* was a-building, and during the growing panic over the imminent appearance of the Confederate *Merrimack,* B. F. Delano submitted a plan for an armored *Ticonderoga.* She was to displace 3,054 tons and be cut down to accept two monitor-type turrets. Her plating was to extend to the waterline and her two masts were to unship when necessary.[34] His was one of many such ideas submitted to the department around this time but not implemented.

In accordance with the policy of increased dependence on engine power, the original rigs of these sloops were greatly abbreviated. They were barkentines rigged only to topgallants; only the *Canandaigua* and *Lackawanna* received cutwater knees and bowsprits.[35]

Three of the vessels, the *Monongahela, Shenandoah,* and *Ticonderoga,* received wire standing rigging for their earliest commissions.[36] This was one of the earliest instances of the use of wire rigging in the navy, though it had been in use earlier in Britain. It appears that in the U.S. Navy it was mainly for vessels on foreign service during the war where the weight savings would be most significant.

Despite a difference in displacement ranging up to 500 tons between the *Ossipee*-class ships and the newer sloops, the engines were identical for all (42 inches by 30 inches). Furthermore, the same size and number of boilers were used.[37]

Five of the ships were originally fitted with three pivot guns each, two of which were 11-inch Dahlgrens. The third gun was a 150-pounder Parrott, except in the case of the *Monongahela.* The rifles were mounted on the gun deck except for the *Canandaigua*'s, which was on an extended forecastle. The *Ticonderoga* was unique in having six broadside 9-inch Dahlgrens and two (150- and 50-pounder) rifles, while the *Lackawanna* had the heaviest battery of the lot, with four 9-inchers and one 50-pounder, over and above the three pivoting heavy guns.[38]

Variations in battery were frequent in the war years, particularly when the individual vessels were assigned to roles for which they were not designed. The *Monongahela* was the object of much concern to Farragut during his Mississippi operations, because her small number of large guns made her rate of fire slow. Her lack of direct forward fire also impressed him as inappropriate for river operations. He promptly added five 57-hundredweight 32-pounders to her broadsides.[39]

The *Sacramento*'s battery was an unusual combination in 1864: three 100-pounder Parrotts, six 8-inch (63-hundredweight) smoothbores, and one 30-pounder rifle. With this lightweight armament she would have been little threat to the armored ram *Stonewall* during their near-meeting in 1865.

At the close of the war, the sloops' batteries were standardized. The heavy forward pivot rifle was replaced by a 50- or 60-pounder, and two 9-inch broadside guns were shipped with the two 11-inch pivots. Subsequently, they received six additional 9-inch guns. When the 8-inch converted rifle became available, these replaced the 11-inch guns, and on the *Ticonderoga* and *Shenandoah,* two of the 9-inch Dahlgrens were removed.[40]

In their original configuration, without bowsprits or cutwater knees, these ships presented a distinctly modern appearance, which no doubt repelled traditionalists. In the profile of the lightly rigged *Monongahela,* there is a striking resemblance to early twentieth-century freighters—simply reduce her to pole masts and erect a bridge structure amidships. This is not to say the vessels were attractive, by any means—their blunt endedness would have been softened and their symmetry improved by adding a bowsprit.

All these ships eventually received several modifications: among them, bowsprits and forward relocation of the foremast. As early as February 1864, both the *Ticonderoga* and *Shenandoah* were fitted out for foreign service. Lenthall directed: "As they are cruisers under sail, so as to economize their fuel, they will both be fitted with square sails on fore and main masts and can have a light bowsprit."[41] By 1873 all had bowsprits, cutwater knees, ship rigs, and were reduced from three pivot ports to two per side. As photographs reveal, the length and proportions of their hulls, surmounted by substantial masts, made them particularly handsome ships—with the longer *Ticonderoga* and *Lackawanna* especially pleasing to the eye.

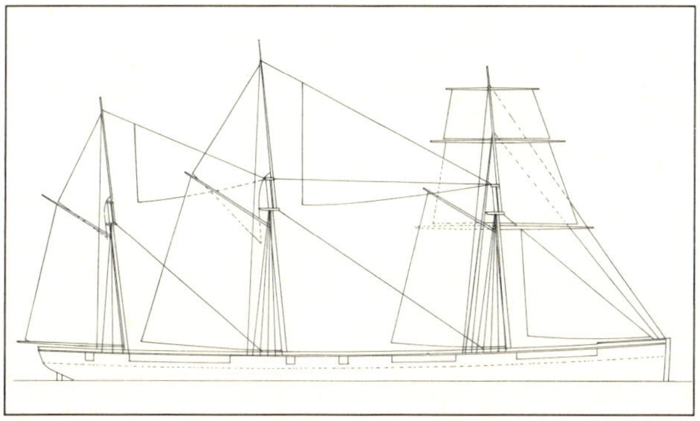

Sail Plan of the Ticonderoga *in 1862 with Minimal Barkentine Rig. A remarkable series of plans shows the growth of this sail plan to the more substantial rig shown in the photograph of the vessel taken in Venice in 1865, p. 100. (Tracing of NARS 134-10-29, National Archives)*

The performance of these ships did not contradict their positive externals. The *Sacramento* was used as an example by Isherwood in defending his machinery after the breakdowns on the *Ossipee.* He cited the commanding officer's report of her trials, with the vessel reaching 12½ knots without the use of her blowers. A subsequent commanding officer, Henry Walke, reiterated her capability of reaching 10 to 12½ knots under "moderate steam." While she was in company with the *Niagara* in 1865, and after a year of extended cruising, her logs showed her making 8 to 13 knots under sail and steam. She was described as a good and easily manageable sea boat, but on one occasion when her propeller could not be uncoupled in heavy seas, its drag kept her "nearly in the trough," with "the sea breaking over her in every way."[42]

The *Shenandoah* was nearly as fast as her sister, with Daniel B. Ridgely reporting 12 knots maximum under steam and 11 in a seaway. She answered her helm readily, but in her barkentine rig configuration she worked poorly under canvas. After receiving her bowsprit and moving her foremast forward, she was much improved. Her commanding officer in 1866 reported she endured "two cyclones. . . . in both of which this ship sustained her reputation for good sea qualities."[43]

The *Monongahela* also attained 13 knots maximum but had a considerable rolling problem, to the extent that the muzzles of the broadside guns "went under water," according to her commander. Later, in calmer seas, she had been instrumental in capturing a Confederate battery with judicious use of her 11-inch guns.[44]

The slowest of the smaller four was the *Canandaigua,* which also had the fullest lines. She made a maximum of 10¼ and an average of 9.4 knots.[45] The two larger vessels did not measure up to the speeds of the other four, with maximums listed as 11 knots for the *Ticonderoga* and 10.5 for the *Lackawanna.* The captain of the latter complimented her capabilities when "lying to under trysails and low steam."[46]

Finally, the *Ticonderoga*'s sailing qualities were put to the test in 1864 when her engines were disabled and she was forced to rely on her small area of canvas. Charles Steedman, her commanding officer, reported: "The ship would do nothing by the wind. She drifted dead to leeward, and, for want of headsails, carried her helm nearly hard up." Shortly thereafter he expanded on the theme: "My

The Lackawanna *in 1880 on a South American Cruise. Her length and proportions made her a decidedly handsome sloop. She was armed with six 9-inch Dahlgrens in broadside, two 11-inch pivots, and a rifled gun on her long forecastle deck. (Naval Historical Center)*

propeller cannot be triced up, and the extreme length of the vessel unfits her, without the aid of steam, to weather a hurricane or equinoctal gale in safety."[47]

Three years later, according to a sailing qualities report after bowsprit and headsails were added, she was still leewardly, but the extreme problem was solved. She steered well but wore slowly and would not stay. In moderate weather with royals and studding sails, she made 11 knots with the wind two points abaft the beam. Close-hauled she made 8 knots and against a head sea, five. She was characterized as a slow sailer, except in a strong breeze, when her length became an asset.[48]

The only vessel of this class lost to natural causes was the *Sacramento.* She began her active service with the Atlantic blockade, then made passage to European waters in search of Confederate cruisers, assisting in the blockade of the *Rappahannock* in early 1865. She was the *Niagara*'s consort when Commodore Craven refused combat with the ram *Stonewall* in 1865. On her first cruise after the cessation of hostilities she grounded off Madras. All hands were saved but the vessel was lost.

The *Shenandoah* participated in the blockade, the search for rebel cruisers, and the attacks on Fort Fisher. From the end of the war to 1886, with the exception of an extensive refit from 1874 to 1879, she was on active duty in South American, European, or Asiatic waters. She was decommissioned 23 October 1886 and sold 30 July the next year.

The *Ticonderoga* was also part of the North Atlantic blockade and the attacks on Fort Fisher. At the termination of the war, she was part of the South Atlantic blockading squadron, then was assigned to the European and South American squadrons. After a four-year refit, she was sent on a circumnavigation of the globe, to extend trade relations. On the two-year cruise she visited forty ports and steamed over thirty-six thousand miles without major mishap. She was decommissioned in 1882 and sold on 5 August 1887.

The *Canandaigua* was part of the South Atlantic squadron and of the attacks on Charleston. After the war, she made two cruises, the first in European waters, from 1865 to 1869; the second from 1872 to 1875, in the West Indies and the gulf. From 15 May to 10 August 1869 she was named *Detroit.* On 8 November 1875 she was paid off, then was broken up in 1884.

Both the *Monongahela* and *Lackawanna* were part of the Battle of Mobile Bay and the *Monongahela* took part in the battle at Port Hudson, Louisiana. At Port Hudson, the *Monongahela* grounded under the fire of a Confederate battery, was towed free, then lost her engines and drifted out of the action. In preparation for the Mobile Bay action, the bows of both vessels were given iron plating with the intention of ramming the Confederate ironclad *Tennessee.*[49] The *Monongahela* twice made contact with the *Tennessee,* and the *Lackawanna* followed, with the *Hartford* only landing a glancing blow on the ironclad.

After the war, the *Lackawanna* served in the Pacific until decommissioning on 7 April 1885. She was sold in 1887.

The *Monongahela* was part of the West Indies squadron in 1867 when a tidal wave washed her ashore at Saint Croix. She was not materially damaged and was refloated after a four-month effort. She was repaired and served as a training ship. Her engines were removed and she rejoined the fleet as a sailing supply ship in 1883, then was a training vessel until 1904. She was destroyed by fire at Guantánamo Bay in 1908.

The *Sacramento*-class ships were generally successful. Their use of identical engines made their steaming performance more uniformly acceptable than that of the *Mohican*-class ships, and it seems that the newer class had somewhat fewer rolling problems. Also, the newer ships had twice the coal capacity as the old vessels and attained better speeds on average. The latter characteristic tended to validate the general steam expansion theories of B. F. Isherwood (though the increased length of the vessels was also a factor), showing that it was not larger cylinders but a larger boiler capacity that was requisite for increased power in simple expansion engines.

Kansas Class

In the first year of the war, the ninety-day gunboats had met a critical need. They would continue giving reliable service throughout the conflict and would become, along with the purchased vessels, the mainstay of the blockade. By mid-1862, however, their shortcomings were evident. With maximum speeds of 8 to 9 knots, they, along with many of the slow improvised blockading vessels, were derisively referred to as "armed buoys" by the Confederates.[50] This slowness, and their inability to make use of their large pivot guns in any but light seas, put them at a distinct disadvantage when faced with either faster or more heavily armed adversaries. In essence, however, on the blockade the battery of the gunboats was a secondary question: the sine qua non was speed, and as built-for-the-purpose runners came on the scene, the ninety-day gunboats' deficiency in this area was further emphasized.

Consequently, a second class of shallow-draft gunboats was begun by August 1862. In all, eight were built and they are usually denominated the *Kansas* class. The vessels were in some cases test beds for bizarre or at least unusual machinery, with only three receiving Isherwood's back-acting engines, which were becoming standard for U.S. naval vessels.

It has been assumed that the hulls of all eight were built to the same design, because Bennett and others list the dimensions for all the vessels as 179 feet 6 inches by 30-foot beam (29 feet molded, according to the plans), with 836 tons displacement. The plans for the gunboats, however, show two entirely different hull designs: one for the *Yantic, Kansas, Nipsic, Shawmut, Saco,* and *Nyack;* and a second for the *Pequot* and *Maumee,* the latter having a length between perpendiculars of 171 feet 6 inches. The lines of the larger group were apparently by Lenthall. The plans of the *Pequot* and *Maumee,* on the other hand, are identical to William H. Webb's plans for a Russian government steamer. Only the bowsprit was removed for the U.S. Navy version.[51] Measurement in both cases was to the aft of the forward stern post.

The disparity in length is of less importance than the difference in hull forms. The most striking contrast was in the vessels' stems, with the Lenthall design having a vertical, straight stem and moderately rounded forefoot, compared to a sharply raked stem and angular junction with the keel on the *Pequot* and *Maumee.*

The entrance angles for each design were similar but the Lenthall ships were marked by straight floors rising some 7 degrees, while the *Pequot* and *Maumee* had flat floors and rounder bilges. Aft, the *Pequot* and *Maumee* were sharper by some 10 degrees but the run of the Lenthall ships was somewhat finer below the waterline. Finally, the *Nipsic* and others had very little sheer while the other pair

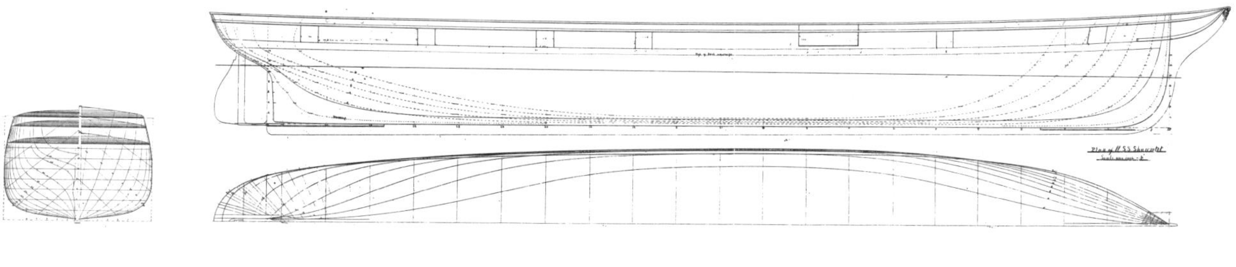

Lines of the Shawmut (Nipsic, Saco, Kansas, *and* Nyack). *These gunboats were considered follow-ons to the ninety-day ships of 1861. This plan is from a postwar refit and shows the cutwater knee added at that time. (NARS 136-9-46, National Archives)*

59. *Russian Government Steamer, n.d.* [65]
Hull plan: 6′=1″

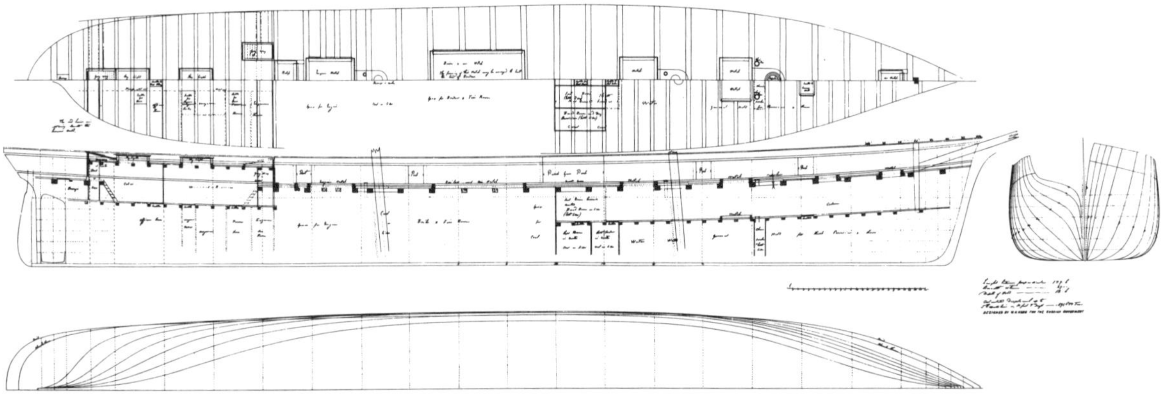

Lines, inboard, and deck plans of the U.S. sloops Pequot *and* Maumee, *1862. Hull lines of these two ships differed substantially from those of the remainder of the class. Lines published here were originally found in William H. Webb's book of ship plans, compiled in the 1890s and recently reprinted in the Nautical Research Guild's* Journal. *In the Webb book they are labeled "Russian Government Steamer," with no date or further identification. These plans, however, are in all respects identical to those labeled* "Pequot" *in the National Archives (NARS 108-10-8C). The only change on the NARS plan is a penciled notation indicating the elimination of the bowsprit. No indication has been found that such a vessel was actually built by Webb for the Russian navy.*

had a pronounced sheer with the lowest point somewhat aft of the midship line.

In appearance, the *Maumee* and *Pequot* suffered from their excessive sheer, further exaggerated by a topgallant forecastle and straight-raking stem. Built without benefit of a bowsprit, they presented the unfortunate aspect of a fishing dory. The ships designed by Lenthall were conventional in appearance, with less prominent forward profiles and straighter sheers. The *Saco* was instantly recognizable, however, with two very tall stacks to provide sufficient draft for her fourteen boilers.

All eight vessels were originally rigged as two-masted topsail schooners, continuing the de-emphasis on sail power begun in the earlier gunboats. Further evidence of this was in the lack of bowsprits and the consequent reduction in headsails.

The Isherwood machinery for the *Nipsic, Shawmut,* and *Nyack* consisted of two back-acting cylinders, of 30-inch diameter and 21-inch stroke, with standard Sewell surface condenser and Martin water-tube boilers. The latter had over twice the grate surface (198 versus 88 square feet) and nearly double the heating area (4,950 versus 2,700 square feet) of the boilers of the ninety-day gunboats, while the engines maintained the same piston size but increased the stroke by 3 inches.[52] Thus, given an increase of only 145 tons displacement (20 percent) over the *Unadilla* class, any substantial increase in speed not accounted for in the hull lines of the *Kansas* class would have been because of the doubling of the boiler capacity alone, in accordance with Isherwood's theories on steam expansion.

The engines of the five remaining vessels present the most interest, because of their variety

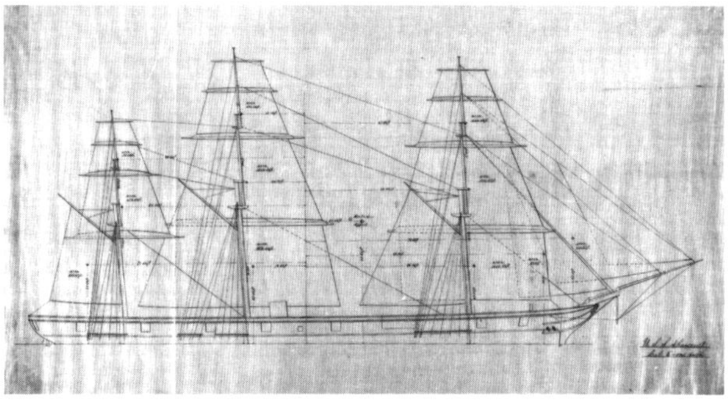

Sail Plan of the Shawmut, *1870s. Compare this plan with the wartime appearance of the* Kansas, *below. (NARS 79-2-45, National Archives)*

The Kansas, *As Originally Built. A wartime photograph, showing minimal masting. Solarization has destroyed the image of the funnel. (Library of Congress)*

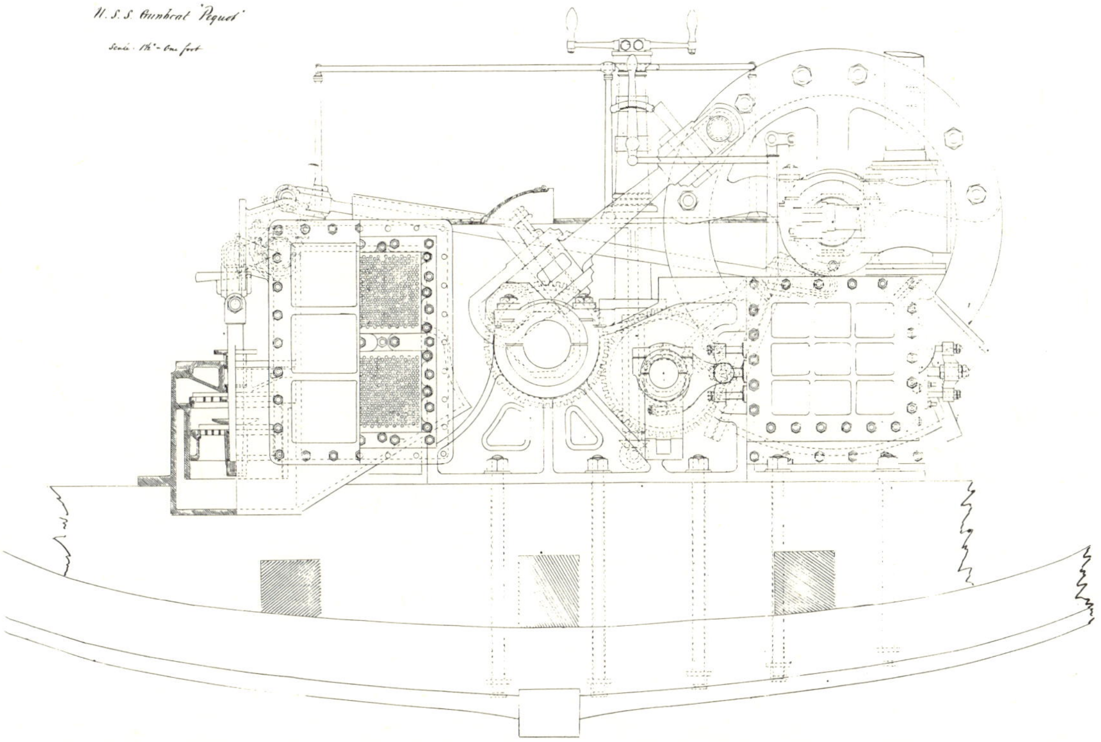

Wright Segmental Engines of the Pequot. *The piston swung in an arc through a curved cylinder. (NARS BSE plan, National Archives)*

in design and origin. Two, the *Kansas* and *Yantic,* had direct-acting engines, the engines of the former having been part of the cargo of the British blockade runner *Princess Royal,* intended to power a Confederate ram. The *Saco* and *Maumee* were fitted with vibrating-lever engines, the former built by Corliss, famous for stationary industrial engines; the latter by Ericsson. Finally, the *Pequot*'s powerplant was of a type not seen before or since, on land or sea: the Wright "segmental" engine.[53]

The use of fire-tube boilers in the *Saco* and *Kansas* was unusual for U.S. naval vessels. The *Kansas*'s boilers were much like those used in locomotives while the *Saco*'s machinery contractors opted for no less than fourteen small fire-tube boilers, all placed below the waterline.

The vibrating-lever type of engine had been used by Ericsson in both the *Monitor* and *Galena.* Two pistons operated in tandem, in a single cylinder, working athwartships. Each connecting rod was attached to one end of a pivoting lever, the other end of which rotated the propeller shaft. The cylinders of the *Saco* measured 28 inches, and the stroke, 24 inches.[54] This was somewhat smaller than the cylinder capacity of the Isherwood engines of this class.

William Wright of the Woodruff and Beach establishment of Hartford, Connecticut, designed the unique machinery of the *Pequot.* The pistons, rather than reciprocating on a straight line within the cylinders, traveled an arc of 60 degrees within a curved cylinder. Rather than a single piston rod, a rod emanated from each side of the piston, curving up and out of the cylinder heads and connecting to form a circle. Steam was alternately provided on each side of this swinging piston, and the piston's travel was sufficient to allow the connecting rod, attached to the upper third of the circular piston rod, to accomplish one revolution of the crankshaft. Two such cylinders were employed, mounted opposite the condenser. This peculiar engine design was apparently not used in any other application other than the *Pequot,* although it was suggested in 1864 by S. M. Pook for use in a few proposed 120-ton torpedo vessels. He recommended these engines because of their "extraordinary lightness and compactness."[55]

The deck arrangement of all these vessels was a variety not seen previously in naval steamers. The quarter deck, which was some 35 feet in length, extended from just abaft the mainmast to about 16 feet from the taffrail. At that point, a sunken poop was incorporated. This was the cockpit, containing the binnacle and helm.

The sunken poop may have also been required for a type of steering apparatus referred to in a letter from the commanding officer of the *Nipsic* as "Reed's patent" mechanism. This apparatus may have been a geared arrangement, and it was said to allow one man to steer the vessel.[56]

The batteries of the eight gunboats were centered around the single large pivot gun, located between the funnel and foremast. This gun was usually a 100- or 150-pounder Parrott rifle, though by late in the war, a few were replaced by 11-inch Dahlgrens. The broadside guns ranged from 30-pounder Parrotts, to 32-pounder smoothbores, to 9-inch Dahlgrens. The *Pequot* and *Saco* seem to have had the largest batteries, with six 32-pounders, one 30-pounder rifle and one 150-pounder Parrott on each, in 1864. The *Yantic* was unusual in having four 9-inch Dahlgrens and one 30-pounder rifle; the latter type gun was usually mounted on the topgallant forecastle of these vessels.[57]

The performance of these gunboats and their various engines was significantly better than that of the ninety-day gunboats. Given their variety of engines, however, across-the-board success could not be expected.

The *Pequot,* despite her strange machinery, retained a positive reputation until the last year of the war. She was, indeed, considered a fast vessel, with her commanders reporting 11½ to 12 and up to 14 knots at various times. She was, however, a wet ship and a heavy roller. In cross seas she at times submerged her hammock rails and waist boats.[58]

Her engines were problematic at the outset and end of her active service. Though they were completed by the contract date, modifications were necessary. Mr. Wright had in the meantime moved to other employment, resulting in an eight-month delay in correcting the problems. By April 1865 the engines were in need of complete overhauling to make her, according to her engineer, "one of the most efficient of her class." Her new engineer in May 1865, however, disagreed violently with the earlier judgment, calling the engines "unsafe and unreliable. . . . being liable at any time to have a great smash up."[59] The chief defect of these machines may have been their uniqueness, a factor that would put off engineers who were responsible for them—men who without a doubt had never dealt with such idiosyncratic machinery.

The *Maumee* was credited with 11½ knots under steam. She was burdened with a propeller that could not be disconnected, a feature that did nothing to enhance her sailing qualities, which were as poor as could be expected with the small sail area provided.[60]

Of the three vessels with machinery not designed by Isherwood, the *Saco* was by far the least satisfactory. In six months time, machinery defects forced her out of service. A survey found that the basic engines "worked admirably," but the "other parts of the apparatus [required] so much and such unremitting attention and [gave] such unsatisfactory results" that the difficulties could not be remedied short of removing all except the main engines. The fourteen boilers and their dependencies created a pipe-fitter's nightmare, and her condenser was not of adequate size to maintain sufficient water feed to the boilers. Furthermore, her coal consumption was excessive at eighteen tons per twenty-four hours at moderate speed. Her maximum speed under steam was 9½ knots.[61] After the war, Isherwood back-acting engines and new boilers (four) were installed, as well as a superheating apparatus. She retained her two funnels, and then could attain 11 knots with sail and steam. Structurally she was sound and well built. In heavy weather she performed well, though with 30 to 40 degrees of roll.[62]

The *Kansas,* with captured English engines, had rather unusual difficulties. When first in commission in 1864, the forward location of the engines affected her weight distribution to the extent that her screw could not be "got under water." This problem was short-lived because she was credited with "upwards of 11 knots" when on the blockade less than four months after the earlier report. She continued to have similar problems, however, with a tendency to race her engines a great deal because her prop was easily exposed in a seaway, an affliction aggravated by heavy rolling.[63]

The *Yantic,* with direct-acting engines, had the best reputation of the three: the *Yantic, Saco,* and *Kansas.* On her trials her engines were judged positively, showing "satisfactory strength, reliability, and practical efficiency." At sea, her commanding officer reported she passed through a gale and "terrific seas," proving herself "a most admirable sea boat, and has passed through . . . unscathed." The *Official Records* record her maximum speed as 10 knots.[64]

The last three vessels were those with Isherwood back-acting engines. The three were rated at 12.5 knots in the congressional report of 1865 on Marine Engines.[65] No specific figures have been found

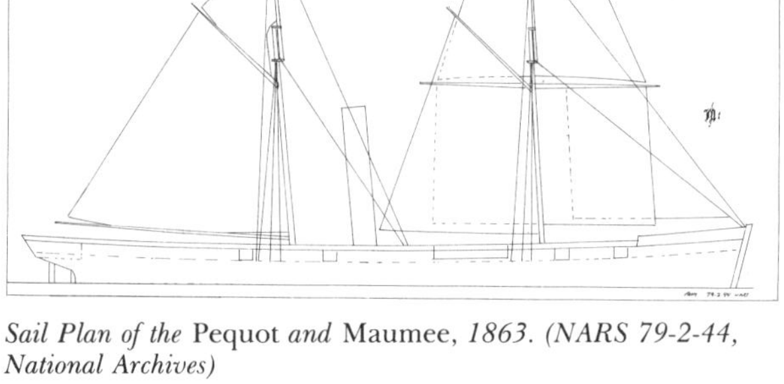

Sail Plan of the Pequot *and* Maumee, *1863. (NARS 79-2-44, National Archives)*

Looking Aft on the Nipsic, *with a 150-pounder Parrott Rifle on Pivot Rails, 9-inch Dahlgrens in Broadside, and Howitzer Aft. (U.S. Army Military History Institute)*

Looking Forward on the Nipsic. *Note the galley stack exhausting into the funnel, and the forecastle pivot gun. (U.S. Army Military History Institute)*

for the *Shawmut.* The *Nyack,* however, on a seventeen-day passage under steam alone in 1867, averaged 8¾ knots and 209 miles per day. In calm weather and smooth seas, she made 12 knots, but in the course of this 3,650-mile run, she encountered both head winds and seas. Because of the postwar economy, she did all this on half power, as per regulations. She was reasonably economical and with the hardest driving burned not over 18 tons of coal per day.[66]

The *Nipsic* received the most encomiums of the eight vessels. Shortly after her trials, John A. Dahlgren commented in a letter to Secretary Welles that he considered her class "a valuable addition to the Navy. She is very fast under steam (11 knots) and steers well. Her armament is also powerful the only defect being the contiguity of the mainmast with the two XI-inch [sic] guns. . . . The vessel pleased me much." After encountering heavy weather some five months into her first commission, her commanding officer suggested reducing the weight of her armament. She labored heavily, rolled her hammock rails under, and took water over the stern and quarter. Her chief engineer confirmed the extent of her rolling and also attributed it to her Parrott rifle and other heavy guns. The former gun also appeared to "have a material effect on [her] boilers when discharged even "at less than 20 degrees elevation."[67]

Through all the foul conditions the *Nipsic*'s engines "worked most beautifully." Her engineer extolled the "signal success of this vessel & machinery," which several times propelled her to 13 or 13¼ knots (by the log as well as landmarks), and the engines could maintain that pace "for any length of time." Her repairs since commissioning (about eight months by 14 April 1864) "would not exceed $175," despite constant use and approximately "3 million revolutions." Ayers's summation was that she was the "fastest vessel in the squadron."[68]

Five of these vessels underwent drastic alterations in rig and appearance in the postwar years. The *Maumee* and *Pequot* escaped these changes owing to their immediate decommissioning at the close of the war and their sale soon afterward. The *Nyack* remained in commission for a time and plans were made to rebuild her, but they were not carried out.

As part of the reactionary regimen instigated by Admiral Porter in the late 1860s, the remaining five gunboats were rerigged as ships between 1869 and 1871 (though the *Nipsic* for a short time had square sails on two masts and was the only brig in the service). They not only carried royals, but the *Shawmut,* at least, had a flying jib and jibboom. In the process of reverting to tradition, all five also received cutwater knees and suitable decoration.[69]

Gone was the spare and functional combination of austere lines and minimal rig. Replacing it were lofty masts and spars that may have complemented a vessel such as the old *Constitution* with her high and architecturally pleasing tiers of strakes and ports. The low-lying and undistinguished hulls of these vessels, however, were simply overwhelmed by this mass of sparring.

Because of these ships' relatively late entrance into the war, their combat records are less impressive than those of the ninety-day gunboats. The *Kansas,* for instance, did not join the blockade until December 1863. She was in action with the Confederate ram *Raleigh,* however, and made several important captures while part of the North Atlantic squadron. After participating in the assaults on Fort Fisher and in support of other minor army operations, she was decommissioned at war's end. Re-

The Saco *with Twin Funnels, Taken during Wartime. She had fourteen small boilers at this time. (U.S. Army Military History Institute)*

The Saco, *after the Removal of Her Original Boilers. She retained her two funnels and gained a third mast and cutwater knee. (Naval Historical Center)*

commissioned in 1865, she remained on the Atlantic until 1875, then was decommissioned and later sold (1883) at Portsmouth Navy Yard.

The *Maumee* joined the North Atlantic Blockading Squadron in October 1863. She was engaged in the search for the raider *Tallahassee,* then was part of the Fort Fisher expeditions. She was decommissioned in June 1865 and sold in 1869.

The *Nipsic* was stationed off Charleston for her entire war career, then served in the South Atlantic and West Indies until 1873. When recommissioned in 1879, the *Nipsic* was no longer the gunboat built in 1862–63, but a vessel of the *Enterprise* class, nearly five hundred tons larger than the original.

The *Nyack* was not commissioned until 28 September 1864 and was in the Fort Fisher assaults. After the war she was in the Pacific, cruising off South America. She was decommissioned and sold in 1871.

After a considerable delay, in part caused by her strange machinery, the *Pequot* was commissioned in February 1864, then was on the Atlantic blockade and in the Fort Fisher attacks. She was laid up immediately following the cessation of hostilities and was sold in 1869 to the Haitian navy.

Boiler difficulties limited the war career of the *Saco* to six months, from July 1864 to January 1865, when she was an element of the North Atlantic Blockading Squadron. After the war she was stationed in the Atlantic, Mediterranean, and Far East. She was decommissioned in 1876 and sold in 1883.

The *Shawmut*'s war career extended from November 1864 to Lee's surrender at Appomattox. She cruised in search of the raider *Tallahassee,* was in the second Fort Fisher expedition, and on the North Atlantic blockade. After service in the South and North Atlantic in the postwar years, she was sold in 1877.

The *Yantic* was commissioned 12 August 1864 and immediately set out in search of the *Tallahassee,* then joined the North Atlantic squadron. In the first operation against Fort Fisher, her 100-pounder Parrott rifle burst, killing six of her crew. She provided support for the second assault on that fort, then on Fort Anderson, North Carolina. She was in commission on various stations nearly continuously until 1897, when she was loaned to the naval militia of Michigan. From 1917 she served in various training capacities until being decommissioned in June 1926. She sank at her dock on 22 October 1929, with the cause described as "structural deterioration."[70]

In retrospect, the *Kansas*-class vessels were a mixed group, particularly in their initial commissions. The *Saco* was a failure in her machinery, with the *Pequot* a close second. The other vessels with non-Isherwood engines were not signally deficient compared to those with engines of his design. The *Nipsic* seems to have been the fastest of the lot. All except the *Saco* with her original boilers appeared to have attained the speeds necessary for effective blockade duty. The stability problem of the earlier vessels remained, however, with the rounder-bilged *Pequot* and *Maumee* somewhat worse in that respect than the others. In general, these vessels' greatest shortcoming was their late entrance into the war. Their speed could have had a significant effect on the blockade had they appeared earlier in the conflict.

CHAPTER 8

Double-Ended Gunboats, 1861–1866

Next to the monitors and ninety-day gunboats, the type of vessel popularly identified with the Civil War is the "double-ender." These were side-wheel, light-draft ships intended for river service and therefore designed with both stem and stern lines ostensibly identical, to obviate the need to turn broadside to reverse directions. These ships were fitted with a minimal fore-and-aft rig but in essence were dependent on their engines. A precedent for the idea of the identical fore and aft lines can be found in 1837 in the *Fulton II;* and the British had built smaller paddle-wheel, light-draft gunboats specifically for the Crimean War.

Octorara Class

There were three groups of double-enders begun during the war, totaling forty-eight ships. Of these, nine were not completed before Appomattox, and two of the latter were never commissioned. The later two groups, the *Sassacus* and *Mohongo* classes, were homogeneous within their classes and built from standard plans. They adhered to the accepted definition of "double-ender": identical fore and aft lines as well as paddle wheels located at the midship section. The initial group of twelve, however, usually denominated the *Octorara* "class," was composed of vessels built to nine disparate designs, by four navy yards and three civilian contractors. Of the twelve vessels, only three were strict double-enders, while the majority deviated at least to the extent of having the side wheels abaft the midpoint of their length. Six not only exhibited hull lines that differed significantly fore and aft but had round sterns. Above water they appeared to be conventional side-wheel vessels, and beneath the waterline their only concession to being double-ended was a second rudder at the bow.

The Department of Navy's newspaper advertisement of August 1861 for bidders called for a load draft of 6 feet 9 inches, the capability of carrying a 7,000-pound rifled gun at each end, and a complement of one hundred men. They were to carry provisions for sixty days and sufficient coal to maintain their maximum speed for eight days.[1]

There are no plans or only partial lines for four of the vessels: *Cimarron* (also called *Cimerone*), *Maratanza, Sonoma,* and *Conemaugh.* The latter two, built at Portsmouth Navy Yard, were identical. The *Maratanza* was constructed at Boston Navy Yard, and the *Cimarron* was contracted to D. Merschon, Jr., of Bordentown, New Jersey.

Of the existing plans of these vessels those of the *Miami, Paul Jones, Port Royal,* and *Octorara* show certifiably identical fore and aft lines. Available cross sections of the sister ships *Sonoma* and *Conemaugh* show minor differences between the two ends. The side wheels of the latter pair, however, were located at least fifteen feet aft of center, and those of the *Octorara,* built at New York Navy Yard, were offset ten feet aft.[2] The *Maratanza* was 207 feet by 32.6 inches. Available cross sections show differences in her fore and aft lines. A wartime photograph shows a rounded stern.[3]

The *Miami,* built at Philadelphia, was the only true double-ender constructed in a navy yard. She was 208 feet 2 inches by 33 feet 2 inches and 730 tons. She had distinctive raked rudder posts with perpendicular stem posts outboard of the rudders for their protection, protective posts required by contract. The differences between the stem and the stern on the *Miami* were the figurehead and the stern rudder, which was 6 feet wide as opposed to 5 for the fore rudder. Also, the aft protective post jogged outward to accommodate the wider rudder.

The Miami *during Wartime, with Topmasts Sent Down and Ports Open. Note that four of the forward (left) gunport shutter stanchions are still in place, while the remainder have been unshipped. The protective stem posts can be clearly seen. Assistant Secretary Fox had little good to say about this vessel—particularly about her looks. Two sailing vessels can be seen on her far side. (Naval Historical Center)*

Gustavus Fox considered her an example of what a U.S. naval vessel should not be: "She is a great clumsy, ugly, eight knot boat, and will never go faster without driving her blower. The guns are put in the eyes of her, consequently she looks like a bowl at each end."[4]

The *Port Royal* was 207 feet between perpendiculars by 34 feet 4 inches (Note that the perpendiculars used for length measurements were on the load line and therefore to the stems, not to the rudder posts.) This vessel was nearly identical in its rudder and stem arrangements with the *Paul Jones* (216 feet 10 inches by 35 feet 4 inches) and *Octorara* (205 feet by 34 feet 5 inches). Their stems were virtually perpendicular and below the load line doubled as protection for the rudders. The rudder posts, therefore, did not double as stem posts and were approximately 6 feet long. The *Paul Jones* was built by J. J. Abrahams of Baltimore.

A letter from Lenthall and Isherwood to Welles discussing desirable characteristics for the second class of the double-enders indicates that "the features of the Port Royal" (built by Thomas Stack at New York) were shown to prospective contractors as examples.[5] The *Port Royal,* built and designed by civilians, was considered the optimum example for the next class of these ships.

The remaining vessels of the 1861 prototype double-enders were the *Sebago* and *Mahaska* (built at Portsmouth) and the *Tioga* and *Genesee* (built at Boston). The *Sebago* and *Mahaska,* which measured 228 feet 2 inches by 33 feet 2 inches, each had different stems and sterns, with a conventional stern and rudder post aft. The fore rudder of each was inset and faired into a conventional-appearing stem. The result was a rudder of rather small surface area angled aft, reducing its effectiveness on the water. Their fore and aft bodies were dissimilar, particularly from about thirty feet from the stern, with a finer run than entrance in the lower waterlines. Their paddle wheels were some twenty-five feet aft of the midships line, at the fore end of the vessels' run.[6]

The Maratanza, *Built at the Boston Navy Yard. Note her round stern disguising her status as a "double-ender." (Naval Historical Center)*

The final pair were the *Tioga* and *Genesee,* which were 209 feet by 34 feet 11 inches. In these two, the designers made no pretense of attaining identical

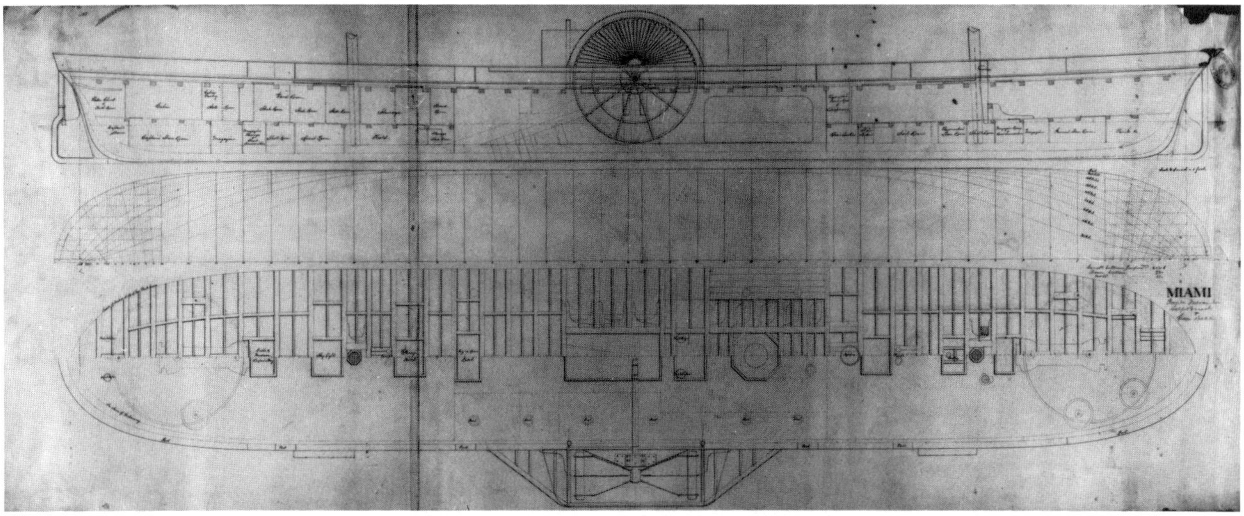

Lines and Deck of the Miami. *The added width of the stern rudder is not shown on this drawing. (NARS 41-9-9C, National Archives)*

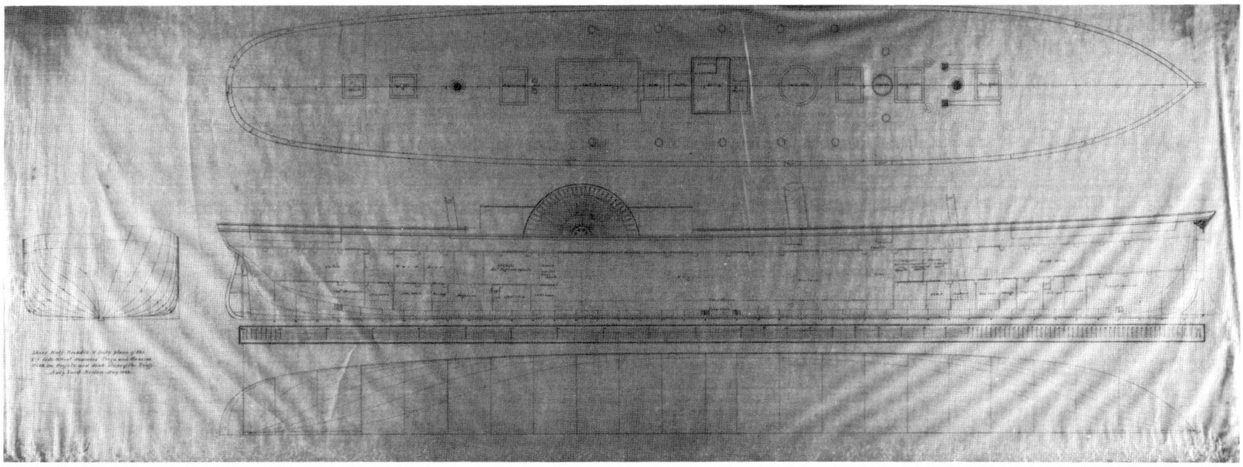

Lines, Deck, and Inboard Plan of the Tioga *and* Genesee, *showing distinct differences between fore and aft lines and small triangular fore rudder. (NARS 107-9-10E, National Archives)*

fore and aft lines, employing conventional high buttocks lines and a cruiser stern. The paddles were over thirty feet from midships, and the sole concession to double-ender criteria was a triangular rudder implanted in the corner of the right angle formed by the keel and stem. This rudder was pivoted so as to be housed within the stem post when not in use, then rotated outward when needed, but its triangular shape and small surface certainly could have gained little purchase on the water. Though none of the double-enders were known for their beauty, the addendum of a small decorated knee atop the vertical stems of the *Tioga* and *Genesee* smacked of affectation.[7]

The machinery in the *Octorara*-class vessels, fore-and-aft rigged, was designed by B. F. Isherwood and consisted of a single-cylinder, inclined, direct-acting engine mounted on a wooden frame. Two vertical water-tube boilers were fitted with forced draft blowers. The least costly were the *Octorara* and *Cimarron,* about $100,000 each, and the *Miami* was the most expensive at $179,051.[8]

The largest pair, the *Conemaugh* and *Sonoma,* mounted formidable batteries. In 1864 the *Conemaugh* had six 9-inch Dahlgrens in broadside and an 11-inch Dahlgren and 100-pounder rifle on the pivot rails. The companion vessel had four 9-inch Dahlgrens in addition to the larger guns.

The *Octorara,* with the smallest dimensions of the group, did not mount any of the larger Dahlgrens but had one 100-pounder rifle and three 9-inch smoothbores, plus four 24-pounders. The 207- to 209-foot ships usually mounted two large pivot guns and four to six smaller guns. At times two to four of the 9-inch shell guns replaced the 24- or 32-pounder broadside guns.[9]

The commanding officer of the *Cimarron* effectively summarized the sailing qualities of this class

The Genesee *on River Service. Her small area fore rudder is entirely below the waterline. (Naval Historical Center)*

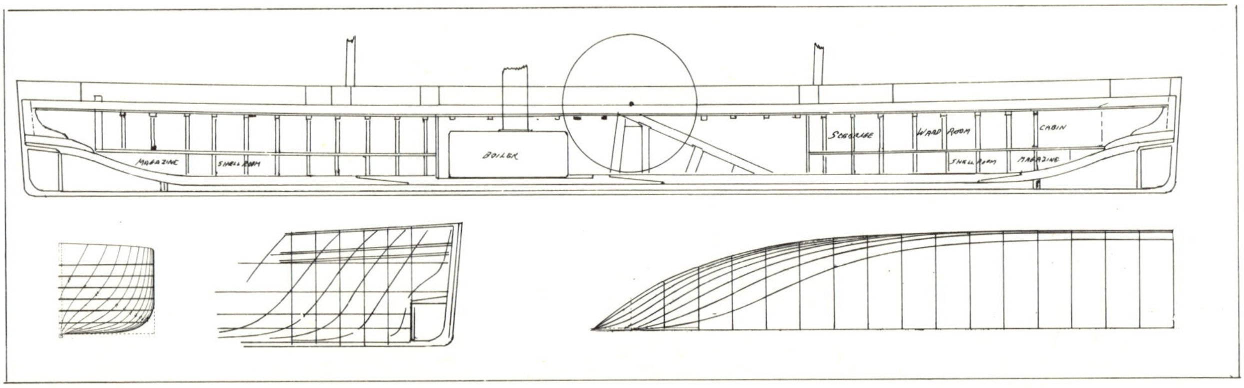

The double-Enders Octorara *and* Port Royal. *Lines and inboard plans show* Octorara, *one of the few of the class with identical fore and aft lines. The partial—aft—plan of the* Port Royal, *showing her very similar rudder arrangement, was used as an example to show contractors for the vessels of the* Sassacus *class.* Port Royal's *aft lines were slightly fuller than those forward. (Traced and reproduced from NARS 79-11-30 and 79-12-24, National Archives)*

of vessel: "The Cimarron is without doubt the best shallow river craft in the service and will for that very reason be the worst one for sea service." His letter of complaints on the vessel reflected the general performance was to be expected from shallow-draft, flat-bottomed craft on the high seas: "She does not rise on a sea, but disposes of it by scooping part of it . . . over her bows and passes staggering through the remainder." She rolled "frightfully and with the slightest provocation," making it a risk to cast loose the guns. Her steering was another detriment, varying two to three points from the set course because of her light draft. He later recommended her rudder be enlarged.[10]

Rudder problems arose with the other vessels also. On the *Maratanza,* which may have incorporated the same small triangular contrivance as had the *Tioga* and *Genesee,* her commander stated, "Her forward rudder is not to be relied upon." The *Miami* was also noted for having too little rudder surface.[11]

The area of canvas of the *Octorara*-class vessels was inadequate to overcome a hull form not suited to open seas. The *Maratanza* was credited with 3 knots maximum under her canvas and would not tack or wear. The *Miami* had her spars and rigging taken out by 1864, which may have been a general pattern for river service.[12]

The Conemaugh, *Sister Ship of the* Sonoma, *Built at Portsmouth. The only available plan of this vessel indicates the ends were nearly identical. Her paddles, however, are significantly aft of centerline. (Naval Historical Center)*

Their flat-bottomed and wall-sided hull form contributed to the strains placed on the ships in rough seas, but on the *Cimarron,* shoddy construction was an additional problem. On her first cruise, directly from the hands of the contractor, her hull and engine frame were "much strained," with supporting knees broken and "nearly all the deck (perpendicular) knees on both sides amidships . . . displaced, loosened." Her commander complained she was of the "poorest kind" of materials, a large portion of which was green timber or "commerce third or fourth cullings." The firing of her heavy guns served to exacerbate these problems.[13]

Little has been found that indicates any significant machinery problems and most of the double-enders averaged 7 to 9 knots. The *Official Records* credits the *Conemaugh* with the highest maximum speed, 11.5 knots, with the *Octorara* second at 11 knots.[14]

The main duties of these vessels were on the rivers, including army support operations and reconnaissance. For several months, three—the *Sonoma, Octorara,* and *Tioga*—were assigned to the West Indies with Captain Wilkes's Flying Squadron and performed remarkably well, despite their congenital sea-keeping difficulties.[15]

During this nine-month period the *Sonoma* gave chase to the CSS *Florida,* and the double-ender's commander reported: "I have no doubt under steam alone Sonoma is a faster vessel." Only a fresh breeze and heavy seas enabled the escape of the cruiser.[16]

Besides participation in the battles at Mobile Bay and Port Hudson, these vessels served in relatively light support duties. The *Miami,* however, was one of the unlucky wooden vessels to encounter a Confederate ram. In this case, she was lashed to the exferryboat *Southfield* when attacked by the ironclad *Albemarle,* resulting in the sinking of the *Southfield* and severe damage to the double-ender.

All twelve survived the Civil War. They were unsuited to cruising duty, however, and in any event had been superceded by the later, better designed double-enders. All were sold out by the end of 1868.

Sassacus Class

Although the first group of double-enders were built from several designs, the second class of the gunboats was based on one pattern. These twenty-eight vessels of the *Sassacus* class made it the largest class of ships built in the United States before World War I, with the possible exception of Jefferson's diminutive gunboats in the first decade of the nineteenth century.

Of the Sassacus class, eighteen were built under contract at civilian yards, the other ten at navy yards. All save three saw wartime service, and one, the *Algonquin,* was never commissioned. The latter ship played a part in the continuing feud between chief engineer Isherwood and the amateur engineer E. N. Dickerson. One of the twenty-eight was built of iron by Reany, Son, and Archbold. The specifics of this vessel, the *Wateree,* will be discussed separately.

The specifications of the class were laid down in "Proposals for Building side wheel Gunboats," which was published in 1862 to attract prospective contractors. This called for a length of 236 feet, breadth 35 feet, and 12-foot depth of hold from the throats of the floor timbers to the lower side of the deck plank. Frames and keel were to be of white oak and filled to the throat of the floors with white pine. Two tiers of iron diagonal braces, 3½ inches by ½ inch or 7⁄16 inch, were called for, as well as a head strap. The bulwarks were to be 5⁄16-inch iron plates, backed by substantial planking. This early use of light protective plating is distinguishable in photographs of these ships. The contractors were required to submit a plan showing only "the shape of one half of the vessel . . . as both ends are alike." Proposals were to be submitted by 30 July 1862.[17]

The following information on these vessels is found in a description of the *Mackinaw,* built at New York Navy Yard, published in 1863 in B. F. Isherwood's *Experimental Researches in Steam Engineering.*[18] Isherwood describes the ships as "in all respects alike," but some minor differences are apparent: the *Mackinaw* had a length of 240 feet and incorporated both chestnut and hackmatack (tamarack, or larch) in the framing.

The rudders were framed in iron, covered in brass, and placed in rectangular openings protected by brass stems. A light lookout deck spanned the gun deck between the wheelhouses, with a pilothouse, "made bullet proof with brass plates," on each end.

Below decks, the central area of 75¾ feet was devoted to machinery and coal from the keelsons to the spar deck. Berth decks on each end provided quarters for officers and crew, and stores were below these.

The engine was a single inclined cylinder of 58-inch diameter and 105-inch stroke, mounted on two 22-inch by 16-inch yellow pine frame members. These two timbers formed the fore and aft base of the cylinder, and one of the deck beams doubled as an athwartship engine support. The lower ends of the inclined timbers were secured to the keelsons by knees. Each inclined timber was supported at the upper end by a vertical 16-inch by 20-inch yellow pine timber. Two 16-inch-square cross beams connected these vertical supports.

Running the length of each inclined timber was an iron frame, which on the upper end incorpo-

The Mendota *with Topmasts Down. Her bulwarks were of sheet iron. Note the octagonal pilothouse, also covered with sheet iron. (U.S. Army Military History Institute)*

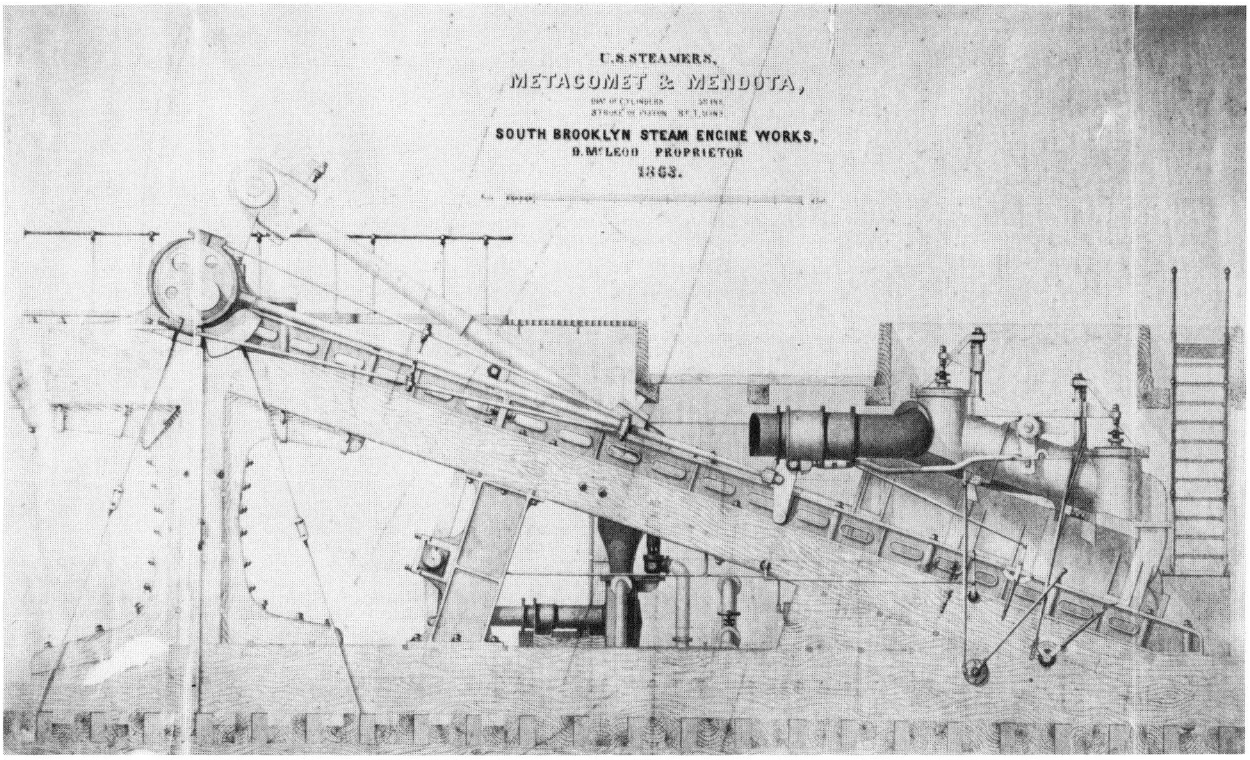

Inclined Engine for the Mendota *and* Metacomet, *Typical of the Class. Note the wooden frame and opening in deck for crank. These single-cylinder engines were capable of pushing the vessels to 14 knots. (National Archives)*

rated the pillow blocks for the paddle shaft, and on the lower extremity, supported each side of the piston. The pillow blocks were secured to the vessel itself by twelve $1\frac{5}{8}$-inch iron rods running downward to the keelsons. Therefore, the engine's framework was an integral part of the ship's structure. And, judging by the substantial nature of the timbers, the engine framing added strength to the hull.

Two boilers were installed, front to front. This allowed a fireroom of 8 feet 6 inches between them. Forced draft was provided to each boiler by an auxiliary engine that also worked bilge pumps, boiler feed pumps, and a distilling apparatus. A few of the ships, including the *Mackinaw,* were given superheating boilers. The machinery of these ships, with the exception of the *Algonquin,* which was the unsuccessful brainchild of E. N. Dickerson, produced 712 horsepower without blowers and 1,272 with forced draft.

The ships were given four watertight bulkheads, two of iron, one at each end of the engine spaces, and one of wood near each end. Wood or iron stanchions were to be unshipped to allow use of the pivot guns. The $\frac{5}{16}$-inch iron port shutters were hinged at the bottom.[19]

The gunboats were schooner-rigged with wire standing rigging and four shrouds to each mast. They had a complement of 163, which included fourteen officers. The battery placed on each was two 100-pounder rifles on fore and aft pivots, four 9-inch Dahlgrens, and two 24-pounder howitzers. Few variations in this arrangement were made during the war, except where 11-inch Dahlgrens replaced the rifles on the *Tacony,* and two additional 9-inchers were placed on the *Shamrock.* (The tabulation in the *Official Records* of vessels and armament lists a 15-inch Dahlgren on the *Mackinaw* in 1865, but the weight of that gun makes this report suspect.) The *Shamrock* was unique in receiving a ram in 1864, specifically intended to cope with the ironclad *Albemarle,* but was never so used. The *Osceola* also received a ram during the war, but no plans or specifications of these rams have been located.[20]

Generally, the performance of these ships was satisfactory and emphasized speed. All averaged over 8 knots. The *Tacony* and *Osceola* were reported to attain 15 knots, while the *Sassacus, Wyalusing,* and *Mattebessett* could achieve 14. Isherwood's report on the *Mackinaw* showed 10.16 geographical miles per hour with natural draft and 12.39 using the blowers.[21]

In 1864, the *Eutaw,* which was fitted with superheating boilers, was subjected to a trial for the benefit of a congressional committee investigating charges made by E. N. Dickerson against both Isherwood and the navy. The *Eutaw*'s performance

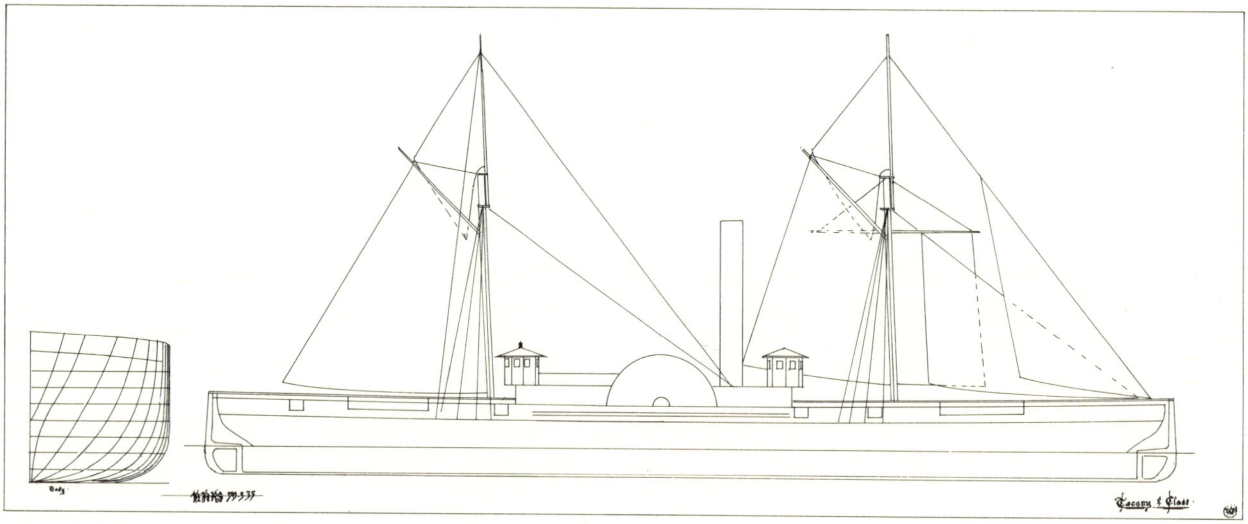

Sail and Lines of the Tacony (Sassacus *Class). (NARS 79-3-35, National Archives)*

did nothing to embarrass Isherwood, running 42.67 knots at an average speed of 13.11 knots and attaining 14.5 knots at times "without any unusual effort," according to a consulting engineer hired for the occasion. He also was impressed by her economy—the vessel used half the amount of coal used by most commercial steamers. The committee's report termed the vessel "one of the fastest steamers afloat" and in general discounted Mr. Dickerson's claims that the navy's vessels were inferior in machinery and speed to foreign naval vessels.[22]

In actual service, the *Sassacus,* in late 1864, pursued the raider *Tallahassee,* reaching 12½ knots under steam in a 26-hour stint. Her commander claimed that she had been faster when lighter and when more experienced firemen were available.[23]

Like their earlier counterparts, these ships were not sailers by any means. The *Mattebessett* was reported unable to make steerageway under sail, and the *Sassacus* was described as "unmanageable" under canvas. In gale conditions they were wet and rolled excessively. A report on the *Tacony* stated she was very buoyant, "but being of a light draft, she comes down with a crash upon a sea."[24]

At least two of the class suffered early in their careers because of poor workmanship and weak construction, aggravated by their rolling in heavy seas. The *Ascutney* (contract built) was condemned by a board of survey less than two months after commissioning and was sent north for "extensive repairs and strengthening." Another contract vessel, the *Chicopee,* had much green timber in her decks. Shrinkage of this wood was so extensive that "caulk [was] impossible." Her beams and knees were also described as too "frail to confine the sides of the ship or the decks."[25]

Navy-built vessels were not immune to similar maladies. The deck under the pivot guns of the *Tallapoosa* was "sprung by the weight of the metal thereon" conjoined with the rolling of the vessel and heavy seas coming aboard. Her decks were shored up to prevent the guns from "forcing their way through." She was a product of the Boston Navy Yard. It is noteworthy that few complaints have been found concerning the engines of the vessels built by the navy.[26]

During the war, the *Metacomet* was present at Mobile Bay as the consort of the *Hartford.* She captured the *Selma* and transported the wounded to Pensacola afterwards, her speed a definite asset. Five of the class were at Fort Fisher: the *Osceola, Pontoosuc, Sassacus, Tacony,* and *Pawtuxet.* The *Sassacus* rammed the ironclad *Albemarle* and remained in contact for over ten minutes, receiving a solid shot through one boiler in the engagement. Her fore rudder was stove in to the extent that she subsequently was obliged to steam backwards to Hampton Roads for repair. The only wartime casualty from this class of vessels was the *Otsego,* which was sunk by two mines in the Roanoke River.

In the postwar period, all were sold with the exception of the *Tallapoosa.* This vessel remained active and was rebuilt in 1874 (the secretary of the navy's report of 1888 lists her as built in 1874 at Baltimore). The new vessel retained the same basic measurements but was shorn of her fore rudder and received a conventional round stern and rudder. A cabin was built on her spar deck and she completed her career as an armed transport. In 1884 she was sunk in a collision and salvaged to continue in active service until her sale in 1892.[27]

Two vessels of the *Sassacus* class deserve separate attention: the iron *Wateree* and the *Algonquin,* which was the only vessel of this class that did not receive engines designed by Isherwood.

The dimensions and model of the *Wateree,* as far as we know, were identical to the rest of the class, and she carried the same armament. Her frames were of 4-inch × 4-inch × ½-inch flanged iron, with 18 inches between centers, and her keel was ¾-inch plate iron. She had eight keelsons (possibly combined into four box keelsons) and was plated with ½-inch iron except under the engines where the plates were ⅝ inches. Her stems were 4-inch × 7-inch and 3-inch × 6-inch hammered iron. In 1868 this vessel was the victim of an earthquake and tidal wave and was deposited one-quarter mile inland. Though relatively undamaged, the expense of returning her to sea was prohibitive and she was sold where she lay, in the streets of Arica, Peru (now Chile).[28]

The *Algonquin* was a disaster of another variety. E. N. Dickerson, undeterred by the *Pensacola* fiasco, had convinced the Navy Department that his ideas would be vindicated if his machinery was placed on one of the new double-enders and tried in direct opposition to an Isherwood engine in an identical vessel. With the influential support of Paul S. Forbes, a New York businessman, the lawyer gained an agreement to allow such a trial, using the *Algonquin* as a test-bed for Dickerson's engine,

A Sassacus-*Class Ship, Probably the* Agawam. *This view shows her hurricane deck. Other photographs of these vessels indicate there were minor variations, such as the number of portholes in the paddle-wheel housings (where the water closets were located). Note that shrouds were run inboard of the bulwarks. (U.S. Army Military History Institute)*

boilers, and surface condenser. Isherwood's machinery would be represented in the double-ender *Winooski.*[29]

The Dickerson engine had a stroke of 10 feet and bore of 48 inches, not differing greatly in cubic capacity from the standard Isherwood installation. The boilers were significantly smaller, however, having 132 square feet of grate surface, compared to 200 for the Martin boilers of the competition.

The trials were to be staged at New York, with both vessels tied to the dock and given identical coal supplies. Dock trials would eliminate wind and sea conditions as well as trim factors from skewing the outcome.

As with the *Pensacola,* the completion of the *Algonquin*'s machinery was long past the contract date, and she was not prepared for the formal trials until September 1865, some two years late. In the interim, Dickerson and friends had been working to discredit Isherwood in the public media, making extravagant claims for the Dickerson machinery, heaping invective upon Isherwood, and complaining of the conditions set for the trial.

It was also in this period that the congressional probe of Dickerson's allegations occurred as well as the publication of a satirical story "Uncle Samuel's Whistle and What It Costs." This masterpiece of nineteenth-century humor, rife with classical and biblical allusions, made even the starting of Dickerson's engines in the *Pensacola* a saga of epic proportions. Crowds of engineers wielding "handspikes, beetles, hydraulic jacks, oil cans and wrenches" were scattered among the myriad of mechanical contrivances that characterized the engine, and, with superhuman efforts and gallons of oil, got her under way—while the captain was ashore, purchasing a picture of "D——n."

By the date of the trial, 21 September 1865, public interest in the proceedings had reached an intensity that today is difficult to credit to a humdrum trial of differing types of machinery. By sundown a crowd of 10,000 had gathered and the carnival atmosphere was heightened by widespread betting on the outcome.

At the end of fifty-one hours of the ninety-six-hour competition, Dickerson stopped his engine, claiming a broken steam pipe. Six weeks were required to repair the defect. Dickerson then halted the second trial at seventy-one hours for no apparent reason other than the fact that he was losing. A trial board reported the *Winooski* developed 545 horsepower using 2.9 pounds of coal per horsepower, while the rival engines produced 517 horsepower and consumed 3.1 pounds per horsepower.

Dickerson and Forbes then demanded a sea trial, claiming their machinery was built to "navigate the sea, and not to strain hawsers and pull docks." The department complied reluctantly and a one-thousand-mile course was determined upon and run in

The Winooski, *the Double-Ender Used to Test Isherwood's Engines against Those of E. N. Dickerson in the* Algonquin. *The contest was one-sided in favor of the navy engine and vessel. (Naval Historical Center)*

February 1866. Despite the bluster, the outcome was expected: when the trial was terminated because of weather conditions, the *Winooski* had outdistanced the *Algonquin* by some seventy miles in twenty-nine hours.

The statistics were all unfavorable to Dickerson. Using forced draft, the *Algonquin* had averaged 9.8 knots and used 4.1 pounds of fuel per horsepower. Without blowers, Isherwood's engines used 3.47 pounds per horsepower and drove the *Winooski* at 11.7 knots. Furthermore, the Dickerson machinery weighed 39 percent more and took up 11 percent more space than that designed by Isherwood.

The *Algonquin* was declared "totally unfit for the naval service." In 1869, after further confrontations with Dickerson over his contractual agreement to remove the useless machinery at his own expense, the vessel was sold, complete with machinery.

Though Dickerson lost much of his credibility and popular support in this contest, he had yet another chance to plague Isherwood and the navy before his final defeat involving the machinery of the new steam sloop *Idaho,* discussed in chapter ten.

Mohongo Class

The third group of double-enders marked the only use of iron for an entire class of unarmored vessels before the 1870s. This iron construction necessitated their construction in civilian shipyards that had iron-working capabilities. These were the seven *Mohongo*-class double-enders, which included the *Ashuelot, Monocacy, Muscoota, Shamokin, Suwanee,* and *Winnepec.* All were laid down in 1863, but only one saw Civil War service.

These were the largest and longest lived of all the double-enders, measuring 255 feet by 35 feet with 1,370 tons displacement. Each had a single inclined engine of 850 horsepower (58 inches by 105 inches cylinder) and two boilers with a superheating apparatus.[30]

Their iron construction was based on frames 18 inches apart, measuring 12 inches in depth inside the turn of the bilge but 4 inches in depth from the bilge to the rail. Four box keelsons formed the hull's longitudinal strength, with the inner pair made up of vertical plates 14 inches in height. The top of each "box" was a plate 24 inches wide. The outer keelsons were equal in height but with top plates of 16 inches. The deck beams were of wood, 10 inches by 12 inches. Plans of the *Ashuelot* confirm that two watertight bulkheads defined the engine spaces and allow the possibility that two more were installed fifteen feet from each bow. The bulkhead forward of the engine spaces was pierced for a passage through the coal bunkers.[31]

Though of hull lines similar to the earlier classes, these iron vessels withstood ocean navigation with considerably more aplomb than those ships. The first in commission was the *Suwanee,* which received high praise from her commander after riding out a gale "handsomely" in April 1865. In a "tremendous sea," battened down and hove to, she

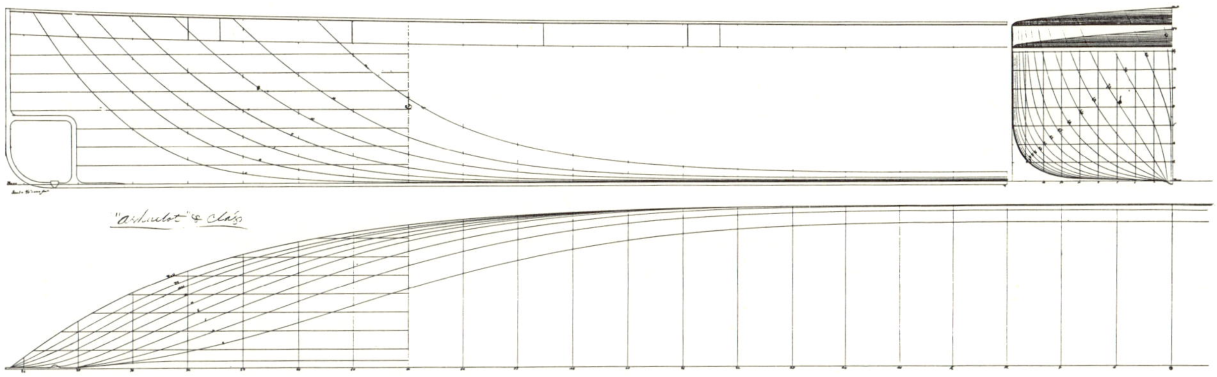

Lines of the Mohongo *and Class. (NARS 107-12-1C, National Archives)*

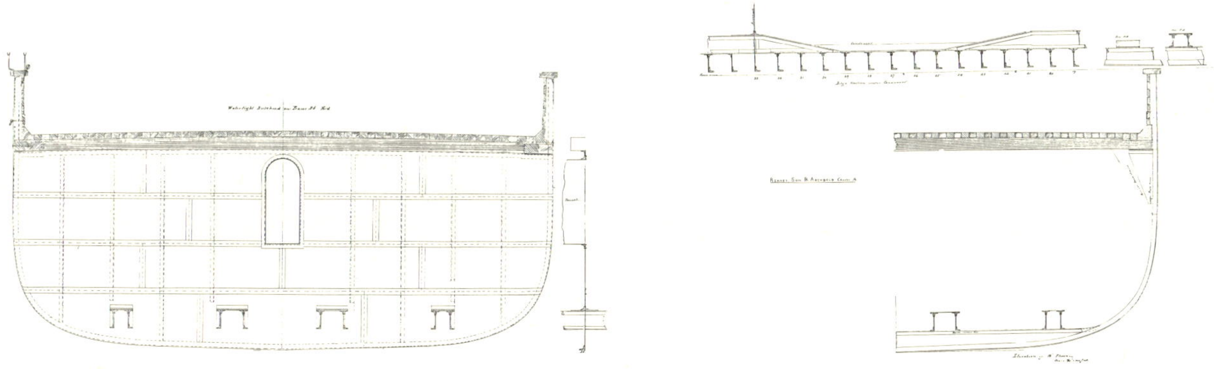

Iron Watertight Bulkhead (left) and Half Cross-Section of Frame of Double-Enders (right). Top right shows spacing of iron frames. Note wooden decks and box keelsons. (NARS 107-12-1F, 107-12-1H, National Archives)

The Mohongo, *Iron Double-Ender, a Larger Version of the* Sassacus-*Class Ships. Not all of these saw wartime service, but* Ashuelot *and* Monocacy *served for decades on foreign stations. (Naval Historical Center)*

"excited my admiration by the seaworthy qualities she exhibited. We took a little water in over the bows, but shipped no heavy seas." The contrast between this sea-keeping performance and that of the early versions of this type is clear-cut.[32]

They remained, however, heavy rollers and poor sailers. They quickly fell off to leeward in beam seas and winds and would not wear under sail alone. One of their captains stated it simply: "Cannot sail."[33] They were reasonably speedy, averaging over 10 knots. The *Muscoota* maintained 12 knots for an equal number of hours, and in one instance, ran 12 hours on one boiler and superheater, averaging 9 knots.[34]

Armament on some of these ships was four 9-inch Dahlgrens and two pivoted 100-pounders. The *Ashuelot* carried two 60-pounder Parrotts and four 8-inch Dahlgrens. An assortment of 20- and 24-pounder howitzers was placed on the hurricane decks. During the Spanish-American War, the *Monocacy* listed four 37-mm and three 47-mm Hotchkiss guns, with 8-inchers in place of the 9-inch smoothbores, and two 60-pound rifles.[35]

Two of these ships, the *Monocacy* and the *Ashuelot,* were longtime fixtures on the Asiatic station. Both were well suited to shallow river operation as well as to the climate. A report by a medical officer in the 1880s commented favorably on the "ample accommodations for all hands under all circumstances." In warm weather many of the officers and crew slept on or under the hurricane deck on bamboo beds with mosquito netting. The cabins were described as "unusually large" and the berth deck was "large, airy and comfortable." Steam heat was used for all accommodations as well as for the heads, which were in the paddle-wheel guards. The condensed water from the heating system was used for bathing, cooking, and drinking. The heating was efficient enough to keep the vessel "comfortable" even in single-digit temperatures. Such salubrious living quarters were virtually unknown in wooden naval vessels of any era.[36]

After the *Ashuelot* was lost in 1883, the *Monocacy* remained in Chinese waters, to be sold in 1903. She was so identified with that station that her replacement was given her name.

These three groups of similarly designed ships, despite their unconventional hull forms and their continued use of obsolescent machinery, marked an orderly progression in vessel design. The original group was an assortment of attempts on the double-ender theme; the second class was based on the most satisfactory of the original set; and the third was an enlarged, improved, and strengthened version of the successful *Sassacus* class. The shortcomings of the ships, once the initial unsatisfactory designs were discarded, were only those inherent in such special-use vessels.

Admiral Farragut reported late in the war that he had had "little service" from the double-enders "compared with the screw gunboats." He was, however, referring to blockading duties, for which most of the vessels were manifestly unsuited in any kind of seaway. The admiral softened his criticism by admitting that the *Sebago* and *Metacomet* and a few others had been capable of offshore operations. Therefore, it seems that these ships fulfilled their designers' intentions as far as river operations are concerned, and, in some cases, exceeded those expectations.[37]

CHAPTER 9

Fast Gunboats and Spar-Decked Cruisers, 1863–1869

The chronological boundaries 1863 to 1869 appear to ignore what would seem to be a more historically important dividing line: the end of the Civil War in 1865. In an operational study of the navy, 1865 would be a more valid date. In the era of wooden ship construction, however, vessels laid down in 1863 in many cases were not in service until after the war ceased. This factor, as well as the fact that many of these vessels were not necessarily designed for the domestic conflict, require a later date to close the subject.

Five classes of screw vessels were begun in 1863 and 1864: gunboats of the *Swatara* and *Algoma* classes, cruisers of the *Contoocook* and *Guerriere* classes, and the group of "super-cruisers" sometimes referred to as the *Wampanoag* class. As will be seen, the latter three classes were among the largest wooden vessels of the steam navy and were intended for operation on the open seas. The policy rationale for the building of these ships can be found in the words of Secretary of the Navy Gideon Welles late in 1864: "If I should not build, and we have not only continued hostilities, but war with England or France, I shall be denounced for being unprepared. Yet it is patent that powerful, and expensive because powerful, structures are conducive to peace. A few strong, powerful vessels will conduce to economy because they will deter commercial nations from troubling us, and if not troubled, we need no large, expensive navy." Thus the defeat of the Confederacy was not the primary reason for these vessels, unless one of the "commercial nations" would come to their aid. This need of large vessels had been ignored since the beginning of the war, while a fleet of coasting and blockade vessels had been abuilding.[1]

Welles prefaced the above statement with the remark that if peace took place, "I shall be blamed for extravagance." This prophecy was accurate and peace left the nation with a great number of vessels for which there was no perceived need, as the navy reverted to its prewar cruising role. This anomalous position, as well as the use of inferior construction materials, relegated some otherwise outstanding vessels to short and obscure careers.

The timber used for these vessels was a mixture of species. As far as can be determined, only two of the nineteen government-built ships were entirely of live oak: the *Wampanoag* and *Madawasca* (later the *Tennessee*), both built at New York Navy Yard. (The *Ontario,* later the *New York,* though never launched, was also of live oak.) The vessels of the *Nantasket* class were entirely of white oak, and those of the *Alaska, Contoocook,* and *Guerriere* classes were constructed of a combination of woods. The major part of their timbers were white oak—usually the frames. In the case of the *Antietam,* the frames were of live oak, white oak, locust, hackmatack, and red cedar. The *Contoocook*-class cruisers were generally of white oak frames and live oak ends (cants, aprons, and so on). Though the *Alaska*-class vessels used the same combination, their longer careers indicate either that a larger proportion of live oak was used or more seasoned materials.

The potential problems these materials posed was anticipated. In October 1864 John Lenthall elucidated the situation in his report to the secretary of the navy:

> Could the new vessels have remained on the stocks for a year or eighteen months, their durability would have been much increased; but that could not be permitted . . . and in a year or two will be felt the full weight of this evil, for they will decay with great rapidity.
>
> The demand for materials . . . for the past two or three years has absorbed all the supplies that

were in the yards. The appropriations for years past have made no provision for supplies beyond the want of the then passing year, and there could be thus no accumulation of timber or other materials for future wants. . . .

"For many years no white oak was received . . . that had not grown within a short distance of salt water, and that had not been cut at a particular season of the year; but latterly it has been found impracticable to adhere to these requirements, and timber has been used that has grown in all sections of the country and cut at any time. Our supply of southern yellow pine timber has been exhausted, and other kinds are being used to supply the deficiency, and among them the American larch or hackmetack from the State of Maine.[2]

Lenthall added in his 1865 report that the navy's ships "particularly those built in the last eight or ten years . . . have been mostly made with unseasoned timbers." He described the white oak as "little else than refuse of the past years" and that there was no supply of white oak knees, except by purchase on the open market at "exorbitant prices." The shortage was threatening to cause suspension of work on some vessels unless a method of replacing the knees was found.[3]

By 1867 the pressure for the quick completion of vessels had abated considerably. Therefore, Lenthall reported he would allow vessels then on the stocks to remain there "as long as possible, that the green timber of which they are necessarily composed may season."[4] Unseasoned timber had been used for several years, and these five classes were not the only vessels built of such materials. The *Sassacus*-class double-enders had been built of white oak and, as has been seen, were plagued by structural weaknesses, both in contract- and navy-built vessels. The *Kansas*-class gunboats were generally made of white oak and postwar reports on their condition reflect this.

The substandard quality of materials foreordained short operational careers for most of the five classes begun in 1863 and 1864. In other ways, however, they were noteworthy vessels. The engines for all but three ships were designed by Benjamin Isherwood, and many of these engines were built in navy yard shops. Only a few engines had been built before this time at navy facilities: those of the *Wabash* and the original engines of the *Pensacola* and *Richmond* had been built at Washington Navy Yard.

Isherwood reported in December 1864 that the construction of engines in navy facilities was necessary as a wartime expedient: the few civilian establishments capable of such work were "extensively engaged" in other machine work, for other navy bureaus, the War Department, and the merchant service. In all, sixteen engines were built in the navy yards. The largest was a 100-inch by 48-inch geared powerplant built at the Washington yard, and the remainder were back-acting cylinders, ranging from 36 inches by 36 inches to 68 inches by 42 inches. The latter engine was constructed at Boston and installed in the *Franklin.* A pair of 60-inch by 36-inch cylinders from Washington replaced the original engines of the *Richmond.* Three of the 36-inch by 36-inch installations were built at Washington and two at Kittery. Eight 50-inch by 42-inch engines were completed, four at Boston and four at New York. Not all these engines were used immediately; four were converted to compound in the 1870s. The *Bonhomme Richard,* for which the large geared engine was intended, was never ordered by the department. All the vessels of the *Alaska* class and three of the *Nantasket* class had navy-built engines. No further engines were undertaken in the navy yards until the triple-expansion machinery of the rebuilt *Monadnock,* and those of the *Raleigh* and *Cincinnati,* of the 1890s.[5]

The armament of the new vessels marked a significant turn away from the policy of using large pivot guns in place of broadside guns on large vessels. In 1863, R. B. Forbes wrote, "Large pivots are going out of fashion and . . . broadside guns are coming into fashion."[6] Forbes was reflecting a growing dislike in naval circles of the large pivot guns, because of their limited use in any but smooth seas. In June of the same year, Farragut stated in a letter to Welles his objections to the armament on board the *Monongahela* (two 11-inchers, one 150-pounder, and four howitzers) and generalized to apply to all batteries composed of a small number of large pivot guns. He compared his vessel to the English frigate *Rinaldo,* which was armed with two 68-pounders and sixteen broadside guns:

The frigate has more than six times as many chances, and although the shot is not as large or as destructive, it will nevertheless go through the ship and kill and wound many men; they would also be enabled to keep up such a continual fire upon the three large guns as to render them useless, and at close quarters, our men having no protection, the enemy's musketry would be able to prevent their reloading the guns.

Such has been the case in two or three instances here; nearly every man was wounded at the pivot gun on board the *Owasco.*

"It is said these guns are intended for distant shooting; but are these vessels so fleet as to enable the commander to choose his distance? No! And if he could, is there sufficient steadiness in the vessel to enable him to fire with any accuracy at a great distance? No! If, on the contrary, there is any sea running at all, it is with imminent danger that he ventures even to cast loose his gun, and the motion is so rapid and violent that he really must be an expert to hit a vessel at the distance of a mile or even a half a mile; and in the meantime a small vessel with more stability, more guns, and perhaps

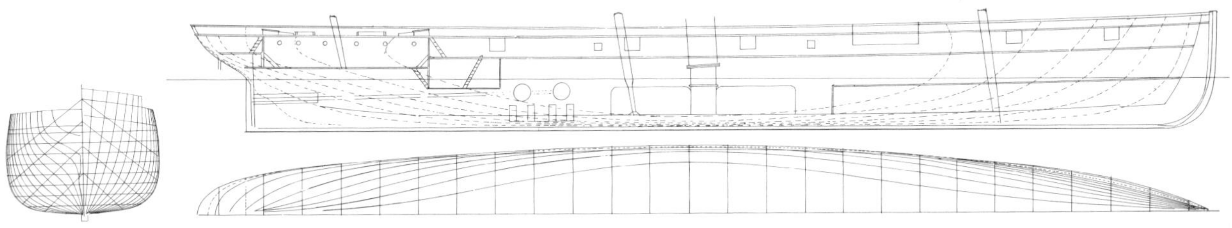

Lines, Inboard, and Sheer of the Resaca *and* Nantasket. *The plans show their extreme sharpness forward and 7-to-1 length-to-breadth ratio. The simplified inboard plan shows the location of cylinders on the back-acting engines, boilers, and decks. Note the sunken poop and resulting "partial" quarterdeck. Plans for near–sister ships* Swatara *and* Quinnebaug *show a similar inboard arrangement, but their lines are marginally fuller. (Drawn from NARS 108-11-2C and 108-11-3D, National Archives)*

> more speed, is keeping him close aboard and pouring in broadside after broadside until the leviathan surrenders to a pigmy.
>
> I assure you, sir, that I am afraid to trust one of these gunboats, with nothing but their original armament, even among the miserable cotton-made gunboats in the river, but I have placed on them two or more broadside guns . . . and I fear that the country will find, should we have a foreign war (when it is too late), that these vessels, armed with the big pivot guns, will be no match for the enemy's vessels half their size.

In the same letter Farragut also complained of the *Monongahela*'s lack of forward fire and recommended she have "twenty VIII-inch guns on the broadside, with two 100-pounder rifles on the topgallant forecastle."[7]

Farragut's letter was essentially ignored by Welles at the time. The batteries of four of the five ship classes begun late in the war, however, showed that Farragut's objections had been taken into consideration. All were given substantial broadside batteries, and only the *Algoma* class ships had large pivot guns.

Two overriding factors dictated the hull designs of all five of these classes of vessels: higher speed and increased size over earlier vessels of comparable classes. Two examples serve to illustrate the increments in size. The vessels of the *Swatara* class were no more heavily armed than the earlier *Yantic*-class ships yet were 36 feet longer and displaced 200 tons more, and the *Guerriere*-class ships were similar in armament to the 1857 sloops such as the *Pensacola* but were 80 feet longer and exceeded them by nearly 1,000 tons of displacement. (The reversion to broadside batteries also required extra length to prevent overloading the ends of these ships.) Furthermore, these increases in lengths were not accompanied by proportionally larger breadth or draft dimensions.

The dominating factor in all these hull designs was the search for higher speeds. Increased length without significant augmentation of breadth dimensions enabled both finer and sharper lines, which theoretically would enable the vessels to attain high velocities. And, increased length in itself resulted in higher speeds.

The one vessel completed in this era that did not meet the above design criteria was the frigate *Franklin,* commissioned in 1867 (see chapter 4). The *Wampanoag*-class vessels are also treated in a separate chapter because of their unique hull designs, divergent engineering characteristics, and the controversy they engendered.

Swatara Class

The four gunboats of the *Swatara* class were follow-ons to the *Kansas* class and by extension to the ninety-day gunboats. At 216 feet, their design was a 36-foot stretching of the earlier gunboat model. Resemblances to the *Kansas* class are obvious, from the sunken poop to the 30-foot beam. It is assumed that they also used the geared steering apparatus of the earlier ships. The new vessels were not proportionately beamier than either the *Kansas* or ninety-day vessels, which reveals the department's preoccupation with finer lines in the later war years. The ships were begun in 1864 and none were completed until after Appomattox. Three—the *Swatara,* the *Nantasket,* and the *Resaca*—were initially authorized and were termed "fast gunboats." The *Quinnebaug* was added to the class and was scheduled to receive engines imported from England.[8]

Like the *Kansas* class, these gunboats used two distinct hull designs. Above the waterline, all four were nearly indistinguishable; the only differences were minor variations in port spacings. Below the waterline, the *Swatara* and *Quinnebaug* were on one plan (with allowances for twin screws on the latter), and the remaining ships were on a dissimilar model. Aft, the waterlines of both pairs were not vastly different. Both the length and angle of the entrance lines on the *Resaca* and *Nantasket,* however, were more extreme than those of the other pair of gunboats. At 26 degrees on the 12-foot line, these were six degrees sharper than the *Swatara*

The Resaca, *One of the Few Photographs of This Class of Vessel. Because of their unseasoned timber, all had exceedingly short life spans and were out of service by 1873. (Naval Historical Center)*

and *Quinnebaug,* the sharpest hulls on any U.S. Navy steamship. The fineness of their entrance further emphasized the literal point: though they were 30 feet wide, they reached this breadth over 100 feet aft, compared to the other pair's 88 feet to their widest sections. Nearly one-half of the length of the *Resaca* and *Nantasket* design was in the entrance lines.

These vessels were constructed entirely of white oak, a wood usually satisfactory for maritime construction (it was the basis of a great deal of merchant vessel hulls), but in this case it was apparently unseasoned. Furthermore, the fastenings used were tree nails, in lieu of bolts in some areas of the hull. In this class of vessels, iron diagonal strapping was employed extensively to counteract potential longitudinal weakness. The engines and boilers of the *Nantasket* were not supported by normal first futtocks but rather by "long floor[s] reaching from bilge to bilge"; in other words, single large timbers straddled the keel, providing solid base timbers for the machinery.[9]

The midship sections of the two pairs of vessels diverged somewhat also, with the *Swatara* having flatter floors and harder bilges. The *Nantasket* and *Resaca,* with much rounder bilges, were more on a par with the *Maumee* and *Pequot* in this respect.

The engines of all but the *Quinnebaug* were designed by Isherwood and built in navy yards. They were 36-inch by 36-inch back-acting installations with three boilers and disconnecting (but not hoisting) screws. The engines for the *Quinnebaug* were contracted to Jackson and Watkins of London in order to provide machinery competitive with Isherwood's engines. Two sets of two-cylinder engines measuring 38-inch by 21-inch stroke were installed. Each pair drove one of her twin screws. The English engines were allotted the same hull space as the department's powerplants. The steam cut-off of the English engines was one-fourth of the stroke, considerably less than that of Isherwood's valve settings.[10]

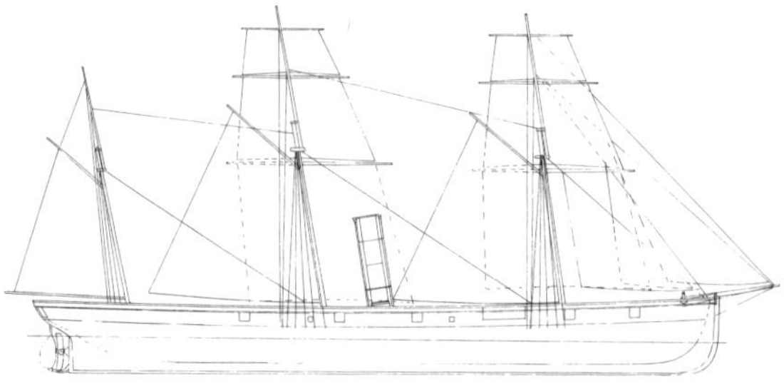

Sail and Spar Plan of the Swatara, *1865. (Traced from NARS 107-10-12G, National Archives)*

All four ships were three-masted and were originally bark-rigged and lightly sparred. Later the *Nantasket* and *Swatara* were ship-rigged and given bowsprits and jibbooms.[11] The batteries of these gunboats consisted of six 32-pounders (42 hundredweight) and single 60- or 100-pounder pivot rifles.[12] These batteries were actually lighter than that of some of the *Kansas*-class ships.

The *Resaca* was in commission for eleven days in mid-1866 and made 9 to 12 knots under steam alone. Later, when her four-bladed screw was replaced by a two-bladed unit, her maximum dropped to around 10 knots. She was reported as a "success in every sense, both with her canvas and her new screw." She carried her spars and canvas "beautifully," attaining 7 to 8 knots in a "gentle breeze." (As will be seen, in the postwar economy-minded navy the criteria for excellence in a cruising vessel did not include speed under steam.) The mean speed of the *Swatara* in her trials was 12 knots, significantly higher than the 7 knots run by the *Quinnebaug* with her English engines.[13]

As early as 1871, all four gunboats were reported "not worth repairs" because of the deterioration of their timbers. The *Quinnebaug* made one cruise to South America, then returned to be decommissioned in November 1870. Her engines, having proved unsatisfactory, were removed and she was laid up.[14] The *Swatara* was commissioned in November 1865, made two cruises, and was decommissioned in 1871. In that same year, work was begun replacing the *Swatara* and *Quinnebaug* with new vessels carrying the same names but of greater beam and depth, built of live oak. The *Nantasket* was in commission from October 1869 to July 1872 and was broken up in 1876 after her engines were removed for later reuse. The *Resaca* was sold in 1872 at Mare Island and became a passenger vessel, the *Ventura*. She was wrecked in 1875.

Algoma Class

In the construction of all the vessels of this era, the hulls were ordered after the directives for building the engines. With the *Algoma* class, the delay between the two was such that none of the hulls had been ordered before the war's end. The 50-inch by 42-inch engines, however, had been begun at navy shops in 1864 and were to power vessels named *Algoma, Teghkanic, Meredosia, Talladega, Confiance, Serapis, Detroit,* and *Peacock.*[15] The last four were named for vessels defeated by American ships and the first four names were in accordance with Secretary Welles's desire for distinctively American (Indian) names—regardless of their cacaphonous pronunciations.[16]

Four of the unused engines were assigned to hulls begun in 1867, designated *Algoma, Alaska, Astoria,* and *Kenosha.* The mass name changes of 1869 resulted in the *Algoma* becoming the *Benicia;* the

The Alaska *with Her Funnels Down. All five of her broadside guns are out, but the pivot part is only partially open. (Courtesy Peabody Museum)*

Astoria, Omaha; and *Kenosha, Plymouth.* The vessels of the class were to be more economical alternatives to the *Contoocook* and *Guerriere* classes and were intended for foreign cruising.

Dimensionally, at 250 feet, the new vessels were lengthened versions of the *Ticonderoga,* with the same 38-foot beam. In all other respects, they differed substantially.[17] These vessels displaced over 100 tons less than the *Ticonderoga* and *Lackawanna,* reflecting finer lines as well as lighter building materials. Their midship sections were considerably rounder in the bilges than the older vessels with a rather unusual bilge-like angle below the actual turn of the bilge.

The *Algoma* class vessels were armed with single 11-inch pivot guns plus ten broadside 9-inch guns and single 60-pounder rifles forward. This was a distinct divergence from the two or three pivot guns on the earlier vessels.[18]

The engines for this class were designed by Isherwood and were back-acting with surface condensers. They had four boilers and twin funnels, along with a superheating apparatus located in the uptakes. The latter could be bypassed allowing steam directly from the boilers to the engines. Several steam-operated auxiliaries were incorporated into this machinery, including a steam-reversing gear.[19]

The main portions of these hulls were of white oak. The cant frames, counter, and top timbers were of live oak. Diagonal bracing was used, along with a head strap and bracing for the stern deadwood.[20]

The vessels were fitted with disconnecting screws and a new type of hoisting mechanism. This was a crank-operated screw gear mounted on an iron frame. The arrangement was disliked by both proponents and opponents of shipboard labor-saving devices. (The latter group tended to favor labor intensive practices as a tool for keeping large crews busy.) It was reported that the device required nearly an hour to raise the propeller and half that

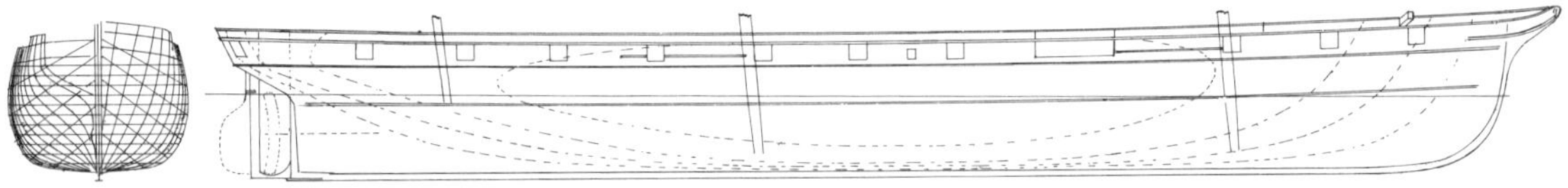

Sheer and Body Plan of the Algoma *Class, 1866. Note the single pivot port. In size these vessels were comparable to the* Sacramento *class but exemplified the move away from big pivot guns to broadside armament. (Traced from NARS 77-13-1E, National Archives)*

to lower it—compared to less than fifteen minutes for the older rope-purchase method. Furthermore, the long elevating screw was partially below the waterline and therefore required weekly cleaning to keep it free of barnacles. Finally, the above deck frame was vulnerable, fragile, and in the way. On the other extreme, some officers suggested a steam-operated hoisting gear.[21]

The completed ships were exceptionally handsome vessels. The two funnels were sufficiently subdued by their tall rig, and the unattractive gap between the fore and main/masts that was usual in twin-funnel vessels was inobtrusive here. The only exception to this was the *Omaha* in later years, after she had received new boilers and outsized funnels.

Not all the class had hoisting funnels. The *Algoma* and *Alaska* were originally built with telescoping funnels. At least the *Plymouth,* however, had standing pipes. The aft pipe was twenty-three feet from the mainmast and prevented use of the mainsail (unless reefed). In reply to one complaining captain, Lenthall responded: "The steam machinery cannot be placed further aft. . . . To have all the advantages of the combination of sail and steam without any of the disadvantages . . . is not a practical idea . . . the height of the chimney is an engineering question, and is considered of vital importance in the efficiency of the machinery."[22]

Captain Macomb of the *Plymouth* was not swayed by such arguments, however. He simply had the offending funnel cut down to a height he felt suitable. One photograph exists of the unsightly result.[23] It appears from photographs that all the vessels eventually received hoisting funnels.

The performance of these vessels was highly satisfactory, even drawing admiration from the usually negative British. Under steam and sail most would attain 13.5 to 14 knots, and 12 to 13 knots was not unusual under sail. The *Omaha* was reported to reach 14.5 under sail, and the *Benicia,* referred to as a dull sailer, clipped off 14 knots in a quartering gale. The *Plymouth* made 13.2 knots at full steam and 8 to 9 at half power.[24]

There were some notable deviations from general cruising in the careers of these sloops. The *Alaska,* with the *Benicia,* participated in the punitive

Sail Plan of the Omaha, *1872. Armament was ten 9-inch smoothbores in broadside and one large pivot gun, a major departure from the large pivot battery of the* Shenandoah *class. (NARS 77-13-3W, National Archives)*

The Handsome Plymouth *during Her Mississippi River Peace Cruise of 1877. On her stern are false, painted-on quarter galleries, considered fashionable at the time. (U.S. Army Military History Institute)*

expedition against "Corea" in 1871 and served to protect Alaskan settlers from Indians in 1879. She was decommissioned and sold in 1883. The *Benicia* provided transportation for the king of Hawaii in the 1870s, and in 1870 the *Plymouth* escorted the British armored ship *Monarch,* which carried the remains of philanthropist George Peabody to the United States.

In 1877, the *Plymouth,* this time with matching funnels, made a ceremonial cruise up the Mississippi as far as Vicksburg. She and her crew were feted lavishly in this thirty-six-day odyssey marking the end of Reconstruction in the South.[25]

The *Omaha* outlasted them all and was extensively rebuilt of live oak in the 1880s, with one critic claiming that her refit cost half as much as a "small steel cruiser." She gained complete electrical and ventilation systems in this reconstruction and remained active until 1891. She was a quarantine ship until sold in 1915.[26]

Contoocook Class

"The most efficient kind of ships we have had in the navy, and the model of which for steaming and sailing cannot be surpassed" was Admiral Porter's glowing estimate of the vessels of the *Contoocook* class "clipper screw sloops" completed between 1868 and 1871.[27] Regrettably, as with the *Swatara* class, substandard hull materials abbreviated their service life significantly. By 1875, the date of Porter's statement, two were already out of service.

The class was to have had ten ships, six of which were cancelled: the *Arapahoe, Keosauqua, Mondamin, Tahgayuta, Wanaloset,* and *Willamette.* The remaining sloops were originally designated the *Contoocook, Manitou, Moshulu,* and *Pushmataha.* Only the *Contoocook* saw service under her original designation, which was changed to *Albany* on 15 May 1869. On that date the *Manitou* became the *Worcester;* the *Moshulu, Severn;* and the *Pushmataha, Cambridge.* On 10 August, the last was again changed to *Congress.*

These vessels were 290 feet by 41 feet, with a resulting length to breadth ratio of 7 to 1. They displaced 3,100 tons and had an 18-foot draft. Length-to-breadth ratios of prewar steamers had been 5 to 1 in the *Merrimack* class and 5.1 to 1 for the *Hartford* sloops. Had such proportions been applied to the new vessels they would have been a mere 205 feet in length. The leaner proportions of the newer vessels represented the emphasis on speed as well as a deemphasis on the breadth considered necessary to enable a vessel to stand up to her canvas.

The hulls of the *Contoocook* class were designed by John Lenthall and were similar in their lines to

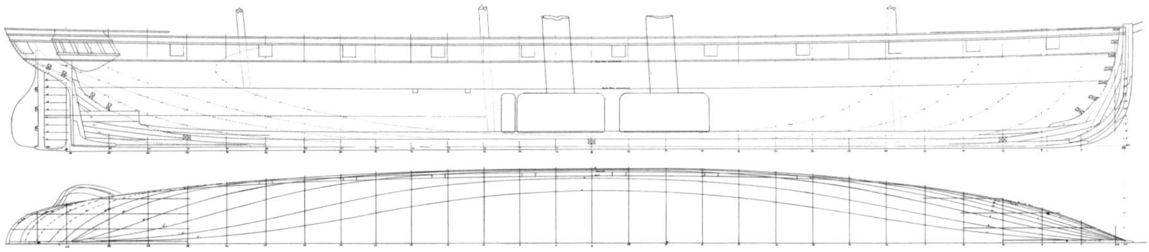

Sheer and Lines of the Contoocook *Class. With fourteen broadside 9-inch guns, this was essentially a new class of steam vessels. Poor construction materials, however, prevented long service lives. (Reproduced from BSE Plan, RG 19, National Archives)*

those of the *Swatara* and *Quinnebaug.*[28] Both classes of vessels measured about 32 degrees on the entrance waterline and had little deadrise or tumble home. The original design was without a spar deck and had no cutwater knee. The majority of the timber in the ships was white oak, though some live oak was incorporated in the *Severn.*[29] Plans of the latter vessel also show iron knees supporting her spar deck. This use of iron no doubt was spurred by the severe shortage of white oak knees noted by Lenthall earlier.[30]

As these vessels were originally designed, they were to have rams incorporated on their stems. The ram itself was to be a cast-metal bulge protruding a foot from the stem at the 14-foot waterline. Measuring aft along that waterline, the timber backing was 10 feet deep and 4 feet thick at its maximum cross section. Further strength was imparted by diagonal iron or timber braces reaching downward and forward from deck beams to this mass of deadwood. With the cessation of hostilities, this plan was not implemented.[31]

B. F. Isherwood designed the 60-inch by 36-inch back-acting engines for the class, and four main and two superheating boilers were used. The propeller was fixed but could be disconnected from the shaft. A few published statistics delineate the proportions of this machinery: the main shaft was 130 foot long and 13½ inches in diameter, each cylinder and steam chest weighed 22½ tons, each of three main pillow blocks weighed 5 tons, and the crankshaft journals were 45 inches long.[32]

The *Severn* and *Congress* had two standing smoke pipes, but the *Worcester*'s funnels had hoisting sections. Later, the *Congress* was fitted with hoisting funnels and it is assumed that the other two were similarly equipped.[33] The vessels were to be bark-rigged, though at least the *Congress* and *Worcester* were later ship-rigged. The former carried canvas to royals and over 32,000 square feet of sail.[34]

The *Severn* and *Worcester* were given quarter galleries, and all the vessels had cutwater knees added.

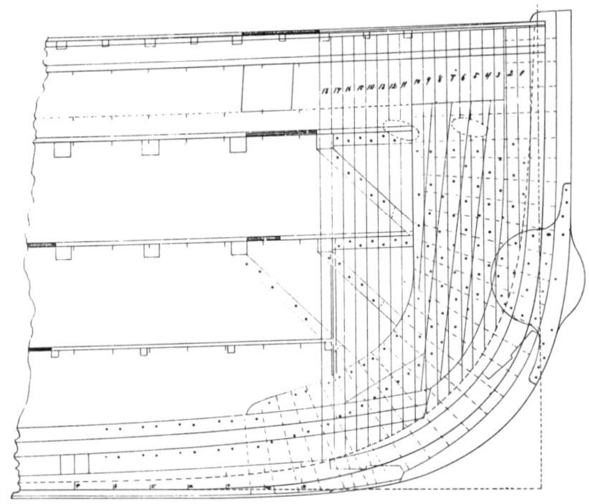

Forward Timbering of the Contoocook. *The proposed ram and substantial solid structure behind it are evident. (NARS 78-10-19, National Archives)*

The knees of the *Congress* and *Worcester* were somewhat fuller and less angular than those on the other vessels.[35]

The *Contoocook* was armed in 1868 with eight 9-inch Dahlgrens on the gun deck and a 60-pounder on the forecastle deck. A year later, after the addition of her spar deck, six additional Dahlgrens were added. The remaining three vessels were armed with fourteen 9-inch guns from their commissioning, plus one or two 60-pounder Parrotts.[36]

Admiral Porter's praise of this class of ships was in direct contrast to the verdict rendered by the Goldsborough board in 1869. As will be seen, this group roundly condemned the *Wampanoag* class for having excessive length in proportion to breadth and depth and for being over-engined. Maintaining their consistency, they labelled the *Severn* as "a diminished pattern of the same tribe, but not yet loaded perhaps with steam appliances to quite the same exorbitant degree." They recommended the removal of two main boilers and one of the funnels, changing the propeller to one of two blades, building a complete spar deck, and rerigging her as a ship with altered mast locations.

The *Congress* and *Worcester* were to be modified in the same manner. The *Albany* was overlooked by this board, but her commander had suggested similar changes earlier.[37] As has been seen, spar decks were built and the rerigging took place. No changes were made, however, in the number of boilers or funnels.

The first sea trials of the vessels were encouraging, with the *Contoocook* logging 12 knots under steam, until her crankshaft journals overheated and her boilers foamed. She was easy in her motions and was expected to be a fine sea boat.[38]

The commander of the *Congress* wrote that under steam alone she could maintain 12½ to 13 knots under the best circumstances. Under sail alone she attained 11.6 knots and her commander expected 14 with sail and steam in favorable conditions. She was easy in her motions and tacked under royals, topgallants and top sails "without once missing stays." She was, however, slow in answering her helm. Surprisingly, she was regarded as a weatherly ship, due in part to the addition of a 14-inch false keel, as recommended by the Goldsborough board.[39]

As has been stated, these handsome ships led short careers. The *Severn* was in commission twenty-eight months (from 1869 to 1871), in repairs until 1875, and sold to John Roach in 1877 for $250,000. Her building cost had been $489,176.34. The *Albany*'s career began in March 1868, and she was decommissioned in January 1870. She was sold on 12 December the same year. The *Congress* lasted six years, 1870 to 1876, and was sold in 1883. The last to go out of commission was the *Worcester*, in 1879; she was sold in 1883. Their aggregate cost to the government had been in excess of $2.5 million.[40]

Guerriere Class

The ocean cruiser program of 1863 included ten spar-decked sloops, each measuring 300 feet by 46 feet, and displacing 3,934 tons. This class was to be more heavily armed than the *Contoocook* class, with less emphasis on speed. The names of the proposed ships were: the *Java, Ontario, Piscataqua, Illinois, Minnetonka, Guerriere, Kewaydin, Antietam, Wautaga,* and *Hassalo.*[41]

Four of the vessels were renamed in 1869: the *Kewaydin* became the *Pennsylvania;* the *Minnetonka, California; Ontario, New York;* and *Piscataqua, Delaware.*

In September 1864, 12½ feet was added to their length, to accommodate increased armament. The secretary of the navy's report of 1864 noted that two of the vessels would be "covered with a thin iron armor to resist shells, but not of sufficient weight to interfere with the nautical qualities of the vessels." The plating was to protect the gun spaces only and was probably intended for the *Hassalo* and *Wautauga,* which were never built.[42]

Hull lines are available for only two of these sloops. Other plans, however, indicate that the *Java, Antietam,* and *Guerriere* were 312 feet 6 inches long by 46 feet. No plans of the *Kewaydin* are available, but since she was built at Boston with the *Guerriere,* the latter's plan may have been used. The

The Congress, Contoocook *Class, off Spezia. (Courtesy Peabody Museum)*

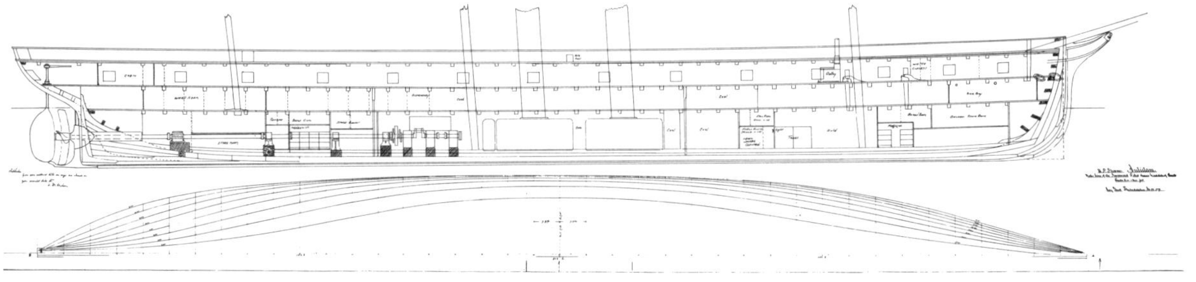

Inboard Profile of the Guerriere. *Some details have been omitted, such as diagonal hull bracing. Below is a half breadth of* Antietam *to the eighteen-foot waterline, showing the sharp entrance lines of these cruisers. Very few plans of the lines of these ships exist. (Tracing from NARS 108-8-7F, 79-2-4, National Archives)*

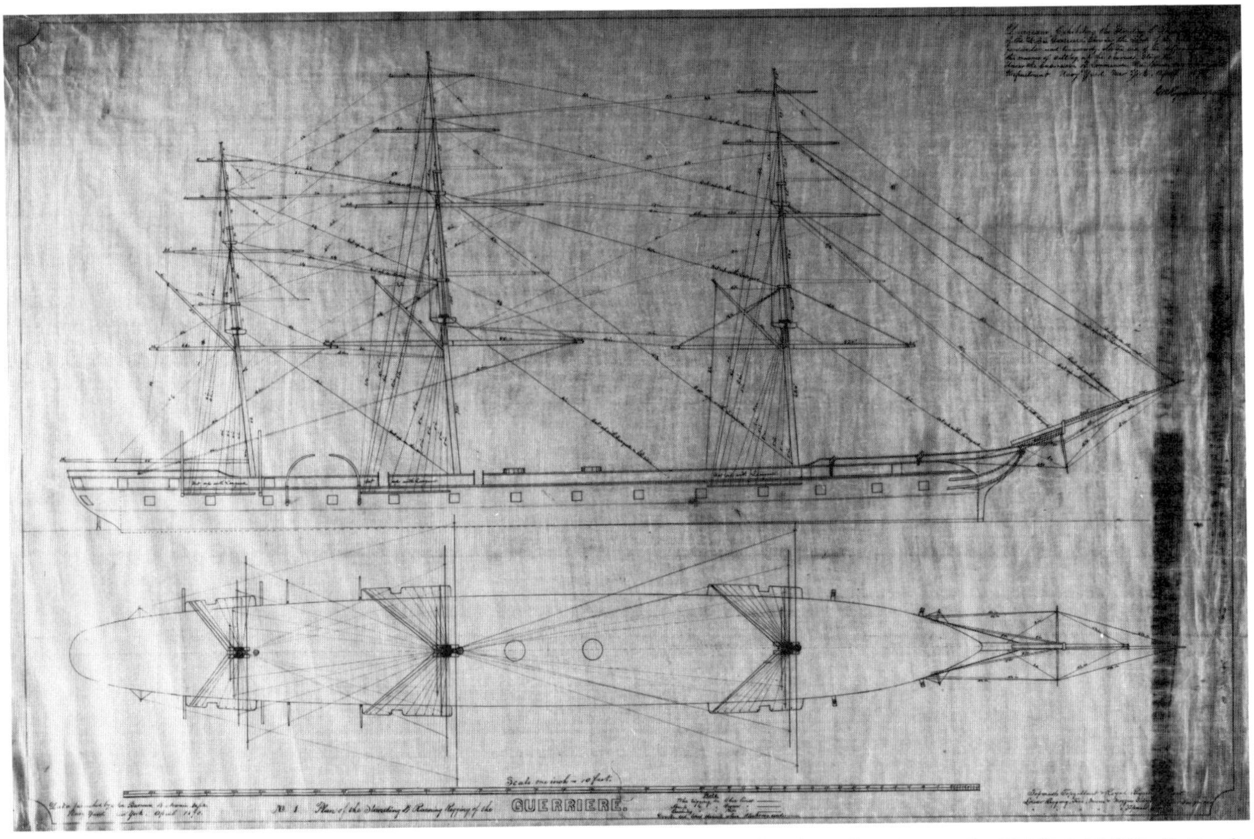

Sail Plan of the Guerriere, *1870. Note the significant increase in her masting compared to the earlier photograph. (NARS 5-12-20L, National Archives)*

Ontario was 315 feet by 47 feet (both of these breadth dimensions are to the outside of the planking). Bennett lists the *Minnetonka* as 316 feet 6 inches but also lists *Ontario* incorrectly as 312 feet 6 inches. Bennett also indicates that all the vessels were of identical displacements, when at least the *Ontario* was of greater tonnage (over 4,000). The *Minnetonka* and *Piscataqua* were built at Kittery, and the latter was 312 feet 6 inches according to her offsets.[43]

As an aside, some plans in the National Archives are for the model called the *Antietam,* originally built as a training aid for the Naval Academy. The model is currently part of the Smithsonian Institution's re-creation of the 1876 Centennial Exposition. The 1½-inch scale, 39-foot (between perpendiculars) reproduction shows her as a fully armed warship, although as completed the original vessel was only a storeship.[44]

The hull forms of the *Ontario* and *Antietam* differ from each other in the fineness of their forward underwater lines (the *Ontario* was a bit fuller), and had slightly more deadrise amidships. Only the *Ontario* was built of live oak, with the others being constructed of white oak or a combination of the latter and locust, hackmatack and red cedar.[45]

They were powered by Isherwood-designed engines of the same dimensions as those of the *Contoocook*-class sloops, with both superheating and main boilers. The *Minnetonka* may have been unique in having horizontal fire-tube boilers rather than the standard water-tube variety, though both types were designed to produce the same amount of steam.[46] The ships had twin funnels, with the aft pipe only fifteen feet from the mainmast. This proximity and height prevented the use of the main course.[47] This was later remedied with telescoping pipes.[48]

These sloops were ship-rigged, and some may have carried canvas only as high as topgallants. Later plans, however, indicate royals were used. The *California* reportedly carried 23,820 square feet of canvas in her main sails alone.[49] All were to have had straight stems without cutwater knees; instead, three distinctive knee designs were actually used. The *Delaware*'s knee had a high and shallow curve, ending above the line of the ports; the *Guerriere* and *Java,* a rather flat curve ending at the lower port line. The *California,* at the behest of Admiral Porter himself, had a fully curved knee ending below the port line, reminiscent of the sailing seventy-four-gun ships. Also, the *California*'s bowsprit was stepped on the gundeck rather than the spar deck.[50] The gundeck battery consisted of sixteen or eighteen 9-inch Dahlgrens and two 100-pounder rifles in broadside. On the spar deck each carried one 60-pounder rifle.[51]

The Goldsborough board had little complimentary to say about the *California,* the one member of the class they inspected. They frowned upon her lack of depth and "extravagant sharpness of ends." They found her length-to-breadth ratio, however, not as objectionable as that of either the *Wampanoag* or *Contoocook* classes. The board concluded that the *California* was "but a poor specimen of an efficient vessel of war," implying similar criticism of the entire class.[52] Specifically, however, performance reports reflect that their sailing qualities easily outshone their steaming capabilities. An early report on the *Delaware* credited the vessel with 12 knots under steam, courses, and topgallants.[53] The *Guerriere* attained 13 knots under similar circumstances in 1869. Earlier, without her mainsail and when rigged only to topgallants, she

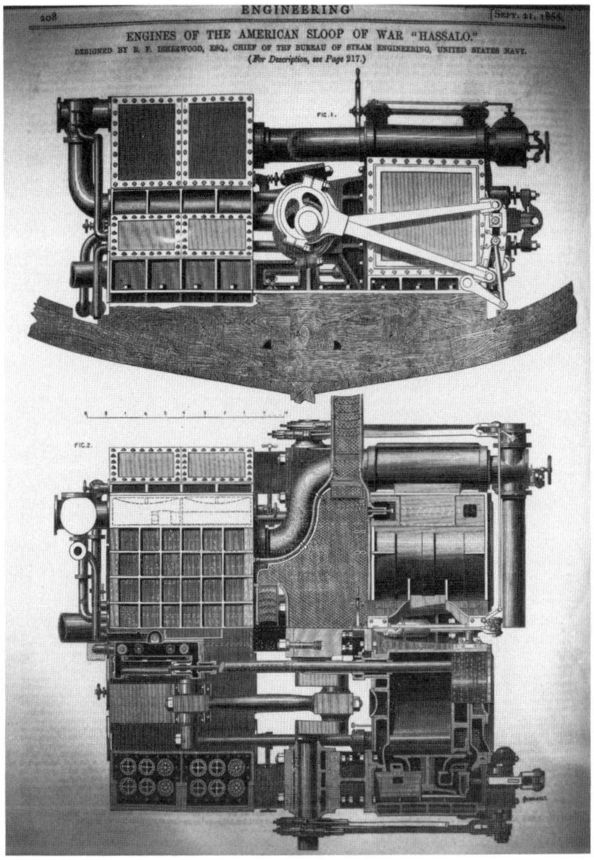

Isherwood's Back-Acting Engines Designed for the Hassalo. *These were to be 60-inch diameter by 36-inch stroke cylinders—identical to the remainder of the* Contoocook *and* Guerriere-*class powerplants. These were the largest Isherwood back-acting engines except those for the frigate* Franklin, *which measured 68 inches by 42 inches. At the top is a view of the aft end, showing the propeller shaft in the center, with eccentrics and rods leading to the valve mechanism; cylinders are on the right with steam pipes above leading from boilers to cylinders, then to condensers on the left. The lower illustration is a top view with cutaway of cylinder showing double piston rods working a crosshead on the opposite side of the crankshaft. From the crosshead to the crankshaft is the connecting rod. Note engineer's platform in the center between the cylinders and the condenser. The entire installation was approximately 25 feet wide, 20 feet long, and 10 feet high. From* Engineering *magazine, 21 September 1866. (Naval Historical Center)*

The Guerriere *as the Flagship of the Brazil Squadron, before 1870, with Her Original Masts and Sparring. (U.S. Army Military History Institute)*

averaged 10 knots and required twelve and one-half minutes to tack. Under steam alone she made 11 knots—with a foul bottom.[54]

The *California* made 11 knots on her trials without sails and 13 under steam and sail (under topgallants, jib and foresail, in force 4 and 5 winds. Her dragging prop slowed her from 7 to 4½ knots, but with it revolving, the reduction was limited to 1 knot.[55]

When assigned to the Pacific, the vessel's passage from New York to San Francisco gained considerable notice: 139 days, including a nine-day stop at Callao. This was outstanding for any vessel (the record of 89 days was set by the *Flying Cloud*) and certainly the best time for a naval ship. Her best day's run was 276 knots—averaging 11.5 knots under sail alone.[56] The *Delaware* occasionally reached 13 knots under light steam. In the postwar years full steam was rarely used, particularly after 1869. Consequently, the maximum speeds of these ships may have never been reached.[57]

Again, white oak was the greatest nemesis of these vessels. The *Delaware,* after one cruise to the Far East, was found "very rotten" and was in ordinary from 1871 until sinking at her dock in 1876. The *California* was sold in 1875, after years in ordinary, having been found "not worth the cost of repairs." The *Guerriere* was flag vessel in the South Atlantic, then transported the body of Admiral Farragut in 1870, though she grounded off Nantucket in the process. She again grounded in the Mediterranean in 1872, damaging her extensively. She was brought home and sold. The *Antietam* was launched as a storeship and sold in 1888, but the *Illinois, Java, Kewaydin* (*Pennsylvania*), and *New York* were never launched.[58]

The *New York* remained on the stocks in Brooklyn for many years with minimal deterioration of her live-oak frame. The secretary of the navy's report of 1882 urged she be finished and provided with new engines and boilers, which were on hand. Many advanced ideas were proposed for the vessel, including 6-inch breechloaders in broadside as well as in sponsons and embrasures for forward fire. A request of $500,000 was made to complete the ship. As late as 1885, plans were still being made for her, but she was finally sold in 1888—after more than twenty-five years on the stocks.[59]

The Short-lived California *(Formerly* Minnetonka*). One of the fastest steam naval ships under sail, she made the New York–to–San Francisco run in 130 days. (National Archives)*

CHAPTER 10

Commerce Destroyers, 1864–1869

Donald McKay, in a letter incorporated into Secretary Welles's annual report of 1864, predicted that the *Wampanoag*-class cruisers would be "the fastest and most formidable ocean cruisers ever built by any power."[1] He was more accurate than critics of the navy would admit, and the conflict engendered by these "supercruisers," two of which proved to be the swiftest wooden steamships ever built, rattled the foundations of the navy and reflected basic policy changes that would affect the service until the 1880s.

The seven vessels were designed to maintain 16 knots and "sweep the oceans and chase and hunt down the vessels of the enemy," according to the annual report of 1864, and their high speed was to be had by "some sacrifice of armament." Even this early the goals of the department with these vessels, as well as the two other classes of ocean cruisers, totaling twenty-seven projected ships, looked beyond the defeat of the Confederacy and encompassed "any enemy." The vessels were to augment the "position and influence" of the navy "among the commercial and maritime powers of the world."[2]

For convenience, these seven vessels have been denominated the *Wampanoag* class. The ships, however, were a diverse group, with three distinct hull designs and four engine types. Five hulls were built at navy yards, with a hull design by B. F. Delano: these were the *Wampanoag, Madawasca, Ammonoosuc, Neshaminy,* and *Pompanoosuc.* Four of these had engines designed by B. F. Isherwood, with the fifth vessel—the *Madawasca*—having a powerplant designed by John Ericsson. Two ships, the *Idaho* and *Chattanooga,* were entirely the products of civilian contractors. The *Chattanooga* was built by William Cramp in Philadelphia, with engines by the Merrick firm. The *Idaho*'s hull was by Paul S. Forbes at New York, with a design by Henry Steers, the brother of George Steers, the designer of the *Niagara.* Her engines were designed by the unabashed E. N. Dickerson.

The awarding of civilian contracts for some of these vessels was a move intended by the department to defuse continued criticism of Isherwood's engine designs. The competition provided by the *Idaho, Chattanooga,* and the engines of the *Madawasca* would provide a basis of comparison with vessels designed and built by the navy.

The "Isherwood Cruisers"

The origin of the hull lines of the navy-designed vessels is the subject of some contention. Isherwood, in an article written in 1900, states that he designed "the engineering department, including machinery, and coal bunkers . . . and arranged for all the other objects forming the completed vessel, the form of the hull was approximately modelled around the whole so as to just include it." These ideas were presented by Isherwood to B. F. Delano at New York Navy Yard but were rejected as too extreme. Isherwood persisted and prevailed, according to his recollections, and the result was a ship designed "engineering fashion, not naval construction fashion. . . . probably the first time that a steamship was ever so produced."[3] Therefore, if the engineer was accurate, the hull lines of these ships, particularly the two constructed at New York under Delano's supervision, should show a significant departure from earlier naval designs.

In studying these hull lines and comparing them to those of the *Guerriere* and the other classes of 1863 and 1864, however, one is not struck by any radical divergence among them. The hulls of these vessels were logical extensions of those of the *Contoocook* and *Guerriere* classes. They were extreme in

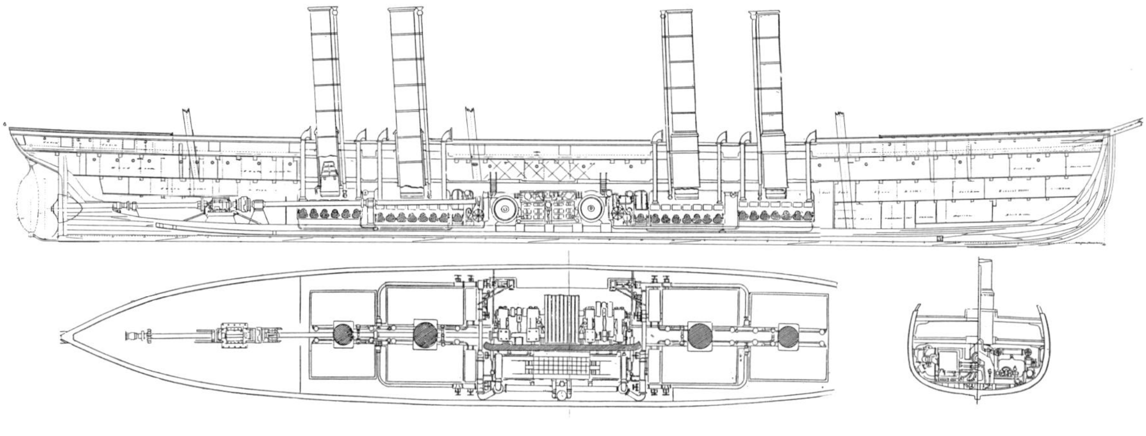

Inboard Profile and Machinery of the Wampanoag. *The plan of engines has been superimposed on the plan of 1875 at the same scale to show the amount of space devoted to Isherwood's geared engines and twelve boilers. Note that coal was also carried on the berth deck. The overhead view shows the size of the geared drum and location of fire rooms. Small boilers at each end of the engine spaces are the superheating units. The hull lines of the* Wampanoag *were identical to those of the* Madawasca *(later* Tennessee*), seen in chapter 11. (Engine plan from Bennett,* Steam Navy of the United States, *1896; 1875 plan from NARS 107-10-12B, National Archives; overhead view from Bennett.)*

one respect: the adding of thirty-five feet to the original length of the *Guerriere* design was not accompanied by an increase in beam and resulted in the incredible length-to-beam ratio of 7.4 to 1. Before 1863, the extremes had been set by the *Ticonderoga,* which exhibited a ratio of 6.23 to 1, and the *Niagara,* at 5.78 to 1.

As has been seen, the growth of the *Nipsic* into the *Nantasket* class, in the pursuit of speedier lines, involved retaining nearly the same midship section while adding thirty-five feet to the length of the newer class. This resulted in a length-to-breadth ratio of about 7 to 1. This process was further exaggerated for the *Wampanoag* sloops, where the cross-section design of the *Guerriere*-class cruisers was similar and 35 feet (again) was added, enabling considerably finer lines fore and aft. Isherwood's recollection of Delano's objections to his design may well have been faulty. In fact, the naval constructor's complaints were probably not about the "engineering" methods supposedly used by Isherwood but the hull's narrowness and the massive spaces necessary to accommodate Isherwood's prodigious machinery. In that sense, the hulls were indeed "modelled around the whole, so as to just include it."

Specifics of these hulls reinforce their resemblance to the smaller vessels of that era. Lines of the *Ammonoosuc* and the identical *Neshaminy* exist, as well as those of the *Madawasca,* dated 1875 (after her name change to *Tennessee*). The mold loft dimensions of the *Madawasca* were identical to those of the *Wampanoag*. No plans of the *Pompanoosuc* have been found.[4]

All were 335 feet long and ranged from 44 to 48 feet wide with the broadest measurement applying to the *Pompanoosuc* and the narrowest to the *Madawasca* and *Wampanoag*. The *Ammonoosuc* measured 44 feet 6 inches. The mean draft of the vessels was 19 feet. Therefore, only the *Pompanoosuc* showed an increase in breadth over the *Guerriere* class, and all the vessels were a foot deeper than the spar-decked cruisers.

The most striking similarity among all the vessels of the *Wampanoag* and *Guerriere* classes is in the midships cross sections. The amount of deadrise is 7½ or 8 degrees in every case, the bilges have the same curvature, and the amount of tumble home is indistinguishable among them. The vessels' entrance lines in every case are approximately 32 degrees at the load line, but the *Madawasca* and *Wampanoag* exhibit hollowness above the 20-foot line, whereas the *Guerriere*'s entrance lines become straight at the 18-foot level. All have extremely fine runs. It is noteworthy that the *Wampanoag* and *Madawasca* are hollower in entrance lines than the others of their class. Also, the *Contoocook*-class design is as sharp as the other two classes.

The most convincing proof of the unbroken lineage of the *Wampanoag*'s hull design, however, is the most graphic. Simply compare the lines of the *Kansas* (excepting the *Maumee* and *Pequot*), the *Swatara,* the *Contoocook,* and *Guerriere* classes with those of the *Wampanoag*. (The *Algoma*-class hull lines can also be included in this comparison in most respects, but the unusual curvature of bilges was unique to that class.)

There is little discernible in the hull lines to justify any claim to a significant change in form in the *Wampanoag* class. There is much to indicate, however, that speed was of the essence in these vessels, more so than in any earlier U.S. naval warships.

The engines Isherwood designed for these fast vessels were unorthodox and massive. Each 100-inch piston was fitted with two piston rods actuating a connecting rod. The latter, rather than operating the screw shaft, rotated nine geared wheels 10 feet in diameter, securely bolted together forming a toothed drum over 9 feet long. This drove pinion gears 5 feet in diameter mounted on the propeller shaft. The resultant ratio was one turn of the large gear to 2.05 revolutions of the propeller. The pinion teeth were of iron, but those of the main gear were of lignum vitae, an exceedingly dense South American wood that was also used for propeller shaft bearings. The engine was given a surface condenser, located between the cylinders, and a steam reversing gear. The engine alone occupied 26 feet athwartships and 46 feet fore and aft in the hull.[5]

Geared engines were not favored in this era because of the lack of suitably tough material for the teeth. In these vessels, however, Isherwood felt the need to reduce engine vibration and therefore eliminate as much reciprocating motion as possible. Back-acting cylinders would place undue athwartships strains on an already narrow wooden hull.[6] The obvious disadvantages of the gearing were in its weight and space requirements (as well as the tendency for primitive gearing to create a considerable grinding din).

There were three earlier geared-engined vessels in the U.S. Navy: the engines of the *Dacotah,* those of the *Pawnee,* and the second powerplant of the *San Jacinto.* The former two each used single large gears. It is obvious, however, that the *Wampanoag*-class engines were enlarged versions of the *San Jacinto*'s design (built by the Merrick firm of Philadelphia), modified for a different hull shape and using an alternate type of valve gear. The similarities are impressive: both had a stroke of 48 inches and used wooden-toothed gears of approximately 10 feet in diameter bolted to form a drum. The Merrick machinery also used iron-toothed pinions on the propeller shaft, yielding a gear ratio of more than 2 to 1, and the general arrangement of condensers is similar. The 70-inch cylinder diameter of the older machinery was enlarged, and the doubled piston rods of the Isherwood engines were a consequence of this 40 percent increase in the diameter of the piston, and 100 percent increment in area.[7]

An unprecedented number of boilers was used for these engines: eight Martin water-tube main boilers and four superheating boilers. The total grate surface was 1,128 square feet, and the aggregate heating surface was 28,000 square feet. This

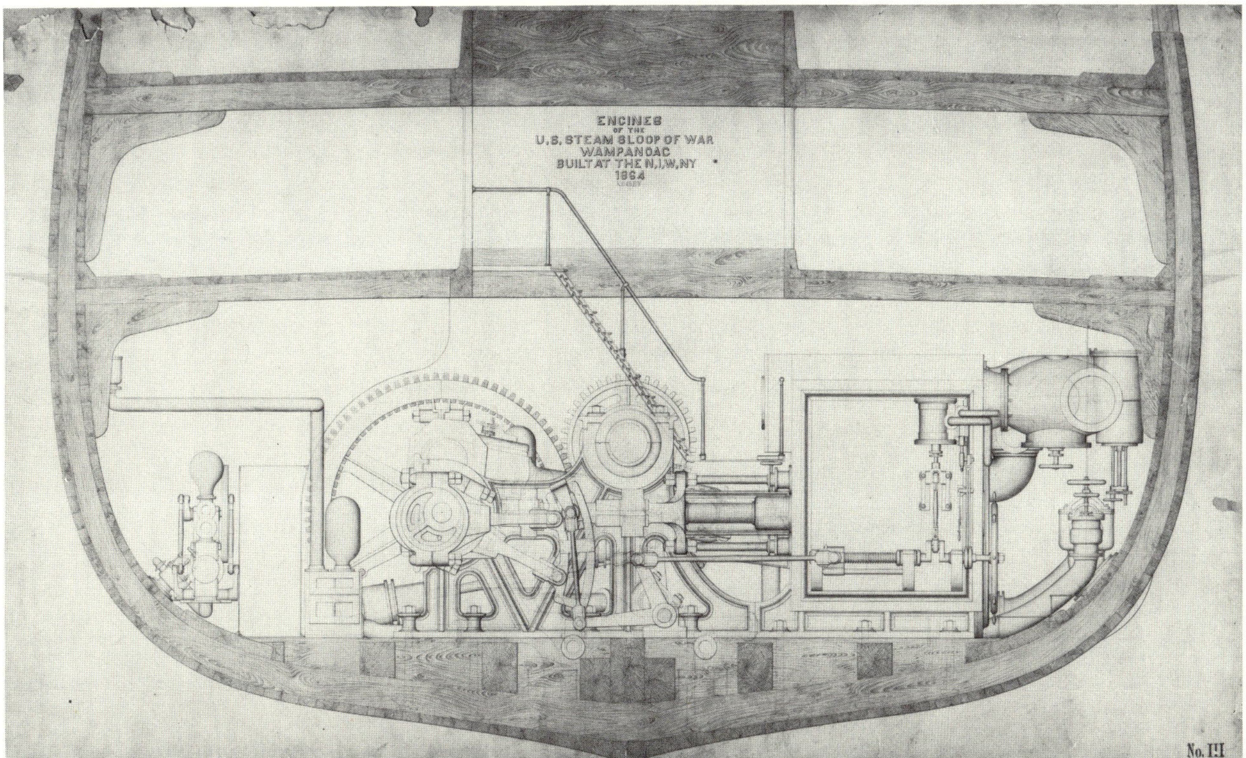

Cross Section showing Engines of the Wampanoag, *Looking Forward. Cylinders (100 inches in diameter) are on the right. Large gears to the left operated center pinions on the propeller shaft. The condenser was between the cylinders. (NARS BSE Plan, National Archives)*

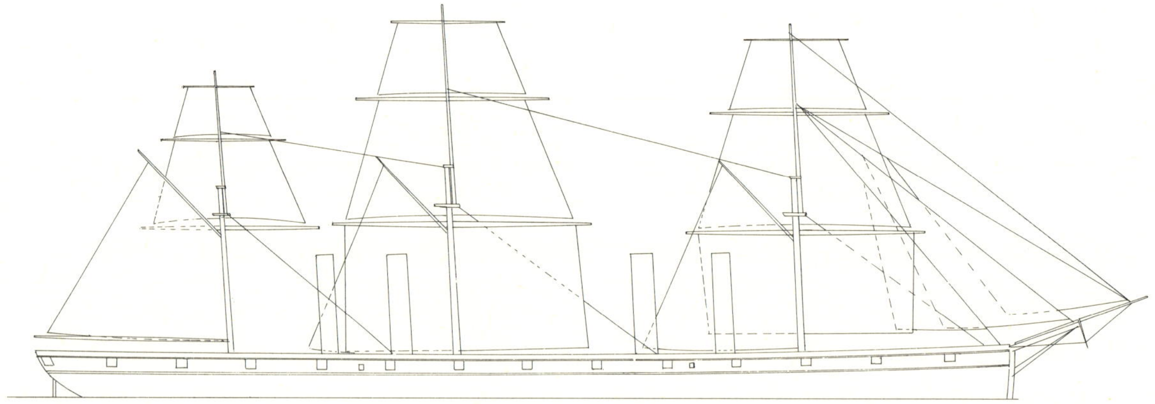

Sail Plan of the Fast Cruiser Neshaminy, *December 1867, with Bowsprit and Three Head Sails. Indications are that* Wampanoag *had a similar arrangement on her record-breaking speed trial. (Traced from NARS 79-4-1B, National Archives)*

grate surface was more than twice that of the *Guerriere*, and the *Merrimack*-class frigates had about 300 square feet. The heating surface of the latter vessels was approximately 40 percent that of the *Wampanoag*-class boilers. The boilers were arranged in pairs, with fire rooms running fore and aft between each pair and fifty-eight furnaces. Two superheating boilers were arranged with the forward four main boilers and two with the aft boilers. The engines were between each set of main boilers. The total length of engines and boilers was over 166 feet (the length of a ninety-day gunboat), and the weight of the powerplant, including water in the boilers, was 1,267.5 tons. This included the four nontelescoping funnels, one to each pair of main boilers. All the machinery was two feet below the waterline at the designed mean draft.[8]

A bronze four-bladed screw 18-feet in diameter was provided for each vessel. There is disagreement on the pitch of these screws. An original plan shows an expanding pitch, from 23 feet 6 inches to 26 feet 6 inches. Isherwood, in 1900, however, stated that the plan was not followed correctly by the workers making the casting, and the resulting propeller had a 28-foot constant pitch. A later study cites Admiral George W. Baird, who had been present at the time of the trials, staunchly affirming the 28-foot pitch.[9] Whether the original plan was followed for each vessel's screw is not known.

The two ships built at New York, the *Madawasca* and *Wampanoag*, were of live oak framing. The *Neshaminy*, built at Philadelphia, however, and the *Pompanoosuc* and *Ammonoosuc*, built at Boston, were of lighter construction. The *Neshaminy* used white oak, locust, hackmatack, and red cedar in her frames; and white oak in her keel, deadwood, and stem. These three also made liberal use of treenails rather than through-bolts.[10]

The sloops were among the first in the navy fitted with balanced or "equipoise" rudders. These required no rudder posts but were mounted on a prolongation of the keel and braced by a composition casting. Above the counter timbers a massive collar supported the structure.[11]

As originally designed, the ships were to have a light bark rig and no bowsprit. Isherwood felt their length precluded any need of a bowsprit and further argued that this protrusion would hinder use of the vessels' knifelike prow as a ram. As later modified with a bowsprit and head sails, they would carry 20,000 square feet of sails. The rigging was wire rope. The *Wampanoag* was armed with ten 9-inch smoothbores and three 60-pounder Parrott rifles, with one of the latter on the topgallant forecastle.[12]

The appearance of these sloops was unique, with their unbroken sheer and raked funnels, a visual analog of their speed and power. Their profile had never before been approximated in this or any other navy, and they cannot fail to bring to mind the four-pipe, flush-deck destroyers of this century, though the destroyers were smaller than these wooden cruisers.

Madawasca

Except for their engines, the *Madawasca* and *Wampanoag* were identical vessels. Though both ships employed cylinders of 100-inch diameter and 48-inch stroke, Ericsson's vibrating lever arrangement acted directly through rocking shafts onto the propeller shaft. They were identical in dimensions to the engines of the monitor *Dictator*, completed in 1864 and displacing over 4,400 tons.[13]

The vibrating-lever engine was certainly an unusual arrangement, particularly in the awkward appearing rock-shaft connecting rod. The design

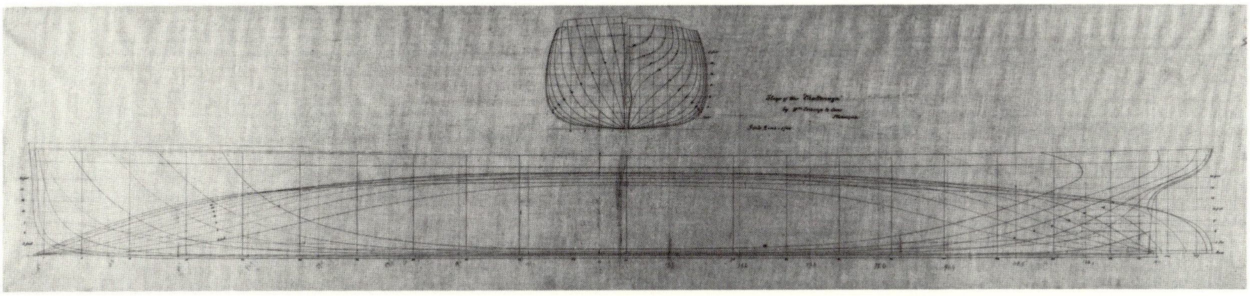

Lines of the Chattanooga. *Note the hollowness of her entrance lines. (NARS 108-10-5N, National Archives)*

Launch of the Chattanooga *at Cramp's Shipyard, Philadelphia, 13 August 1864. She was powered by Merrick back-acting engines. (Courtesy Peabody Museum)*

was indeed unique to John Ericsson and not even approximated by other marine engineers. Ericsson, however, had used variations of these levers since the mid-1840s. Since 1862, approximately twenty-five naval vessels had been powered by vibrating lever engines, including the *Galena, Maumee,* and the original *Monitor.*

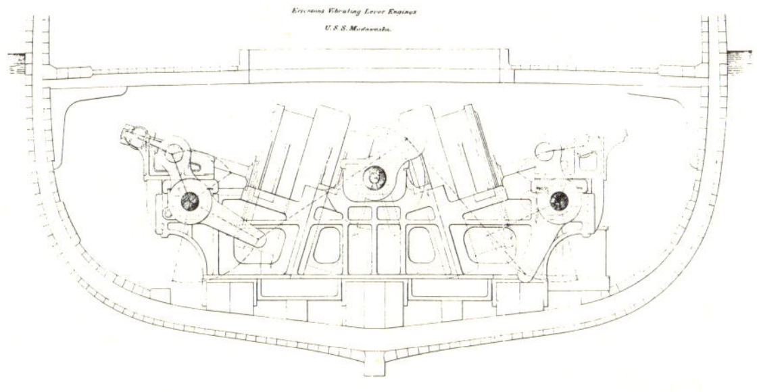

Ericsson's Vibrating Lever ("Grasshopper") Engines of the Madawasca. *Piston rods work outward in this* V *configuration. (From Bennett,* Steam Navy of the United States, *1896)*

Therefore, unlike Isherwood's geared machinery, Ericsson's engine for the *Madawasca* was a known quantity, with the only unanswered question the compatibility of the engine with the hull of the *Madawasca* and with the boilers Isherwood had ordered for the vessel. The *Dictator,* which was credited with 11 knots, had six Martin boilers, compared to the eight main boilers of the *Madawasca.*

Chattanooga

The *Chattanooga*'s hull cross section showed little deadrise and resembled that of the *Wampanoag.* Her entrance lines were also remarkable in their hollowness, with at least 12 inches of concavity at the 18-foot waterline and an angle of 34 degrees. These lines show less fineness than those of the *Wampanoag,* resulting from the *Chattanooga*'s broader beam and shorter length. The Cramp-built ship was, despite her 315-foot length, the shallowest and lightest of these cruisers, displacing 3,043 tons and drawing about 15 feet at the time of her trials, with an immersed midship section measuring 535 square feet. The next largest immersed section was that of the *Idaho,* with 606 square feet.[14]

Sail Plan of the Chattanooga *before She Was Fitted with a Bowsprit. (NARS 79-2-48, National Archives)*

The engines of the ship were, like those of the *Madawasca,* of a standard design: back-acting with 84-inch cylinders and a 42-inch stroke. The *Army and Navy Journal* described them as identical (except for surface condensers) to those built for the *General Admiral,* a 5,600-ton frigate constructed for the Russian navy by William Webb of New York—"one of the best pairs of screw engines in existence." Indeed, the Russian vessel had made a run from New York to Cherbourg in eleven days under steam alone, a record for a warship.[15] The *Chattanooga* was given eight boilers and a superheating apparatus. The total grate surface was 980 square feet, 148 square feet less than that of the *Wampanoag.*[16]

The ship was originally intended to have a bark rig without bowsprit or fore and main trysails. In 1866, bowsprit, jibboom, and trysails were ordered for the vessel because she was planned for foreign service. She was fitted with a topgallant forecastle and a poop cabin.[17]

Idaho

The last vessel of the *Wampanoag* class marked the final segment in the long-standing feud between Isherwood and E. N. Dickerson. The *Idaho,* however, seems to have been anticlimactic since the lawyer-cum-engineer had lost much of his support after the *Winooski-Algonquin* confrontation.

Though the competition among these commerce destroyers centered on their machinery, an equally outstanding feature of the *Idaho* was her hull. She was 298 feet by 44 feet 6 inches, with a draft of 17 feet and displacement of 3,240 tons. Unfortunately, as is the case with many contract-built vessels, there is a paucity of plans for this ship. The National Archives's sheer and half-breadth drawing is essentially useless and shows only the planksheer, port, and deck lines. We have only comments by R. B. Forbes and the *Army and Navy Journal* to describe what must have been an exceedingly fast design. The journal noted, her "model is narrow, running out both forward and aft very sharp, and not unlike that of the famous *Niagara.*" Forbes called her a "perfect clipper model" and expected great speed of her, "if not spoiled by want of good machinery or overlading with guns."[18]

The construction of the vessel was unique. Steers used a variety of iron bracing not seen before. This was, according to Forbes, "a system of trussing made of massive rods fastened to the keelsons, and setting up by buckles [turnbuckles] to the beams. These rods cross each other at right angles, and give great support to the ship." A partial inboard plan shows diagonals some 26 feet long, running upward from the keelsons to alternate upper-deck beams, and crossing midway between the berth and orlop decks. It is not clear whether these rods crossed athwartships, from the sister keelsons to the deck beams, or how they were arranged around the engines and boilers.[19] As will be seen, they proved eminently successful in strengthening this hull. The vessel had ten feet of deadwood in the bow—an asset in ramming, according to the *Army and Navy Journal*—and four watertight bulkheads. Her original rig was as a bark without a bowsprit.[20]

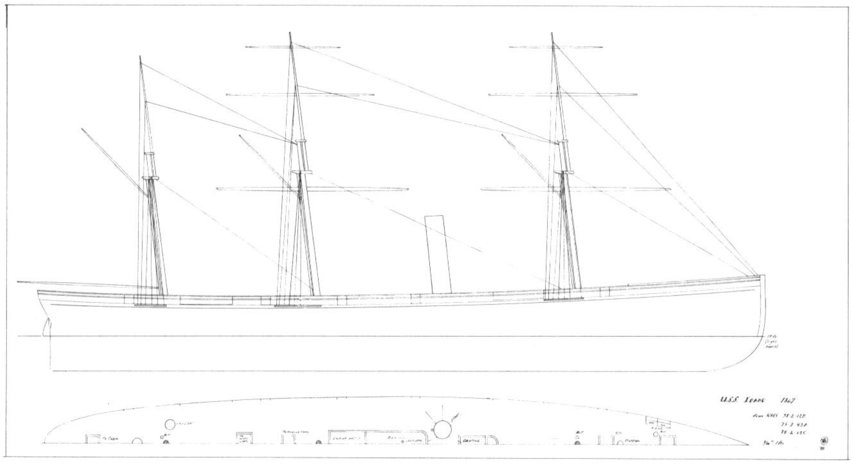

The Idaho, *1867. E. N. Dickerson's entry into the competition, drawn by author from sail and other original plans. The curvature of forefoot is estimated. When she was later converted to sail, her masts were moved forward and she was given three headsails and royals. In this configuration she was one of the fastest sailing vessels of the time. (From NARS 38-2-12B, 79-3-43A, and 38-2-12C, National Archives)*

Historic View of New York Navy Yard in Late 1866. Three of the "super cruisers" are in the image. On the right is the Idaho, *subsequent to her trial failure (note side-by-side funnels); the* Wampanoag *is fitting out at left. The four funnels of the* Madawasca *can be discerned in the background. The* Susquehanna *is just astern of her. (Naval Historical Center)*

The Dickerson machinery, already unorthodox in theory, in this case was pressed further from orthodoxy in driving twin screws. Four cylinders, of 36-inch diameter and 8-foot stroke, composed these engines, with two cylinders acting directly on each shaft. The boilers were designed by Dickerson and had a total of 396 square feet of grate surface, much less than half that of the *Chattanooga* or the Isherwood cruisers.[21] Her two funnels were placed side by side, the first such arrangement since the *Fulton* in 1837. Little information is available on the engines of this ship or her hull.

THE SEA TRIALS

In studying the sea trials and relative merits of the commerce destroyers, one is immediately overwhelmed by the controversy they engendered. The fracas was of such scope and intensity that writing a relatively unbiased account is an onerous task. First, the cost of the ships and the timing of their completion immediately invited unfavorable comments. The government eventually paid $550,000 for the *Idaho* and $950,000 for the *Chattanooga,* and the navy-built ships cost over $1.2 million each (with the exception of the *Pompanoosuc,* which was not completed). Million-dollar warships were rarities in this era. The only prewar vessel to cross this line was the *Niagara,* at $1.05 million, and the average *Kearsarge*-class ship cost around $300,000.[22] Had wartime necessity called for such expenditures, less public attention might have arisen, but the first of the sloops ready for trials was the *Idaho,* in May 1866, in the midst of postwar retrenchment.

The involvement of eminent public figures brought even more public interest. Ericsson was the mechanical genius of *Monitor* fame; Dickerson, through years of fulminations against the department and Isherwood, had become notorious in the public press; Merrick and Cramp were among the most reputable shipbuilders of the era. The navy's chief engineer, B. F. Isherwood, however, who designed the majority of the navy's engines used in the war, was the undisputed center of attention. The presence of other notables was secondary; Isherwood and what he stood for were the issues at hand.

The ostensible basis for the conflict was the performance of these vessels, and, more particularly, their machinery. The *Wampanoag* and her sisters were seen as the apotheosis of Isherwood's engineering concepts. His detractors labeled his engines excessively heavy, inefficient, uneconomical, underpowered, and based on unsound engineering principles. The failure of these new vessels and his monstrous engines, or the signal success of any of the competing engines, would certainly end Isherwood's dominance in the Bureau of Steam Engineering.

One of the main difficulties in determining the validity of the verbiage used against Isherwood was that another, less public conflict was at work. The issue was an outcropping of the old line–versus–staff imbroglio, which had ominous implications for the future of steam power in the navy. Isherwood and his fellow steam engineers were pressing for increased rank in relation to the officers on the quarterdeck. Allowing such a realignment in rank would have been tantamount to admitting that these "mechanics" were as essential to naval warfare as the ships' commanders.[23]

Unfortunately for Isherwood, his opposition was singularly well organized and was led by the powerful and outspoken "second Admiral," David Dixon Porter. Porter and his friends, including dissatisfied engineers and contractors, orchestrated unrelenting attacks in the public press, particularly in the *Army and Navy Journal,* which became the semiofficial organ for the anti-Isherwood group. Furthermore, the blunt and sometimes tactless Isherwood did not always contribute to his own best interests. In the midst of this contest, he presumed to the rank of rear admiral, an eminence only recently created, and unnecessarily reopened an old conflict with Ericsson over the ventilation system of the *Monitor.* Finally, Isherwood was a Democrat in a political atmosphere that equated that party with disloyalty.[24]

IDAHO

By 15 May 1866, the day the *Idaho* began her sea trails, E. N. Dickerson's reputation was ebbing; he had had two unqualified failures, the *Pensacola* and *Algonquin,* and walked away from the second without attempting to publicly rationalize or explain the defeat. Even the *Army and Navy Journal* disdained to take up his cause, referring to him as a "prestidigitateur." Indeed, it was patently obvious that political influence, not mechanical genius, sustained his efforts. Secretary Welles seems to have been echoing a common sentiment in a letter of January 1866: "His vessel is likely to prove a failure."[25]

Definitive proof of this was delayed by episodes of the engines' unreliability. Mechanical difficulties prevented her from achieving any consecutive twenty-four-hour run until she had been five days at sea. Then, rather than meeting or exceeding the contract speed of 15 knots, the *Idaho* averaged an unimpressive 8.27 knots over smooth water off New Jersey. She used the highest pressure steam of all the cruisers, at 37.9 pounds; expanded steam an incredible 7.7 times, compared to 1.5 for the *Wampanoaq;* and consumed an uneconomical 7.6 pounds of coal per horsepower. For the final time, Dickerson's claims were shown to be palpably false and far short of reality.[26]

The navy refused to accept the ship, although Dickerson's influential friend Paul S. Forbes wangled a congressional resolution forcing the acceptance of the vessel. A board subsequently surveyed her and administered the ultimate insult to her machinery: "It . . . occupies much of the space in the vessel which should have been appropriated for other purposes." They recommended she be auctioned off.[27]

The subsequent career of the ship is more intriguing than her beginnings. The navy had her machinery removed and rig altered to that of a fully rigged ship carrying canvas to royals and a bowsprit. She was then sent as a store ship to Nagasaki.[28] On the passage to the Far East she proved the excellence of Steers's lines, often running three hundred miles per day, and on one occasion was said to have exceeded 18 knots for two hours running. With heavier sparring, it was claimed, she could attain 20 knots.[29] In any case, she was certainly the possessor of all the attributes of the true clipper ship, not the least being a pristine heritage dating from George Steers's *America.*

Opportunities to test her speed were to be few, however. On a passage from Yokohama in 1869, she rode out a typhoon of titanic proportions (barometric readings of 27.62), in which she was dismasted and at times taking water fore, aft, and amidships at the same moment.[30] It was a tribute to Steers's construction techniques that she brought her crew home, though she was battered and jury-rigged. Her hulk was sold in 1874 in Yokohama.

CHATTANOOGA

The second sloop ready for trials was the *Chattanooga.* In May of 1866, this ship underwent a short trial of her engines, running twelve hours until a jammed valve ended the trip. The "general working of the engines was very good," according to the report of her engineers, but she only attained 8.4 knots against the tide.[31]

Two other abortive attempts were made until she reached an unbroken twenty-four-hour run on 17 August. In smooth water off Delaware she averaged 13.2 knots at 50 revolutions per minute and thus failed to reach the contract speed. The reason given for her shortcomings was the engine's inability to work off the steam produced without damaging the journals. As it was, during the twenty-four-hour trial, some two hundred gallons of "the best sperm oil" was consumed in lubricating the crankshaft journals, and the crank pins were continually deluged with water to prevent their overheating.[32]

The next month, the *Army and Navy Journal* charged ominously that "a strong effort [was] made to condemn the engines of the *Chattanooga*," and that the twenty-four-hour contract run was unrealistic for new engines, which required running-in at moderate revolutions to wear smoothness onto the bearing surfaces. And, on this sloop, where some journals measured 45 inches in length, the possibility of great unevenness was considerable.[33]

Despite allegations that Isherwood was determined to prevent the success of any of his civilian competitors, accommodations were made between Cramp and the navy, and the *Chattanooga* was accepted in August 1867. She was on the North Atlantic station for a short time, then, in December 1871, was holed by ice at the League Island Navy Yard. She was sold shortly thereafter.

MADAWASCA

The final competitor against the vessels with Isherwood engines was to be the most significant, because the sole difference between the *Madawasca* and the Isherwood-engined cruisers was their powerplants. While preparing his vessel for the trials, Ericsson protested the conditions imposed by the department. He objected to the use of superheaters, wished to have his own crew aboard on the trials, and insisted that a twenty-four-hour run at high speed would destroy engines not yet properly run-in. Isherwood relented on each issue Ericsson raised. In particular, he was allowed as many preliminary trials as he wished, at sea or at the dock, at any speed or boiler pressure, and with his or the navy's crews aboard.[34]

One of the early dock trials ran thirty-one hours before overheating journals curtailed it. Then, in September 1866, the sloop ran no less than 13 knots for several hours in a sea trial. Isherwood raised some doubts as to the accuracy of the speeds recorded on the run, and, in any case, Ericsson believed the vessel could better her speed.[35]

On 14 January 1867 the *Madawasca* steamed out of New York and remained at sea for seven days on her official trial. The weather, however, was unpropitious for such an undertaking. Though she logged over a thousand miles, only forty-one hours could be used for her performance report, and the longest unbroken run amounted to sixteen hours. Of the time at sea, the last fifty hours were in hurricane-force winds, and rough seas had been the norm throughout the week. Ericsson credited her with five consecutive hours at 15¼ knots, two hours at 15½ knots, and he maintained that "no attempt was made to ascertain the speed with full throttle, as Isherwood's boilers did not admit of such a test." The average speed for the aggregate forty-one hours was 12.73 knots, using 5.17 pounds of coal per horsepower produced.[36]

Her commander complimented her machinery as "near perfect." Her seakeeping, however, left much to be desired. He had never seen a ship "take seas into her so viciously," and she had displayed a penchant for riding into the waves, rather than over them.[37]

Despite her failure to meet the department's requirements by two knots, the *Madawasca* was accepted by the navy, though she was immediately laid up. In the interim, until the *Wampanoag*'s steam trial, she was the fastest steamship afloat. She was later substantially modified, which will be described in the next chapter.

WAMPANOAG

The *Wampanoag* was not ready for her trials until February 1868. She had been launched more than three years before, on 15 December 1864, and had gone into commission 17 September 1867. Though mechanical setbacks encountered in erecting the huge engines had accounted for the delays, Isherwood's adversaries attributed them to a reluctance to meet any of the competing vessels under the same conditions. It was also implied that the engines were failures and the dilatory progress was simply a ploy to stave off the inevitable public disaster.

As early as December 1866, the *Army and Navy Journal* had taken up the cudgels in earnest with a series of articles on "Our New Navy," attacking Isherwood and his cruisers. The articles characterized the hulls as the "sharpest ever adopted for war vessels," and heaped praise on this element of the vessels' design. Then they deduced that ordinary direct-acting engines would suffice to propel such sharp hulls at 15 knots, with the powerplant taking up 40 percent less space and weight than Isherwood's geared "relics." The "cogs" only served to add 40 feet to the engines and proportionally reduced coal bunkerage and stowage space. These engines were, in their words, "a monument of mechanical incapacity . . . in the annals of steam engineering." The major portion of the articles was taken up in lengthy comparisons of contemporary British armored warships with the expected performance of the *Wampanoag*.[38]

These articles were not the only weapons used against Isherwood in the *Army and Navy Journal.* Attacks on the man and his "regime" were standard fare for nearly three years, to the extent that the researcher becomes certain that any stories favorable to Isherwood would have been conveniently overlooked by the editors, usually in favor of any half-truth usable against him. Anti-Isherwood articles also found their way into British journals, usually planted by semidisguised members of Porter's followers.[39]

The *Wampanoag* went to sea on 2 January 1868 for a thirteen-hour run, covering 192⅜ miles at 14.99 knots. She encountered a "considerable swell" and rolled 20 degrees each way. Her commander characterized her movements as "easy" and stated that at her greatest speed "she scarcely made a ripple on the water." The trial ended because of heating of the propeller shaft.

Her second trial was under sail on 7 February, with the prop disconnected and revolving. Under topgallants, jib, and courses—with a fresh wind abeam and smooth sea—she reached 10.5 to 11 knots. Captain Nicholson reported her steering to be easy, with her helm amidships. No sail was carried on her mizzen.

In an economy steam trial she ran twenty-five hours maintaining 11.3 knots to determine her coal consumption at a moderate, steady speed. A gale curtailed this run, and she anchored at Sandy Hook with spar damage. She had averaged 1.875 tons of coal per hour.

The long-anticipated full power trial began at 9 P.M., 11 February, and ended at 11 A.M. on the thirteenth, when her engines were stopped to "fix a washer on the after crank." In these thirty-eight hours, in increasingly rough seas and with a breeze abaft the beam, the *Wampanoag* covered 630.875 nautical miles, from Barnegat Light to Tybee Light off Savannah. This was an average of 16.6 knots each hour. An unprecedented 17.75 knots was recorded in four separate half hours, and 17.25 knots was maintained for six consecutive hours.

After the *Wampanoag* heaved to, heavy seas and approaching bad weather ended the run. It was obvious that B. F. Isherwood had created a magnificent ship. As Commander Nicholson put it in his report: "I consider the Wampanoag as a ship, to be faultless in her model, and, as a steamship, the fastest in the world."[40]

The news of this accomplishment drew both astonishment and scepticism. The nearest approach to such speeds had been by the Collins liner *Adriatic,* with a speed of 15.91 knots on a measured course—and that was two knots over what she could sustain. The typical fast transatlantic run of this era was at 14½ knots.

The *Army and Navy Journal* made much innuendo of "the wind abaft the beam" portion of the report but generally reiterated its space and weight objections. A British journal, however, stated flatly that sail must have been used to obtain such speeds.[41]

Charges that the *Wampanoag* was an aberration and fluke were made but were quickly set to rest with the trial of the *Ammonoosuc* in June 1868. In smooth water on runs of 30 and 49.8 miles, she made 16.82 and 17.11 knots respectively.[42]

A more official certification that the vessels met the navy's expectations and requirements was provided by two members of a board formed by Secretary Welles to evaluate the *Wampanoag* in a short passage at sea. Melancton Smith and Thornton A. Jenkins reported that she had fulfilled the requirements: "a vessel of the greatest obtainable speed, with sufficient armament for destroying the enemy commerce, and for self-defense in case of need has been attained." The committee's third member attacked the vessel along lines pioneered by the *Army and Navy Journal.* The passage itself had been lackluster, with heavy fog preventing another maximum speed run.[43]

These vessels were not to be allowed further tests of their speed, however. The *Wampanoag* was decommissioned less than three months after her trials and was condemned as over-engined. She was renamed *Florida* and spent the major part of her career as a store ship at New London. She was sold in 1885. The *Ammonoosuc* was even less fortunate: she was immediately placed in ordinary at Boston. Renamed the *Iowa,* she saw no service and was sold in 1883. The *Neshaminy,* later renamed the *Arizona,* then *Nevada,* was surveyed and found to have a "marked twist, or cant" in her white-oak hull.[44] Though launched in October 1865 having had engine trials, she was never completed and was sold in 1874. The *Pompanoosuc* survived to be renamed the *Connecticut,* and deteriorated at Boston, unlaunched, until 1883.

B. F. Isherwood met a fate analogous to his vessels. With the advent of the Grant administration came the appointment of Adolph Borie as titular head of the Navy Department and Admiral Porter as the true center of authority. Isherwood's removal was then inevitable and occurred on 16 March 1869.[45]

The public, of course, was entitled to a rational explanation for discarding the fastest steamships in the world, as well as for the waste of the $4 million spent on their construction. Porter obliged the taxpayers in the "Report on Board of Steam Machinery Afloat" issued 25 September 1869. Though purported to be a survey of all naval steam vessels, it was essentially a diatribe against Isherwood and his designs, most importantly, the *Wampanoag* class. Over twelve of the document's sixty-seven pages were devoted to the *Wampanoag,* and the balance of the report was divided among 104 other vessels.[46]

The space and weight problem emphasized by the *Journal* was the main defect emphasized in various contexts by this board, headed by L. M. Goldsborough. Calculations presented by the board projected a shortage of accommodations and stowage space for the 375-man crew. Other defects were found in her immense grate surface, arrangement of sails, lack of depth, insufficient armament, uneconomical engines, and potential lack of longitudinal rigidity. For good measure, the *Neshaminy,* and by implication the entire class, was characterized as an "overgrown Indian canoe . . . [built] to obtain speed at all hazards."

The Florida *(originally the* Wampanoag*) in Ordinary at New York, 1874. She was deemed overengined and decommissioned shortly after her high-speed run in early 1868, in which she achieved over 17 knots. (Naval Historical Center)*

In order to rectify these defects, the board recommended removing two of the superheating boilers and four of the main boilers, reducing the number of funnels to two and making them telescopic, replacing the four-bladed propeller with a two-bladed one, building a complete spar deck, and giving her full sail power. The expense these changes would entail, however, was considered more than the ship was worth, and they were never carried out.

The cloud that fell over the last years of the old steam navy has obscured the *Wampanoag* as well, and the controversy and recriminations have left many of these and other questions concerning the vessels still unanswered. Space does not allow a full analysis here, but the major points can be addressed.

There remain lingering doubts that these ships attained the impressive speeds claimed. In 1927 in a paper published in the *Transactions of the Society of Naval Architects and Marine Engineers,* James Swan pointed out that given the original vessel's recorded engine revolutions, it was unlikely that the *Wampanoag* exceeded 16 knots on her trial. Using the results of tests run with a model at the navy's model basin, Swan noted that the discrepancy could have been caused by considerable inaccuracy in estimating the length of the original trial run, the action of favorable winds and current, or the use of a propeller with a greater pitch than the one recorded. The article discounted the effect of the wind, because it would have been counteracted by the heavy rolling of the ship. The current could also be discounted, because it would have been unfavorable on that particular course.[47]

Upon further study, however, it appears that the possibility of inaccurate course measurement was the least likely explanation of the *Wampanoag*'s fast trials. The run was made with reference to coastal lighthouses and in familiar waters. Furthermore, both the chip and patent log were used and compared. The latter device remained in the water and recorded the speed and distance on a counter on board.[48] Moreover, though Isherwood himself was not present on board, he characteristically insisted on massive and accurate documentation.

Therefore, the possibility that the *Wampanoag*'s propeller was of a larger pitch than that shown on the original plans (28-foot constant pitch, as opposed to a 25-foot increasing pitch) may be relevant to the accuracy of the claimed speeds of the vessels.

With the question of speed comes a comparison with the British cruiser *Inconstant*, which was completed in 1868 as a counterweight to the *Wampanoag* class, and which was labeled "the fastest ship in the world." Like most of the published speeds of British warships, the 16 knots credited to this vessel were achieved on the Stokes Bay measured mile. No less an authority than Admiral G. A. Ballard, historian of the Victorian navy, stated that these trial speeds were generally 20 percent higher than the vessels maintained at sea in ordinary conditions.[49] This inflation of trial speeds was also recognized at the time: John Ericsson wrote that his *Madawasca* would have made 17 knots on the British measured mile.[50]

Doubts concerning the Isherwood cruisers' longitudinal rigidity are still raised today. History has provided a partial answer to this in the experience of the *Tennessee,* the spar-decked rebuilding of the *Madawasca.* She was not taken out of service until 1885, and there was never any question raised concerning the integrity of her live-oak hull. It is not unlikely, however, that the three white oak and mixed wood vessels would have displayed such hardiness. The canted hull of the *Neshaminy* was an augury of potential problems with these vessels.

The economy of these ships was shown in 1875 when the navy published statistics showing the amount of coal consumed hourly per indicated horsepower for various vessels. The *Wampanoag* was rated at 3.129 pounds per hour. This was significantly better than any of the competing cruisers, and only the double-ended paddle-wheel ships approached it, at 3.276 pounds per hour. The majority of the navy's ships exceeded 3.5 pounds per hour consumption.[51] Furthermore, as the economy trial proved, at 11 knots she burned some 45 tons of coal daily. With a coal capacity of 750 tons, her range at that speed was over more than four thousand miles and sixteen days. For a comparison, the *Inconstant* would have exhausted her fuel at 2,700 miles at 10 knots.[52]

The question of a vessel's economy as a cruiser, however, involved her sailing as well as steaming capabilities. No complete sailing trial was made on the *Wampanoag,* but she did have merit as a sailer. Her greatest weakness was apparently in light breezes, and her machinery could have been used quite economically to compensate for this lack.

The most repeated objection to the *Wampanoag* was her supposed lack of stowage space and crew accommodations. Dissenting engineers on the Goldsborough board made a minority report including a statement that by physical measurements there was sufficient stowage for bread and provisions for 375 men for six months. Her commander, on the contrary, reported she could only stow bread enough for sixty-five days and other provisions for forty-five days.[53] Such a wide discrepancy indicates that neither figure could be relied upon.

In the matter of accommodations for the crew, however, the ship was caught short. Significantly, when defending his vessel, Isherwood quietly overlooked this issue. Even the engineers of the minority report agreed that a complete spar deck was necessary to obviate the problem. Such an addition would not have significantly slowed the vessel.[54]

A more general objection made to these vessels bordered on the philosophical: since the Civil War had ended and there was no foreign conflict, these fast cruisers were not needed. It could as easily have been said that neither the army nor navy was necessary in time of peace. Any nation, however, must balance the need of keeping a trained fighting force on hand with that of peacetime economy. The U.S. Navy had chosen in this era to keep in commission some of the more satisfactory monitors, which served no practical purpose whatever in a cruising navy (although they were certainly a visible example of "taxes at work" for the voting constituents). Certainly the prestige and deterrent value of the fastest cruisers in the world would have been of more account than the maintenance of a great number of nonseagoing monitors or obsolete 11-knot sloops of war.

Having defended the *Wampanoag,* one must address the more general question of the engineering accomplishments of Benjamin F. Isherwood. Much of the criticism of Isherwood in the last years of his tenure was at least in part the result of his advocacy of increased recognition for the engineer corps. His engine designs were under intense attack during these same years. Before and after the controversy just described, however, his engines were much more favorably received. In the earlier years of the war, for instance, Admiral Porter himself had declared them a "monument to the skill and perseverance of . . . Isherwood."[55] In 1873, when the department was searching for suitable engines for newly rebuilt ships, an engineer evaluated those Isherwood-designed engines that had been built before the end of the war but had not yet been used. He concluded that they were "all of excellent design. . . . [and their] performance has always been excellent. The engines are simple, durable, substantial in construction, and convenient of management. In these respects they are certainly not inferior to any marine engines now on board naval vessels, whether of the compound or any other type."[56] As late as 1882, six of his engines were converted to compound engines for vessels being launched. Even more remarkable, the last of the Isherwood engines erected in a U.S. Navy ship were those that had been removed in 1872 from the *Nantasket* and were used to re-engine the *Kearsarge* in 1888.[57]

CHAPTER 11

The "Dark Ages," 1869–1885

The fate of the *Wampanoag* did not occur in isolation and in fact was part of a pattern that began to surface as early as 1864 and reached fruition in 1869, when Admiral David D. Porter was allowed free reign in a department whose titular head was political appointee Adolph Borie. The historian Robert G. Albion identifies Porter as the man who singlehandedly "turned off the light," plunging the navy into its "Dark Ages," a period of retrenchment and reaction that would not end until the construction of the navy's steel "ABCD" ships—the *Atlanta, Boston, Chicago,* and *Dolphin*—in the early 1880s.

The era was one of institutionalized stagnation. While foreign navies pursued advances in all areas of warship construction and armament, American naval vessels remained essentially on the plane reached in the midst of the Civil War. Indeed, in some respects American practice deliberately regressed from that level. The result was not a happy one: in 1875 a British journal administered this salute: "There never was such a hapless, broken down, tattered, forlorn apology for a Navy as that possessed by the United States."[1]

If any single phrase could be termed a rallying cry for the era, it would be "full sail power." With Porter at the helm, any factor that detracted from a vessel's efficiency under canvas was subject to elimination or severe reduction. Porter was an inverted visionary, whose prescribed cure for all the service's ills was a return to what he might have termed the "spiritual purity" of sail. In his report to the secretary of the navy in 1870, Porter gave his assessment of the state of the navy: "Since 1846, the quality of our seamen has fallen off. . . . Up to 1846 we possessed . . . the finest body of seamen in the world. At about that time period steam was introduced, but merely as an auxiliary. . . . Even at the first introducing of steam power . . . a deterioration in the crews of ships could be perceived, owing, in great measure to the seamen being employed in coaling ship and hoisting out ashes, to the exclusion of their more agreeable and legitimate duties." Furthermore, he continued, the increased use of steam power "enormously enlarged the expenses of our vessels. . . . so that during the war our expenditure of coal was at least $18,000,000." One is left with the impression that Porter felt the war should have been fought under sail—for economy's sake.

Other evils that Porter attributes to the encroachments of steam power in his report are the decline in competitiveness among ships' crews (a result of the decreasing number of sail-handling drills), the deterioration of wooden hulls because of the heat of the engines, and the decline of seamanship. That attribute he regarded as intrinsically valuable both for efficiency under sail as well as for the morale of the men.

The report concludes, "No seagoing vessel can be a perfect machine unless she is rigged with full sail power and managed in the most seamanlike manner." Interestingly, Porter's examples came from the "lessons of the War of 1812," rather than the Civil War.[2]

In the three months of Porter's primacy over the department, he issued a stream of directives that effectively translated his views into law. Orders went out requiring the use of full sail power whenever possible, with steam for emergency uses alone. Stringent recording of all coal use as well as written justification for each use was required from each commanding officer. Unnecessary coal use would be paid for by the offending commander. To facilitate sailing, all four-bladed propellers were to be replaced with two-bladed units. Constant sail drills were required, and proficiency in drills was to have a significant impact on officers' promotions.[3]

Though these were drastic measures, their precursors dated back to December 1864. At that time, Secretary Welles directed that all ships constructed for foreign service be efficient as "cruisers at sea under sail alone," maneuvering as purely sailing vessels. This resulted in a spate of refittings in which bowsprits and more head sails were added to a great number of vessels.[4]

In April 1867, Welles directed that in the future, the "essential qualities and appointments of a man-of-war be not surrendered to motive power." Speed was desirable in some vessels but not where attained by sacrificing "the health and comfort of the crew."[5] Commanders were to record the use of steam in red ink, and steam propulsion was solely for "urgent necessity" or necessity "so strong that the public interest would obviously be materially injured by not using it." Such economy measures were urgent, because Congress had reduced Welles's appropriation request by $22 million.[6]

The reversion to full sail power was far from the extent of the navy's malaise, however. Although other navies had progressed from wood construction to iron, composite, and steel, with sophisticated watertight compartmentation as well as double bottoms, the U.S. Navy relied on live oak, building only three smaller iron vessels in the remaining years of the old steam navy. Though watertight bulkheads were sometimes used in wooden hulls, they were obviously inefficient versions of those in rigid metal ships.

European progress in ordnance centered around immense breechloading rifles and cast-steel construction, whereas in the American navy, the Dahlgren smoothbore and lighter varieties of the Parrott rifle remained the standard weapons. (The larger Parrotts had been withdrawn after several burst in the last months of the war.) The only new weapons were rifled conversions of the Dahlgren and breechloading conversions of the Parrott, developed in the 1870s.

Although some have pointed out that the budgets of the postwar years were not significantly smaller than earlier peacetime allotments, from 1864 to 1882 Congress authorized only eight new vessels and limited both their aggregate tonnage and, of course, their cost. At no time had Congress authorized the navy to invest in the machinery necessary to build iron or steel vessels. Therefore, five of the new ships were of wood and the three built of iron were contracted out.[7]

Congressional recalcitrance concerning new construction left the navy to accomplish its ends with a great number of elderly vessels. The majority of the purchased wartime ships were unsuitable for cruising and were sold off. Numerous otherwise satisfactory ships built of poor materials late in the war were rotten after one cruise. Consequently, the active navy of the 1870s had a higher percentage of prewar and early wartime vessels than newer ships.

The official and unofficial reports on the condition of vessels in this era are appalling. Phrases such as "very rotten," "a little soft in the upper works," "signs of weakness topside, endangering mainmast," "spar deck has settled on both sides," pieces of bulwarks "falling out," are common. Probably the most telling story is of the *Yantic*, whose weakened condition and "altered shape" induced her commander to dismount her battery and mail her Dahlgrens to the U.S. "on favorable terms" before bringing his ship home from the Cape of Good Hope.[8]

The two main forces that molded the obsolete fleet of the 1870s were budgetary constraints imposed from above and romantic, reactionary leadership within the navy itself. This is not to say that the navy was satisfied with its growing obsolescence. On the contrary, agitation for a new, armorclad, ocean-going fleet was continuous but was ignored by Congress until the decrepitude of the Old Navy was patently obvious. (One significant warning came in 1879 when the warring Chilean navy was shown to be more formidable than the American fleet.)

Unfortunately, the "Dark Ages" of the American navy is not a myth that can be demolished by dramatic historical revisionism. Much as recent scholarship has reduced the perceived intensity of Europe's Dark Ages, however, more accurate knowledge may dispel the generally accepted impression that this era in the U.S. Navy was one of unrelieved depression. In evaluating the navy of this era some redeeming factors should be kept in mind. First, many extremely unfavorable comparisons have been made with sea-going armor-clad navies. The U.S. Navy had no pretensions toward such a fleet and only maintained a cruising presence world-wide. Thus American cruising ships ought only be compared with their counterparts in other navies. If one is to denigrate the United States for failure to keep pace with first-class navies, the problem was one of policies made by presidents and legislators, not by naval constructors and line officers.

Second, much of the criticism of the navy came from within—from the very individuals who were lobbying for a new fleet. Thus, it was in their interest to portray the navy in the worst possible light. Such tactics eventually achieved the desired results but in the process left a legacy of negativism not easily counteracted. In some respects the navy was keeping pace with contemporary technology, particularly engines and auxiliary equipment. Also important was the intellectual creativity of the era,

The Tennessee *(Formerly the* Madawasca*) New York, 1875, during Her Radical Rebuilding. This angle affords an excellent view of the ship's extreme length-to-breadth ratio. (Naval Historical Center)*

exemplified by the establishment of the Naval War College, the Naval Institute, and the Office of Naval Intelligence—and the writings of Alfred Thayer Mahan. These areas ought not be overlooked—nor overemphasized. Only when a balanced presentation is made can the navy's "Dark Ages" be put into perspective.

Tennessee

The vessel that became virtually an object lesson portraying the best and worst of the navy of this era was the *Madawasca,* which was renamed the *Tennessee* in 1869. In two major rebuildings between that year and 1875, she underwent an extraordinary—and expensive—metamorphosis from the "fastest steamship in the world" to a "9-knot frigate."

The first step in redeeming the ship from her "worthless" condition (according to the Goldsborough board's standards) was to modify her along the lines recommended for the *Wampanoag.* Four of her main boilers were removed, along with their two funnels, and the remaining smokepipes were made telescopic. A complete spar deck was built, with a forecastle deck, poop cabin, and quarter galleries. Her fore and mizzen masts were restepped further forward, and a bowsprit and cutwater knee were added. She was then ship-rigged, and as such spread some 34,000 square feet of canvas, with studding and storm sails rounding the figure out to more than 43,000 square feet. Compared to the 25,000 square feet carried originally, she now exemplified "full sail power."[9] The contrast between her new and old appearance is as striking as the dichotomy between Victorian and modern architecture.

Admiral Porter was no doubt pleased with her sailing performance, judged as "very fast," "readily making 10 to 11 knots on a wind." Her dragging propeller hampered her performance to windward, however, unless steam was used to keep the screw turning.[10] Under steam she hobbled along averaging 8.16 knots on her only cruise after this rebuilding. When the drag of the four-bladed propeller was addressed by replacing it with a two-bladed unit, only 6.19 knots could be got out of her. Her commander reported that not more than thirty revolutions were possible with her engines, and Ericsson later wrote that her remaining boiler power was "utterly insufficient . . . for the two 100-inch cylinders without running at so slow a rate that the centers could not be passed."[11] In other words, the steam available was not sufficient to run the engines, no less propel the vessel. (This statement is curious in view of the inventor's complaints in 1867 that the boilers were far too numerous for the engines.)

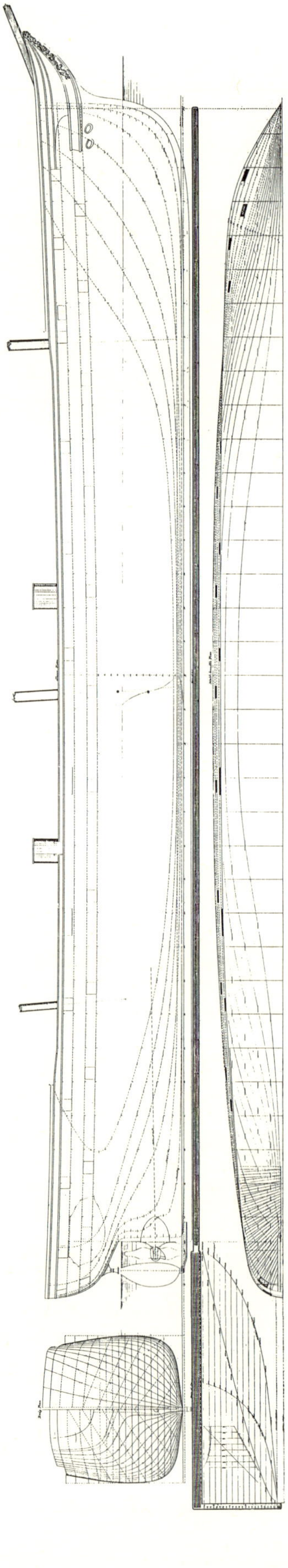

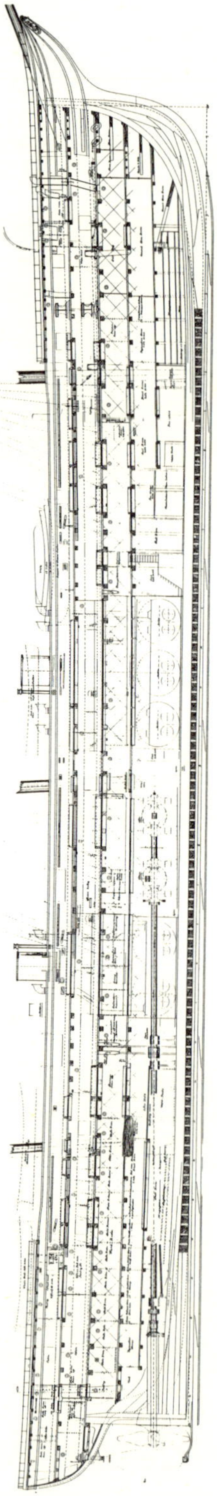

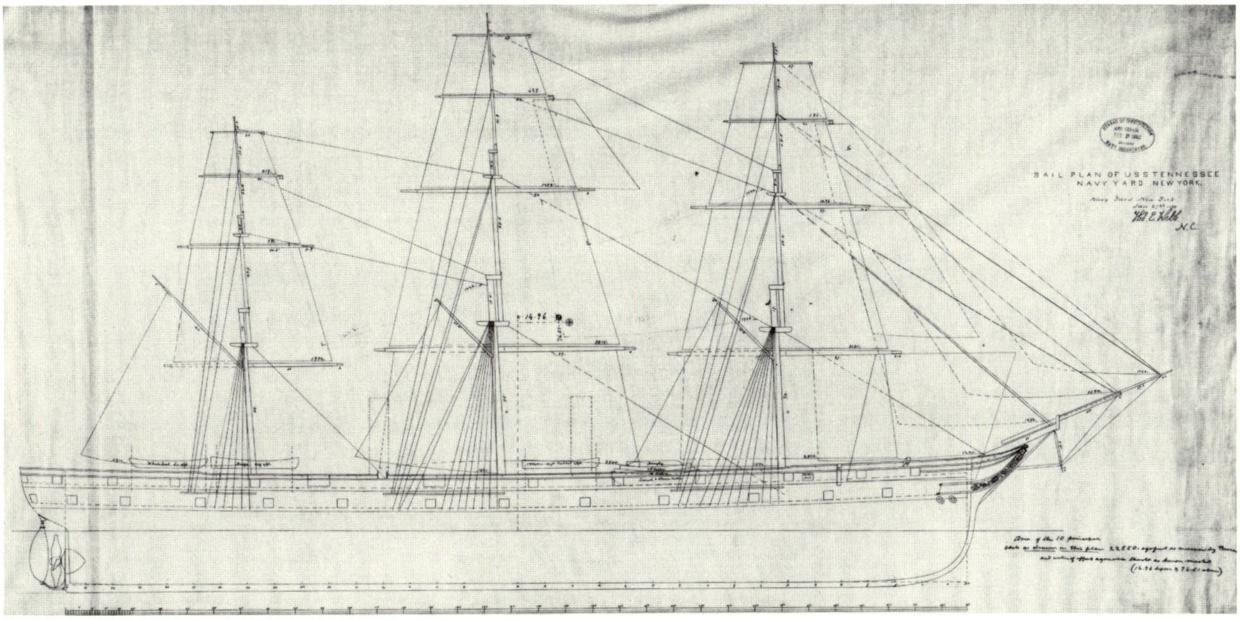

Sail Plan of the Tennessee. *Because of the spaciousness of her accommodations, this vessel was a favorite command. (NARS 79-8-11, National Archives)*

Though the department continued to downplay the importance of performance under steam, the *Tennessee* was re-engined in the years 1871 to 1875 (despite the $576,000 already spent on the initial rebuilding). This transaction was part of many in the scandals involving John Roach of Philadelphia. More than $800,000 was pumped into this rebuilding, plus Ericsson's engines (which had not been officially condemned). They were traded to Roach for his services—over and above the monetary payment for the new engines and boilers.

The contract for the engines, which were of the new compound type, was made by the secretary of the navy without consulting Chief Engineer J. W. King, who was in Europe at the time, investigating the latest developments in this type of engine. According to one source, Roach and Secretary Robeson intended to consult King, but the chief engineer then indefinitely extended his visit to Europe. Not wishing to delay the process, the contract was signed in King's absence. Criticism that the contract was unbid was answered by the contention that the engines were experimental and as such did not require the bidding process.[12]

The Frigate Tennessee, *1875. The sharpness of the* Wampanoag *can be judged from these lines. The Goldsborough board recommended identical changes to the Isherwood-engined vessel: complete spar deck, removal of two funnels, and other modifications. By this date the* Tennessee *had been reengined with experimental compound machinery and had ten cylindrical boilers. (NARS 79-8-7, 79-8-5, National Archives)*

Compound engines were designed to take advantage of additional expansion of steam by allowing it to expand twice, first in a small high-pressure cylinder and then in a larger, low-pressure cylinder. Use of separate chambers significantly reduced the steam condensation (and loss of power) that resulted when pressure was allowed to reduce significantly within a single cylinder. Engineers such as Dickerson had attempted to eliminate condensation in simple expansion engines by using wood lagging on the outside of the cylinders to reduce heat loss, but the results had been unsatisfactory.

Roach's engines were unusual because four cylinders were used, arranged in pairs. A single piston rod was used in each pair, connecting the high- and low-pressure pistons of each pair. The large cylinders measured 78 inches in diameter; the low, 40 inches. The stroke of the pistons was 40 inches. This cylinder arrangement was unusual in that most compound engines used separate rods for each cylinder.[13]

Ten cylindrical boilers rated at 50 pounds per square inch were used. The entire engine, boiler, and coal space measured 106 feet in the hull. The vessel was also refitted with a four-bladed propeller.[14] (By the mid-1870s, after much undeniable proof of the inefficiency of the two-bladed propellers, four-bladed screws were again adopted as standard in the navy.)

In a twenty-four-hour economy trial in 1875 under fore-and-aft sails, the *Tennessee* averaged 10.1 knots and used 32.6 tons of coal. In a fair weather passage in the Mediterranean she averaged 9 knots, reaching 10 for a single hour. Her coal consumption was estimated at 30 tons per day.[15]

These official reports are a great deal more positive than later accounts of her economy. One of her later commander's notebooks on the vessel gave her coal consumption at full power (10 knots) as 60 tons per day. At two-thirds power and 8 knots, she used 38 tons per day. Another indication of her voracious appetite was that 35 tons of coal was stored in bags on deck. According to tabulations published in 1875 in the report of the secretary of the navy, she used 3.46 pounds per indicated horsepower—better than the old *Madawasca,* but worse than the *Wampanoag*'s 3.129 figure. Other compound engines of the era ranged between 2.03 and 2.79 pounds per indicated horsepower.[16]

Under sail, her early reports of speed evaporated similarly. She could attain 6.6 knots without steam assistance, in smooth seas with a strong wind. This was the greatest speed she reached under sail in five years, from 1880 to 1885, according to her commanding officer, Oscar F. Stanton. With steam assisting her canvas, she made 10.5 knots. As would be expected with a vessel of such shallow draft and proportionately excessive length, she was not weatherly. Tacking required 6 knots, a smooth sea, and a fresh breeze, and took more than fifteen minutes. Wearing required 15 to 30 minutes.[17]

By the end of her service life, the *Tennessee* was armed with sixteen 9-inch Dahlgrens on the gun deck, and two 8-inch converted rifles and four 80-pounder converted breechloading Parrotts on her spar deck. Four spar torpedoes and an equal number of Hotchkiss 1.5-inch breechloaders rounded out her battery. She was a favorite vessel, at least among the admirals, with her commodious apartments well insulated from the lower ranks. As to her capabilities as a fighting ship, she resembled a few equally sedate wooden steam frigates of the French navy of the 1880s, which were characterized as "nothing but nice accommodations."[18]

Her career was spent as the flagship of the Asiatic squadron and then the North Atlantic squadron. She was condemned as unseaworthy and sold in 1887. According to Bennett, she had cost, including repairs, over $3.8 million: $3.2 million was

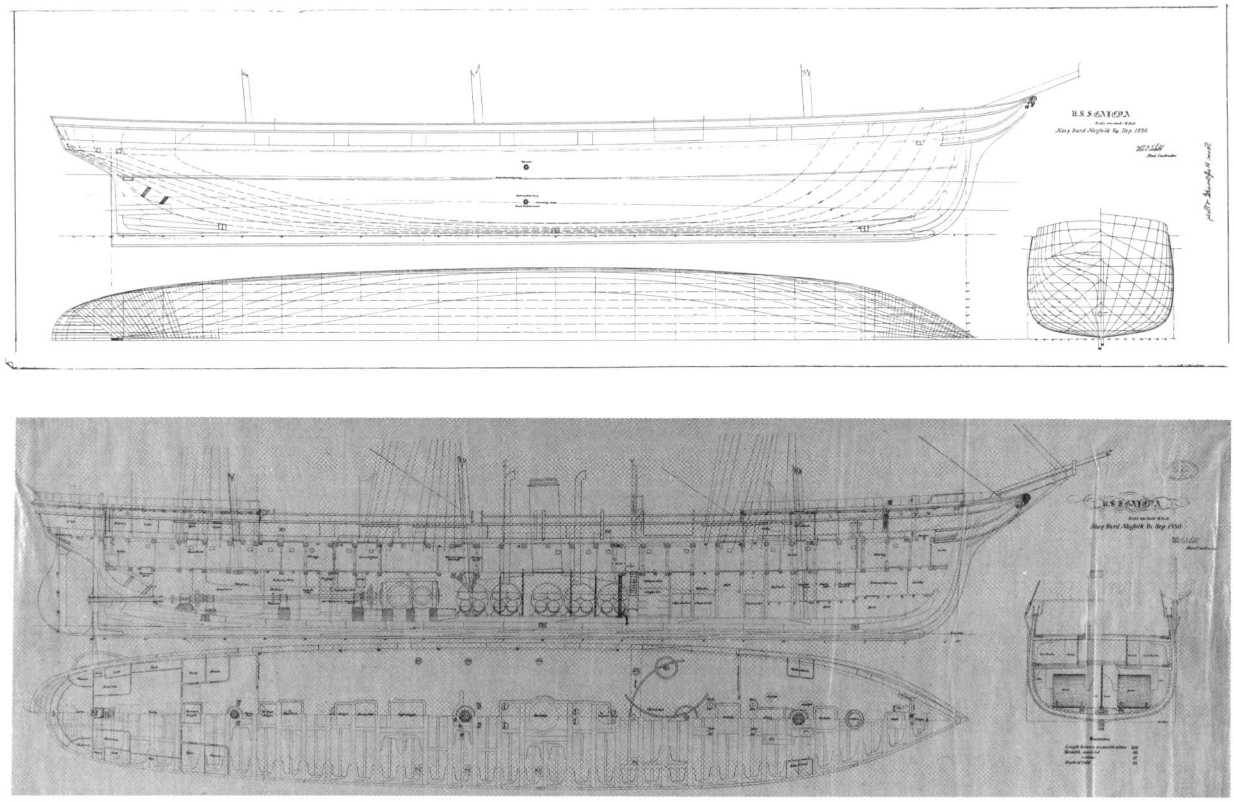

Lines and Inboard Plans of the Galena-*Class Rebuilt Sloops. Any resemblance between these vessels and their predecessors of the same names is entirely accidental. The hull lines are much fuller than late wartime cruisers, and all were built with greater sail area. (NARS 78-3-3J, 78-3-3I, National Archives)*

*The Former Double-Ender (*Sassacus *Class)* Tallapoosa. *She was sunk, salved, and rebuilt in the 1870s. She is an excellent example of the extremes to which rebuilding was taken in the postwar era. Compare this vessel with the appearance of the* Winooski *and* Agawam*—her original sister vessels—in chapter eight. The* Tallapoosa *was apparently nicely appointed as an admiral's barge and remained in service until the 1890s. (Naval Historical Center)*

consumed in her original cost and in the two major refits. For comparison, the original cost of the new steel cruiser *Chicago* was $1.25 million.[19] A congressional investigation of Roach's rebuilding of the vessel and other questionable dealings between the contractor and the navy resulted in 420 pages of testimony but no solid conclusions.[20]

Galena Class

After 1873, Congress was as averse to new construction as before. Consequently, the navy reverted to administrative "rebuilding" of worn-out vessels. Although rebuilding earlier had been piecemeal, on individual vessels, in 1871 it became the basis for an entire class of six sloops-of-war.

The ships selected to be rebuilt were two sailing sloops, the *Vandalia* and *Marion;* one prewar steam sloop, the *Mohican;* a former ironclad, the *Galena;* and the *Quinnebaug* and *Swatara.* Therefore, from six disparate vessels, ranging in length from 118 feet to 216 feet, came six nearly identical vessels, 216 feet in length. Five were 37 feet in breadth and 1,900 tons; and the sixth, the *Vandalia,* was 39 feet and 2,033 tons.

The administrative fiction was papered over lightly in the annual reports, with rather ingenuous phrasing. In the case of the *Swatara,* "It was considered in the interests of the government that her frame should be of live oak timber instead of white oak. . . . It became necessary in carrying out this idea to increase her capacity, which was done sufficiently to increase her speed and fighting power."[21]

The department was somewhat cavalier in carrying out the finer points of the ruse, because the *Army and Navy Journal* reported that the skeleton of the *Quinnebaug* was on the ways at Gosport while a fragment of her timber was taken to Philadelphia: "She is now being rebuilt there." A subsequent Congressional inquiry elicited testimony, probably exaggerated, that when the new ships were laid down "the old vessels being repaired were on the high seas, miles away."[22]

The rebuilds were indeed illegal, because all repairs over $3,000 required a board of survey, according to congressional action of 21 February 1861. At least three of these vessels, the *Marion, Vandalia,* and *Galena,* had no such nicety performed. (Two other vessels, the *Tallapoosa* and *Nipsic,* were also rebuilt at this time without legal justification.)[23] Because funds for construction were from the repair budgets, the actual work was spasmodic and the first of the *Galena* class commissioned was the *Swatara,* in November 1874. All except the *Mohican,* built at Mare Island, were in service by 1880. The latter was not commissioned until 1885 and was the last wooden warship built for the U.S. Navy, requiring fourteen years for completion.

The new ships were similar to the *Swatara* class of 1864 only in length. Their breadth was increased from 30 feet to 37 feet and 39 feet, and their draft was approximately 16 feet, compared with 12 feet for the earlier ships. Though the port arrangement for the new vessels was similar to the old, the rebuilt ships showed some four feet additional freeboard and had quarter galleries and an

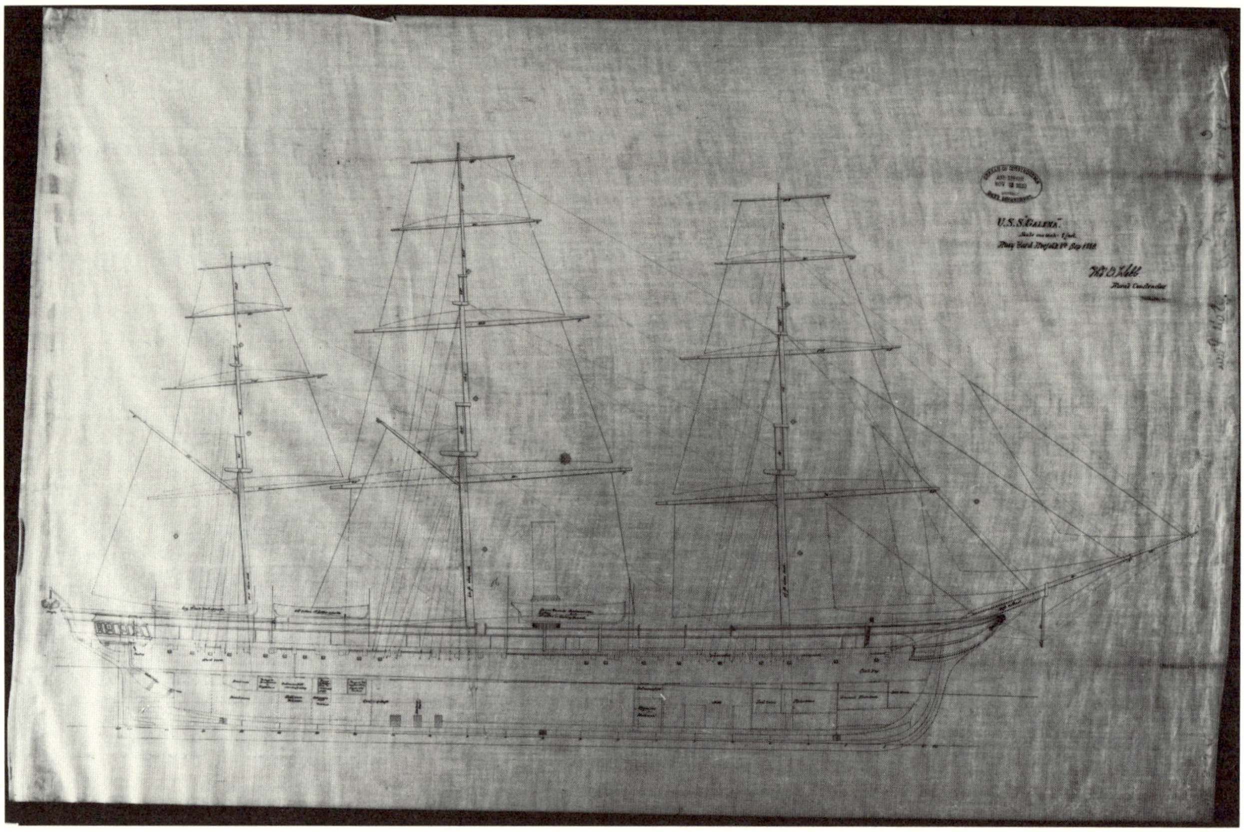

Outboard Plan of the Galena *and Class (Except the* Vandalia*). (NARS 78-3-3K, National Archives)*

The Quinnebaug *in a Classic Pose at Venice. (Library of Congress)*

angular knuckle at the stern, instead of the single curve from rudder to taffrail of the early ships.

The department described the rebuilt vessels as "not designed purely for speed, but [for] general . . . cruising. . . . They were to have greater beam in proportion to their length than the vessels built during the previous few years. . . . to allow room to work their batteries, and to carry comparatively heavy ones, and to stand up well under canvas."[24]

The compound engines of all the vessels had originally been Isherwood back-acting 50-inch by 42-inch powerplants. They now had one 42-inch high-pressure cylinder and a 64-inch low-pressure cylinder, working horizontally as had the original engines. The cylinders were jacketed to reduce condensation. Boiler pressure now was above 60 pounds per square inch, and steam, supplied from ten cylindrical boilers, was expanded 6.5 times.[25]

In hull form, the extremes of the wartime ships were eliminated. Where the first *Swatara* had a 32 degree entrance angle, the second measured 42 degrees, and the wider *Vandalia*'s measured 44 degrees. The cross section of the *Vandalia* shows a considerably rounder bottom than the others of the class, more closely resembling that of the *Nantasket* and *Resaca* than the cross section of the original *Swatara* and *Quinnebaug*.

The batteries of the new ships were indeed more substantial than those of the older vessels. Although the old ships carried six 32-pounders in broadside, the rebuilt sloops mounted an equal number of 9-inch Dahlgrens. The standard 11-inch pivot gun was mounted amidships and a 60-pound Parrott was on the forecastle of each ship. They were rigged as barks or ships and carried up to 14,000 square feet of canvas.[26]

The *Mohican* obtained much unwelcome public attention because of her protracted construction time and subsequent expenses. On the defensive for obvious reasons, the department defended the long obsolete vessel as well as they could: her live oak was "brought from Florida at great expense," and she was "provided with all the leading improvements in naval architecture. . . . A staunch, fast wooden vessel is still the best for cruising purposes and that the foreign navy officers appreciate."[27] She did indeed have electric lighting, an efficient ventilation system, and iron deck beams, plus an 8-inch muzzle-loading rifle. Her cost, however, was estimated at $908,000, although the *Vandalia* had cost only $325,000.

Explanations for this effusion of funds centered around the difficulties incurred in building on the West Coast, including both freight expenses and the lack of ironworking facilities. (Roach, in Pennsylvania, built the crankshaft for the engine.) Additional waste occurred because of her deterioration during periods when lack of funds stopped progress. One source reported that she was six inches wider on one side because of the settling of the stocks through the years. The secretary of the navy, William C. Whitney, called this "most extraordinary mismanagement and wastefulness" "incapable of explanation."[28] Though it seems that

Stern of the Swatara, *Showing Gilt Decoration and a Plethora of Boats on Iron Davits. (Naval Historical Center)*

Vandalia *Fitting Out. Note the use of wire rope and rigging screws. Primer for hull was white zinc paint. (Naval Historical Center)*

the Mare Island yard was blamed for this, the onus ought to have been upon the leadership at higher levels, who could have halted her construction at any point in more than fifteen years of work.

All of the vessels proved generally successful in performance. The one with the reputation for speed was the *Vandalia,* which made 12 knots under steam alone on trials, and the *Marion* recorded over 12 knots against a head swell in one instance. The *Swatara* inaugurated her career with a cruise around the world to observe the transit of Venus, and her compound engines met the economy levels expected of them, using 2.03 pounds of coal per indicated horsepower. This was the lowest figure recorded for a U.S. naval vessel to that date.[29]

All of these sloops had lengthy careers, though as contemporaries of the newer steel ships they were soon relegated to training or auxiliary uses. The *Vandalia* was wrecked at Samoa in 1889, and the last to be sold was the *Mohican,* in 1921.

NEW CONSTRUCTION

A congressional act of 10 February 1873 authorized the construction of new vessels for the navy, the first such authority since before the end of the Civil War. Eight vessels were to be built with an aggregate displacement of 8,000 tons and cost of $3.2 million. This amount did not include engines, funds for which were allotted under a separate head. Four were to be built by contract and all were to have auxiliary sail power.

Enterprise Class

Four wooden gunboats, measuring 185 feet by 35 feet were part of the authorization of 1873: the *Enterprise, Adams, Essex,* and *Alliance.* A fifth, built to the same plans, was officially a rebuild of the *Nipsic* and was not completed until 1879. Two eminent civilian naval architects were responsible for constructing three of the ships: John W. Griffiths for the *Enterprise* and Donald McKay for the *Essex* and *Adams.* All three were built at navy yards, with the Griffiths vessel and one of the McKay ships (the *Essex*) together at Kittery. McKay's vessels were among the last built by the famous clipper ship designer.[30]

The lines of these vessels were considerably fuller than the wartime gunboats of the *Kansas* class which they resembled only in length. In keeping with the department's emphasis on capacity, general cruising, and the ability to stand up to their canvas, the new ships were five feet wider and had some four feet greater draft than the gunboats of the Civil War era. Thus, although the wartime gunboats displaced less than 900 tons, the *Enterprise*-series vessels displaced 1,375 tons. Construction of the hulls used standard techniques, with iron diagonal bracing, head straps, and straps bracing the stern deadwood to the upper timbers.[31]

Griffiths, on the *Enterprise,* added bilge keels. In this case there were three on each bilge, with the topmost about eight feet below the waterline; the second, a foot lower at about the maximum curve of the hull; and the third, another foot below that. They were a foot square in cross section and measured 72 feet 6 inches, 60 feet 6 inches, and 49 feet 6 inches, respectively. Griffiths had used the same number of keels on his steamer *New Era* and explained that they were analogous to the rifling in a gun barrel in keeping the vessel "steady and longitudinally on course."[32] It seems, however, that there was great potential for drag with this array of protuberances.

Eventually, a controversy arose between the department and Griffiths over the quality of work on the vessel, which was leaking from improperly driven copper hull bolts. After lying incomplete and neglected for several months at the wharf, the government reclaimed the ship, had her docked, recoppered, and the keels removed.[33]

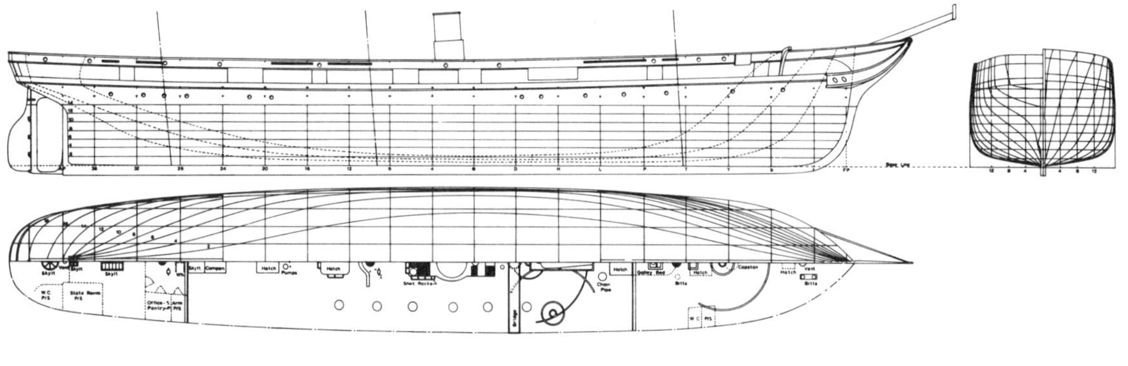

Lines of the Essex. *(From* Ship Modeller's Shop Notes, *edited by Merritt Edson, 1979)*

The Essex *in the Late 1880s. These vessels were generally unremarkable, though their compound engines made them relatively economical, a plus in the austere postwar years. (U.S. Naval Institute)*

The Essex *during the Spanish-American War, armed with modern 4-inch breechloaders. (Naval Historical Center)*

For the engines, the department again was not reluctant to adopt new technology, particularly if it promised improved economy, and all these gunboats were given compound engines. They were built by contract, with costs ranging from $120,000 to $175,000. Although competitive designs were solicited, the Bureau of Steam Engineering judged its own plan to be superior, and all the engines were built to those specifications. The two cylinders were 34 inches and 51 inches in diameter, and the stroke was 42 inches. Eight cylindrical boilers and a telescoping smoke pipe completed the steam machinery for each vessel.[34]

All five were bark-rigged, though the *Adams* was originally given less canvas—without royals and with shorter yards.[35] Though the congressional mandate indicated they were to be "auxiliary" sailers, the total square footage for each (except the *Adams*) was over 15,000, including royals and three head sails. This was a greater area of canvas than that given the larger *Galena*-class ships.[36] The sloops were armed with four 9-inch Dahlgrens in broadside and on 11-inch smoothbore or 8-inch converted rifle on a waist pivot mounting.[37] In appearance, this class was difficult to distinguish from the *Galena* class, because members of that class were also bark-rigged at times. The mizzen channels of the smaller ships were not broken by gun ports, and their mizzen spanker booms extended beyond the taffrail.

The performance of the new ships was up to the economical levels expected by the department, with the *Adams* rated at 2.25 pounds of coal per hour per horsepower.[38] At 8½ knots she theoretically could make 3,582 miles on her coal capacity of 140 tons. The rebuilt *Nipsic* ran 300 nautical miles at 9½ knots per hour, using about 12 tons per day. Their stodgy lines precluded great speed, and 10 to 11 knots under steam and sail was a general average for these sloops.[39]

The *Enterprise*, by virtue of the snarl with Griffiths, was the last congressionally authorized wooden steamship commissioned in the navy (April 1877). She was a training vessel for the state of Massachusetts as early as 1891 and was sold in 1909. The *Essex* was assigned to training duties in the early 1890s and was stricken in 1927. The *Adams* saw training duties as of 1897 and was a station ship at Samoa in 1907 and on the Delaware until her sale in 1920. The *Alliance* was involved in the search for the *Jeannette* Arctic expedition in 1881 and was an apprentice training ship beginning in 1895. She was sold in Puerto Rico in 1911. The *Nipsic* was beached during the Samoan hurricane of 1889, then was refloated and returned to Mare Island for repairs. In 1892 she was a receiving ship on Puget Sound, where she was sold in 1913.[40]

The introduction of the compound engine in this era also had its critics. One officer wrote that the economy gained was at the expense of simplicity of design and increased danger from higher boiler pressures. Furthermore, he contended that the funds expended on new machinery would have been better spent on modern vessels. He concluded with a comment appropriate to the current sail-oriented dispensation: "On cruising ships, economy counts for nothing."[41] In other words, expensive steam machinery, regardless of its economical operation, was rarely used.

Alert Class

Iron was used for the hulls of the three gunboats built by contract in the authorization of 1873. These were the *Alert, Ranger,* and *Huron,* measuring 175 feet by 32 feet, with a draft of 12 feet and displacement of 1,020 tons. Among the smallest steamships built during the sailing steam era, two (the *Alert* and *Huron*) were built by Roach at Philadelphia, and the *Ranger* was constructed by Harlan and Hollingsworth of Wilmington, Delaware, the first firm to build iron steamships in the United States.

The Roach company built the two-cylinder compound engines for the three vessels. The high-pressure cylinder measured 28¼ inches; the low-pressure, 42½ inches; both with a 42-inch stroke. The engines developed 560 indicated horsepower and each vessel's five cylindrical boilers were rated at 80 pounds pressure per square inch. Though these were the smallest compound engines used in this era, they weighed 122,000 pounds each.[42]

The frames of the hulls were of angle iron, 3 inches by 4 inches by ½ inch in thickness, on 20-inch centers. Alternating frames (every 40 inches) were strengthened by 2½-inch by 3-inch reversed angles. The deck beams were of T-iron, 8 inches wide and 6 inches across the T, flaring out to 24 inches to form the knees, which were riveted to the sides of the vessel. The decks were ¼-inch iron, planked with wood. Thirteen strakes made of plates ⅝ inch to 11/16 inch thick and 26 inches wide formed each half of the hull. The strakes lapped alternately over and under on their edges. The keel was formed by a 1-inch thick longitudinal plate that protruded about 12 inches from the bottom, and the garboard strakes were angled to butt up on each side of it. Strengthening the frames at the keel were web plates 5/16 inch thick and 18 inches high at the center line, which extended to the turn of the bilge. The watertight bulkheads were of 3/16-inch plates, 21 inches wide, strapped at the seams with T-iron.[43] The general arrangement and proportions of the ironwork of these hulls followed the accepted practice of the era and resulted in a sturdy, long-lasting vessel.[44]

Their hull design was unremarkable, with about a 42-degree entrance angle and the fullest section slightly forward of midships. The *Huron* and

The Huron *with Schooner Rig. Others of her class (the* Alert *and* Ranger*) remained active beyond the turn of the century, usually in training roles. (Naval Historical Center)*

Ranger were schooner-rigged originally, while the *Alert* was bark-rigged. Each was armed with an 11-inch pivot gun, two 9-inch Dahlgrens in broadside, and a 60-pound rifle on the topgallant forecastle.[45] Though economical, they were lacking in speed. The *Huron* recorded 10 knots with a new screw and full power in 1877. Her commander reported her rolling as 20 to 30 degrees and her bottom "quite foul" after three weeks at sea.[46]

The career of the *Huron* ended just short of her second anniversary in commission, when she grounded in a severe gale off Kitty Hawk, North Carolina, in November 1877. Only 34 of her 138-man crew survived. The cause of the disaster was thought to be related to compass variations caused by her iron structure—a continuing problem in such ships.[47]

The *Alert* was sold in 1922 after service as a submarine tender (AS-4) in the Pacific.[48] The *Ranger*, rerigged as a bark after the *Huron* disaster, survived in various training roles until stricken from the navy list in 1940 and taken over by the Merchant Marine Academy. Under the name *Emery Rice*, she was first a training ship, then a museum. She was finally scrapped in 1958—the last surviving relic of the Old Navy, outliving the *Hartford* by two years.

The original engines of the *Ranger*, however, were saved from the scrappers; an annex is presently being prepared for their display at the American Merchant Marine Museum at Kings Point, Long Island. These are the only known engines from the steam navy era to survive.[49]

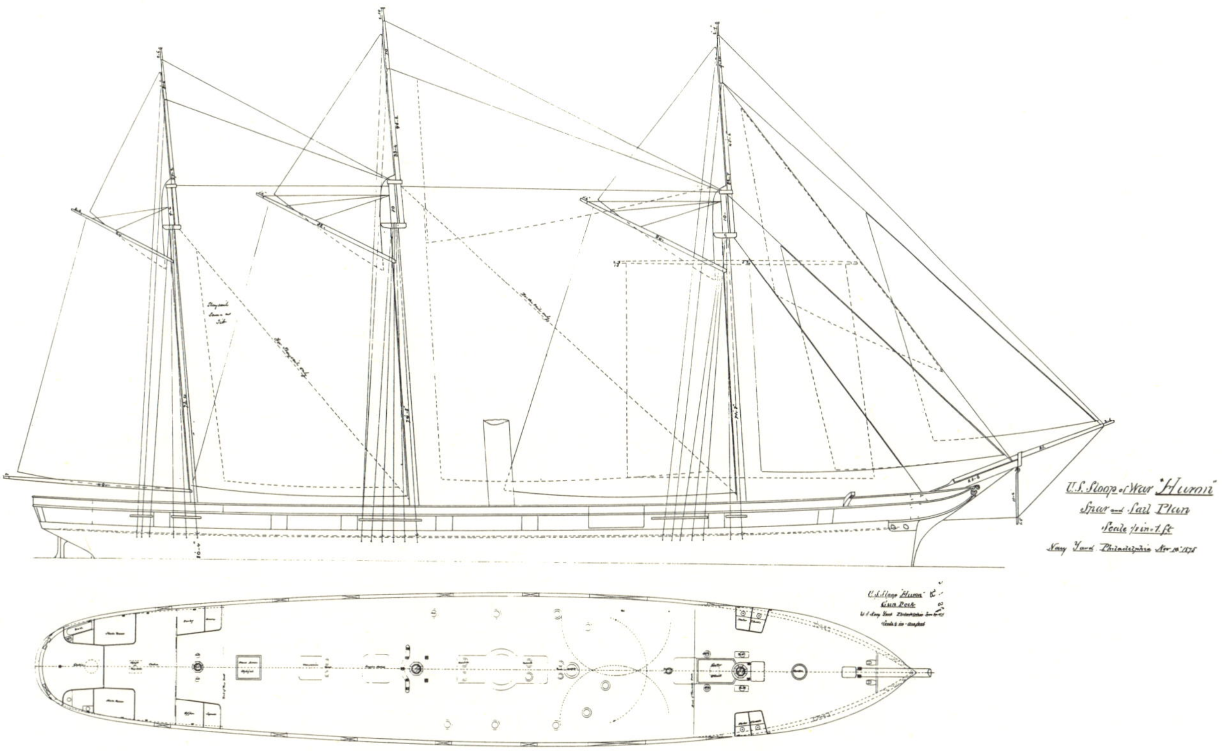

The Iron Sloop Huron, *As She Was Fitted When Lost in 1877. (NARS 40-8-2A, 40-8-2B, National Archives)*

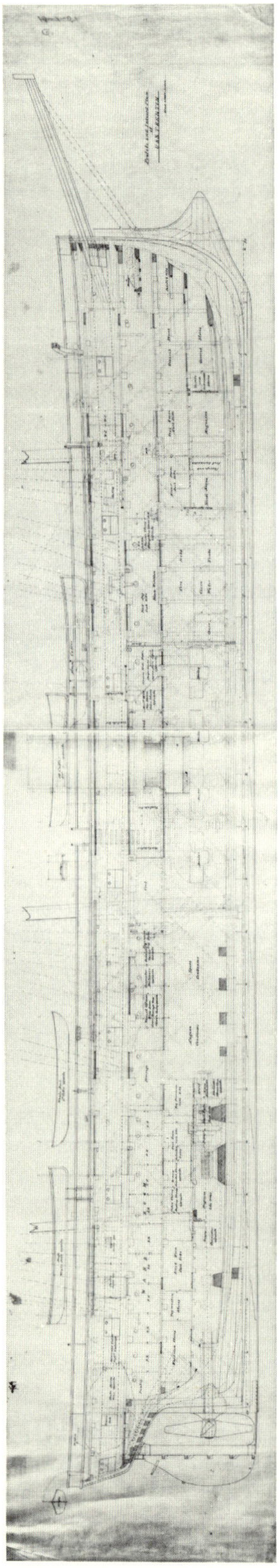

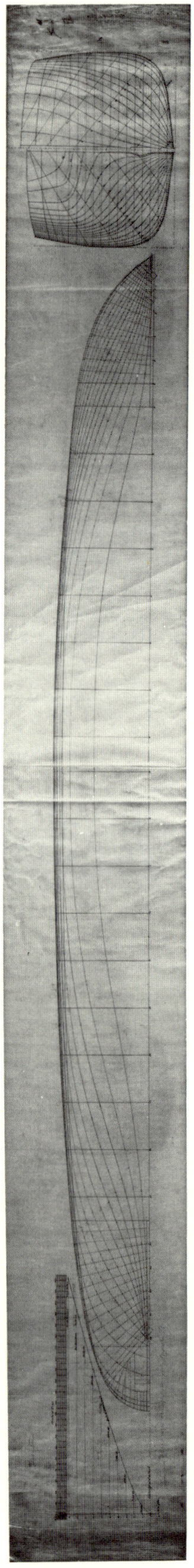

Trenton

The vessel that may be considered the epitome of the wooden steam navy emerged from the authorization of 1873. This was the *Trenton,* variously described as a "frigate-built cruiser," "screw corvette, 1st rate," and "screw steamer, 2nd rate." Officially she was characterized as "a new type for flagships" and Bennett described her as "the most formidable cruising ship in our neglected navy, and the only one that in type and armament at all approached the practice of other navies."[50] Her defects have hitherto merited much attention and were generic for the American navy of the period. Positive aspects of the vessel, however, have been ignored.

If hull form is considered a criterion for modernity, the 3,900-ton *Trenton* was technically a throwback. The annual report of the secretary of the navy in 1883 described her as "an enlarged copy of the United States steam frigate *Lancaster,* having about one-sixth more displacement. The forms of the immersed solids . . . are almost precisely the same." The older frigate was described as "primarily a sailing vessel." Under sail and steam at a maximum of 11 knots, "the model of the vessel was admirably adapted. . . . maneuvering and working . . . wonderfully fine."[51]

At 253 feet by 48 feet, the new sloop was eighteen feet longer and two feet wider than the prewar ship. Though both ships' cross section at midships was nearly identical below the waterline, the *Trenton* was sharper both fore and aft than the *Lancaster.*

The most prominent feature of the *Trenton*'s hull was the composition (bronze) ram bolted to the stem and protruding nine and one-half feet, with its forward point seven feet below the waterline. This was the first such item used on any U.S. naval unarmored cruiser, and its use placed this ship in the midst of the fashionable naval trends of the day. An early plan for the vessel would have rendered her bow nearly indistinguishable from that of the *Lancaster,* with a customary cutwater knee and rounded forefoot.[52]

As with her predecessor, the *Trenton* was of live oak, heavily strapped. Her plans show two watertight bulkheads forward of the engines, one approximately thirty feet aft of the fore perpendicular, with the second twenty-five feet aft of the first. The structure of these is not known, though the *Lancaster* was reported to have had iron bulkheads.[53] Again, however well caulked, such bulkheads in intrinsically flexible wooden hulls were unlikely to be effective.

Inboard and Lines of the Trenton. *Her design was an enlarged* Lancaster. *She was originally intended to have a traditional head with cutwater knee. (NARS 79-1-13C, 108-8-6K, National Archives)*

A seemingly inconsequential difference between this ship and others was the location of her hawseholes. These were on the berth deck, one deck below standard practice, leaving the forward gun deck free of anchor chains and hoisting apparatus.[54] This was to allow a shifting bowsprit to be worked on the gun deck and thus prevent that spar from interfering with ramming. Though the location for the hawseholes was found to be beneficial for the vessel's ventilation, its drawbacks became clear at the close of the frigate's career.[55]

A three-cylinder compound engine powered the vessel, combining two low-pressure cylinders of 78 inches and a 58½-inch high-pressure cylinder, fitted with steam jackets to reduce condensation. The stroke was 48 inches. With eight cylindrical boilers and a superheating apparatus, the installation developed 3,100 indicated horsepower.[56]

For the first time since the *New Ironsides,* the main battery consisted of 11-inch Dahlgrens. These guns had been converted, however, to rifled weapons by the introduction of a 2.75-inch wrought iron tube or sleeve into the original bore, which had been enlarged to 13.5 inches to accept the rifled tube. The weapon fired an 8-inch shell weighing 180 pounds, with a 35-pound charge.[57]

As originally fitted, the *Trenton* had eight of the rifled Dahlgrens on the gun deck, and three on the spar deck—one aft and two forward. The forward-firing guns could be trained both on the same side or on opposite bows of the vessel. They could be pivoted from direct forward fire to two points abaft the beam. The aft pivot had an arc of fire of 270 degrees. Four of the broadside guns were on Ericsson-designed friction-compressor pivot carriages, run in and out by gearing. Hydraulically operated recoil buffers were employed on the remaining four broadside guns.[58] Some sources indicate the vessel could fire four guns forward. Though the plans show bridle ports on the gun deck as well as provisions for securing the carriages below the port sills, the fore-most broadside gun was more than fifty feet aft of these ports, indicating tackle and manhandling were necessary to obtain four-gun bow fire. In later years, one of the spar-deck guns was removed from the ship. The vessel was also equipped with spar torpedoes on the quarters and bows, as well as two Harvey towing torpedoes.

A few other modern conveniences were first seen in the U.S. Navy on the *Trenton.* On the forward berth deck was a steam-powered windlass, which was essentially a horizontal drum and shaft, mounted athwartships with a spiral gear in its center, run by an engine beneath the deck. A hand gear was attached to allow manual assistance to the engine when breaking the anchor off the bottom.[59]

A second steam auxiliary was a steering mechanism, mounted on the gun deck and consisting of a two-cylinder engine attached to the tiller by hide

The Trenton *in 1876. Before her loss at Samoa in 1889 she was the most advanced wooden cruiser of the old navy. (Naval Historical Center)*

ropes. The above-deck wheel could be "worked by a child" with this mechanism in use. Two steam winches were also employed for hoisting ashes or coaling ship. They were originally intended to hoist the telescopic funnel.[60]

Though electric lights and generators were a few years away on naval vessels, as early as 1877 electric power was used on the *Trenton* to provide communication between individual gun captains and the commanding officer. An annunciator mounted on the bridge was designed to show a red marking when the captain of the corresponding broadside gun closed his circuit, thereby indicating that his gun was ready to fire. Keys on the commander's annunciator could be pressed to fire simultaneously all guns ready at any particular instant. Power for this device, as well as for firing the spar torpedoes, ringing alarm bells, and operating thermostats placed in potential danger areas, was provided by three galvanic batteries.[61]

The frigate was ship-rigged and carried 22,900 square feet of canvas in her ten principal sails. When carrying canvas to her royals, and with her flying jib, she spread over 30,000 square feet of sail.[62]

The performance of this curious modern-antique hybrid was satisfactory to the department, which obviously had none too high expectations, given their choice of hull lines for the ship. In a maximum performance trial in 1878, she attained 12.6 knots over a six-hour run in the Mediterranean, using 2.29 pounds of coal per indicated horsepower. Under ordinary practice, using five of her eight boilers, she had a mean speed of 8.43 knots, and with the assistance of sail, 10.22 knots.

Sail and Outboard Plans of the Trenton, *1878. The area of her ten principal sails was 22,900 square feet. (NARS 108-8-6U, National Archives)*

Her overall coal usage was 3.1 pounds per indicated horsepower. At her maximum speed (12½ knots), her cruising range was 1,650 miles, with coal consumption at 60 tons per day. In ordinary service, at less than 9 knots, a distance of 2,455 geographical miles was possible.[63]

Few major changes were made in the ship during her service life. She became the first U.S. naval vessel to have electric lights. By 1883 a pilothouse had been added to her forward bridge, and by 1888 her armament had been augmented by the addition of four 47-mm Hotchkiss rifled cannon, a Gatling machine gun, and a 3-inch breechloading field piece.[64]

In 1889, when British, German, and American interests were approaching a collision over the Samoan Islands, the *Trenton, Nipsic,* and *Vandalia* were dispatched to the scene. In the famous typhoon of May that year, the *Trenton*'s fate was sealed by the low position of her hawseholes. No jury-rigged obstructions placed in them were sufficient to prevent the seas from putting out her fires early in the course of the storm, and she was forced to the bottom of the shallow harbor, a total loss. Less than two years before, her commander had recommended the pipes be raised to her gun deck because it was "dangerous to bend the chains in rough weather."[65]

THE LAST REBUILDINGS, 1877–1885

Between 1877 and 1885 the department maintained its numbers by both administrative rebuildings and periodic overhauls of old vessels. These refits or rebuildings were in many instances so extensive that the vessels were taken down to the bare frames—or further. The practice of "pulling vessels to pieces" under the guise of "repairs" was widespread and abused, becoming a method by which the navy yards justified their expenses and their existence. Admiral Porter vigorously attacked the system, citing examples such as the *Kearsarge,* which had consumed $1,123,415 in repairs beyond her construction cost of $286,918, and the *Shenandoah* and *Ossipee,* which had both absorbed twice their original cost in repairs.[66]

Porter recommended that future repairs be under the purview of a single board of survey rather than carried out by navy-yard boards with vested interests in keeping their yards active. In 1882 and 1884 Congress limited repairs on individual vessels to first 20 then 30 percent of their original cost.[67] The percentage of the original vessels retained through these rebuildings cannot be determined, but some ships were modified extensively and some of the major alterations can be described here.

The *Lancaster,* having been officially extolled for her perfection and copied in the *Trenton,* received the most thoroughgoing refit and alteration of the last years of the wooden steam navy. The result was virtually a new ship.

Boards of survey reports of 1876 and 1878 specified the extent of her delapidation: "large portion of frame bad," "ceiling . . . fore and aft defective; thick strakes defective; forward and center engine keelsons defective." All her masts and spars were rotten and all the "joiner work of cabins, ward room etc. will not answer to be put back again." The estimate for repairing her spars and hulls was $691,390.61. Her original cost–including machinery–had been $670,000.[68]

The completed vessel, however, was not merely a refurbished 1858 *Lancaster.* By recommissioning, in August 1881, she had been out of service since 1875, and the repairs had become simply a starting point. She was given new 60-inch by 36-inch engines and boilers, and a steam capstan and steering gear. Her hull was fitted with bilge keels, 6-inch watertight bulkheads, and a ventilation system based on an arrangement used on the *Richmond.* This was composed of ducts to all parts of the vessel, connected to a large steam-driven blower on the berth deck.

Her bow was reconfigured as the *Trenton*'s, with a ram and running-in bowsprit. Some of the same castings were used for both ships.[69] Her gundeck battery, formerly of twenty-four 9-inch guns, was replaced by eight converted 8-inch rifles, and two additional rifles were on fore and aft spar deck pivot rails.[70]

No statistics have been found on the cost of the new *Lancaster,* but it no doubt exceeded the million-dollar mark. All the modifications listed above and many minor ones were termed "expenditures over and above the estimate per Survey." (The engines and boilers had been on hand, therefore their use could be touted as an economy move.)[71]

Though patterned on the *Trenton,* and boasting an outsized spread-eagle figurehead, the *Lancaster*

The new Lancaster *under construction at Portsmouth, 1881. The cost of her rebuilding far exceeded her original cost. Note the composition ram casting and bilge keels. (Naval Historical Center)*

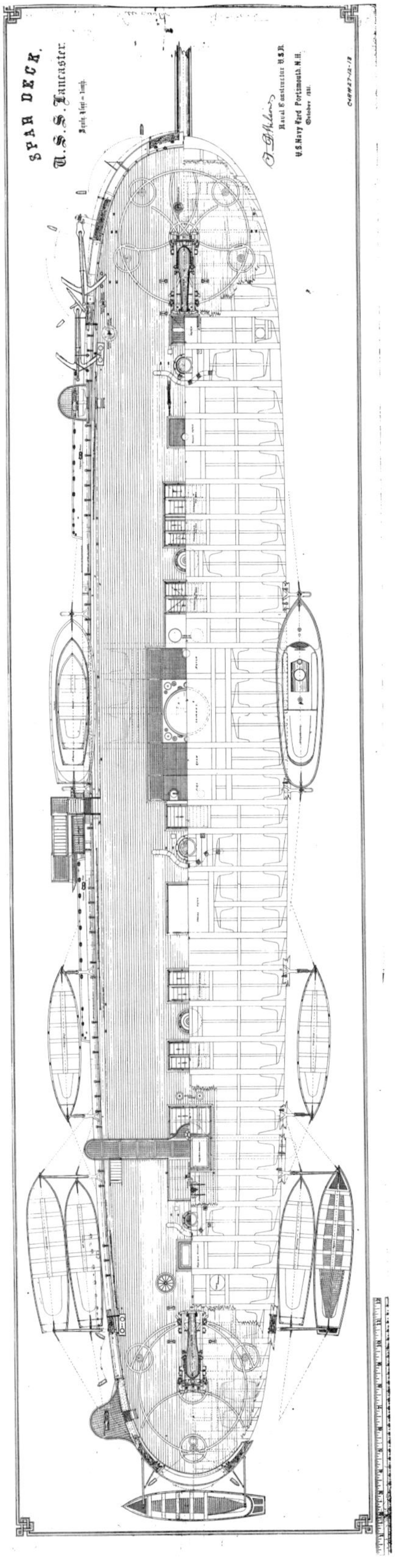
SPAR DECK.
U.S.S. Lancaster.

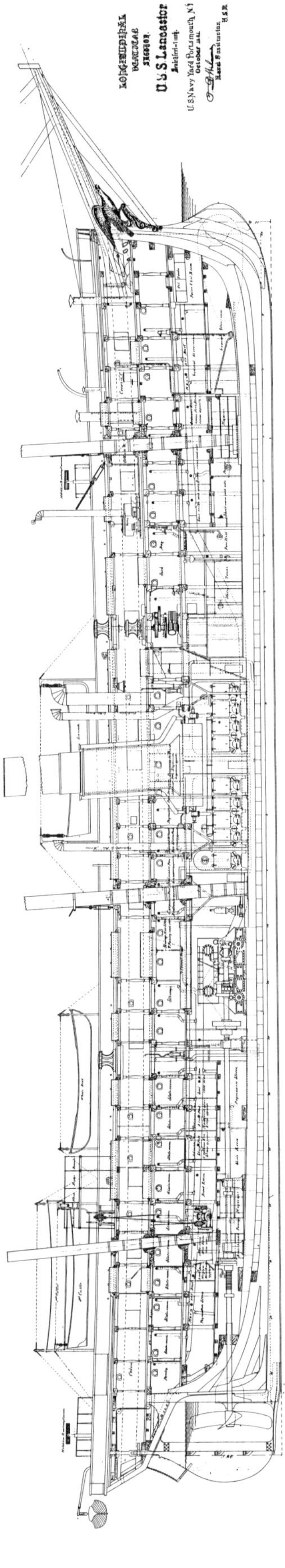
U.S.S. Lancaster
U.S. Navy Yard Portsmouth, N.H.

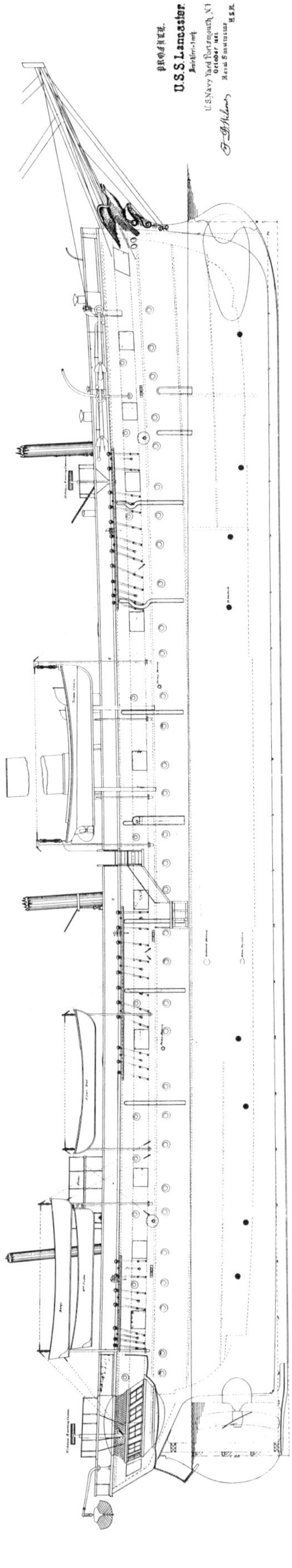
U.S.S. Lancaster
U.S. Navy Yard Portsmouth, N.H.

The Lancaster *Later in Her Career, with Searchlights and a Second Bridge. (National Archives)*

failed to measure up to the older ship. She was disinclined to steer well and lacked weatherliness. Her maximum speed under sail and steam was about 12 knots, and 9 knots was her limit under sail alone.[72]

After the loss of the *Trenton*, she was the most heavily armed vessel in the old fleet. Even then the navy had yet to finish with her. Her battery was removed in 1895 and replaced with ten 5-inch rapid-fire guns and two 5-inch breechloaders. In 1896 launchers for Whitehead self-propelled torpedoes were mounted on her gundeck aft. This advanced armament was probably the ultimate incongruity for a wooden sailing steam warship.[73]

Spar Deck, Inboard, and Outboard Plans of the Rebuilt Lancaster, *1881. She was given steam steering and capstan, with blower ventilation. (NARS 27-12-18, 27-12-20, 27-12-21, National Archives)*

She was placed in a gunnery training role after the Spanish-American War, then was a receiving ship and Public Health Service quarantine vessel. She was broken up in 1933, but her magnificent one-and-a-half-ton eagle figurehead, carved by John Bellamy, survived. It is now on prominent display at the Mariners' Museum at Newport News, Virginia.

Other prewar vessels received significant but much less comprehensive rebuilds in the 1870s and 1880s. The most noticeable changes were the addition of spar decks to the *Hartford, Pensacola,* and *Brooklyn*. The *Pensacola* received the boilers from the *Benicia* in 1878 and thus became the only one of that class to have twin funnels.[74]

The *Hartford* had much attention lavished on her over many decades. Compound engines were installed in the early 1880s, and a ram bow was proposed but not added. In rebuildings of the 1880s

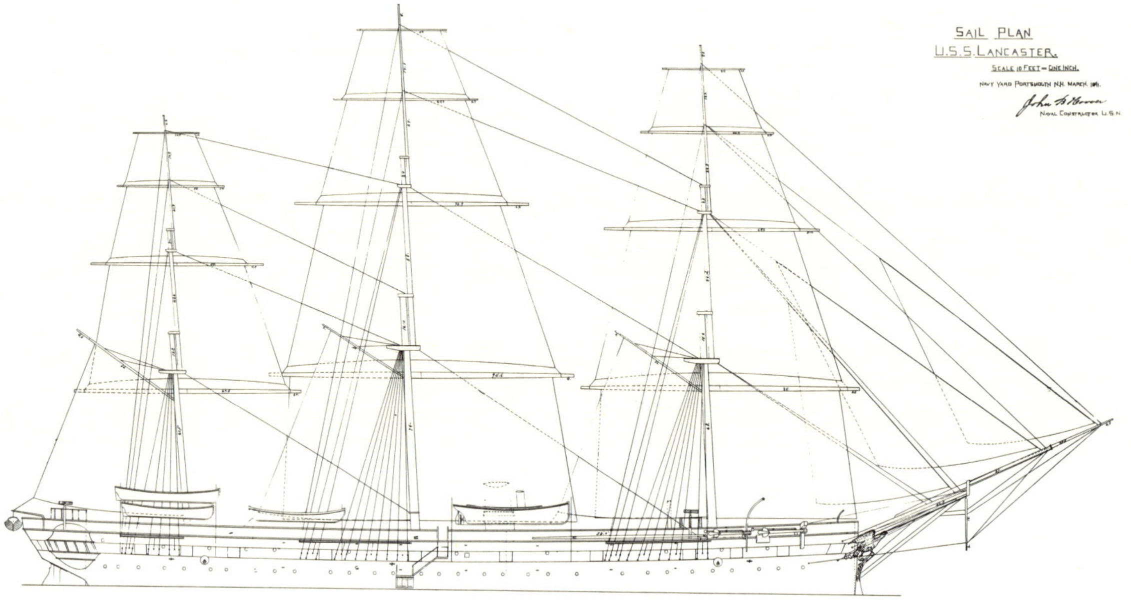

Sail Plan of the Lancaster, *1891. (NARS 27-11-38, National Archives)*

and 1890s she was given a blower ventilation system, electric lights, bilge keels, steam capstan and steering, and thirteen 5-inch rapid-fire guns. She was kept in training roles in the 1890s and was a station ship at Charleston until 1926. From 1945 to November 1956, she was classified as a relic and remained at Norfolk, awaiting appropriations for her restoration. These never materialized. She sank on 20 November 1956 and was broken up. She was the last survivor of the wooden steam era still part of the navy inventory.[75]

Similar updates and alterations were carried out on many of the wooden steamers, with the larger vessels the recipient of more of these improvements. Also typical of the later years were bridges forward of the mainmasts, topped by pilothouses, effectively eliminating any grace the old ships may have retained through the years.[76]

The Pensacola *As She Appeared in 1886. Note the complete spar deck, twin funnels, and forward bridge. (Naval Historical Center)*

APPRAISAL, 1869–1885

An evaluation of U.S. naval ships of the undistinguished era Robert Albion called the "Dark Ages" must take into account both the functional expectations of the navy at the time and comparisons with appropriate vessels of foreign fleets.

First, the American navy was a cruising fleet—an arm of the State Department and essential transportation for the Marines to various minor hot spots around the globe. There was no battle fleet and Congress was far from authorizing one. The monitors were suitable only for coastal and river operations. Only the Spanish-American War would bring the revolution in policy that would bring about an American sea-going battle fleet. The relative inactivity of the period immediately explains the first and most repeated criticism of the navy in this era, that it was twelfth-rate or worse.

To further place the navy's doldrums in perspective, the major powers were facing their own "Dark Ages," particularly in the 1870s. Technological and tactical confusion reigned because of the advent of guns powerful enough to smash the heaviest armor compatible with efficient vessels. This defensive-offensive stalemate left a vacuum quickly filled by exaggerated claims for rams, torpedoes, small gunboats, and amazingly, something the French called "decuirassement"—dearmoring. In this, "freely penetrable" hulls were built that nonetheless would remain, in theory, viable fighting units. While the Americans watched with interest from the sidelines, the major powers were treading gingerly, attempting to avoid massive expenditures on technologies that might prove tangential to those with lasting value. American naval leadership sometimes claimed to be waiting for the Europeans' technological dust to settle and reveal the true direction to follow. Had Congress voted the funds, however, the navy would no doubt have been as deeply in the confusion as the Europeans. (The ship plans of this era include numerous proposals for American "state-of-the-art" armorclads, further revealing the true level of interest in the subject on this side of the Atlantic.)[77]

Specific criticisms of American cruising vessels center around their construction, motive power, and armament. The continued use of wooden hulls, dependence on sail as the primary propulsion, and reliance on antiquated smoothbores by the United States were considered proofs of the navy's tattered, worn-out condition.

In cruising vessels, however, iron hulls were not advantageous because of their quick fouling. This was generally acknowledged and the solution favored was composite construction. A second drawback of iron was its brittleness: when struck by shot, splinters more lethal than wood endangered the personnel. Iron and steel were of course longer lasting and more rigid. Furthermore, watertight subdivisions and double bottoms were only truly effective in rigid hulls.

The relative weights of such arguments in the eyes of contemporaries can be judged not only by the ships of the U.S. Navy but by those of other fleets, in particular those vessels belonging to nations with adequate iron and steel industries. In France the nostalgia for wooden ships resulted in the commissioning of four full-fledged wooden frigates comparable to the *Merrimack* in size in the 1880s, the last in 1886. French cruising corvettes were made of wood until about 1876, when iron-beamed wooden hulls were introduced. The first French steel cruiser was completed in 1885.[78]

In Britain, five iron corvettes were built in the 1870s, with seven of steel, six composite, and twelve of wood. The final turn away from wood construction in British corvettes occurred with the composite *Emerald* class, completed between 1876 and 1878. The Royal Navy's sloops (less than 175 feet) were all of composite construction in the same decade.[79] In comparison, after 1877, the only U.S. naval wooden ships launched were the rebuilt vessels not authorized by Congress.

The continued use of sail on cruising vessels was not just an American idiosyncrasy and was justified in foreign navies in exactly the same ways: the shortage of coaling stations and the need for propulsion should the engines fail on the open sea. If indeed the British and French, both with farflung empires, used the coaling station argument, American opponents of full sail power were left with little arguing ground. British capital ships retained their rigs until 1887, and masted sloops intended for foreign stations were launched as late as 1904. In the French navy, fully rigged gunboats and frigates were common through the 1880s.[80]

In steam technology, the U.S. Navy was comparable to its foreign counterparts. In both French and British navies, compound engines were first seen in 1868 or 1869, compared to the first contract for American compound engines made in 1871 for the *Tennessee*. The American use of steam capstans, steerers, and other auxiliaries was not significantly behind that of other navies. Forced draft was not seen in the Royal Navy until 1882 but had been used intermittently in American vessels since Ericsson's *Princeton*.[81]

The armament of American vessels was their weakest component. Though breechloading had been adapted to the medium Parrott rifles, the 8-inch converted Dahlgren remained a hand-trained muzzleloading weapon, though run out by gearing. European navies had adopted steel breechloaders, though many of these were still trained by hand. Little can be said in favor of these modified Dahlgrens, except that breechloading guns still retained time-consuming elements of the firing process: both types required running out and retraining by hand or gears. (Steam-operated gun training was for the most part limited to capital ships.)

To summarize, it can be said that American naval vessels of the 1870s and 1880s were woefully deficient in one area: firepower. In propulsion and auxiliary machinery they were on a par with cruisers of other nations. In their construction they were deficient in principle, but in practice their wooden structure was well adapted to their role as cruising vessels.

Of course the key problem with all the American cruisers was in the role they were expected to play. It somehow escaped the attention of legislators and other policymakers that these very poorly armed and protected ships were the very vessels that would be called upon to defend the nation in the event of attack by any power—whether militarily backward or advanced. Showing the flag was deemed a peaceful and somewhat symbolic occupation. The contradiction implicit in sending seemingly obsolete vessels to represent the nation's prestige, however, was not sufficient to dislodge policymakers from the economy-minded priorities that prevented the improvement of the situation.

The Venerable Hartford, *with 5-inch Breechloaders and Prominent Pilothouse and Bridge. Around the turn of the century she received compound engines in one of her last rebuilds. She remained afloat until 1957, but ideas of restoring her never came to fruition. She was the last wooden ship of the old steam fleet. (U.S. Naval Institute)*

ON SAMOA

To conclude, we should return to Apia, Samoa, in 1889, and the expected confrontation involving American, British, and German warships. Considering the description of the qualities of the American vis-à-vis foreign cruisers given above, it cannot be said that the American ships would have fared well in any exchange of fire, whether in the rapidity or range of fire, or in the ship's survivability if holed at the waterline. Both the British and German vessels mounted 6-inch rifled breechloaders (four on the British *Calliope* and one on the German *Adler*) as well as smaller breechloaders, while the *Trenton, Nipsic,* and *Vandalia* mounted a total of twelve 8-inch muzzleloading rifles and ten 9-inch smoothbores, plus two 60-pounder Parrott rifled breechloaders. All told, the German and British ships mounted some 36 breechloaders ranging from 4½ inches to 6 inches in bore.

None of the German or British vessels were ironclads. All the vessels were in fact fully rigged iron cruising ships, except the *Calliope,* which was constructed of steel with a steel protective deck over her engines and magazine. Finally, both the American and foreign vessels were powered by compound engines. The *Olga* and *Calliope* were rated at over 13 knots, and the *Eber* and *Adler* were 11-knot gunboats. The American vessels were equal to or faster than the *Eber* and *Adler* but outclassed by the *Olga* and *Calliope.*[82]

The storm that determined the outcome of the clash provided an anticlimactic finale to an entire era of anticlimax. The confrontation passed without embarassing the United States militarily. With two German and two American vessels destroyed, and one vessel of each nation surviving the storm, the episode ended in a disastrous draw. Only the Royal Navy enhanced her status, because of the *Calliope*'s powered escape from the hurricane.

* * *

The era of the sailing steam navy was long past by the storm in Samoa in March 1889, and the process of sweeping away these outdated vessels was expeditious—although some remained in auxiliary roles for decades afterward. By the Spanish-American War, only five remained on active service: the *Alert, Monocacy, Lancaster, Mohican,* and the old *Michigan.* Eight were engaged in various auxiliary and training roles, with the *Hartford* rebuilding at Mare Island. Ten more were listed in the annual report of the secretary of the navy as "unfit for sea service"—ranging from the *Wabash* to the *Iroquois* and *Pensacola.*[83] Although the heyday of such hybrids was over, another seventy years would pass before the disdained species was extinct. When the *Hartford,* dowager aunt of the fleet, dignified despite the ramshackle barn of her deck, sank quietly at her wharf in 1956, she was already an appropriate symbol for an entire era of forgotten ships.

Appendix A

CONSTRUCTION AND FATE OF VESSELS

NAME	HULL/MACHINERY	LAUNCHED	COMMISSIONED	FATE
Demologos (Fulton I)	A. & N. Brown/Robert Fulton, New York	29 Oct 1814	Never	Blew up 4 Jun 1829
Fulton II	New York Navy Yard/West Point Foundry/H. R. Dunham	May 1836	13 Dec 1837	Laid up 1842, burned 9 May 1862
Mississippi	Philadelphia Navy Yard/Merrick & Towne	1841	22 Dec 1841	Burned 15 Mar 1863
Missouri	New York Navy Yard/West Point Foundry	7 Jan 1841	Feb 1842	Burned 23 Aug 1843
Union	Norfolk Navy Yard/Washington Navy Yard	1842	1843	Laid up 1848
Michigan	Stackhouse & Tomlinson Pittsburgh/Erie, PA	5 Dec 1843	9 Aug 1843	Broken up 1949
Water Witch (iron)	Washington Navy Yard/Washington Navy Yard	1844	1844?	Decommissioned 25 April 1851
Allegheny	Stackhouse & Tomlinson Rebuilt 1851, Norfolk	22 Feb 1847	Apr 1847	Sold 15 May 1869
Princeton	Philadelphia Navy Yard/Merrick & Towne	1843	9 Sep 1843	Broken up Oct 1849
Susquehanna	Philadelphia Navy Yard/Murray & Hazlehurst, Baltimore	6 Apr 1850	24 Dec 1850	Decommissioned 14 Jan 1868, sold 27 Sep 1883
Powhatan	Norfolk Navy Yard/A. Mehaffy	14 Feb 1850	3 Sep 1852	Decommissioned 2 Jun 1886, sold 30 Jul 1886
Saranac	Portsmouth Navy Yard/Coney & Co.	14 Nov 1848	12 Oct 1850	Wrecked 16 Jun 1875
San Jacinto	New York Navy Yard/Merrick & Towne	16 Apr 1850	1851	Wrecked 1 Jan 1865
Princeton II	Boston Navy Yard/Merrick & Towne Murray & Hazlehurst rebuilt engines, 1852	29 Oct 1851	18 May 1852	Sold 9 Oct 1866
Water Witch II (wood)	Washington Navy Yard NY/Washington Navy Yard	1852	1852	Captured 3 Jun 1864, destroyed Dec 1865
Merrimack	Boston Navy Yard/R. P. Parrot	15 Jun 1855	20 Feb 1856	Burned/scuttled 1861
Wabash	Philadelphia Navy Yard/Merrick	27 Oct 1855	18 Aug 1856	Sold 15 Nov 1912
Minnesota	Washington Navy Yard/Washington Navy Yard	1 Dec 1855	21 May 1857	Sold Aug 1901
Roanoke	Norfolk Navy Yard/Tredegar	13 Dec 1855	4 May 1857	Converted to ironclad, sold 1883
Colorado	Norfolk Navy Yard/Tredegar	10 Jun 1856	13 Mar 1858	Sold 1885
Niagara	New York Navy Yard/Pease & Murphy	23 Feb 1855	6 Apr 1857	Decommissioned 1865, sold 1885
Brooklyn	J. Westervelt, New York/James Murphy	1858	26 Jan 1859	Decommissioned 14 May 1889, sold 25 Mar 1891
Franklin	Portsmouth Navy Yard/Boston Navy Yard	17 Sep 1864	3 Jun 1867	Sold 26 Oct 1915
Hartford	Boston Navy Yard/H. Loring	22 Nov 1858	27 May 1859	Sank 20 Nov 1956, broken up
Lancaster	Philadelphia Navy Yard/Reanie & Neafie	20 Oct 1858	12 May 1859	Decommissioned 1902, broken up 1933
Richmond	Norfolk Navy Yard/Washington Navy Yard, new engines c. 1866, Washington Navy Yard	26 Jan 1860	Oct 1860	Sold 23 Jul 1919
Pensacola	Pensacola Navy Yard/E. N. Dickerson	15 Aug 1859	5 Dec 1859	Sold 1912
Saginaw	Mare Island Navy Yard/Union Iron Works	3 Mar 1859	5 Jan 1860	Wrecked 29 Oct 1870
Mohican	Portsmouth Navy Yard/Woodruff & Beach	15 Feb 1859	29 Nov 1859	Decommissioned 25 Jun 1872
Iroquois	New York Navy Yard/Fulton Iron Works	12 Apr 1859	24 Nov 1859	Sold 26 Aug 1910
Wyoming	Philadelphia Navy Yard/Merrick	19 Jan 1859	Oct 1859	Sold 9 May 1892
Dacotah	Norfolk Navy Yard/Murray & Hazlehurst	23 Mar 1859	1 May 1860	Sold 30 May 1873
Narragansett	Boston Navy Yard/Boston Locomotive Works	15 Feb 1859	6 Oct 1859	Decommissioned 3 Oct 1883
Seminole	Pensacola Navy Yard/Morgan Iron Works	25 Jun 1859	25 Apr 1860	Sold 20 Jul 1870
Pawnee	Philadelphia Navy Yard/Reanie & Neafie	8 Oct 1859	11 Jun 1860	Sold 3 May 84
Pocahontas	Norfolk Navy Yard/Harrison Loring	Jan 1860	19 Mar 1860	Sold 30 Nov 1865, (*Abby Bacon* to 1868)

formerly (*Dispatch*)	Medford, Mass. as *City of Boston*	1852	Purchased 20 Mar 1855	Decommissioned 2 Jan 1859
Aroostook	N. W. Thompson/Novelty Iron Works		20 Feb 1862	Sold Hong Kong Oct 1869
Cayuga	Gildersleeve & Son/Woodruff & Beach	21 Oct 1861	21 Feb 1862	Sold 29 Oct 1865
Chippewa	Webb & Bell/Morgan Iron Works	14 Sep 1861	13 Dec 1861	Sold 30 Nov 1865
Chocura	Curtis & Tilden/Harrison Loring	5 Oct 1861	15 Feb 1862	Sold 13 Jul 1867
Huron	Paul Curtis/Harrison Loring	21 Sep 1861	8 Jan 1862	Sold 1869
Itaska	Hillman & Streaker/I. P. Morris	1 Oct 1861	28 Nov 1861	Sold 30 Nov 1865, *Aurora*, 1866
Kanawha	Goodspeed/Pacific Iron Works	21 Oct 1861	21 Jan 1862	Sold 13 Jun 1866
Katahdin	Larrabee & Allen/Morgan Iron Works	12 Oct 1861	17 Feb 1862	30 Nov 1865, sold *Juno*, 1866
Kennebec	G. W. Lawrence/Novelty Iron Works	5 Oct 1861	8 Feb 1862	Sold 30 Nov 1865
Kineo	J. W. Dyer/Morgan Iron Works	9 Oct 1861	8 Feb 1862	Decommissioned 9 May 1865, sold 1866
Marblehead	G. W. Jackman/Highland Iron Works	16 Oct 1861	8 Mar 1862	Sold 30 Sep 1868
Ottawa	Westervelt/Novelty Iron Works	1861	7 Oct 1861	Sold 25 Oct 1865
Owasco	Maxson & Fish/Novelty Iron Works	6 Oct 1861	23 Jan 1862	Sold 25 Oct 1867
Pembina	Thomas Stack/Novelty Iron Works	1861	16 Oct 1861	Decommissioned 22 Sep 1865
Penobscot	C. P. Carter/Allain	19 Nov 1861	16 Jan 1862	Sold 19 Oct 1869
Pinola	J. J. Abrahams/Charles Reeder	1861	29 Jan 1862	Sold 1865
Sagamore	A. & G. T. Sampson/Atlantic Works	1 Sep 1861	7 Dec 1861	Sold 13 Jun 1865
Sciota	Jacob Bireley/I. P. Morris	15 Oct 1861	15 Dec 1861	Mined 14 Apr 1865, sold 25 Oct 1865
Seneca	Jeremiah Simonson/Novelty Iron Works	27 Aug 1861	14 Oct 1861	Sold 10 Sep 1868
Tahoma	W. & A. Thatcher/Reany & Son, Archbold	2 Oct 1861	20 Dec 1861	Sold 1867
Unadilla	John Englis/Novelty Iron Works	17 Aug 1861	30 Sep 1861	Sold 9 Nov 1869, Hong Kong
Winona	C. & R. Poillon/Allain	14 Sep 1861	11 Dec 1861	Sold 30 Nov 1865
Wissahickon	John Lynn/Merrick	2 Oct 1861	25 Nov 1861	Sold 25 Oct 1865, *Adele*, 1866
Cimarron (orig. *Cimerone*)	D. S. Merchon, Jr./Merchon	16 Mar 1862	5 Jul 1862	Sold 1865
Conemaugh	Portsmouth Navy Yard/Novelty Iron Works	1 May 1862	16 Jul 1862	Sold 1 Oct 1867
Genesee	Boston Navy Yard/Neptune Iron Works	2 Apr 62	3 Jul 62	Sold 3 Oct 1867
Mahaska	Portsmouth Navy Yard/Morgan Iron Works	10 Dec 1861	5 May 1862	Sold 20 Nov 1868
Maratanza	Boston Navy Yard/Harrison Loring	26 Nov 1861	12 Apr 1862	Sold 1868
Miami	Philadelphia Navy Yard/Merrick	16 Nov 1861	29 Jan 1862	Sold 1865
Octorara	New York Navy Yard/Neptune Iron Works	7 Dec 1861	28 Feb 1862	Sold 9 Nov 1866
Paul Jones	J. J. Abrahams/Reany, Son, & Archbold	30 Jan 1862	9 Jun 1862	Sold 13 Jul 1867
Port Royal	T. Stack/T. Stack	17 Jan 1862	26 Apr 1862	Sold 3 Oct 1866
Sebago	Portsmouth Navy Yard/Novelty Iron Works	30 Nov 1861	26 Mar 1862	Sold 19 Jan 1867
Sonoma	Portsmouth Navy Yard/Novelty Iron Works	15 Apr 1862	8 Jul 1862	Sold 1867
Tioga	Boston Navy Yard/Morgan Iron Works	18 Apr 1862	30 Jun 1862	Sold 15 Oct 1867
Juniata	Philadelphia Navy Yard/Pusey, Jones	20 Mar 1862	4 Dec 1862	Decommissioned 1889, sold 25 Mar 91
Adirondack	New York Navy Yard/Novelty Iron Works	22 Feb 1862	23 Aug 1862	Wrecked 23 Aug 1862
Housatonic	Boston Navy Yard/Jabez Coney	20 Nov 1861	29 Aug 1862	Sunk 17 Feb 1864, raised & sold 1891
Ossipee	Portsmouth Navy Yard/Reliance Machine Co.	16 Nov 1861	6 Nov 1862	Decommissioned 1889, sold 25 Mar 91
Kearsarge	Portsmouth Navy Yard/Woodruff & Beach	11 Sep 1861	24 Jan 1862	Sunk 2 Feb 1894

NAME	HULL/MACHINERY	LAUNCHED	COMMISSIONED	FATE
Oneida	New York Navy Yard/J. Murphy	10 Jun 1861	28 Feb 1862	Sunk 24 Jan 1870
Tuscarora	Philadelphia Navy Yard/Merrick	24 Aug 1861	5 Dec 1861	Sold 20 Nov 1883
Wachusett	Boston Navy Yard/Morgan Iron Works	10 Oct 1861	3 Mar 1862	Decommissioned 1885, sold 30 Jul 1887
Canandaigua	Boston Navy Yard/Atlantic Works	28 Mar 1862	1 Aug 1862	Decommissioned 8 Nov 1875, broken up 1884
Lackawanna	New York Navy Yard/Allaire Works	9 Aug 62	8 Jan 1863	Decommissioned 7 Apr 1885, sold 30 Jul 1887
Monongahela	Philadelphia Navy Yard/Merrick	10 Jul 1862	15 Jan 1863	Fire 17 Mar 1908, Guantanamo
Sacramento	Portsmouth Navy Yard/Taunton Locomotive Works	28 Apr 1862	7 Jan 1863	Aground 19 Jun 1867
Shenandoah	Philadelphia Navy Yard/Merrick	8 Dec 1862	20 June 1863	Decommissioned 23 Oct 1886, sold 30 Jul 1886
Ticonderoga	New York Navy Yard/Allaire Works	17 Oct 1862	12 May 1863	Decommissioned 10 Sep 1882, sold 5 Aug 1887
Kansas	Philadelphia Navy Yard/Captured, English manufacturer not known	29 Sep 1863	21 Dec 1863	Decommissioned 10 Aug 1875, sold 27 Sep 1883
Maumee	New York Navy Yard/Stover Machine Co.	2 Jul 1863	29 Sep 1864	Decommissioned 17 Jan 1865, sold 15 Dec 1869 (Hong Kong)
Nipsic (I)	Portsmouth Navy Yard/Woodruff & Beach	15 Jun 1863	2 Sep 1863	Decommissioned 1873, broken up
Nyack	New York Navy Yard/S. Brooklyn Engine Works	6 Oct 1863	28 Sep 1864	Decommissioned 15 Mar 1871, sold 30 Nov 1883
Pequot	Boston Navy Yard/Woodruff & Beach	4 Jun 1863	15 Jan 1864	Decommissioned 3 Jun 1865, sold 1869
Saco	Boston Navy Yard/Corliss St. Engine Co.	28 Aug 1863	11 Jul 1864	Decommissioned 13 Jul 1876, sold 20 Nov 1883
Shawmut	Portsmouth Navy Yard/Corliss St. Engine Co.	17 Apr 1863	1 Nov 1864	Laid up, sold 27 Sep 1877
Yantic	Philadelphia Navy Yard/Merrick	19 Mar 1864	12 Aug 1864	Sunk 22 Oct 1929
Agawam	G. W. Lawrence/Portland Locomotive Works	21 Apr 1863	9 Mar 1864	Sold 1867
Algonquin	New York Navy Yard/Providence St. Engine Co.	21 Dec 1863	——	Sold 21 Oct 1869
Ascutney	G. W. Jackson/Morgan Iron Works	4 Apr 1863	28 Jul 1864	Decommissioned 22 Sep 1864, sold 28 Oct 1868
Chenango	J. Simonson/Morgan Iron Works	19 Mar 1863	29 Feb 1864	Decommissioned 1 July 1865, sold 28 Oct 1868
Chicopee	Paul Curtis/Neptune Iron Works	4 Mar 1863	7 May 1864	Decommissioned Dec 1866, sold 8 Oct 1867
Eutaw	J. Abrahams/Vulcan Iron Works	Feb 1863	2 Jul 1863	Sold 1867
Iosco	Larrabee & Allen/Globe Works	20 Mar 1863	26 Apr 1864	Decommissioned 28 Jul 1865
Lenapee	E. Lupton/Washington Iron Works	28 May 1863	30 Dec 1864	Sold 1868
Mackinaw	New York Navy Yard/Allaire	22 Apr 1863	23 Apr 1864	Decommissioned 4 May 1867, sold 3 Oct 1867
Massasoit	Curtis & Tilden/Globe Works	8 Mar 1863	8 Mar 1864	Decommissioned 27 Jun 1865, sold 15 Oct 1867
Mattabessett	A. & G. Sampson/Allaire	1863	7 Apr 1864	Decommissioned 31 May 1865, sold 15 Oct 1865
Mendota	F. Z. Tucker/S. Brooklyn Engine Works	13 Jan 1863	2 May 1864	Decommissioned 12 May 1865, sold 7 Dec 1867
Metacomet	T. Stack/S. Brooklyn Engine Works	7 Mar 1863	4 Jan 1864	Decommissioned 18 Aug 1865, sold 28 Oct 1865
Mingoe	D. S. Merchon/Pusey Jones Co.	6 Aug 1863	29 Jul 1864	Sold 3 Oct 1867
Osceola	Curtis & Tilden/Atlantic Works	29 May 1863	10 Feb 1864	Sold 1867
Otsego	Westervelt/Fulton Iron Works	31 Mar 1863	Apr 1864	Sunk 9 Dec 1864
Pawtuxet	Portsmouth Navy Yard/Providence St. Engine Co.	19 Mar 1863	28 Aug 1864	Sold 1867
Peoria	New York Navy Yard/Etna Iron Works	29 Oct 1863	26 Dec 1866	Sold 1868
Pontiac	Hillman & Streaker/Neafie, Levy, & Co.	1863	7 Jul 1864	Sold 15 Oct 1867 (J. Roach)
Pontoosuc	G. W. Lawrence/Portland Locomotive Works	1863	10 May 1864	Decommissioned 5 Jul 1865, sold 3 Oct 1866

Sassacus	Portsmouth Navy Yard/Atlantic Works	23 Dec 1862	5 Oct 1863	Sold 1868
Shamrock	New York Navy Yard/Poole & Hunt	17 Mar 1863	13 Jun 1864	Sold 1868
Tacony	Philadelphia Navy Yard/Morris, Towne Co.	7 May 1863	12 Feb 1864	Decommissioned 7 Oct 1867, sold 26 Aug 1868
Tallahoma	New York Navy Yard/Stover Machine Co.	28 Nov 1863	1867	Sold 1868
Tallapoosa	Boston Navy Yard/Neptune Iron Works	17 Feb 1863	13 Sep 1864	Sold 1892
Wateree	Reany, Son & Archbold/Reany, Son & Archbold	12 Aug 1863	20 Jan 1864	Wrecked 13 Aug 1868
Winooski	Boston Navy Yard/Providence St. Engine Co.	30 Jul 1863	27 Jun 1865	Sold 25 Aug 1868
Wyalusing	C. H. & W. H. Cramp/Pusey, Jones	12 May 1863	2 Aug 1864	Decommissioned 10 Jun 1865, sold 15 Oct 1867
Ashuelot	D. McKay/D. McKay	12 Jul 1865	4 Apr 1866	Wrecked 18 Feb 1883
Mohongo	Z. Secor/Fulton Foundry	9 Jul 1864	23 May 1865	Decommissioned 29 May 1869, sold 17 Nov 1870
Monocacy	A. & W. Denmead/A. & W. Denmead	14 Dec 1864	1866	Sold 22 Jun 1903
Muscoota	Continental Iron Works/Continental Iron Works (T. S. Rowland)	1864	5 Jan 1865	Sold 1869
Shamokin	Reany, Son & Archbold/Reany, Son & Archbold	1864	17 Oct 1865	Sold 1869
Suwanee	Reany, Son & Archbold/Reany, Son & Archbold	13 Mar 1864	23 Jan 1865	Wrecked 9 Jul 1868 British Columbia
Winnepec	Harrison Loring/Harrison Loring	20 Aug 1864	1865	Sold 1869
Ammonoosuc (Iowa)	Boston Navy Yard/Morgan Iron Works	21 Jul 1864		Trials 1868, Laid up, sold 27 Sep 1883
Neshaminy (Arizona) (Nevada)	Philadelphia Navy Yard/J. Roach	5 Oct 1865		Sold 1874 (J. Roach)
Wampanoag (Florida)	New York Navy Yard/Novelty Iron Works	15 Dec 1864	17 Sep 1867	Decommissioned 5 May 1868, sold 1885
Madawasca (Tennessee)	New York Navy Yard/Allaire; 2nd engines, Roach	8 Jul 1865	—	Sold 1886
Pompanoosuc (Connecticut)	Boston Navy Yard/Corliss	Never launched		Broken up 1883
Chattanooga	Cramp/Merrick	13 Aug 1864	16 May 1866	Decommissioned 3 Sep 1866, sunk Dec 1871, sold Jan 1872
Idaho	Henry Steers/Morgan Iron Works	8 Oct 1864	2 Apr 1866	Decommissioned 31 Dec 1873, sold 1874
Antietam	Philadelphia Navy Yard/Morris & Towne	13 Nov 1875	1876	Sold 8 Aug 1888
Guerriere	Boston Navy Yard/Globe Works	9 Sep 1865	21 May 1867	Decommissioned 22 Mar 1872, sold 12 Dec 1872
Illinois	Portsmouth Navy Yard/Corliss	Never launched		Broken up 1872
Java	New York Navy Yard/J. Roach	Never launched		Broken up 1884
Kewaydin (Pennsylvania)	Boston Navy Yard/Harrison Loring	Never launched		Broken up 1884
Minnetonka (California)	Portsmouth Navy Yard/Woodruff & Beach	3 Jul 1867	12 Dec 1870	Decommissioned 3 Jul 1873, sold May 1876
Ontario (New York)	New York Navy Yard/J. Roach	Never launched		Sold 1888
Piscataqua (Delaware)	Portsmouth Navy Yard/Woodruff & Beach	11 Jun 1866	21 Oct 1867	Sank 1876

NAME	HULL/MACHINERY	LAUNCHED	COMMISSIONED	FATE
Contoocook (Albany)	Portsmouth Navy Yard/Providence St. Engine Co.	3 Dec 1864	14 Mar 1868	Decommissioned 7 Jan 1870, sold 12 Dec 1870
Manitou (Worcester)	Boston Navy Yard/Woodruff & Beach	25 Aug 1866	27 Feb 1871	Laid up 1879, sold 1883
Moshulu (Severn)	New York Navy Yard/S. Brooklyn Engine Works	22 Dec 1867	27 Aug 1869	Decommissioned 31 Dec 1871, sold 2 Mar 1877
Pushmataha (Cambridge) (Congress)	Philadelphia Navy Yard/Morris & Towne	17 Jul 1868	4 Mar 1870	Decommissioned 26 Jul 1876, sold 20 Sep 1883
Algoma (Benicia)	Portsmouth Navy Yard/Boston Navy Yard	18 Aug 1868	1 Dec 1869	Decommissioned 29 Nov 1875, sold 3 May 1884
Alaska	Boston Navy Yard/Boston Navy Yard	31 Oct 1868	8 Dec 1869	Decommissioned 13 Feb 1883, sold 20 Nov 1883
Omaha (Astoria)	Philadelphia Navy Yard/New York Navy Yard	10 Jun 1869	12 Sep 1872	Decommissioned 1891, sold 17 Apr 1815
Plymouth (Kenosha)	New York Navy Yard/New York Navy Yard	8 Aug 1868	20 Jan 1869	Decommissioned 17 May 1879
Galena (II)	Norfolk Navy Yard/Norfolk Navy Yard	13 Mar 1879	26 Aug 1880	Sold 9 May 1892
Mohican (II)	Mare Island Navy Yard/Mare Island Navy Yard	27 Dec 1883	25 May 1885	Sold 1922
Nantasket	Boston Navy Yard/Portsmouth Navy Yard	15 Aug 1867	22 Nov 1869	Decommissioned 8 Jun 1872 (?)
Quinnebaug	New York Navy Yard/Jackson & Watkins (London)	31 Mar 1866	19 Jul 1867	Decommissioned 29 Nov 1870, broken up 1871
Resaca	Portsmouth Navy Yard/Washington Navy Yard	18 Nov 1865	9 Jul 1866	Decommissioned 1872, sold 1873, wrecked 4 Apr 1875, Ventura
Swatara	Philadelphia Navy Yard/Washington Navy Yard	23 May 1865	15 Nov 1865	Decommissioned 20 Dec 1871, broken up
Marion	Portsmouth Navy Yard/Boston Navy Yard	22 Dec 1873	12 Jan 1876	Decommissioned 11 Dec 1897, sold 24 Jul 1907
Quinnebaug (II)	Philadelphia Navy Yard/New York Navy Yard	28 Sep 1875	28 Sep 1875	Sold 1891
Swatara (II)	New York Navy Yard/New York Navy Yard	17 Sep 1873	11 May 1874	Decommissioned 7 Feb 1891, sold 2 Nov 1896
Vandalia	Boston Navy Yard/Boston Navy Yard	23 Oct 1874	10 Jan 1876	Wrecked 16 Mar 1889
Alert	J. Roach/J. Roach	1 Sep 1874		Sold 1922
Huron	J. Roach/J. Roach	23 Sep 1874	15 Nov 1875	Wrecked 24 Nov 1877
Ranger	Harlan & Hollingsworth/J. Roach	3 Dec 1876	27 Nov 1876	Decommissioned 16 Aug 1908, scrapped 7 Mar 1958
Adams	D. MacKay/Atlantic Works	24 Oct 1874	21 Jul 1876	Decommissioned 5 Aug 1919, sold 5 Aug 1920
Alliance	Norfolk Navy Yard/Quintard	8 Mar 1875	18 Jan 1877	Decommissioned 7 Jul 1911, sold 13 Nov 1911
Enterprise	J. W. Griffiths/Woodruff Iron Co.	13 Jun 1874	16 Mar 1877	Sold 1909
Nipsic (II)	Washington Navy Yard/W. Wright	11 Jun 1878	11 Oct 1879	Sold 1913
Essex	D. McKay/Atlantic Works	26 Oct 1874	3 Oct 1876	Decommissioned May 1889, sold 23 Dec 1930
Trenton	New York Navy Yard/Morgan Iron Works	1 Jan 1876	14 Feb 1877	Wrecked 16 Mar 1889

Appendix B

DIMENSIONS, HORSEPOWER, AND ARMAMENT OF VESSELS

Note: Most of the maximum speed statistics would be more accurately called "maximum cruising" speeds and were obtained in operational or nearly operational conditions. There were no systematic, uniform, controlled-condition maximum speed trials in the USN. An asterisk (*) indicates a figure from congressional document H. Doc. 65 (33-1), 1854; or H. Doc. 8 (38-2), 1865. Lengths given are between perpendiculars except where otherwise indicated. N = nominal horsepower. M = measurement tonnage.

NAME	DISPLACEMENT (TONS)	DIMENSIONS (LENGTH × BREADTH × DEPTH OF HOLD)	INDICATED HORSEPOWER	KNOTS	ORIGINAL ARMAMENT
Demologos (Fulton I)	1,450	153′2″ × 56′ × 20′	120?	5.5	26 32-pdr
Fulton II	1,011	181′6″ × 34′10″ × 12′2″	700+	14	4 32-pdr
Mississippi	3,220	220′ × 39′ × 23′6″	685	8.7	2 10-in, 8 8-in
Missouri	3,220	220′ × 39′ × 23′6″	515 N	8.9	2 10-in, 8 8-in
Michigan	604	162′6″ × 27′ × 12′	110 N	*12	1 8-in
Princeton	1,046	156′ × 30′6″ × 21′6″	330+	8.7	2 12-in, 10 42-pdr
Union	956	185′6″ × 33′ × 16′9″	87 N	7.25	4 8-in
Water Witch	190	100′ × 21′ × 10′	32 N	6.5	
Water Witch II (1846)	255	130′ × 21′ × 10′	54 N	8.7	1 8-in, 2 32-pdr
Allegheny	1,020	185′ × 33′ × 13′6″	243 N	7	4 8-in
Powhatan	3,600	249′9″ × 44′ × 26′6″	*1,500	*11	3 10-in, 6 8-in
Susquehanna	3,550	250′ × 44′ × 26′6″	*1,450	*11	3 10-in, 6 8-in
Saranac	2,200	210′ × 37′ × 23′6″	*700	*9.2	2 8-in pivot, 4 8-in broadside
San Jacinto (1854—new engines)	2,200	210′ × 37′ × 23′6″	782 *550	9.9 *8.5	2 8-in pivot, 4 8-in broadside
Princeton II	1,385	176′7″ × 32′ × 21′9″	480+	*8.7	4 8-in, 6 32-pdr
Water Witch II (1852 rebuild)	450	150′ × 22′ × 11′6″	195	9.5	1 30-pdr (1861)
Merrimack	4,635	256′10½″ × 50′2″ × 26′2½″	972	8.8	2 10-in, 14 8-in, 24 9-in
Wabash	4,774	262′4″ × 50′2″ × 26′2″	1,038	9.1	2 10-in, 28 9-in, 14 8-in (1861)
Minnesota	4,833	264′8½″ × 50′2″ × 26′2″	995	8.9	1 10-in, 28 9-in, 14 8-in

NAME	DISPLACEMENT (TONS)	DIMENSIONS (LENGTH × BREADTH × DEPTH OF HOLD)	INDICATED HORSEPOWER	KNOTS	ORIGINAL ARMAMENT
Roanoke	4,772	263′8¼″ × 51′4″ × 26′2″	996	8.8	1 10-in, 28 9-in, 14 8-in (1861)
Colorado	4,772	263′8¾″ × 51′4″ × 26′2″	996	8.8	2 10-in, 28 9-in, 14 8-in
Niagara	5,540	328′10½″ × 53′8″ × 23′ (load line)	1,995	10.9	12 11-in
Franklin	5,298	265′ × 53′ × 27′3″	1,900+	10.25	1 11-in, 34 9-in, 4 100-pdr
Hartford	2,550	225′ × 44′ × 23′3″	696	9.5	20 9-in
Richmond	2,604	225′ × 42′ × 20′8″	*450	7.5	16 9-in
Brooklyn	2,532	223′ × 43′ × 22′8″	*705	*9.2	16 9-in, 2 10-in
Pensacola	3,000	230′8″ × 44′6″ × ?	——	8.8	20 9-in, 1 11-in, 1 100-pdr (1863)
Lancaster	3,290	235′8″ × 46′ × 22′3″	*810	*9.5	24 9-in, 2 11-in
Wyoming	1,457	198′6″ × 32′2″ × 14′7″	*717	11.2	2 11-in, 4 32-pdr
Tuscarora	1,457	198′6″ × 32′2″ × 14′7″	*717	11.2	2 11-in, 6 32-pdr
Mohican	1,461	198′8″ × 32′2″ × 16′	*822	*11.8	2 11-in, 4 32-pdr
Kearsarge	1,461	198′8″ × 32′2″ × 16′	*822	*11.2	2 11-in, 4 32-pdr
Iroquois	1,488	198′10½″ × 33′10″ × 16′	*813	*11.7	2 11-in, 4 32-pdr
Oneida	1,488	198′10½″ × 33′10″ × 16′	*813	*11.7	2 11-in, 4 32-pdr, 1 30-pdr
Wachusett	1,488	198′10½″ × 33′10″ × 16′	*717	*11.2	2 11-in, 4 32-pdr, 2 30-pdr
Dacotah	1,369	198′5″ × 32′9″ × 15′8″	*873	*12	2 11-in, 4 32-pdr
Seminole	1,230	188′ × 30′6″ × 14′	——	9	1 11-in, 1 30-pdr, 4 32-pdr
Narragansett	1,043	188′6″ × 30′6″ × 14	——	7.75	1 11-in, 4 32-pdr
Pawnee	1,533	221′6″ × 47′ × ——	——	8	4 11-in
Saginaw	508	155′ × 26′ × 11′6″	——	9	1 50-pdr Dahl., 1 32-pdr, 2 24-pdr
Pocahontas	694	154′ × 30′4″ (extreme) × 13′6″	60 N	8	1 10-in Dahl., 4 32-pdr
Aroostook	691	158′4″ × 28′ × 12′	400	10	1 11-in, 2 24-pdr, 1 20-pdr
Cayuga	691	158′4″ × 28′ × 12′	400	10	1 11-in, 2 24-pdr, 1 20-pdr
Chippewa	691	158′4″ × 28′ × 12′	400	10	1 11-in, 2 24-pdr, 1 20-pdr
Chocura	691	158′4″ × 28′ × 12′	400	10	1 11-in, 2 24-pdr, 1 20-pdr
Huron	691	158′4″ × 28′ × 12′	*400	*10	1 11-in, 2 24-pdr, 1 20-pdr
Itasca	691	158′4″ × 28′ × 12′	*400	*10	1 11-in, 2 24-pdr, 1 20-pdr
Kanawha	691	156′4″ × 28′ × 12′	*400	*10	1 11-in, 2 24-pdr, 1 20-pdr
Katahdin	691	156′4″ × 28′ × 12′	*400	*10	1 11-in, 2 24-pdr, 1 20-pdr
Kennebec	691	156′4″ × 28′ × 12′	*400	*10	1 11-in, 2 24-pdr, 1 20-pdr
Kineo	691	156′4″ × 28′ × 12′	*400	*10	1 11-in, 2 24-pdr, 1 20-pdr
Marblehead	691	156′4″ × 28′ × 12′	*400	*10	1 11-in, 2 24-pdr, 1 20-pdr

NAME	DISPLACEMENT (TONS)	DIMENSIONS (LENGTH × BREADTH × DEPTH OF HOLD)	INDICATED HORSEPOWER	KNOTS	ORIGINAL ARMAMENT
Ottawa	691	156′4″ × 28′ × 12′	——	——	1 11-in, 2 24-pdr, 1 20-pdr
Owasco	691	156′4″ × 28′ × 12′	*400	*10	1 11-in, 2 24-pdr, 1 20-pdr
Pembina	691	156′4″ × 28′ × 12′	——	——	1 11-in, 2 24-pdr, 1 20-pdr
Penobscot	691	156′4″ × 28′ × 12′	*400	*10	1 11-in, 2 24-pdr, 1 20-pdr
Pinola	691	156′4″ × 28′ × 12′	*400	*10	1 11-in, 2 24-pdr, 1 20-pdr
Sagamore	691	156′4″ × 28′ × 12′	*400	*10	1 11-in, 2 24-pdr, 1 20-pdr
Sciota	691	156′4″ × 28′ × 12′	*400	*10	1 20-pdr, 2 24-pdr
Seneca	691	156′4″ × 28′ × 12′	——	11.5	1 20-pdr, 2 24-pdr
Tahoma	691	156′4″ × 28′ × 12′	*400	*10	1 10-in, 2 20-pdr, 2 24-pdr
Unadilla	691	156′4″ × 28′ × 12′	——	——	1 11-in, 2 24-pdr, 1 20-pdr
Winona	691	156′4″ × 28′ × 12′	*400	*10	1 11-in, 2 24-pdr, 1 20-pdr
Wissahickon	691	156′4″ × 28′ × 12′	*400	*10	1 11-in, 2 24-pdr, 1 20-pdr
Ossipee	1,934	205′ × 38′ × 16′9″	*1,304	*12	1 100-pdr, 1 11-in, 6 32-pdr, 3 30-pdr
Adirondack	1,934	205′ × 38′ × 16′9″	1,304	11.6	2 11-in, 4 32-pdr, 2 24-pdr
Housatonic	1,934	205′ × 38′ × 16′9″	1,304	11.6	1 100-pdr, 3 30-pdr, 1 11-in, 2 32-pdr
Juniata	1,934	205′ × 38′ × 16′9″	1,304	11.6	1 100-pdr, 1 11-in, 4 30-pdr
Sacramento	2,100	229′ × 38′ × 17′	*1,304	12.5	1 150-pdr, 2 11-in, 1 30-pdr
Monongahela	2,078	225′ × 37′8″ × 16′10″	*1,304	*12	1 150-pdr, 2 11-in, 2 24-pdr
Shenandoah	2,030	225′ × 37′6″ × 17′1″	*1,304	*12	1 150-pdr, 2 11-in, 1 30-pdr
Canandaigua	2,030	226′ × 38′4″ × 17′2″	*1,304	*12	1 150-pdr, 2 11-in, 3 20-pdr
Lackawanna	2,526	232′ × 38′ × 17′7″	*1,304	*12	1 150-pdr, 4 9-in, 1 50-pdr, 2 11-in
Ticonderoga	2,526	232′ × 38′ × 17′7″	*1,304	*12	1 150-pdr, 6 9-in, 1 50-pdr
Kansas	836	179′6″ × 30′ × 12′	——	11.6	1 100-pdr, 2 9-in, 2 20-pdr
Saco	836	179′6″ × 30′ × 12′	——	9.5	1 100-pdr, 6 32-pdr, 1 30-pdr
Maumee	——	171′6″ × 29′ × 12′	——	11.5	1 100-pdr, 2 32-pdr, 1 30-pdr
Pequot	——	171′6″ × 29′ × 12′	——	11	1 150-pdr, 6 32-pdr, 1 30-pdr
Yantic	836	179′6″ × 30′ × 12′	——	10	1 100-pdr, 2 9-in, 1 30-pdr
Nipsic	836	179′6″ × 30′ × 12′	*670	12	1 150-pdr, 2 9-in, 1 30-pdr

NAME	DISPLACEMENT (TONS)	DIMENSIONS (LENGTH × BREADTH × DEPTH OF HOLD)	INDICATED HORSEPOWER	KNOTS	ORIGINAL ARMAMENT
Shawmut	836	179′6″ × 30′ × 12′	*670	*12.5	1 100-pdr, 2 9-in, 1 30-pdr
Nyack	836	179′6″ × 30′ × 12′	*670	*12.5	1 100-pdr, 2 9-in, 1 30-pdr
Miami	730	208′6″ × 33′2″ × 11′	—	8	1 80-pdr, 1 9-in, 4 24-pdr
Octorara	981	205′ × 34′5″ × 12′	*590	*11.3	1 80-pdr, 1 9-in, 4 24-pdr
Port Royal	1,163	207′ × 34′4″ × 11′6″	*630	*11	1 100-pdr, 1 10-in, 6 24-pdr
Paul Jones	1,210	216′10″ × 35′4″ × 11′8″	*630	*11	1 100-pdr, 2 9-in, 1 11-in, 2 50-pdr
Maratanza	—	207′ × 32′6″ × 11′8″	*590	*10	1 100-pdr, 1 9-in, 4 24-pdr
Sonoma	1,105	232′ (overall) × 34′8″ × 12′	*630	*11.3	1 100-pdr, 1 11-in, 6 24-pdr
Conemaugh	1,105	232′ × 34′8″ × 12′	*630	*11.3	1 100-pdr, 1 11-in, 6 24-pdr
Tioga	1,120	209′ × 34′11″ × 12′6″	*630	*10.9	1 100-pdr, 1 10-in, 6 24-pdr
Genesee	1,120	209′ × 34′11″ × 12′6″	*630	*10.9	1 100-pdr, 1 10-in, 6 24-pdr
Sebago	1,070	228′2″ × 33′2″ × 11′4″	*590	*11	1 100-pdr, 1 9-in, 4 24-pdr
Mahaska	1,070	228′2″ × 33′2″ × 11′4″	*590	*11	1 100-pdr, 1 9-in, 4 24-pdr
Cimarron	993	217′6″ × 35″ × 12′4″	*630	*11.6	1 100-pdr, 1 9-in, 6 24-pdr
Ascutney	1,173	236′ × 35′ × 12′	*1,468	*13.7	—
Agawam	1,173	236′ × 35′ × 12′	*1,468	*13.7	2 100-pdr, 4 9-in
Chenango	1,173	236′ × 35′ × 12′	*1,468	*13.7	2 100-pdr, 4 9-in
Chicopee	1,173	236′ × 35′ × 12′	*1,468	*13.7	2 100-pdr, 4 9-in
Eutaw	1,173	236′ × 35′ × 12′	*1,468	*13.7	2 100-pdr, 4 9-in
Iosco	1,173	236′ × 35′ × 12′	*1,468	*13.7	2 100-pdr, 4 9-in
Lenapee	1,173	236′ × 35′ × 12′	*1,468	*13.7	2 100-pdr, 4 9-in
Mackinaw	1,173	236′ × 35′ × 12′	1,272	12.4	2 100-pdr, 4 9-in
Massasoit	1,173	236′ × 35′ × 12′	*1,468	*13.7	2 100-pdr, 4 9-in
Mattebessett	1,173	236′ × 35′ × 12′	*1,468	*13.7	2 100-pdr, 4 9-in
Mendota	1,173	236′ × 35′ × 12′	*1,468	*13.7	2 100-pdr, 4 9-in
Metacomet	1,173	236′ × 35′ × 12′	*1,468	*13.7	2 100-pdr, 4 9-in
Mingoe	1,173	236′ × 35′ × 12′	*1,468	*13.7	2 100-pdr, 4 9-in
Osceola	1,173	236′ × 35′ × 12′	—	15	2 100-pdr, 4 9-in
Otsego	1,173	236′ × 35′ × 12′	*1,468	*13.7	2 100-pdr, 4 9-in
Pawtuxet	1,173	236′ × 35′ × 12′	*1,468	*13.7	2 100-pdr, 4 9-in
Peoria	1,173	236′ × 35′ × 12′	*1,468	*13.7	2 100-pdr, 4 9-in
Pontiac	1,173	236′ × 35′ × 12′	*1,468	*13.7	2 100-pdr, 4 9-in
Pontoosuc	1,173	236′ × 35′ × 12′	*1,468	*13.7	2 100-pdr, 4 9-in
Sassacus	1,173	236′ × 35′ × 12′	—	14	2 100-pdr, 4 9-in
Shamrock	1,173	236′ × 35′ × 12′	*1,468	*13.7	2 100-pdr, 4 9-in
Tacony	1,173	236′ × 35′ × 12′	*1,468	*13.7	2 100-pdr, 4 9-in
Tallahoma	1,173	236′ × 35′ × 12′	*1,468	*13.7	2 100-pdr, 4 9-in
Tallapoosa	1,173	236′ × 35′ × 12′	*1,468	*13.7	2 100-pdr, 4 9-in
Wyalusing	1,173	236′ × 35′ × 12′	—	14	2 100-pdr, 4 9-in

NAME	DISPLACEMENT (TONS)	DIMENSIONS (LENGTH × BREADTH × DEPTH OF HOLD)	INDICATED HORSEPOWER	KNOTS	ORIGINAL ARMAMENT
Winooski	1,173	236′ × 35′ × 12′	——	11.7	——
Algonquin	1,173	236′ × 35′ × 12′	——	9.8	——
Wateree	——	236′ × 35′ × 12′	*1,468	*13.7	2 100-pdr, 4 9-in
Mohongo	1,370	255′ × 25′ × ——	850	12	2 100-pdr, 4 9-in
Ashuelot	1,173	255′ × 25′ × ——	850	12	2 60-pdr, 4 8-in
Monocacy	1,173	255′ × 25′ × ——	850	12	2 60-pdr, 4 8-in
Muscoota	1,173	255′ × 25′ × ——	850	12	——
Shamokin	1,173	255′ × 25′ × ——	850	12	——
Suwanee	1,173	255′ × 25′ × ——	850	12	2 100-pdr, 4 9-in
Winnepec	1,173	255′ × 25′ × ——	850	12	——
Swatara	1,113	216′ × 30′ × 13′3″	——	12	1 60-pdr?, 6 32-pdr
Quinnebaug	1,113	216′ × 30′ × 13′3″	273(N?)	9	1 60-pdr?, 6 32-pdr
Resaca	1,129	216′ × 30′ × 13′3″	——	12	1 100-pdr, 6 8-in
Nantasket	1,129	216′ × 30′ × 13′8″	——	10	1 60-pdr, 6 32-in
Algoma (Benicia)	2,394	250′6″ × 38′ × 19′2″	1,165	12	1 60-pdr, 1 11-in, 10 9-in
Alaska	2,394	250′6″ × 38′ × 19′2″	1,165	12	1 60-pdr, 1 11-in, 10 9-in
Omaha (Astoria)	2,394	250′6″ × 38′ × 19′2″	1,165	12	1 60-pdr, 1 11-in, 10 9-in
Plymouth (Kenosha)	2,394	250′6″ × 38′ × 19′2″	1,165	12	1 60-pdr, 6 8-in, 1 11-in
Contoocook (Albany)	3,003	290′ × 41′ × 20′8″	1,300	12	8 9-in, 1 60-pdr
Worcester (Manitou)	3,003	290′ × 41′ × 20′8″	1,300	12	1 60-pdr, 14 9-in
Severn (Moshulu)	3,003	290′ × 41′ × 20′8″	1,300	12	1 60-pdr, 14 9-in
Pushmataha (Congress) (Cambridge)	3,003	290′ × 41′ × 20′8″	1,300	12	2 60-pdr, 14 9-in
Antietam	——	312′6″ × 46′ × 21′2″	——	——	——
Guerriere	4,034	312′6″ × 46′ × 21′2″	1,145	10.2	2 100-pdr, 16 9-in, 1 60-pdr
California (Minnetonka)	3,954	312′6″ × 46′ × 21′2″	1,300	11	2 100-pdr, 18 9-in, 1 60-pdr
Delaware (Piscataqua)	3,954	312′6″ × 46′ × 21′2″	1,300	11	2 100-pdr, 16 9-in, 1 60-pdr
New York (Ontario)	——	315′ × 46′ × ——	——	——	——
Ammonoosuc (Iowa)	3,850	335′ × 44′6″ × 22′7″	——	17	3 60-pdr, 10 9-in
Neshaminy (Arizona) (Nevada)	3,850	335′ × 44′6″ × 22′7″			3 60-pdr, 10 9-in
Wampanoag (Florida)	4,215	335′ × 44′ × 23′	4,100	17.7	3 60-pdr, 10 9-in
Pompanoosuc (Connecticut)	4,446	335′ × 48′ × ——			
Madawasca	4,105	335′ × 44′ × 23′	2,142+	15.5	3 60-pdr, 10 9-in
(Tennessee)	4,840	335′ × 44′ × 23′	1,800	10	2 11-in, 16 9-in, 2 100-pdr, 1 60-pdr

NAME	DISPLACEMENT (TONS)	DIMENSIONS (LENGTH × BREADTH × DEPTH OF HOLD)	INDICATED HORSEPOWER	KNOTS	ORIGINAL ARMAMENT
Idaho	3,241	298′ × 44′6″ × 24′	645	8.2	——
Chattanooga	3,043	315′ × 46′6″ × ——	1,736	13.3	——
Galena (II)	1,900	216′ × 36′ × 19′	1,172	12	1 11-in, 6 9-in
Marion	1,900	216′ × 36′ × 19′	1,172	12	1 11-in, 6 9-in
Mohican (II)	1,900	216′ × 36′ × 19′	1,172	12	1 11-in, 6 9-in
Quinnebaug (II)	1,900	216′ × 36′ × 19′	1,172	12	1 11-in, 6 9-in
Swatara (II)	1,900	216′ × 36′ × 19′	1,172	12	1 11-in, 6 9-in
Vandalia	2,110	216′ × 39′ × 20′	1,172	12	1 11-in, 6 9-in
Enterprise	1,375	185′ × 35′ × 16′2″	930	11.5	1 11-in, 4 9-in
Adams	1,375	185′ × 35′ × 16′2″	930	11.5	1 11-in, 4 9-in
Alliance	1,375	185′ × 35′ × 16′2″	930	11.5	1 11-in, 4 9-in
Nipsic (II)	1,375	185′ × 35′ × 16′2″	930	11.5	1 11-in, 4 9-in
Essex	1,375	185′ × 35′ × 16′2″	930	11.5	1 11-in, 4 9-in
Alert	1,020	175′ × 32′ × 15′1″	656	10.5	1 11-in, 2 9-in, 1 60-pdr
Huron	1,020	175′ × 32′ × 15′1″	656	10.5	1 11-in, 2 9-in, 1 60-pdr
Ranger	1,020	175′ × 32′ × 15′1″	656	10.5	1 11-in, 2 9-in, 1 60-pdr
Trenton	3,814	253′ × 48′ × 23′4″	3,100	13	11 11-in

Notes

Works frequently cited have been abbreviated as follows:

ANC	*Army and Navy Chronicle*
ANJ	*Army and Navy Journal*
BSE	Bureau of Steam Engineering
Conway's	*Conway's All the World's Fighting Ships, 1860–1905*
DANFS	*Dictionary of American Naval Fighting Ships*
JFI	*Journal of the Franklin Institute*
NARS	National Archives and Records Service
ORN	*Official Records of the Union and Confederate Navies in the War of the Rebellion*
SecNav Reports	*Annual Reports of the Secretary of the Navy*

1. FROM HARBOR BATTERIES TO PADDLE-WHEEL FRIGATES, 1815–1840

1. Carter, *Blaze of Glory,* 115, 234.
2. Hutcheon, *Robert Fulton,* 132–33.
3. Chapelle, *Fulton's "Steam Battery,"* 151; Hutcheon, *Robert Fulton,* 134; Marestier, *Memoir on Steamboats,* 23, 24, 36.
4. Chapelle, *Fulton's "Steam Battery,"* 151–52.
5. Ibid.
6. Ibid., 152–54.
7. Ibid.
8. Bennett, *Steam Navy,* 8; Chapelle, *Fulton's "Steam Battery,"* 159–61.
9. Chapelle, *Fulton's "Steam Battery,"* 159–61.
10. Ibid., 149.
11. Bennett, *Steam Navy,* 12.
12. Hutcheon, *Robert Fulton,* 124–28.
13. Chapelle, *Fulton's "Steam Battery,"* 144–45.
14. Hutcheon, *Robert Fulton,* 139–40.
15. Ridgely-Nevitt, *American Steamships,* 54; Bennett, *Steam Navy,* 16; Marestier, *Memoir on Steamboats,* 27, 82.
16. Hutcheon, *Robert Fulton,* 138.
17. *American State Papers: Naval Affairs* 1:584, 685, 803, 805; John Rodgers to Mahlon Dickerson, 22 June 1835, Letters of Commissioners to Secretary of the Navy, RG 45, Entry 213.
18. *American State Papers: Naval Affairs* 1:685.
19. Chapelle, *American Sailing Ships,* 128–29; Ridgely-Nevitt, *American Steamships,* 52.
20. *American State Papers: Naval Affairs* 4:8.
21. Samuel Humphreys to John Rodgers, 17 December 1831, Letters from Naval Constructors, RG 45/224.
22. J. Rodgers to I. Hull, 3 March 1833, AC, box 1, Letters from Commissioners and Secretary of the Navy, RG 45/212; Secretary of the Navy to Navy Commissioners, 16 Jan 1833, AC, box 3, RG 45/212.
23. Mahlon Dickerson to John Rodgers, 26 June 1835, *Construction of the Steam Frigate Fulton,* 25th Cong., 2d sess., letter 4, H. Exec. Doc. 433.
24. Commissioners to Humphreys, Hartt, and Lenthall, undated memorandum attached to report by Humphreys et al. to Commissioners, 14 July 1835, RG 45/224.
25. S. Humphreys, S. Hartt, and J. Lenthall, Report, 14 July 1835, RG 45/224.
26. Report on Steam Battery, Commissioners to Dickerson, 29 July 1835, Letters to Secretary of the Navy from Naval Commissioners, RG 45/213.
27. 29 August 1835, Navy Commissioners' Journal, RG 45/209.
28. Commissioners to I. Chauncey, 27 November 1835; Commissioners to Ridgely and William and Governeur Kemble, 22 February 1836, RG 45/212 EM, Box 9.
29. Bennett, *Steam Navy,* 19, 40.
30. S. Hartt to M. C. Perry, 28 May 1836, Commandants' Letters, New York Navy Yard, RG 45/220.
31. M. C. Perry to Commissioners, 16 January 1837, letter 99, 25th Cong., 2d sess., H. Doc. 433; Ridgely to Commissioners, January 1837, letter 106, ibid.
32. S. Humphreys to Commissioners, 20 January 1837, letter 102, H. Doc. 433.
33. M. C. Perry to Commissioners, 6 September 1837, letter 137, H. Doc. 433; Board Memorandum to

Humphreys et al., on Report by Humphreys, 14 July 1835, RG 45/224; *ANC,* 21 June 1838.
34. Stuart, *Naval and Mail Steamers,* 13–18.
35. B. F. Isherwood, "Trial Trip of the Steamship Fulton," *JFI* 23, no. 1 (January 1852): 123; Stuart, *Naval and Mail Steamers,* 18.
36. M. C. Perry to Commissioners, 4 October 1837, letter 148, H. Doc. 433.
37. Report by Humphreys et al., 14 July 1835, RG 45/224.
38. *ANC,* 5 April 1838, 221–22.
39. Bearss, *Boston Historical Park,* 2:839; M. C. Perry to M. Dickerson, 17 February 1838, letter 196, H. Doc. 433; *ANC,* 5 July 1838, 10.
40. *ANC,* 5 April 1838, 222.
41. Bennett, *Steam Navy,* 28–29.
42. M. C. Perry to Commissioners, 16 December 1837, letter 166, H. Doc. 433; ibid., 15 January 1838, letter 184.
43. Bearss, *Boston Historical Park,* 2:839; *ANC,* 28 June 1838, 413.
44. *ANC,* 21 June 1838, 394.
45. *ANC,* 5 July 1838, 10.
46. *ANC,* 19 July 1838, 37; W. F. Lynch to M. C. Perry, 15 February 1838, H. Doc. 433.
47. *ANC,* 19 July 1838, 37.
48. M. C. Perry to Commissioners, 16 January 1837, letter 99, H. Doc. 433; ibid., 15 March 1838, letter 202; M. C. Perry to Commissioners, 30 July 1842, RG 45 Old Subject File (OSF), AD, box 42; Report to Secretary of the Navy William A. Graham from Shubrick, 1 March 1853, Records of the Bureau of Construction and Repair, RG 19, Entry 49, Letters to the Secretary of the Navy.
49. "Statement of Gradual Increase of the Navy, on Steam Vessels," *Naval Magazine* 1, no. 6 (1836): 20.
50. *Conway's,* 43, 285.
51. "Steam Navy of the United States," H. Doc. 65 (33–1), 65–69.
52. Commissioners to S. Humphreys, 9 April 1839, Letters to Naval Constructors and Steam Engineers, 1838–42, RG 45/218; Commissioners to H. Paulding, 28 May 1839, RG 45/213.
53. *ANC,* 26 March 1842, 158.
54. *ANC,* 19 March 1842, 140.
55. Notes on U.S. Naval and Mail Steamers, Letters from Constructors, RG 45/224; Ridgely-Nevitt, *American Steamships,* 106.
56. Notes on U.S. Naval and Mail Steamers, Letters from Constructors, RG 45/224.
57. Board to Lenthall, 26 February 1840, RG 45/218; NARS Plan 108-7-14K.
58. Stuart, *Naval and Mail Steamers,* 37.
59. Ibid., 40.
60. *ANC,* 2 September 1841, 278–79, 30 December 1841, 410; B. F. Isherwood, "United States Steam Frigate Mississippi," *JFI* 24 (December 1852): 385.
61. Ibid.
62. S. Humphreys to Morris, 15 January 1841, RG 45/224; *ANC,* 26 March 1842, 158.
63. Isherwood, "Mississippi," 385.
64. Stuart, *Naval and Mail Steamers,* 40.
65. William C. Redfield, "Steam Navigation," *JFI* 60, no. 6 (June 1846): 369; Stuart, *Naval and Mail Steamers,* 38.
66. Van Riemsdijk and Brown, *Steam Power,* 83.
67. NARS Plans, BSE.
68. Ridgely-Nevitt, *American Steamships,* 100, 129.
69. C. Copeland to Morris, 14 September 1839, RG 45/224.
70. Stuart, *Naval and Mail Steamers,* 41.
71. *ANC,* 5 February 1842, 44; 26 March 1842; C. Copeland to L. Warrington, 19 March, 4 March 1842, RG 45/224; Stuart, *Naval and Mail Steamers,* 41–42.
72. *DANFS* 4:390.
73. A. Upshur to B. Kennon, 10 July 1843, letters to Chiefs of Bureaus, RG 45/M480.
74. *ANC,* 2 September 1841, 278–79; 5 February 1842, 44.
75. *ANC,* 12 February 1842, 57; Stuart, *Naval and Mail Steamers,* 39.
76. Morison, *"Old Bruin,"* 343.
77. Ibid., 411.
78. *SecNav Reports,* 1842, 535.
79. Stuart, *Naval and Mail Steamers,* 164–66.
80. Report of Wm. Sewell, 15 September 1845, Reports of Engineers RG 45/279; *U.S. Nautical Magazine and Naval Journal,* 5 (October 1856–March 1857): 157; C. H. Haswell to Morris, N. D., RG 45/224; *ORN,* series no. 2, 1:146.
81. Bennett, *Steam Navy,* 387.

2. EXPERIMENTS IN CONSTRUCTION AND PROPULSION, 1841–1846

1. Chapelle, *American Sailing Navy,* 426–57.
2. *Conway's,* 43.
3. *SecNav Reports,* December 1841, 350.
4. C. Copeland to L. Warrington, 2 February 1842, 1 May 1842, RG 45/224; Commissioners to Hartt, 19 February 1842, 12 May 1842, RG 45/218; S. Humphreys to L. Warrington, 6 September 1841, RG 45/224; L. Warrington to S. Humphreys, 10, 25 September 1841, RG 45/218; Proposals for Engines, 1 June 1842, RG 45 OSF, box 169, box EE; NARS Plan 107-13-12H.
5. *SecNav Reports,* 1842, 536.
6. Chapelle, *American Sailing Navy,* 458, 553–54; Report of Survey of *Southampton,* 14 August 1852, RG 19/233.
7. Chapelle, *American Sailing Navy,* 457.
8. L. Warrington to S. Humphreys, 10 September 1841, RG 45/218.
9. C. Copeland to L. Warrington, 23 February 1842, RG 45/224; Musham, "Early Great Lakes Steamboats," 56.
10. Spencer, *USS Michigan,* 7.
11. Commissioners to S. Humphreys, S. Hartt, C. Copeland, 17 February 1842, RG 45/218.
12. Ridgely-Nevitt, *American Steamships,* 281–82.
13. Spencer, *USS Michigan,* 7–8.
14. Spencer, *USS Michigan,* 9; Musham, "Early Great Lakes Steamboats," 141; Rodgers, "Iron Sentinel," 34.
15. L. Warrington to S. Hartt, 25 March 1842, RG 45 OSF, AD box 42; NARS Plans 79-7-15B, 79-7-15C.
16. White, "USS Michigan Renamed Wolverine," 46; Rodgers, "Iron Sentinel," 33.
17. Spencer, *USS Michigan,* 9.

18. White, "USS Michigan Renamed Wolverine," 46; Musham, "Early Great Lakes Steamboats," 141; S. Hartt to L. Warrington, 25 March 1842, RG 45 OSF, AD box 42; Rodgers, "Iron Sentinel," 41.
19. B. F. Isherwood, "Notes on the U.S. Steamship "Michigan," *JFI* 21 (April 1851): 218; Stuart, *Naval and Mail Steamers,* 26–28; Spencer, *USS Michigan,* 11.
20. *U.S. Nautical Magazine* 1 (July 1845): 324; *ORN,* series no. 2, 1:143–44.
21. Isherwood, "Notes," 217–18; Stuart, *Naval and Mail Steamers,* 217–18.
22. Spencer, *USS Michigan,* 18; Musham, "Early Great Lakes Steamers," 142.
23. Stuart, *Naval and Mail Steamers,* 28; White, "USS Michigan Renamed Wolverine," 47.
24. Rodgers, "Iron Sentinel," 143.
25. Spencer, *USS Michigan,* 26–27.
26. Robert H. Thurston, *History of the Steam Engine,* 293–96; Ridgely-Nevitt, *American Steamships,* 83–86; Commissioners to Foster Rhodes, N.D., RG 45/218; Commissioners to C. Copeland, 1 February 1841, RG 45/218.
27. *DANFS,* 5:383; Baxter, *The Introduction of the Ironclad Warship,* 13.
28. Stuart, *Naval and Mail Steamers,* 44–47; Bennett, *Steam Navy,* 63–66.
29. Bennett, *Steam Navy,* 64.
30. B. F. Isherwood, "The U.S. Steamship Princeton," *JFI* 25 (June 1853): 380–83.
31. Church, *John Ericsson,* 1:121–22; NARS Plans 103-14-10F, 40-6-4A, 40-6-4B, 40-6-4E.
32. Stuart, *Naval and Mail Steamers,* 43–44.
33. Bennett, *Steam Navy,* 68.
34. Ibid.
35. R. Stockton to Secretary of the Navy, 2 October 1843, Captain's Letters, RG 45/M125.
36. F. Engle, Report on Sailing Qualities, December 1845, RG 45/277.
37. Isherwood, "U.S. Steamship Princeton," 101–7.
38. B. F. Isherwood, "U.S. Screw Steamship Princeton," *JFI* 26 (July 1853): 43–45.
39. J. Faron Report, 24 February 1846, Reports of Engineers of Vessels, 1844–49, RG 45/279.
40. *U.S. Nautical Magazine* 1 (1 March 1845): 59.
41. Stuart, *Naval and Mail Steamers,* 49–50; B. F. Isherwood, "The United States Steam Frigate Mississippi," *JFI* 24 (December 1852): 388.
42. Isherwood, "U.S. Screw Steamship Princeton" *JFI* 26 (July 1853): 49–50.
43. Church, *Ericsson:* 1:137.
44. Bennett, *Steam Navy,* 71–72.
45. F. Engle Report, December 1845, RG 45/277.
46. Bennett, *Steam Navy,* 74.
47. *Conway's,* 44.
48. Clark G. Reynolds, "Hunter's Horizontal Wheels," *American Neptune* 24 (January 1964): 10.
49. *SecNav Reports,* December 1841, 350.
50. Reynolds, "Hunter's Horizontal Wheels," 10; Stuart, *Naval and Mail Steamers,* 22–23; Bennett, *Steam Navy,* 49–50.
51. NARS Plans 41-4-1C, 41-4-1CE.
52. W. W. Hunter to D. Henshaw, 25 November 1843, *SecNav Reports,* 1843, 562–64.
53. Stuart, *Naval and Mail Steamers,* 24–25.
54. *SecNav Reports,* 1843, 551–63.
55. Stuart, *Naval and Mail Steamers,* 24–25; B. F. Isherwood, "U.S. Steamship Princeton," *JFI* 25 (August 1853): 101–2.
56. G. Bancroft to C. Morris, 30 April 1845, Letters from Secretary of the Navy to Bureau Chiefs, RG 45/M480; C. Haswell to Morris, 13 January 1845, RG 45/224.
57. Information on Steam Navy of the United States, 33d Cong. 1st Sess., H. Doc. 65, 30 ff.
58. Stuart, *Naval and Mail Steamers,* 25.
59. Stuart, *Naval and Mail Steamers,* 52.
60. C. K. Stribling, E. W. Carpenter, John Faron, and William Williamson to G. Bancroft, 27 May 1845, RG 45/OSF, AD, box 42.
61. Stuart, *Naval and Mail Steamers,* 52.
62. Plans in Lenthall Collection, Franklin Institute, Philadelphia; Ridgely-Nevitt, *American Steamships,* 189; Report by John Faron, 9 October 1845, RG 45/279.
63. Stuart, *Naval and Mail Steamers,* 52–54; NARS Plan 108-11-8.
64. Reynolds, "Hunter's Horizontal Wheels," 9–10.
65. Stuart, *Naval and Mail Steamers,* 23, 59.
66. Bennett, *Steam Navy,* 53.
67. Stuart, *Naval and Mail Steamers,* 61; NARS Plan 107-14-12C.
68. Information on Steam Navy of the United States, 33d Cong., 1st sess., H. Exec. Doc. 65, 7; Bennett, *Steam Navy,* Appendix B.
69. Stuart, *Naval and Mail Steamers,* 25, 61–66; Information Respecting Navy Steamers Built since 1835, 32d Cong., 2d sess., H. Doc. 63, 7–8.
70. Reynolds, "Hunter's Horizontal Wheels," 21.
71. Stuart, *Naval and Mail Steamers,* 62; B. F. Isherwood, "Notes on the U.S. Steamship Michigan," *JFI* 21 (April 1851): 219.
72. Bennett, *Steam Navy,* 54; Reynolds, "Hunter's Horizontal Wheels," 22.
73. Bennett, *Steam Navy,* 57.
74. "United States Steamers," *JFI* 27 (February 1854): 188.
75. Ibid., 191.
76. A. P. Upshur to W. W. Hunter, 7 July 1843, *SecNav Reports,* 1843, 556.
77. C. Copeland to Foster Rhodes, 28 October 1841, RG 45/218; ibid., Commissioners to C. Copeland, 13 May 1841; Report from C. Haswell, C. Copeland, J. Faron, and G. Hebard, February 1846, RG 45/224.
78. Reports from Engineers, RG 45/279; Haswell et al., Report, 1846, RG 45/224.
79. Haswell et al., Report, 1846, RG 45/224.
80. Ibid.
81. C. Haswell to Bancroft, 6 February 1845, 3 October 1844, RG 45/224; Pursell, *Early Stationary Steam Engines,* 120–24.
82. C. Haswell et al., Report, 1846, RG 45/224.
83. *SecNav Reports,* 1845, 649.
84. Albion, *Makers of Naval Policy,* 191.

3. CONSERVATIVE EXPANSION, 1847–1853

1. Morison, *"Old Bruin,"* 188.
2. Ibid., 20; Bennett, *Steam Navy,* 93.
3. "Steam Navy of the United States," 33d Cong., 1st sess., H. Doc. 65, 113 ff.
4. Ibid.
5. Rodger, "Design of the Inconstant," 16.

6. "Steam Navy of the United States," H. Doc. 65, 113 ff.
7. Ibid.; Haswell et al., Report, February 1846, RG 45/224; *JFI* 4 (August 1841): 120.
8. "Steam Navy of the United States," H. Doc. 65, 113 ff.
9. *Conway's,* 41–43.
10. B. F. Isherwood, "Notes on the United States Steamship Powhatan," *JFI* 25 (February 1853): 131; Isherwood, "Remarks on the U.S. Steamship Susquehanna," *JFI* 24 (October 1852): 252; Ridgely-Nevitt, *American Steamships,* 116, 150.
11. Charles H. Haswell, "Models for Steamships—A Comparison of the Performance of the U.S. Steamships Susquehanna and Powhatan," *JFI* 25 (March 1853): 203; Isherwood, "Notes on the Powhatan," 130.
12. Stuart, *Naval and Mail Steamers,* 169–72.
13. Ibid., 83, 88–90.
14. Isherwood, "Notes on the Powhatan," 131; Isherwood, "Performance of the U.S. Steam Frigate Powhatan," *JFI* 30 (August 1855): 185.
15. Stuart, *Naval and Mail Steamers,* 88; *ORN,* series 2, 1:183, 217; Reports of North Atlantic Blockading Squadron, November 1864, RG 45 OSF, AD box 52.
16. Morison, *"Old Bruin,"* 343, 411.
17. "Naval Steamers," *JFI* 27 (February 1854): 204; "Comparison of the Performance of the U.S. Steamers Mississippi, Susquehanna and Powhatan," *JFI* 30 (August 1855): 121.
18. "Naval Steamers," *JFI* 27 (February 1854): 204.
19. Bennett, *Steam Navy,* 105, 109.
20. Isherwood, "Remarks on the Susquehanna," 252–55; *ORN,* series 2, 1:217.
21. Haswell, "Models for Steamships," 203; Isherwood, "Notes on the Powhatan," 153–55; Bennett, *Steam Navy,* 109.
22. A. T. Pearson to I. Toucey, 19 February 1858, RG 45/M125, reel 359.
23. *U.S. Nautical Magazine and Naval Journal,* vol. 6, 472.
24. Bennett, *Steam Navy,* 109; L. M. Goldsborough to Fox, 3, 5 June 1862; W. M. Thompson and R. Warmaugh, *Correspondence of Gustavus Vasa Fox,* 1:279, 285.
25. 20 January, 28 July 1870, Letters to Commandant, Philadelphia Navy Yard, RG 19/54.
26. NARS Plans, 141-14-8A, 141-14-8B, 141-14-8C, 141-14-8D, 141-14-8E, 141-14-8F, (Screw Sloop *Susquehanna,* 1870).
27. Stuart, *Naval and Mail Steamers,* 74–75.
28. Ibid., 75–76; Bennett, *Steam Navy,* 109–10.
29. B. F. Isherwood, "The U.S. Steamship Saranac," *JFI* 25 (May 1853): 316; B. F. Isherwood, "Notes on the U.S. Steamship Saranac," *JFI* 25 (April 1853): 264.
30. Josiah Tatnall to W. Ballard, 14 April 1850, RG 45/M125, reel 347.
31. Josiah Tatnall to W. A. Grantham, 9 December 1850, RG 45/M125, reel 347.
32. N. Scott to Frailey, 20 May 1867, RG 45/M125, reel 373.
33. "Naval Steamers," *JFI* 27 (February 1854): 191; Stuart, *Naval and Mail Steamers,* 80–81; NARS Plan 107-12-12D.
34. C. Haswell to Board, 23 July 1849, RG 45/224; Ridgely-Nevitt, *American Steamships,* 90–94; NARS Plan 38-2-8A (*Massachusetts*).
35. C. Haswell to Skinner, 33d Congress, 1st sess., H. Doc. 65, 143; Stuart, *Naval and Mail Steamers,* 81.
36. Bennett, *Steam Navy,* 114–19.
37. Stuart, *Naval and Mail Steamers,* 80–81; B. F. Isherwood, "The Trial Trip of the U.S. Steamship San Jacinto," *JFI* 22 (November 1851): 341.
38. "Naval Steamers," *JFI* 27 (February 1854): 190; Stuart, *Naval and Mail Steamers,* 81; C. Haswell to Skinner, 22 April 1850, RG 45/224; Bennett, *Steam Navy,* 113.
39. Isherwood, "Trial of San Jacinto," 341–43; "Naval Steamers," *JFI* 27 (February 1854): 192.
40. Isherwood, "Trial of San Jacinto," 341–43; NARS BSE Plan.
41. Stuart, *Naval and Mail Steamers,* 80; *ORN,* series 2, 1:200.
42. Isherwood, "Trial of San Jacinto," 343–45.
43. B. F. Isherwood, "Trial Trip of the United States Screw Steamer San Jacinto with New Machinery," *JFI* 28 (July 1854): 129.
44. Ibid.
45. Ibid.; NARS BSE Plans, *San Jacinto.*
46. NARS Plan 79-5-6; Isherwood, "Trial of San Jacinto with New Machinery," 129.
47. Isherwood, "Trial of San Jacinto with New Machinery," 131.
48. H. H. Bell to G. B. Fox, 19 December 1861, in Thompson and Warmaugh, *Fox Correspondence,* 1:412–13.
49. B. F. Isherwood to Shubrick, 8 September 1852, RG 45/OSF, AD, box 47; Isherwood to Skinner, 22 September 1851, 33d Cong., 1st sess., H. Doc. 65.
50. Chapelle, *American Sailing Navy,* 466–68.
51. Stuart, *Naval and Mail Steamers,* 109.
52. C. Stuart to C. Skinner, 3 June 1851, 33d Cong., 1st sess., H. Doc. 65, 54-5.
53. Chapelle, *American Sailing Navy,* 440–41; Lambert, *Battleships in Transition,* 15.
54. Stuart, *Naval and Mail Steamers,* 111; B. F. Isherwood, "The U.S. Steamship of War Princeton," *JFI* 27 (May 1854): 339.
55. Stuart, *Naval and Mail Steamers,* 111; NARS Plan 14-11-15.
56. W. H. Shook, "Notes on the Application of Lamb and Sumner Boilers to the U.S. Steamer Vixen," *JFI* 28 (September 1854): 257; 33d Cong., 1st sess., H. Doc. 65, 58–60.
57. Morison, *"Old Bruin,"* 414; Wallach, *American Squadron to the China Seas,* 5.
58. Daniel B. Martin, H. Hunt, C. Copeland to J. C. Dobbin, 19 November 1853, in "Report on United States Steamers," *JFI* 27 (February 1854): 190–93.
59. B. F. Isherwood, "U.S. Screw Steamship Princeton," *JFI* 25 (June 1853): 102–6.
60. Bennett, *Steam Navy,* 74.
61. Stuart, *Naval and Mail Steamers,* 104–5; B. F. Isherwood, "The United States Steamer Water Witch," *JFI* 25 (March 1853): 179–80.
62. Stuart, *Naval and Mail Steamers,* 105–6.
63. Isherwood, "Water Witch," 179–85.
64. Bennett, *Steam Navy,* 91; *Civil War Naval Chronology,* 6:323.

65. Stuart, *Naval and Mail Steamers,* 91; W. Shubrick to W. A. Graham, 11 March 1852, Letters Rec'd by Secretary of the Navy, RG 19/49.
66. Stuart, *Naval and Mail Steamers,* 91; Isherwood, *Engineering Precedents,* 477.
67. 33d Cong., 1st sess., H. Doc. 65, 12; Bennett, *Steam Navy,* 29–30.
68. Bennett, *Steam Navy,* 30.
69. C. Morris to H. Paulding, 21 April 1840, RG 45/213.
70. C. Haswell to G. Bancroft, 22 July 1845, RG 45/225.
71. C. Skinner to W. A. Graham, 16 April 1851, RG 19/49; W. Shubrick to W. A. Graham, 18 September 1852.
72. W. Shubrick to W. A. Graham, 2 April 1852, RG 19/49.
73. *SecNav Reports,* 1860, 34–36.
74. Ammen, *Old Navy,* 259–60.

4. THE STEAM FRIGATES OF 1854

1. Bennett, *Steam Navy,* 138–41.
2. Stuart, *Naval and Mail Steamers,* 164–66; B. F. Isherwood, "The United States Steam Frigate Mississippi," *JFI* 24 (December 1852): 385.
3. Bolander, "Introduction of Shells and Shell Guns," 2.
4. *Civil War Naval Ordnance,* 4, 20.
5. J. C. Dobbin to Lenthall, 10 June 1854, RG 45/M480, reel 2.
6. C. Morris, C. Copeland, J. Smith, J. Lenthall, and S. Hartt to J. C. Dobbin, 31 August 1853, RG 19/49.
7. Lenthall to Dobbin, 14 December 1853, RG 19/49; Dobbin to Lenthall, 21 January 1854, Letters from Secretary of the Navy to Bureau Chiefs, RG 45/M480, reel 2.
8. Isherwood, *Experimental Researches,* 1:157.
9. Theodore Wilson, Instructions and Specifications for the Construction of Ships, 1857–1873, RG 19/234; "Trial Trip of the United States Steam Frigate Merrimac," *JFI* 31 (April 1856): 276.
10. Board Report on Engines for Six Steamers from D. Martin, H. Hunt, W. W. Wood, W. Everett, 20 September 1854, RG 45/224.
11. Isherwood, *Experimental Researches,* 1:176.
12. Ibid., 1:188.
13. "Trial Trip of the Merrimac," 275–76; "The New American Steamships of War," from *Mechanic's Magazine* (London), in *JFI* 31 (February 1857): 131.
14. "Trial Trp of the Merrimac," 275.
15. Isherwood, *Experimental Researches,* 1:162–63.
16. "Trial Trip of the Merrimac," 277–78.
17. Isherwood, *Experimental Researches,* 1:163; *ORN,* series 2, 1:141–42.
18. "Trial Trip of the Merrimac," 276; Isherwood, *Experimental Researches,* 1:172–74.
19. *U.S. Nautical Magazine and Naval Journal* (March–October 1856): 253, 309, 335.
20. "Screw Steamers of the Navy," *U.S. Nautical Magazine and Naval Journal* 6 (April–September 1857): 61.
21. "Inefficiency of the Navy," *U.S. Nautical Magazine and Naval Journal* 4 (March–October 1856): 253.
22. "Screw Steamers of the Navy," *U.S. Nautical Magazine and Naval Journal,* 65.
23. Ibid.
24. *The Engineer* 1 (10 October 1856): 208.
25. *Times* (London), 19 May 1855.
26. *Conway's,* p. 45; Dahlgren, "Composition of Naval Batteries," 81–84.
27. Lambert, *Battleships in Transition,* 122–24.
28. Bennett, *Steam Navy,* 147.
29. *ORN,* series 1, 4:281–91.
30. Isherwood, *Experimental Researches,* 1:174, 201–7.
31. Letter, RG 45/OSF, EM, box 172; H. K. Thatcher, Reports of North Atlantic Blockading Squadron, November 1864, RG 45/OSF, AD, box 52.
32. L. M. Goldsborough to Welles, 19 July 1865, *ORN,* series 1, 3:568.
33. Isherwood, *Experimental Researches,* 1:168, 181, 192.
34. Ibid., 183–84, 196–99.
35. Melancton Smith, Reports of North Atlantic Blockading Squadron, November 1864, RG 45/OSF, AD, box 52.
36. Joseph Lanham, ibid.
37. R. R. Forbes to L. Goldsborough, 9 February 1858, RG 45/OSF, AQ, box 88.
38. *Conway's,* 45.
39. Dahlgren, "Composition of Naval Batteries," 83.
40. Bennett, *Steam Navy,* 151.
41. "Efficiency of the Navy: The War Steamer Niagara," *U.S. Nautical Magazine and Naval Journal* 3 (October 1853–March 1856): 286.
42. Hoppin, *Life of Andrew Hull Foote,* 108–9.
43. Isherwood, *Engineering Precedents,* 188.
44. Ibid.; Chapelle, *Search for Speed,* 377, and plate 15.
45. Clark, *Clipper Ship Era,* 274.
46. Chapelle, *Search for Speed,* 378.
47. Lubbock, *Best of Sail,* 2.
48. Isherwood, *Engineering Precedents,* 190–92.
49. *Frank Leslie's Illustrated Newspaper,* 2 May 1857.
50. Ibid.; Isherwood, *Engineering Precedents,* 194–95.
51. Isherwood, *Engineering Precedents,* 190; NARS Plans 79-13-31L, 81-12-2.
52. NARS Plan 79-13-31J; *Times* (London): 21 May 1857.
53. *Frank Leslie's Illustrated Newspaper,* 2 May 1857, 8 January 1858; *Times* (London), 21 May 1857; 28 August 1858; *Illustrated London News,* 6 June 1857.
54. Register of Armament, vol. 2, RG 74/111; NARS Plan 79-13-31B.
55. Isherwood, *Engineering Precedents,* 192–93.
56. Ibid., 198.
57. *Mechanic's Magazine* 66 (30 May 1857): 506.
58. Isherwood, *Engineering Precedents,* 195–204.
59. Ibid.; Ballard, *Black Battle Fleet,* 19.
60. Ridgely-Nevitt, *American Steamships,* 164–65; *Conway's,* 45.
61. *Frank Leslie's Illustrated Newspaper,* 2 May 1857.
62. *U.S. Nautical Magazine and Naval Journal* 6 (April–September 1857): 246.
63. Deck Logs, *USS Niagara,* April 1857, RG 24.
64. *Times* (London), 21 May 1857.
65. *Times* (London), 19 May 1857; *Conway's,* 45; Lambert, *Battleships in Transition,* 55, 149.
66. *Frank Leslie's Illustrated Newspaper,* 3 July 1858.
67. *U.S. Nautical Magazine and Naval Journal* 6 (April–September 1857): 472–73.
68. *Frank Leslie's Illustrated Newspaper,* 4 September 1858.
69. *DANFS,* 5:81; NARS Plan 79-13-31Y.
70. Deck Logs, *USS Niagara,* April–May 1861, RG 24.

71. Charles Boynton, *History of the Navy during the Rebellion,* 2:111.
72. W. W. McKean to Welles, *ORN,* 17:3–5.
73. *ORN,* series 2, 1:160–61; NARS Plans 79-13-31W, 79-13-31X.
74. T. Craven to Welles, 21 October 1863, Craven Court Martial Proceedings, vol. 143, no. 4071, Records of the Judge Advocate General (Navy), microfilm, RG 125.
75. Deck Logs, *USS Niagara,* 1863–65, RG 24; Welles to Paulding, 2 January 1864, RG 45/M625, Area File, 1775–1910.
76. Craven to Welles, 1 August 1864, *ORN,* 3:129–30.
77. Craven to Welles, 28 February 1865, *ORN,* 3:435–36.
78. Testimony, Craven Court Martial Proceedings, Records of the Judge Advocate General (Navy), RG 125.
79. NARS Plans 79-13-31N, 79-13-31L, 79-13-31K.
80. Bennett, *Steam Navy,* 153; Bigelow, *France and the Confederate Navy,* 89.
81. *U.S. Nautical Magazine and Naval Journal* 5 (October 1856–March 1857): 29–34.
82. Hoppin, *Life of Andrew Hull Foote,* 108–9.
83. Lenthall to Toucey, N.D., RG 19/49.
84. NARS Plan 53-12-3, November 1855.
85. Sailing Quality Report, 1 October 1874, RG 19/244.
86. *SecNav Reports,* 1867, 3.
87. A. M. Pennock to Welles, 15 June 1867, RG 45/M125, reel 373; Sailing Quality Report, 1 October 1874, RG 19/244.
88. *ANJ,* (1876): 215.

5. *HARTFORD-CLASS SCREW SLOOPS, 1857*

1. Chapelle, *American Sailing Navy,* 466–69.
2. Ibid., 463–69.
3. J. Smith, J. Lenthall, S. Archbold, Ingraham, to I. Toucey, 26 January 1857, RG 19/49; *Conway's,* 43.
4. *SecNav Reports,* 1857, 585.
5. Jameson and Sternlicht, *Black Devil of the Bayous,* 186; NARS Plan 27-13-4, 1882.
6. Bennett, *Steam Navy,* 157.
7. Jameson and Sternlicht, *Black Devil of the Bayous,* 23.
8. *ORN,* series 2, 1:99; NARS Plan 27-13-5, 1882.
9. C. K. Stribling to I. Toucey, 16 July 1859, RG 45/OSF, AQ, box 88; Jameson and Sternlicht, *Black Devil of the Bayous,* 27; Bennett, *Steam Navy,* 157.
10. D. G. Farragut to Commander Smith, G. V. Fox, and Welles, letters, 21 May–23 October 1864, *ORN,* 3:291, 298, 335, 696–97.
11. "Particulars of the U.S. Steam Sloop-of-War Richmond," *JFI* 41 (February 1861): 123.
12. Ibid.
13. Ibid.
14. Ibid.; *ORN,* series 2, 1:192–93; Roberts, "Recognition Data," (Unpublished).
15. "Particulars of the Richmond," 124.
16. C. H. Bell to I. Toucey, 19 January 1861, RG 45/OSF, AQ, box 88.
17. "Failure of Engines of the Pensacola," 17 February 1863, S. Misc. Doc. 70, 37-2.
18. C. H. Bell to Welles, 3 July 1861, *ORN,* 1:35.
19. NARS Plan 79-4-3B.
20. Isherwood, *Experimental Researches,* 1:219.
21. NARS Plans, 79-4-3B (*Richmond*), 79-8-34A (*Brooklyn*).
22. Ibid.
23. Theodore Wilson, "Instructions and Specifications for the Construction of Ships, 1857–1873," RG 19/234.
24. North Atlantic Blockading Squadron Reports, RG 45/OSF, AD, box 52.
25. Isherwood, *Experimental Researches,* 1:220–21.
26. Ibid.; *ORN,* series 2, 1:48; Roberts, "Recognition Data."
27. *ORN,* series 2, 1:48, 99, 192–93.
28. D. G. Farragut to I. Toucey, 2 February 1859, RG 45/M125, reel 361.
29. Isherwood, *Experimental Researches,* 1:231; North Atlantic Blockading Squadron Reports, RG 45/OSF, AD, box 52.
30. *SecNav Reports,* 1888, 348.
31. Roberts, "Recognition Data"; *SecNav Reports,* 1880, 523.
32. Bennett, *Steam Navy,* 158.
33. *ORN,* series 2, 1:124; Roberts, "Recognition Data."
34. W. W. Wood to John Rudd, 14 November 1859, RG 45/M125, reel 362.
35. *SecNav Reports,* 1883, 307.
36. J. Worden to Welles, 8 November 1866, RG 45/M125, reel 372.
37. Roberts, "Recognition Data"; *ORN,* series, 1:173–74.
38. "Failure of Engines of Pensacola," 17 February 1863, 37th Congress, 2d sess., S. Misc. Doc. 70; Sloan, *Benjamin Franklin Isherwood,* 106–7.
39. Sloan, *Benjamin Franklin Isherwood,* 106–7; Bennett, *Steam Navy,* 159–66; "Failure of Engines of Pensacola," 17 February 1863, 37th Congress, 2d sess., S. Misc. Doc. 70.
40. Welles to H. Morris, 12 November 1861, *ORN,* 16:765.
41. James Glyn to I. Toucey, 28 December 1859, 17 January 1860, RG 45/M125, reels 362, 363.
42. D. G. Farragut to G. V. Fox, 5 March 1862, Thompson and Warmaugh, *Fox Correspondence,* 1:304.
43. "Failure of Engines of Pensacola," 17 February 1863, 37th Congress, 2d sess., S. Misc. Doc. 70.
44. Ibid.
45. Bennett, *Steam Navy,* 165.
46. *ANJ,* (29 September 1866): 90; *SecNav Reports,* 1875, 119.
47. J. L. Worden to C. H. Bell, 2 September 1866, 8 November 1866, RG 45/M125, reel 372; J. L. Worden to S. Godon, 9 December 1866, RG 45/M125, reel 372.

6. *THE SLOOPS OF 1858*

1. *SecNav Reports,* 1857, 1858.
2. Coletta, *American Secretaries of the Navy,* 1:305.
3. Notes by Welles and H. A. Wise attached to letter by D. G. Farragut, 15 June 1863, *ORN,* 20:299–300; Hoppin, *Life of Andrew Hull Foote,* 108–9.
4. "Particulars and Performance of the U.S. Steamer Wyoming," *JFI* 38 (October 1859): 268–69.
5. Ibid.
6. Ibid.
7. J. P. Bankhead to Welles, 7 June 1865, *ORN,* 3:544.
8. *ANJ,* 23 January 1864, 1.

9. Roberts, "Recognition Data."
10. W. A. Parker to Welles, 3 September 1863, *ORN,* 2:435.
11. *DANFS,* 8:492–94.
12. NARS Plan 79-9-34R.
13. NARS Plan 79-9-34J.
14. NARS Plan 79-10-5A, *Mohican;* Roberts, "Recognition Data"; North Atlantic Blockading Squadron Report, RG 45/OSF, AD, box 52.
15. *ANJ,* 23 January 1864, 1; C. W. Pickering to Welles, 22 February 1862, *ORN,* 1:321.
16. Pickering to Welles, 22 February 1862, *ORN,* 1:321; Sailing Quality Report, September 1884, RG 19/244; Roberts, "Recognition Data."
17. Pickering to Welles, 22 February 1862, *ORN,* 1:321.
18. *SecNav Reports,* 1883, 392.
19. S. Glisson to Welles, *ORN,* 1:531; North Atlantic Blockading Squadron Reports, RG 45/OSF, AD, box 52.
20. Porter, *Naval History of the Civil War,* 654; Bennett, *Steam Navy,* 434.
21. Bennett, *Steam Navy,* 432.
22. Hobson, *The Famous Cruise of the Kearsarge,* 164–66; Roberts, "Recognition Data."
23. Bennett, *Steam Navy,* 169–70.
24. NARS Plans, 78-3-2L, 5-26-30.
25. NARS Plan 78-3-2 O; Roberts, "Recognition Data."
26. *ORN,* series no. 2, 1:165.
27. Roberts, "Recognition Data."
28. C. Wilkes to Welles, 11 November 1862, *ORN,* vol. 1.
29. J. S. Missroon to Welles, 16 March 1862, *ORN,* 7:129–30.
30. Letters from Bureau of Construction and Repair to Commandant, 3 August 1863, Philadelphia Navy Yard, RG 19/54.
31. R. Townsend to Welles, 17 March 1865, *ORN,* 3:453.
32. C. R. P. Rodgers to Welles, *ORN,* 3:128.
33. A. Ludlow Case to S. P. Lee, *ORN,* 8:512–13.
34. F. C. Dade to G. H. Preble, Preble to D. G. Farragut, *ORN,* 1:437, 445.
35. NARS Plan, 108-8-2C, 79-5-26.
36. "Particulars of the U.S. Steamer Dacotah," *JFI* 41 (January 1861): 29–31.
37. *Luca's Questions & Answers for Marine Engineers,* 138–64.
38. "Particulars of the Dacotah," *JFI* 41 (January 1861): 30; Roberts, "Recognition Data."
39. "Particulars of the Dacotah," *JFI* 41 (January 1861): 30; Egbert Thompson to J. Dahlgren, 25 December 1866, RG 45/OSF, box 48, AQ.
40. Bennett, *Steam Navy,* 170–73; "Particulars of the U.S. Steam Sloop Narragansett," *JFI* 39 (January 1860): 44.
41. *ORN,* series 2, 1:155.
42. Gillis to Craven, 16 October 1861, *ORN,* 4:719; Dupont to Fox, 16 December 1861, Thompson and Warmaugh, *Fox Correspondence,* 1:80; H. Rolando to Welles, 21 June 1863, *ORN,* 2:296.
43. Report on Faulty Construction of *Seminole,* RG 45/OSF, AC, box 22; H. Rolando to Welles, 21 June 1863, *ORN,* 2:296.
44. T. A. Hunt Report, 28 December 1859, RG 45/M125, reel 362.
45. Ridgely-Nevitt, *American Steamships,* 215–20, 276.
46. J. W. Griffiths and Wm. Morris to I. Toucey, 18 June 1858, RG 45/OSF, AD 47, box 29.
47. Building Instructions for Steam Sloop of War of Ten Feet Draught, RG 45/OSF, AC, box 21.
48. Chapelle, *Search for Speed,* 356; Desmond, *Wooden Ship Building,* 10–13.
49. Bennett, *Steam Navy,* 173.
50. *SecNav Reports,* 1869, Report on Steam Machinery Afloat, 200–1.
51. J. Lenthall to C. Stewart, 29 September 1859, RG 19/54.
52. NARS Plan 35-7-6A; Register of Guns, RG 74/111.
53. S. P. Lee Report, *ORN,* 8:367; M. B. Woolsey to Welles, 1 March 1867, RG 45/M125.
54. G. B. Balch to Dahlgren, 16 July 1863, *ORN,* 14:345; T. Bailey to S. H. Pook, 22 July 1865, Survey of *Pawnee,* RG 19/233.
55. Balch to Dahlgren, *ORN,* 14:416–17.
56. Miller, *Sail, Steam and Splendor,* 74.
57. *ORN,* series 2, 1:197.
58. NARS Plan 40-7-7A; Bennett, *Steam Navy,* 166.
59. Page, "The Great Eastern," 256–60.
60. *ORN,* series 2, 1:197.
61. J. T. Watkins to Welles, *ORN,* 1:387.
62. *DANFS,* 6:230.
63. Bennett, *Steam Navy,* 154; "Particulars of the U.S. Steam Ship Pocahontas," *JFI* 39 (May 1860): 336; NARS Plan 40-13-3B.
64. Register of Ordnance, RG 74/111.
65. B. Kennon to I. Toucey, 1860, NARS Plan 107-11-12A, with NARS Plan 107-11-12B.
66. J. A. Gillis to J. P. Gillis, 5 May 1861, *ORN,* 4:448; B. M. Dove to J. Dahlgren, 4 July 1861, *ORN,* 4:562.

7. GUNBOATS AND CRUISERS, 1861–1862

1. NARS Plan 79-5-17.
2. Laing, *American Ships,* 320.
3. Ibid., 321, 325; *Conway's,* 129.
4. Isherwood, *Experimental Researches,* 2:452; *The Engineer* 13 (10 January 1862): 26–27.
5. Isherwood, *Experimental Researches,* 2:453–56.
6. Ibid.; Bennett, *Steam Navy,* 221.
7. Isherwood, *Experimental Researches,* 2:453–56; Laing, *American Ships,* 324.
8. Isherwood, *Experimental Researches,* 2:453–56.
9. Trials of Machinery, 1862–1865, report, 10 May 1864, RG 19/1017.
10. Letter, 9 February 1862, RG 45/OSF, EM, box 172.
11. S. F. Dupont to Welles, 25 July 1862, *ORN,* 13:211–12; S. F. Dupont to D. Ammen, 26 July 1862, *ORN,* 13:215–16; S. F. Dupont to Fox, 21 August 1862, *ORN,* 13:268–69.
12. North Atlantic Blockading Squadron Reports, RG 45/OSF, AD, box 52.
13. G. H. Preble to D. D. Porter, 30 March 1862, *ORN,* 18:91–92.
14. North Atlantic Blockading Squadron Reports, RG 45/OSF, AD, box 52; A. Bryson to Lockwood, 27 April 1862, *ORN,* 7:280; Dupont to T. Stevens, 21 October 1862, RG 45/OSF, AQ.
15. Laing, *American Ships,* 322–33; Haviland, "American Steam Navigation in China," 306.
16. Welles to Paulding, 27 August 1862, *ORN,* 13:285–86.

17. Laing, *American Ships,* 334.
18. Laing, *American Ships,* 322.
19. Isherwood, *Experimental Researches,* 2:455–56.
20. Welles to Bureau of Construction and Repair, 6 May 1861, Letters from Secretary of the Navy to Bureau of Construction and Repair, RG 19/61.
21. Information on Ossipee and Pensacola, Letter from B. F. Isherwood, 20 February 1863, 37th Congress, 3d sess., S. Exec. Doc. 45.
22. Marine Engines, 38th Congress, 2d sess., H. Rept. 8, 36–37.
23. *ORN,* series 2, 1:116, 167; Roberts, "Recognition Data."
24. S. Doc. 45 (*Ossipee* and *Pensacola*); H. Rept. 8 (Marine Engines).
25. J. L. Lardner to Welles, 17 September 1863, *ORN,* 2:457.
26. S. Doc. 45 (*Ossipee* and *Pensacola*).
27. Welles to Lenthall, 22 August 1861, RG 19/61.
28. *ORN,* 20:300.
29. Dimensions from NARS Plans 107-9-3A, 79-7-11, 10-2-104G, 78-3-8C.
30. NARS Plans 78-3-8C (*Monongahela*) and 78-7-14D (*Shenandoah*); *SecNav Reports,* 1887, 288–89.
31. NARS Plan 79-7-11 (*Lackawanna*), 1861; NARS Alpha File, Midship Section of *Ticonderoga,* 23 April 1874; NARS Plan 79-3-11 (*Ticonderoga*), 1878; Plan of *Ticonderoga,* Portsmouth Navy Yard.
32. Fox to Delano, 21 February 1862, Thompson and Warmaugh, *Fox Correspondence,* 2:426–27.
33. *SecNav Reports,* 1887, 288–89.
34. NARS Plan 78-3-7, 2 March 1862.
35. Roberts, "Recognition Data."
36. Lenthall to Pendergrast, 3 May 1862, 23 October 1862, 30 December 1863, RG 19/54.
37. H. Rept. 8, (Marine Engines), 38.
38. Roberts, "Recognition Data."
39. D. G. Farragut to Welles, 15 June 1863, *ORN,* 20:298–99.
40. Roberts, "Recognition Data."
41. Lenthall to J. B. Hull, 24 February 1864, RG 19/54.
42. S. Doc. 45 (*Ossipee* and *Pensacola*); H. Walke to Welles, 12 February 1864, *ORN,* 2:599–600; *Sacramento* Log Extracts, 24–25 March 1865, *ORN,* 3:466; C. H. Boggs to Welles, 29 April 1863, *ORN,* 8:832.
43. North Atlantic Blockading Squadron Report, RG 45/OSF, AD, box 52; J. R. Goldsborough to Welles, 3 August 1866, RG 45/M125.
44. J. H. Strong to Welles, 8 and 25 November 1863, *ORN,* 20:661, 679.
45. *ORN,* series 2, 1:51.
46. North Atlantic Blockading Squadron Report, RG 45/OSF, AD, box 52.
47. C. Steedman to Welles, 23 September and 20 October 1864, *ORN,* 3:304, 306.
48. Wyman to Welles, 1 July 1867, RG 45/M125, reel 374.
49. Porter, *Naval History of the Civil War,* 576; Scharf, *History of the Confederate States Navy,* 575.
50. Farragut to Welles, *ORN,* 21:644.
51. Plan 65 in William H. Webb, *Plans of Wooden Vessels,* 2 vols., privately published, 1895. Reprinted in Erik A. R. Ronnberg, Jr., "Webb's *Plans of Wooden Vessels,*" *Nautical Research Journal* 34, no. 2 (June 1989): 101.
52. H. Rept. 8 (Marine Engines), 36. Bennett, *Steam Navy,* 514–16.
53. Ibid.
54. Survey of Engines, 11 November 1864, RG 45/OSF, EM, box 172.
55. NARS BSE Plan, *Pequot;* Reports from Superintendents outside Navy Yards, 19 May 1864, vol. 5, RG 19, entry 64.
56. A. W. Johnson to S. C. Rowan, *ORN,* 15:403; *ANJ,* 25 September 1869, 288.
57. Roberts, "Recognition Data."
58. S. P. Quackenbush to S. P. Lee, 17 February and 4 March 1864, *ORN,* 9:489, 525; S. P. Lee to Welles, 23 February 1864, *ORN,* 9:500.
59. D. Knox to F. E. Dayton, RG 45/OSF, EE, box 169; A. H. Fisher to D. L. Braine, 4 April 1865, J. T. Pauchin to Braine, 12 May 1865, RG 45/OSF, EM, box 172.
60. J. Parker to Welles, 8 November 1864, *ORN,* 3:323.
61. Survey of Engines, 11 November 1864, RG 45/OSF, EM, box 172.
62. Sailing Quality Report, 30 September 1874, RG 19/244; *SecNav Reports,* 1869, Report of Steam Machinery Afloat, 170.
63. S. P. Lee to Welles, 23 February 1864, *ORN,* 19:500; P. G. Watmaugh to S. P. Lee, *ORN,* 10:103.
64. T. C. Harris to D. D. Porter, 6 November 1864, *ORN,* 3:321; F. Dade to W. W. Wood, 22 August 1864, RG 19/1017.
65. H. Rept. 8 (Marine Engines).
66. *ANJ,* 18 May 1867, 618.
67. Dahlgren to Welles, 6 November 1863, *ORN,* 15:101; A. W. Johnson to S. C. Rowan, 9 April 1864, *ORN,* 15:403. S. L. P. Ayers to B. F. Isherwood, 14 April 1864, RG 19/1017.
68. S. L. P. Ayers to B. F. Isherwood, 14 April 1864, RG 19/1017.
69. NARS Plan 79-2-45; Roberts, "Identification Data"; *ANJ,* 24 July 69, 772.
70. *DANFS,* 8:517.

8. DOUBLE-ENDED GUNBOATS, 1861–1863

1. 8 August 1861, RG 45/OSF, AD.
2. NARS Plan 78-8-14 (*Paul Jones*); ibid., 79-12-24 (*Octorara*); ibid., 78-11-38 (*Sonoma, Conemaugh*).
3. NARS Plan 78-12-12 (*Maratanza*).
4. G. Fox to B. F. Delano, 21 February 1862, Thompson and Warmaugh, *Fox Correspondence,* 1:426.
5. J. Lenthall, B. Isherwood to Welles, 2 July 1862, RG 19/49.
6. NARS Plan 72-15-5.
7. NARS Plan 107-9-10E.
8. Bennett, *Steam Navy,* 228–29.
9. *ORN, series 2, 1:154.*
10. M. Woodhull to Welles, 5 September 1862, *ORN,* 1:468–69; ibid., 10 September 1862, *ORN,* 1:473–74.
11. North Atlantic Blockading Squadron Reports, RG 45/OSF, AD, box 52; A. D. Harrell to Welles, 5 February 1862, *ORN,* 6:548–50.
12. North Atlantic Blockading Squadron Reports, RG 45/OSF, AD, box 52.
13. M. Woodhull to Welles, 5 September 1862, *ORN,* 1:468–69; ibid., 10 September 1862, *ORN,* 1:473–74.
14. *ORN,* series 2, 1:65, 154.
15. C. Wilkes to Welles, 23 January 1863, *ORN,* 2:55.

16. T. H. Stevens to Welles, 9 February 1863, *ORN,* 2:70.
17. RG 45/OSF, AD, box 48.
18. Isherwood, *Experimental Researches,* 2:79–83.
19. Specifications for Side Wheel Steamers, RG 45/OSF, AD, box 49A.
20. Isherwood, *Experimental Researches,* 2:84; *ORN,* series 2, Welles to S. P. Lee, 6 June 1864, *ORN,* 10:127; Bauer, *Ships of the Navy,* 64.
21. North Atlantic Blockading Squadron Reports, RG 45/OSF, AD, box 52; Isherwood, *Experimental Researches,* 2:84.
22. H. Rept. 8 (Marine Engines), 33, 41–45.
23. North Atlantic Blockading Squadron Reports, RG 45/OSF, AD, box 52; J. L. Davis to Porter, 9 November 1864, *ORN,* 3:324–26.
24. North Atlantic Blockading Squadron Reports, RG 45/OSF, AD, box 52.
25. S. P. Lee to Welles, 1 September 1864, *ORN,* 10:411; Arnold to W. H. Macomb, RG 45/OSF, AR, box 106.
26. J. DeHaven to Welles, 7 November 1864, *ORN,* 3:321–22.
27. NARS Plans 79-14-4R, 79-14-4V.
28. RG 45/OSF, AC, box 28; NARS Plan 28-3-22.
29. The following description of the *Algonquin* disaster is from Bennett, *Steam Navy,* 517–23, 919–948 and Sloan, *Isherwood,* 119–30.
30. *Conway's,* 131; Isherwood to Gregory, 23 June 1866, Letters from Bureau of Steam Engineering to Officers, Reports of Local Inspectors of Machinery, RG 19/966.
31. NARS Plans 28-2-24, 107-12-1J, 107-12-14.
32. P. Shirley to Welles, 8 April, 26 May, 12 June 1865, *ORN,* 13:491, 531, 547.
33. F. Higginson, Sailing Quality Report, 1884, RG 19/244.
34. R. B. Gunnell to Isherwood, 1 July 1864, RG 19/1017.
35. *ORN,* series 2, 1:149; *SecNav Reports,* 1898, 567.
36. *SecNav Reports,* 1881, Bureau of Medicine and Surgery Report.
37. Report by D. G. Farragut, 13 November 1864, *ORN,* 21:725.

9. FAST GUNBOATS AND SPAR-DECKED CRUISERS, 1863–1869

1. Welles, *Diary,* 1:496.
2. *SecNav Reports,* 1864, 1001.
3. Ibid., 1865, 235–36.
4. Ibid., 1867, 147.
5. Ibid., 1864, 1093–94; ibid., 1865, 306; ibid., 1868, 129; Bennett, *Steam Navy,* Appendix B.
6. R. B. Forbes to L. M. Goldsborough, 25 December 1863, RG 45 OSF, AD, box 48.
7. Farragut to Welles, 15 June 1863, *ORN,* 20:298–99.
8. *SecNav Reports,* 1864, xxvii; Department to Bureau of Construction and Repair, 20, 29 July 1864, RG 19/61; Bennett, *Steam Navy,* 477.
9. "General Directions for Building Screw Steam Gunboat (Nantasket)," Hart Nautical Collection, Massachusetts Institute of Technology.
10. Bennett, *Steam Navy,* 477–78; *SecNav Reports,* 1868, 126–27.
11. J. Lenthall to Lanham, 3 April 1869, RG 19/54; Lenthall to Hull, 2 February 1865, RG 19/54; *ANJ,* 28 August 1869, 16.
12. Roberts, "Recognition Data."
13. *ANJ,* 13 November 1869, 193; *ANJ,* 1 February 1868, 377; *SecNav Reports,* 1868, 126–27; RG 45/OSF, AD, box 48.
14. Bennett, *Steam Navy,* 477–78.
15. Department to Bureau of Construction and Repair, 29 July 1864, 29 July 1864, RG 19/61.
16. *ANJ,* 31 October 1863, 774.
17. *SecNav Reports,* December 1866; Bennett, *Steam Navy,* 477–78.
18. Sailing Quality Reports, RG 19/244; Roberts, "Recognition Data."
19. Report of Steam Engineering Afloat, *SecNav Reports,* 1869, 193–94.
20. Theodore Wilson, "Instructions and Specifications for the Construction of Ships, 1857–1873," RG 19/234.
21. W. A. Macomb to A. Borie, 28 May 1869, RG 45/M125, reel 378; Sailing Quality Reports, RG 19/244.
22. Lenthall to Selfridge, 29 January 1868, RG 19/54.
23. Macomb to Welles, 26 January and 18 February 1869, RG 45/M125 reel 377; extant photo is at the Naval Historical Center, NH 85303A.
24. Sailing Quality Reports, RG 19/244 and RG 45/OSF, AD, box 48; Reports of Trial Trips, RG 45/OSF, AQ, box 88.
25. *ANJ,* 2 June 1877, 687.
26. Coletta, *American Secretaries of the Navy,* 1:407; *SecNav Reports,* 1882, 148.
27. *SecNav Reports,* 1875, 303.
28. *ANJ,* 30 November 1867, 233.
29. "Machinery Afloat Rpt.," *SecNav Reports,* 1869, 159.
30. NARS Plan 108-3-19.
31. NARS Plan 78-10-19 (*Contoocook*).
32. *ANJ,* 30 November 1867, 233.
33. "Machinery Afloat Rpt.," *SecNav Reports,* 1869, 159–60, 173–74, 193; Roberts, "Recognition Data."
34. NARS Plan 5-12-34 (*Congress*).
35. Roberts, "Recognition Data."
36. Ibid.
37. "Machinery Afloat Rpt.," *SecNav Reports,* 1869, 159–60; G. Balch to A. Borie, 19 May 1869, RG 45/M125, reel 378.
38. G. Balch to Welles, 4 April 1868, RG 45/M125, reel 374.
39. Harrison to D. D. Porter, 20 May 1870, RG 45/M125, reel 379.
40. *ORN,* series 2, 1:30, 186; Bennett, *Steam Navy,* Appendix B.
41. Welles to Lenthall, 5 November 1863, Letters of Secretary of the Navy to Bureau Chiefs, RG 45/M480.
42. *SecNav Reports,* 1864, xxvii–xxviii.
43. NARS Plans 79-2-4, 79-13-1 L, 108-8-7F, and 79-11-3; Table of Offsets of *Piscataqua,* Portsmouth Naval Shipyard.
44. NARS Plans 79-2-1 and 79-11-2 (model).
45. Theodore Wilson, "Instructions and Specifications for the Construction of Ships, 1857–1873," RG 19/234.
46. "Machinery Afloat Rpt.," *SecNav Reports,* 1869, 199–200.
47. Corbin to Welles, 26 September, 6 June 1867, RG 45/M125, reel 373.

48. NARS Plan 5-12-20C.
49. "Machinery Afloat Rpt.," *SecNav Reports*, 1869, 200.
50. Roberts, "Recognition Data"; NARS Plan 109-5-29 (*California*); H. A. Goldsborough to J. Winslow, 15 September 1869, Letters of Bureau of Construction and Repair to Commandant, Portsmouth Navy Yard, RG 19/54A.
51. Roberts, "Recognition Data."
52. "Machinery Afloat Rpt.," *SecNav Reports*, 1869, 199–200.
53. *ANJ*, 7 March 1868, 457.
54. *ANJ*, 28 December 1867, 298–99; *ANJ*, 7 March 1868, 457.
55. J. M. B. Clitz to G. Robeson, 18 January 1871, RG 45/M125, reel 381.
56. *ANJ*, 9 April 1871, 54.
57. Roberts, "Recognition Data."
58. Bennett, *Steam Navy*, 622; *SecNav* Reports, 1871, 149; ibid., 1874, 203; ibid., 1876, 28.
59. NARS Plan, 79-12-29H (*New York*, 1885); *SecNav Reports*, 1882, 145; ibid., 1884, 184.

10. COMMERCE DESTROYERS, 1864–1869

1. *SecNav Reports*, 1864, 717–18.
2. Ibid., xxvii.
3. Isherwood, "The Sloop of War Wampanoag," (August 1900): 288.
4. NARS Plans 79-12-4 (*Ammonoosuc*), 79-8-7 (*Tennessee*), 142-2-30 (Mould Loft Dimensions, *Florida* and *Tennessee*). The following discussion of specifications are from these hull plans.
5. James L. Swan, "The Wampanoag," 45–47; NARS BSE Plans, *Wampanoag*.
6. Isherwood, "The Sloop of War Wampanoag," (September 1900): 404.
7. NARS BSE Plans, *Dacotah, San Jacinto;* B. F. Isherwood, "Trial Trip of the United States Screw Steamer San Jacinto with New Machinery," *JFI* 27 (July 1854): 129.
8. H. Rpt. 8 (Marine Engines), 36–38.
9. NARS Plan-13-30; Isherwood, "The Sloop of War Wampanoag," (September 1900): 407; Swan, "The Wampanoag," 46.
10. Theodore Wilson, "Instructions and Specifications for the Construction of Ships, 1857–1873," RG 19/234.
11. *ANJ*, 29 September 1866, 94.
12. Isherwood, "The Sloop of War Wampanoag" (August 1900): 288–89; Bennett, *Steam Navy*, 576–77; Swan, "The Wampanoag," 47; *ANJ* (29 September 1866): 94.
13. *Conway's*, 121; Bennett, *Steam Navy*, 343.
14. Bennett, *Steam Navy*, 543.
15. *ANJ*, 1 September 1866, 25; *Warship International* 20, no. 3 (1983): 226.
16. Bennett, *Steam Navy*, 543.
17. Lenthall to Selfridge, 27 February 1866, RG 19/54.
18. *ANJ*, 24 October 1863, 141; R. B. Forbes, Sloops of War under Construction, 1865, 14–15, RG 45/ OSF, AD, box 48; NARS Plans 38-2-9, 38-2-12B.
19. R. B. Forbes, Sloops of War under Construction, 1865, 14–15; NARS Plan 79-3-43.
20. *ANJ*, 15 October 1864, 125.
21. Bennett, *Steam Navy*, 543.
22. Bennett, *Steam Navy*, Appendix B.
23. Sloan, *Isherwood*, 201 ff.
24. Ibid.
25. Beale, ed., *Diary*, 2:418; *ANJ*, 1 September 1866, 25.
26. *SecNav Reports*, 1875, 119; Bennett, *Steam Navy*, 525.
27. Bennett, *Steam Navy*, 526.
28. NARS Plans, 38-2-12C and 38-2-12E.
29. Deck Logs, *USS Idaho*, November 1867–February 1868, RG 24; *ANJ*, 18 July 1868, 761.
30. Bennett, *Steam Navy*, 530–31.
31. Hibbert to Welles, 28 May 1866, RG 45/M125, reel 371.
32. *ANJ*, 25 August 1866, 8.
33. *ANJ*, 29 September 1866, 90; ibid., 22 September 1866, 76.
34. Sloan, *Isherwood*, 153.
35. Isherwood to Gregory, 20 September 1866, RG 19/966.
36. Church, *John Ericsson*, 2:189; Bennett, *Steam Navy*, 532–26; *ANJ*, 26 January 1867, 301.
37. Sloan, *Isherwood*, 155.
38. *ANJ*, 22 December 1866, 1; ibid., 29 December 1866, 1; ibid., 5 January 1867, 1.
39. Sloan, *Isherwood*, 201.
40. J. W. A. Nicholson to Welles, 18 February 1868, RG 45/M125, reel 374.
41. Gurley, "The Wampanoag," 1733.
42. Swan, "The Wampanoag," 49.
43. Bennett, *Steam Navy*, 575–76.
44. "Machinery Afloat Report," *SecNav Reports*, 1869, 155.
45. Sloan, *Isherwood*, 232.
46. "Machinery Afloat Report," *SecNav Reports*, 1869, 143–209. The following complaints and recommendations for the *Wampanoag* class are from this report.
47. Swan, "The Wampanoag," 50.
48. Isherwood, "The Sloop of War Wampanoag," (September 1900): 416.
49. Ballard, "British Frigates of 1875," 43; Ballard, *Black Battle Fleet*, 16–17.
50. Church, *John Ericsson*, 2:189.
51. *SecNav Reports*, 1875, 119.
52. Rodger, "The Design of the Inconstant," 18.
53. "Machinery Afloat Report," *SecNav Reports*, 1869, 144–45, 209.
54. Ibid., 209–10.
55. Sloan, *Isherwood*, 152.
56. *SecNav Reports*, 1873, 121.
57. *SecNav Reports*, 1888, 319.

11. THE "DARK AGES," 1869–1885

1. Albion, *Makers of Naval Policy*, 200.
2. *SecNav Reports*, 1870, 156–77.
3. *SecNav Reports*, 1869, 6–8, 104; Coletta, *American Secretaries of the Navy*, 1:364.
4. Instructions of Bureaus, 6 December 1864, RG 19/49.
5. Welles to Lenthall, 11 April 1867, RG 45/M480, reel 112.
6. Paullin, "A Half-Century of Naval Administration in America, 744.
7. Albion, *Makers of Naval Policy*, 114, 199–200.
8. *ANJ*, 9 June 1877, 702.

9. Bennett, *Steam Navy,* 544–45; Oscar F. Stanton, Captain's Data Book, USFS *Tennessee,* G. W. Blunt White Library, Mystic Seaport; "Steam Machinery Afloat," *SecNav Reports,* 154–55.
10. F. A. Roe to C. H. Bell, N.D., RG 45/OSF, AQ.
11. *SecNav Reports,* 1876, 255; Church, *John Ericsson,* 2:190.
12. *SecNav Reports,* 1872, 121–22; Swann, *John Roach,* 132.
13. NARS BSE Plan, *Tennessee;* Stanton, "Captain's Data Book," G. W. Blunt White Library, Mystic Seaport.
14. NARS Plan 107-10-5A; Stanton, "Captain's Data Book," G. W. Blunt White Library.
15. *SecNav Reports,* 1875, 123.
16. Stanton, "Captain's Data Book"; *SecNav Reports,* 1875, 119.
17. Stanton, "Captain's Data Book"; Sailing Quality Report, 1884, RG 19/244.
18. Stanton, "Captain's Data Book"; Ropp, *The Development of a Modern Navy,* 107–8.
19. Bennett, *Steam Navy,* 544–46, Appendix B.
20. H. Misc. Doc. 201, 42-2.
21. *SecNav Reports,* 1876, 30.
22. *ANJ,* 27 January 1872, 383; H. Rept. 784, "Investigation of the Navy Department," 44-1, 111.
23. H. Rept. 784 (Investigation), 111–12.
24. *SecNav Reports,* 1876, 256.
25. *SecNav Reports,* 1873, 127; ibid., 1875, 119; Bennett, *Steam Navy,* 635–36.
26. *SecNav Reports,* 1882, 146.
27. *ANJ,* 30 May 1885, 84.
28. *ANJ,* 23 May 1885, 861; ibid., (25 April 1885): 782; Report on New Mohican, RG 45/OSF, AC, box 34.
29. *ANJ,* 16 December 1876, 295; ibid., 12 February 1876, 431; *SecNav Reports,* 1875, 118–19.
30. The *Alliance* was launched as *Huron;* Bennett, *Steam Navy,* 643–47.
31. "Instructions for Building Nipsic," RG 19/242.
32. NARS Plan 78-2-11P; Griffiths, *The Progressive Shipbuilder,* 50–51; I. Hanscom to M. Bryson, 13 March 1875, RG 19/54A.
33. *ANJ,* 9 December 1876, 279; ibid., 20 January 1877, 375.
34. *SecNav Reports,* 1873, 127–29; ibid., 1876, 126, 256.
35. Letter [author illegible], 29 March 1879, RG 45/OSF, AD, box 58.
36. Bennett, *Steam Navy,* 643; NARS Plans 78-2-11A, 78-3-3V.
37. Roberts, "Recognition Data."
38. *SecNav Reports,* 1875, 119.
39. Ibid., 1876, 257; W. H. Shock to W. H. Hunt, 16 May 1881, Letters from Bureau of Steam Engineering to Secretary of the Navy, RG 19/963; Sailing Quality Report, 1884, RG 19/244.
40. *DANFS;* Clark, "The Last Years of the Sail Navy," 138.
41. *ANJ,* 14 July 1877, 786.
42. Bejarano, "MS Emery Rice."
43. "Building Instructions for Iron Sloop, 1873," RG 45/OSF, AC, box 35; NARS Plans 28-13-16, 136-13-8.
44. Winton, *Modern Steam Practice and Engineering,* 785–814.
45. Sailing Quality Reports, 1877, RG 19/244.
46. Ibid.; *SecNav Reports,* 1877, 264.
47. *Harper's Weekly,* 15 December 1877, 986; *SecNav Reports,* 1883.
48. Clark, "The Last Years of the Sail Navy," 139.
49. Information courtesy Frank O. Braynard, Curator, Merchant Marine Academy Museum, Kings Point, N.Y., 19 August 1987. The *Ranger* was also known as the *Rockport, Nantucket,* and *Bay State* at various times in her career.
50. Brock Greenhill, *Steam and Sail in Britain and North America,* 56; Bennett, *Steam Navy,* 648.
51. *SecNav Reports,* 1883, 307.
52. NARS Plan 78-7-12.
53. NARS Plan 79-1-13C; Letter, 22 December 1858, RG 19/54.
54. NARS Plan 108-8-6H.
55. Baird, "The U.S. Ship Trenton," 16.
56. *SecNav Reports,* 1883, 309–11; Bennett, *Steam Navy,* 647.
57. *SecNav Reports,* 1876, 195–99.
58. Stone, "General Description of the Ordnance and Torpedo Outfit of the U.S.S. Trenton," 88–93.
59. Baird, "The U.S. Ship Trenton," 5.
60. Ibid., 12–13.
61. Stone, "General Description," 91–93.
62. NARS Plan 108-8-6U.
63. *SecNav Reports,* 1883, 318–53; Baird, "The U.S. Ship Trenton," 18–20.
64. *SecNav Reports,* 1883, 318–53; Sailing Quality Report, RG 19/244; Deck Logs, *USS Trenton,* 1888–1889, RG 24.
65. Vaughan to Secretary of the Navy, 23 August 1887, RG 45/OSF, AF, box 66.
66. *SecNav Reports,* 1884, 15–16.
67. Ibid.
68. Reports of Surveys (*Lancaster*), 1876, 1878, RG 45/OSF, AR.
69. J. Easby to J. C. Beaumont, 3 October 1879, 19 June, 4 February, 4 March, 28 October 1880, RG 19/54A.
70. Sailing Quality Report, 1884, RG 19/244.
71. Reports of Surveys, *USS Lancaster,* RG 45/OSF, AR.
72. Sailing Quality Reports, RG 19/244.
73. NARS Plan 101-7-18; *SecNav Reports,* 1895, 362–63.
74. Roberts, "Recognition Data."
75. *SecNav Reports,* 1881, 243; ibid., 1880, 161; NARS Plan 27-13-39, Alpha File.
76. *SecNav Reports,* 1880–84.
77. Ropp, *The Development of a Modern Navy,* 14–27; *SecNav Reports,* 1879, 26.
78. Ropp, *The Development of a Modern Navy,* 107–8; *Conway's,* 314–20.
79. *Conway's,* 44–60; J. W. King, *Warships and Navies of the World,* 394–97.
80. *Conway's,* 41–60.
81. Ibid.
82. *Conway's,* 54, 252, 260.
83. *SecNav Reports,* 1895, 362–67.

Glossary

Air pump. A device for pumping air and water of condensation from the condenser of a steam engine.

Amidships. The middle of a ship, measured either by length or breadth.

Apron. Timber attached to the aft side of and conforming with the shape of the stem, running from the head downward.

Athwartships. From side to side, as opposed to fore and aft.

Ballast. Heavy substances placed in the hold of a ship to bring the center of gravity of the vessel to its proper place for optimum operation.

Beams. Timbers running horizontally across a ship's hull on which the decks are built. ("On beam ends" indicates the ship has heeled far over on her side.)

Bearing. Those parts of a machine that bear the friction; the block or support on which a shaft or axle turns, and also the part of the axle or shaft resting on those supports.

Bedplate. The foundation piece on which an engine is erected.

Between perpendiculars. A measurement of a ship's hull length, taken from a point at the intersection of the main (or gun) deck and the after part of the stem, to the intersection of the deck with the fore part of the stern post.

Bilge. The bottom of a ship's hull, on which the ship would rest if aground.

Bilge keel. The timbers fastened longitudinally under the bilge of a ship's hull to reduce rolling.

Blowing off steam. Discharging dirty or supersalted water from a boiler.

Body (of a ship). The bulk enclosed within hull planking and the deck. As a design term: fore body and after body are the form of the hull forward and aft of the midship section, respectively.

Body plan. Hull plan, usually showing the lines of the vessel as viewed from both fore and aft.

Boilers. Types include flue and tubular boilers. Flues were simply rectangular ducts or passages for the heated gases through the boiler water. Later, many tubes were used to spread the heated gases more evenly throughout the water in the boiler (in the "fire tube" boiler). "Water tube" boilers were the reverse of fire tubular units: the gases surrounded the water, which ran through the tubes. Locomotive boilers were of the fire tube type.

Bore. The diameter of a cylinder of a steam engine. This dimension, with the length of the stroke (the distance traveled by the piston from one end of the cylinder to the other) determined the cubic capacity—and thus nominal horsepower—of an engine.

Breadth. Side-to-side dimension of a ship's hull.

Break. The termination of a ship's deck: where an upper deck ends and reveals a lower deck ("break of the forecastle").

Bridge. A raised superstructure above and across a deck, which had its origin as a "bridge" from the top of one paddle-wheel housing to the opposite housing, usually forward of the funnel.

Bucket. The parts of the paddle wheels extending beyond the circular framework, which provided the thrust through the water.

Bulkhead. A transverse or longitudinal partition in a ship.

Bulwarks. A planked railing built around a ship, enclosing the upper decks.

Buttocks. The rounding of the after hull of the ship, terminating at the stern post.

Buttock lines. Shown on a sheer (side view) plan of a vessel; cut the ship into vertical longitudinal sections, parallel to the centerline.

Cant frames. Although the majority of the crosswise timber frames of a ship's hull are perpendicular to the keel, the frames of the extreme ends run diagonally (canted) from the centerline to the planking.

Cathead. A piece of timber projecting from the bow of a ship, for the purpose of raising the anchor.

Caulking. Forcing oakum (untwisted fibers of old rope) into the seams of a ship's hull to prevent leakage.

Ceiling. The inside planking of a ship.

Center of effort of sail. A calculated point in the plane of sails at which the whole transverse force of the wind is supposed to be collected.

Condenser. A chamber in which steam discharged from a steam cylinder is reduced to water by either direct or indirect contact with cold water. "Jet condensers" used a stream of water directly into the vapor; "surface condensers" operated by routing water injected through a coil or series of tubes through the vapor chamber.

Connecting rod. An intermediate rod between a steam engine's crank shaft and the piston (in a direct-acting engine). In nondirect-acting engines the piston rod's end connected to a crosshead or beam.

Crankshaft. On paddle-wheel vessels, this shaft was the axle for the paddle wheel and in most screw-propelled ships was the propeller shaft. The shaft was cranked by means of "crank pins" (one per connecting rod) offset some distance from the shaft itself.

Crosshead. A beam or rod forming a T with the end of a piston rod. Rods operating from the ends of the T communicated power to the crankshaft or an intermediate beam.

Cutoff. Device for stopping the admission of steam into the cylinder.

Cutwater knee. See Knee head.

Davits. Pieces of iron or steel projecting over the side of a ship or the stern, for the purpose of raising boats.

Deadrise. The angle or curve of the floors of a vessel, from the keel to the bilge. "Flat floor" indicates a small angle upward from the keel.

Deadwood. Solid timbers, fore and aft, built up on the vessel's keel.

Depth of hold. Ship's dimension, taken at midships, from the floor to the deck.

Donkey engine. A small steam engine for auxiliary uses, such as a bilge pump.

Draft. 1. In steam engineering, the flow of air through a furnace. "Natural draft" is created by the rising column of heated gases in the funnel. "Forced draft" is created by artificial means, such as fans. 2. A ship plan.

Engine keelson. The fore and aft timber or iron framework made fast to the bottom of a ship on which the engine bedplate is secured.

Engines. See Steam engines.

Entrance. The fore part of the hull below the load water line. ("Fine" entrance indicates a very sharp angle.)

False keel. A thin keel, below the main keel, which may be damaged without injuring the main keel.

Floor. The bottom of a ship: the part on each side of the keel that approaches nearer horizontal than vertical.

Floor timbers. Timbers fixed athwart the keel upon which the whole frame is erected.

Flue. A large tube, usually made of plates bent and riveted together.

Forced draft. See Draft.

Forecastle. Forward end of the upper main deck, between the foremast and head.

Forefoot. The foremost part of the keel where it joins the stem.

Frame. The bends of timber that form the body of a ship, composed of a floor timber, two or three futtocks, and a top timber on each side of the keel.

Futtocks. Frame timbers between floors and top timbers.

Garboard strake. The line of planking next to the keel.

Grate bars. Iron bars on which fuel is supported while burning in a furnace.

Half-breadth. Ship plan depicting the curvature of the hull's waterlines as viewed from below, showing half the breadth of the hull.

Hauled fires. The burning fuel is removed from the furnace, leaving the grate bare.

Hawseholes. Forward apertures for the passage of chain cables.

Head. The work fitted forward of the ship's stem, including the figurehead, knee, head rails, and other structures.

Head sails. All sails forward of the foremast.

Heating surface. That surface of a boiler that is exposed to heated gases on one side and water on the other.

Hogging. The arching up of the hull of a ship in the middle because of excessive strain on the ends of the vessel. The opposite of sagging.

Hold. The part of the hull below the lower deck between bulkheads, used for ballast, stores, provisions, and, on merchant vessels, cargo.

Horse blocks. Railed platforms at the level of the ship's rail, used for officer's lookout stations.

Indicated horsepower. The true measure of work done within the cylinder of an engine.

Indicator. An instrument for registering the pressure in a cylinder at all parts of a stroke.

Jib. The triangular sail forward of the foremast.

Jibboom. A spar beyond the bowsprit.

Keel. The main and lowest timber of a ship's hull, extending from stem post to stern post, formed of several pieces scarfed together at the ends. The first timber laid down when building.

Keelson. A timber formed of long pieces fixed exactly over the keel for binding and strengthening the lower part of the hull.

Knee. A piece of timber somewhat in the form of a human knee when bent.

Knee head. Knee-shaped timbers fastened forward of the stem, below the bowsprit, forming the base for head rails, figurehead, and other structures. Enlisted personnel toilet facilities were often located here. Also referred to as a cutwater knee.

Leeway. The amount of forward motion a vessel loses by being forced sideways from the pressure of the wind on the sails and side.

Lie-to. To stop a vessel by reducing sail and keeping her close to the wind, eliminating her headway. On steamers, engines turn only enough to maintain steerageway.

Midships section. The widest point of a ship's hull. Depending on the design, this point may or may not be the same as the exact midpoint of the length.

Military mast. Mast designed to support a platform surrounded by a protected barbette (military top) behind which light guns are worked in action.

Mold (or mould). Light pieces of board made as templates for cutting the timbers of a ship's hull.

Mold loft. Large room used for laying off the lines of a vessel on the floor with chalk marks.

Molded beam. Width of a hull measured to the outside of the frames, not including the width of exterior planking. (The latter dimension, including planking, is the "extreme" beam.)

Natural draft. See Draft.

Nominal horsepower. A theoretical figure derived simply by calculating the cubic capacity of a cylinder, without regard to the actual performance of the engine.

Oakum. Old tarred rope, untwisted and forced between planking and decking to prevent leakage.
Ordinary. The term "in ordinary" indicates the ship is laid up—out of commission.
Ordnance. General term for the guns of a ship.
Orlop deck. The lowest deck in the hold.
Overall length. Strictly speaking, the length of a ship measured on deck; often given a more general sense in popular usage.
Packing. Elastic material confined about piston rods to prevent leakage of steam from the cylinder.
Paddle box. Structure built over a paddle wheel for protection and to prevent spray.
Patent log. Device for measuring a ship's speed through the water using a patented mechanical contrivance, usually with a counter on board.
Pillow block. A self-contained shaft bearing that is secured to the ship's structure by bolts.
Pilothouse. The house on deck or on the bridge where the steering wheel is located and from where the ship is controlled.
Piston rod. A rod with one end attached to the piston and the other to a crosshead or to the crankshaft.
Pitch of the screw. The distance a given point in a screw propeller would move in the direction of its axis if turned through one complete revolution in a solid, fixed medium.
Planking. Broad timbers used to cover the deck beams and the sides and bottom of the hull.
Planksheer. A horizontal band of timbers laid over the ends of timber frames.
Press of sail. All the sail a vessel can carry.
Pump. A machine for drawing water out of the hold by suction.
Quarter. The part of a vessel's side near the stern.
Quarterdeck. The uppermost deck at the stern.
Quarter galleries. Ornamental projections on the sides of a naval vessel at her stern, consisting mainly of windows (as opposed to gun ports) for the commanding officer's cabin. False quarter galleries sometimes were painted on the quarters.
Quartering seas. A sea running so as to break against the quarter of a vessel.
Rabbet. A joint made by a groove or channel in a piece of timber, cut to receive and secure the edge or ends of planks, as planks to the keel, stem, or sternpost.
Rake. The overhanging of the stem or stern beyond the perpendicular; also used to describe masts angling back from the perpendicular.
Rate. The class to which a vessel belongs—according to tonnage or armament.
Razee. A vessel cut down by removing an upper deck.
Ribbands. Horizontal timbers to add longitudinal strength to a hull.
Rock shaft. A shaft that vibrates only—not making a complete revolution.
Run. The narrowing of a hull aft, as the floor towards the sternpost.
Running rigging. All the movable ropes of a vessel's rigging, as opposed to "standing rigging," which is more or less permanently fixed.
Scantlings. The dimensions given for timbers, planks, and other building materials.
Scarf (or scarph). A joint between two timbers in which one piece is let into the other, resulting in one solid and even surface, particularly obvious in the keel.
Shaft alley. Passageway from the engine to the stern through which the propeller shaft passes.
Sheathing. Thin sheet copper covering the hull of a vessel, from the waterline downward for protection from worms and other seawater intrusions.
Sheer. The longitudinal curve of a ship's side.
Sheer plan. Plan of the elevation of a ship's side, showing outboard works.
Sloop-of-war. A naval vessel carrying all guns on a single deck.
Spar deck. An upper deck extending the length of the vessel.
Sponson. A projection from the side of a vessel, in which guns are mounted.
Steam engines, types.
Back-acting. The crank shaft is between the cylinder and the crosshead.
Beam (walking beam, overhead beam). A vertical cylinder with a rocking beam transferring power from the piston rod at one end to the connecting rod working downward at the other.
Compound (double) expansion. Steam is used first in a small cylinder, then transferred to a larger, low-pressure cylinder for further expansion.
Condensing. Steam engine using a condenser. Because the condensation process resulted in the creation of a partial vacuum on the exhaust side of the cylinder (the side temporarily opened to the condenser), such engines could operate on lower steam pressure in the cylinder: hence the term "low-pressure engines." Condensing engines were advantageous at sea because the condensed water could be reused in the boilers, obviating the need to use corrosive seawater.
High-pressure. The engine exhausts into the atmosphere rather than into a condenser.
Low-pressure. Uses steam at less than 60 pounds per square inch.
Oscillating. The cylinder vibrates on trunnions, with the outer end of the piston rod connecting directly to the crank shaft.
Side-lever. Vertical cylinder engine with a crosshead at the end of the piston rod operating rods to the ends of two beams. The opposite ends of the rocking beams work connecting rods upward to the crank shaft in a paddle-wheel vessel.
Simple expansion. Steam is used but once in the cylinder.
Steeple. A vertical back-acting engine with a crosshead operating rods downward parallel to the piston rod.
Triple Expansion. The steam is used consecutively in three cylinders, each larger than the last and at decreasing pressure increments.
Steerageway. The movement of a vessel through the water with only sufficient velocity to make her obedient to the helm.
Stem. The main timber at the fore part of a hull, erected vertically to accept the ends of the bow planks.
Sternpost. The main timber at the vessel's stern, erected vertically to accept the ends of the stern planks. On

sailing vessels, the rudder is mounted on the aft side of this timber.

Strake. A single breadth of plank from one end of a ship to another.

Stroke. The distance a piston travels from one end of its movement to the other.

Swivel gun. A small piece of ordnance turning on a pivot.

Taffrail. The rail around the stern of a vessel.

Telescopic funnel. A ship's smokepipe made to allow the upper portions to be lowered significantly in order to remove obstructions to the sails.

Tiller. A bar fitted into the upper forward side of the rudder to turn it.

Topgallant forecastle. A small deck built level with the rail at the extreme forward part of the vessel.

Top hamper. All the spars, rigging, and other structures above the deck.

Top timbers. The highest parts of the ship's frames.

Torpedo. Explosive device, intended to strike a vessel at or below the waterline. Spar torpedoes were attached to the ends of long spars projecting from the bows of a vessel and exploded by means of an electrical charge from on board the attacking ship. "Torpedo" was also a term designating moored explosive charges intended to explode when struck by an enemy ship. Auto-mobile torpedoes were invented after 1870 and were self-contained, having both explosive and propelling mechanisms in a single casing.

Treenails. Abbreviated to "trunnels," these were wooden pins used for attaching a plank to a timber.

Trim. The way a vessel sits in the water in relation to her waterline. "Trimmed by the head" indicates her forepart is more submerged in relation to the waterline than her stern.

Tumble home. The amount of inward (toward the center) curvature of a ship's hull above the waterline, determining the narrowing of the breadth of the vessel from waterline to upper rail.

Turnbuckle. A simple mechanical device of a thread and screw on standing rigging to regulate its tautness.

Unship. To remove anything from its place.

Valve gear. The combination of parts by which an engine valve is operated.

Waist. The part of the deck between quarterdeck and forecastle.

Wales. Strong planks running fore and aft on a ship's sides.

Walking beam. See Steam engines (beam).

Wall-sided. Having little or no tumble home; the ship's sides are nearly perpendicular to the water.

Ways. The timbers on which a vessel slides into the water at launching.

Wear. To bring a sailing vessel around on the other tack by changing the wind over the stern.

Windlass. The machine by which the anchor is weighed.

Windsail. A funnel-shaped canvas leading below through one of the hatches, with widespread "ears" at the upper end to direct air into the ship for ventilation.

Working to windward. To make progress against the wind.

Working a ship. Handling the yards and sail and rudder.

Yard. A spar suspended horizontally to the forward side of a mast and to which the head of a square sail is set ("bent"). It also spreads the foot of the sail above.

Bibliography

1. ARCHIVAL SOURCES

Franklin Institute, Philadelphia
Lenthall Collection
Hart Nautical Collection, Massachusetts Institute of Technology, Cambridge
Building Instructions for *Nantasket*
Dimensions for *Manitou*
National Archives and Records Service, Washington, D.C.
Record Group 19, Bureau of Construction and Repair
Letters to SecNav (Entry 49)
Bureau of Construction and Repair to Philadelphia Navy Yard, 1858–75 (Entry 54)
Letters to Commandant, Portsmouth Navy Yard (Entry 54A)
Letters from SecNav to Bureaus (Entry 61)
Reports of Surveys (Entry 233)
Theodore Wilson, Instructions and Specifications for the Construction of Ships, 1857–73 (Entry 234)
Sailing Quality Reports (Entry 244)
Letters to Engineers, 1862–81 (Entry 965)
Letters from Bureau of Steam Engineering to SecNav (Entry 963)
Bureau of Steam Engineering to Naval Officers (Local Inspectors of Machinery Reports) (Entry 966)
Trials of Machinery, 1862–65 (Entry 1017)
Plans of Naval Vessels (Entry 1028)
Reports from Superintendents outside Navy Yards, 13 vol. (Entry 64)
Record Group 24, Deck Logs of U.S. Naval Vessels
Record Group 45, Navy Department
Navy Commissioners Journal 1829–36 (Entry 209)
Register (Key to Journal) (Entry 210)
Letters Sent from SecNav and Commissioners (Entry 212)
Letters to SecNav from Commissioners (Entry 213)
Letters to Commandants from Commissioners (Entry 216)
Letters to Naval Constructors and Steam Engineers (Entry 218)
Commandants' Letters, New York Navy Yard (Entry 220)
Letters from Constructors (Entry 224)
Sailing Quality Reports (Entry 277)
Report of Engineer-in-Chief Haswell to Bureau of Construction and Repair (Entry 278)
Reports of Engineers of Vessels, 1844–49 (Entry 279)
Letters to Commandants, New York Navy Yard (Entry 328)
Letters from Naval Constructor Samuel Humphreys to Commissioners, 1815–31
Old Subject File (listed by box and code letter in notes)
Microfilm
Miscellaneous Letters to SecNav (M124)
Captains' Letters (M125)
Letters from SecNav to President and Executive Agencies (M472)
Letters to Chiefs of Bureaus (M480)
Area File (M625)
Record Group 74, Bureau of Ordnance
Record of Armament of Naval Vessels (Entry 111)
Register of Naval Guns (Entry 112)
Record Group 125, Office of the Judge Advocate General (Navy)
Proceedings of Court Martial of T. T. Craven, 1865, vol. 143, no. 4071.
New-York Historical Society, New York City
C. S. Bushnell Papers
John Ericsson Papers
Portsmouth Naval Shipyard, Kittery, Me.
Dimensions of *Piscataqua*
G. W. Blunt White Library, Mystic Seaport, Mystic Conn.
William Ellery Maxson Diaries, 1857–68
Oscar F. Stanton, USN, Data Book

2. GOVERNMENT DOCUMENTS

Annual Reports of the Secretary of the Navy, 1836–1900, U.S. Navy Department.
American State Papers: Naval Affairs. 4 Vols., 1789–1836, Washington, D.C., Gales and Seaton, 1834–64.

Official Records of the Union and Confederate Navies in the War of the Rebellion. 30 Vols. Washington, D.C.: Government Printing Office, 1894–1922.

U.S. Congress. House. *Construction of Steam Frigate Fulton.* 25th Cong., 2d sess., 1837–38. Exec. Doc. 433.

———. *Proposed Alterations of Steam Frigate Fulton.* 25th Cong., 2d sess., 1837–38. Exec. Doc. 434.

———. *Information Respecting Naval Steamers Built Since 1835.* 32d Cong., 2d sess., 3 March 1853. H. Doc. 63.

———. *Letter from the Secretary of the Navy Transmitting Papers Giving Information in Reference to the Steam Navy of the United States.* 33d Cong., 1st sess., 24 February 1854. H. Exec. Doc. 65.

U.S. Congress, Senate. *Letter of Secretary of the Navy Transmitting, in Answer to Resolution of Senate of 15th of January, Information in Relation to War Steamers Ossipee and Pensacola.* 37th Cong., 3d sess., 23 February 1863. S. Exec. Doc. 45.

U.S. Congress, House. *Failure of Engines of Pensacola.* 37th Cong., 1st Sess., 17 Feb 1863. S. Misc. Doc. 70.

———. *Report (Mr. A. H. Rice) of Committee of Naval Affairs (on Subject of) Marine Engines.* 38th Cong., 2d sess., 30 January 1865. H. Rept. 8.

———. *United States Steamer Wampanoag.* 40th Cong., 2d sess., 20 July 1868. H. Exec. Doc. 339.

———. *Investigation of the Navy Department.* 44th Cong., 1st sess., 25 July 1876. H. Rept. 784.

3. CONTEMPORARY PERIODICALS

Army and Navy Chronicle (1838–42)
Army and Navy Journal (1862–95)
The Engineer
Frank Leslie's Illustrated Newspaper
Gleason's Pictorial (1857–)
Harper's Weekly
Illustrated London News
Journal of the Franklin Institute (1837–67)
Mechanic's Magazine
Naval Magazine (1836–37)
Times (London)
U.S. Nautical Magazine (1845–46)
U.S. Nautical Magazine and Naval Journal (1853–57)
U.S. Naval Institute Proceedings (1870–)

4. UNPUBLISHED SOURCES

Roberts, Stephen S., "Recognition Data, U.S. Screw Corvettes, Sloops, and Gunboats, 1859–c.1890," 1979.

Rodgers, Bradley A., "The Iron Sentinel: U.S.S. *Michigan,* 1844–1949." Master's thesis, East Carolina University, Greenville, N.C. 1985.

5. BOOKS AND ARTICLES

Alden, John D. *American Steel Navy.* Annapolis: Naval Institute Press, 1972.

Albion, Robert G. *Makers of Naval Policy, 1798–1947.* Edited by Rowena Reed. Annapolis: Naval Institute Press, 1980.

Ammen, Daniel. *The Old Navy and the New.* Philadelphia: J. B. Lippincott, 1891.

Archibald, E. H. H. *The Wooden Fighting Ship in the Royal Navy,* A.D. 897–1860. London: Blandford Press, 1968.

Baird, George W. "The U.S. Ship Trenton." *U.S. Naval Institute Proceedings* (Record) 4, no. 1 (1877): 5–20.

Ballard, G. A. *The Black Battle Fleet.* Annapolis: Naval Institute Press, 1980.

———. "British Frigates of 1875." *Mariner's Mirror* 22, no. 1 (January 1936): 42–53.

Basoco, Richard M., W. E. Geoghegan, and H. I. Chapelle, eds., "British View of the Union Navy, 1864." *American Neptune* 27, no. 1 (January 1967): 30–45.

Bauer, K. Jack, *Ships of the Navy, 1775–1969,* Troy, N.Y.: Rensselaer Polytechnic Institute, 1969.

———. "Naval Shipbuilding Programs, 1794–1860," *Military Affairs* 29, no. 1 (Spring 1965): 29–40.

Baxter, James Phinney III. *The Introduction of the Ironclad Warship.* Cambridge: Harvard University Press, 1933.

Beale, Howard K., ed. *The Diary of Gideon Welles.* 2 vols. New York: W. W. Norton, 1960.

Bearss, Edwin. *Boston National Historical Park.* 2 vols. Washington, D.C.: National Park Service, 1984.

Bejarano, Luis E. "MS Emery Rice." *Polaris* 10 (Winter 1951–2): no pp.

Bennett, Frank M. *The Steam Navy of the United States.* Pittsburgh: Warren & Co., 1896.

Bigelow, John. *France and the Confederate Navy.* New York: Harper & Bros., 1888.

Bolander, Louis H. "The Introduction of Shells and Shell Guns to the U.S. Navy." *Mariner's Mirror* 17, no. 4 (April 1931): 2–3.

Bourne, John. *A Treatise on the Steam Engine.* London: Longmans Green & Co., 1876.

Boynton, Charles B. *The History of the Navy during the War of the Rebellion.* New York: D. Appleton, 1868.

Brock, P. W., and Basil Greenhill. *Steam and Sail in Britain and North America.* Newton Abbot, U.K.: David & Charles, 1973.

Busk, Hans. *The Navies of the World.* London: Rutledge, Warnes, & Rutledge, 1859.

Carter, Samuel III. *Blaze of Glory: The Fight for New Orleans, 1814–1815.* New York: St. Martin's Press, 1971.

Chapelle, Howard I. *American Sailing Ships.* New York: W. W. Norton, 1935.

———. *The History of the American Sailing Navy.* New York: W. W. Norton, 1949.

———. *Fulton's "Steam Battery": Blockship and Catamaran.* Washington, D.C.: Smithsonian Institution, 1964.

———. *The Search for Speed under Sail.* New York: W. W. Norton, 1967.

Church, William Conant. *The Life of John Ericsson,* 2 vols. New York: Charles Scribner's, 1891.

Civil War Naval Chronology, 1861–1865. 6 vols. Naval History Division. Washington, D.C.: Government Printing Office, 1971.

Civil War Naval Ordnance. Naval History Division. Washington, D.C.: Government Printing Office, 1969.

Clark, Arthur H. *The Clipper Ship Era.* New York: G. P. Putnam Sons, 1910.

Clark, Francis E. "The Last Years of the Sail Navy." *American Neptune* 20, no. 2 (April 1960): 134–45.

Coletta, Paolo, ed. *American Secretaries of the Navy, 1775–1913.* 2 vols. Annapolis: Naval Institute Press, 1980.

Conway's All the World's Fighting Ships, 1860–1905. Edited by Robert Gardiner. Greenwich: Conway Maritime Press, 1979.

Cramp, Charles H. "Evolution of Screw Propulsion in the United States." Parts 1 and 2. *Transactions of the Society of Naval Architects and Marine Engineers* 17 (1908): 145–69; 18 (1909): 49–58.

Dahlgren, John A. "Composition of Naval Batteries." *U.S. Nautical Magazine and Naval Journal* 7, no. 1 (January 1858): 1–9, 77–85.

Desmond, Charles. *Wooden Ship Building.* 1919. Reprint. New York: Vestal Press, 1984.

Dictionary of American Naval Fighting Ships, 8 vols. Washington: Government Printing Office, 1959–81.

Emmons, George F. *The Navy of the United States: From the Commencement, 1775 to 1853; with a Brief History of Each Vessel's Service and Fate as Appears upon Record.* Washington, D.C.: Gideon, 1853.

Forbes, R. B. "Remarks on the Steam Power, Rig, etc., of the U.S. Steam Sloops Building, 1864–5." Pamphlet, published privately, n.d.

Griffiths, Denis. *Brunel's "Great Western."* London: Patrick Stephens, 1985.

Griffiths, John W. *The Progressive Shipbuilder.* New York: D. Appleton, 1874.

Gurley, Ralph R. "The Wampanoag." *U.S. Naval Institute Proceedings.* 63, no. 12 (1937): 1732–36.

Guthrie, John. *Bizarre Ships of the Nineteenth Century.* New York: A. S. Barnes, 1971.

Haviland, Edward Kenneth. "American Steam Navigation in China." *American Neptune* 17, no. 4 (October 1957): 298–314.

Herrick, Walter R. Jr., *The American Naval Revolution.* Baton Rouge: Louisiana State University Press, 1966.

Hobson, H. S. *The Famous Cruise of the Kearsarge.* Bonds Village, Ma.: privately printed, 1893.

Hoppin, James Mason. *Life of Andrew Hull Foote, Rear-Admiral United States Navy.* New York: Harper & Bros., 1874.

Hutcheon, Wallace S., Jr. *Robert Fulton: Pioneer of Undersea Warfare.* Annapolis: Naval Institute Press, 1981.

Isherwood, Benjamin F. *Engineering Precedents for Steam Machinery.* New York: H. Baillierme, 1859.

———. *Experimental Researches in Steam Engineering,* 2 vols. Philadelphia: W. Hamilton, 1863–65.

———. "The Sloop of War Wampanoag." Parts 1 and 2. *Cassier's Magazine* (August, September 1900): 282–89, 403–19.

Jameson, Edwin M. and Sanford Sternlicht. *The Black Devil of the Bayous.* Upper Saddle River, N.J.: Gregg Press, 1970.

King, J. W. *Warships and Navies of the World.* Boston: A. Williams, 1882.

Laing, Alexander. *American Ships.* New York: American Heritage Press, 1971.

Lambert, Andrew. *Battleships in Transition:* The Creation of the Steam Battlefleet, 1815–1860. Annapolis: Naval Institute Press, 1984.

Lubbock, Basil. *The Best of Sail.* New York: Grosset & Dunlap, 1977.

Luca's Questions and Answers for Marine Engineers. New York: Audel, n.d.

Marestier, Jean Baptiste. *Memoir on Steamboats of the United States of America.* 1824. Reprint. Mystic (Stonington), Conn.: Marine Historical Association, 1957.

Miller, Byron S. *Sail, Steam and Splendor.* New York: Times Books, 1977.

Morison, Elting "Inventing a Modern Navy." *American Heritage,* July 1986.

Morison, Samuel Eliot. *"Old Bruin": Commodore Matthew Calbraith Perry, 1794–1858.* Boston: Little, Brown, 1967.

Musham, H. A. "Early Great Lakes Steamboats." *American Neptune* 8 (January, April 1948): 37–60, 132–49.

Page, C. E. "The Great Eastern." *Model Engineer* 114 (16 February 1956): 257–60.

Paget, E. W. *Liverpool City Museum's Illustrated Handbook and Guide to the Steam Marine Engines.* Liverpool: Liverpool City Museum, 1962.

Paullin, Charles Oscar. "A Half-Century of Naval Administration in America, 1861–1911." *U.S. Naval Institute Proceedings* 38 (December 1912): 1309–36 and 39 (March 1913): 735–60.

Porter, David Dixon. *Naval History of the Civil War.* 1886. Reprint. Secaucus, N.J.: Castle, 1984.

Pursell, Carroll W., Jr. *Early Stationary Steam Engines in America.* Washington, D.C.: Smithsonian Institution Press, 1969.

Reynolds, Clark G. "Hunter's Horizontal Wheels." *American Neptune* 24 (January 1964): 134–45.

Ridgely-Nevitt, Cedric. *American Steamships on the Atlantic.* East Brunswick, N.J.: Associated University Presses, 1981.

Ripley, Warren. *Artillery and Ammunition of the Civil War.* New York: Van Nostrand Reinhold, 1970.

Roberts, Stephen S. "An Indicator of Informal Empire: Patterns of U.S. Navy Cruising on Overseas Stations, 1869–1897." In *New Aspects of Naval History,* edited by Craig L. Symonds et al., 253–67. Annapolis: Naval Institute Press, 1981.

Rodger, N. A. M. "The Design of the Inconstant." *Mariner's Mirror* 61, no. 2 (February 1975): 9–22.

Ronnberg, Erik A. R., Jr. "Webb's Plans of Wooden Vessels," *Nautical Research Journal* 34, no. 2 (June 1989): 62–114.

Ropp, Theodore. *The Development of a Modern Navy.* Edited by Stephen S. Roberts. Annapolis: Naval Institute Press, 1987.

Roscoe, Theodore, and Fred Freeman. *Picture History of the U.S. Navy.* New York: Bonanza, 1956.

Scharf, J. Thomas *History of the Confederate States Navy.* New York: Rogers & Sherwood, 1887.

Sloan, Edward William III. *Benjamin Franklin Isherwood, Naval Engineer.* Annapolis: Naval Institute Press, 1965.

Soley, J. Russell. *The Blockade and the Cruisers.* New York: Charles Scribner's, 1883.

Spencer, Herbert Reynolds *USS Michigan USS Wolverine.* Erie, Pa.: Privately printed, 1966.

Stone, Charles. "General Description of the Ordnance and Torpedo Outfit of the U.S.S. Trenton (2nd Rate)." *U.S. Naval Institute Proceedings* (Record) 3, no. 6 (1877): 89–93.

Stuart, Charles Beebe. *The Naval and Mail Steamers of the United States.* New York: C. B. Norton, 1853.

Swan, James. "The Wampanoag." *Transactions of the Society of Naval Architects and Marine Engineers* 23 (1927): 43–54.

Swann, Leonard Alexander, Jr. *John Roach: Maritime Entrepreneur.* Annapolis, Md.: Naval Institute Press, 1965.

Thompson, W. M., and Richard Warmaugh. *Correspondence of Gustavus Vasa Fox.* 2 vols. New York: Naval Historical Society, 1920.

Thurston, Robert H. *A History of the Growth of the Steam Engine.* London: Kegan, Paul, Trench, & Co., 1887.

Van Riemsdijk, J. T., and Kenneth Brown. *The Pictorial History of Steam Power.* London: Octopus, 1980.

Wallach, Sidney, ed. *Narrative of the Expedition of an American Squadron to the China Seas and Japan.* New York: Coward-McCann, 1952.

Webb, William H. *Plans of Wooden Vessels.* 2 vols. Privately published, 1895.

White, W. W. P. "The USS Michigan Renamed Wolverine." *Transactions of the Society of Naval Architects and Engineers* 17 (1909): 45–49.

Winton, John G. *Modern Steam Practice and Engineering.* London: Blackie & Son, 1883.

Index

Donald L. Canney has a B.A. in history from Georgia Southern College and did graduate work at Florida State University. After serving in the U.S. Air Force he taught high school history in Columbus, Ohio, for ten years and later was on the editorial staff of *Blue and Gray Magazine.* He is now a historical consultant for a variety of clients, including Conway Maritime Press, the U.S. Coast Guard, and most recently the U.S. Navy Memorial Foundation. His articles have appeared in *Warship, Naval History,* and *Scale Ship Modeler.*

Canney, who lives in Fort Washington, Maryland, is working on the second volume of *The Old Steam Navy* and a book on U.S. Revenue and Coast Guard cutters.

THE NAVAL INSTITUTE PRESS

THE OLD STEAM NAVY, VOLUME 1

Frigates, Sloops, and Gunboats, 1815–1885

Designed by CR MacLellan and Associates, Baltimore, Maryland

Set in New Baskerville (text & display) and Old Style Baskerville (display)
by Bi-Comp, Inc., York, Pennsylvania

Printed on 60-lb. Glatfelter Antique, B-16 shade, 330 ppi
Bound in Roxite B 51545, with plain, text-matching endsheets,
and stamped in gold by The John D. Lucas Printing Company, Inc.,
Baltimore, Maryland